# The Presence of Self

*To Elinor and Jenom, with best wishe ~ Sidharth 2/28/00*

# The Presence of Self

R. S. Perinbanayagam

ROWMAN & LITTLEFIELD PUBLISHERS, INC.
*Lanham • Boulder • New York • Oxford*

ROWMAN & LITTLEFIELD PUBLISHERS, INC.

Published in the United States of America
by Rowman & Littlefield Publishers, Inc.
4720 Boston Way, Lanham, Maryland 20706
http://www.rowmanlittlefield.com

12 Hid's Copse Road
Cumnor Hill, Oxford OX2 9JJ, England

British Cataloguing in Publication Information Available

**Library of Congress Cataloguing-in-Publication Data**

Perinbanayagam, R. S., 1934–
    The presence of self / R. S. Perinbanayagam.
        p.   cm.
    Includes bibliographical references and index.
    ISBN 0-8476-9384-8 (alk. paper).—ISBN 0-8476-9385-6 (pbk.:
alk. paper)
    1. Self (Philosophy)        I. Title.
BD438.5.P47    2000                              99-35069
126—dc21                                         CIP

Printed in the United States of America

∞™ The paper used in this publication meets the minimum requirements of
American National Standard for Information Sciences—Permanence of Paper for
Printed Library Materials, ANSI/NISO Z39.48–1992.

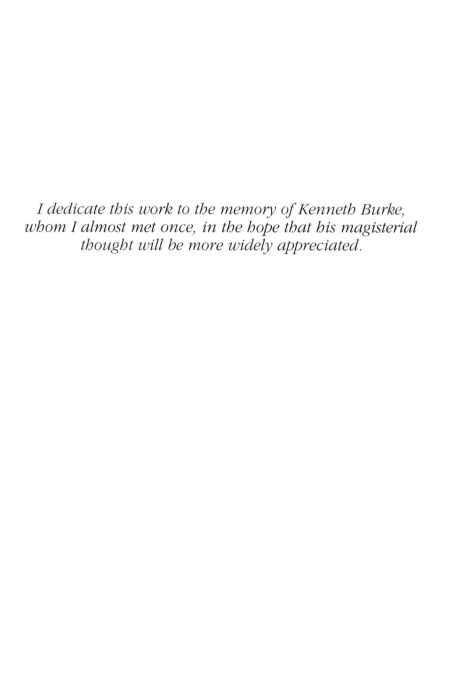

*I dedicate this work to the memory of Kenneth Burke, whom I almost met once, in the hope that his magisterial thought will be more widely appreciated.*

*It acts not from a centre to*
*Its object as remote,*
*But present is, when it doth view,*
*Being with the being it doth note.*
*Whatever it doth do,*
*It doth not by another engine work,*
*But by itself: which in the act doth lurk.*
*Its essence is transform'd into a true*
*And perfect act.*

*Thomas Traherne*

# Contents

# Preface

One of the most frequently debated issues in contemporary sociological theory is the nature and form of the agent, of the human being as an actor in his or her own right. Many recent works have sought to provide theories of the agent as a social and socialized actor. The sociology and social psychology that is derived from the work of American pragmatism did not, however, have to self-consciously and deliberatively concoct a theory of the agent. It was, from the beginning itself, a theory of the agent, conceiving him or her as *both* a voluntary actor *and*, the rumors to the contrary notwithstanding, as a structurally defined and interactionally sensitive one, a minded organism and a self. The theory is not only a *symbolic interactionism* but also a *structuralist interactionism.*

In these pages I develop this pragmatic theory of the agent further, contrast it with certain other theories of the agent and agency and then examine the implications of such a theory to selected areas of sociological interest. I begin with a discussion of the concept of the act, drawing mainly from the work of G. H. Mead and Susanne Langer, and proceed to use it to examine various perspectives on the human actor that are current in the social sciences. This examination yields a view of the individual as, inescapably and irrefutably, a discursive actor with a discursive mind, who engages in richly textured acts that dialogically involve the other and resist him or her at the same time. Actions, then, occurring as they do in terms of the other, and of the environment as an other too, are dialectical adjustments to both. The product of these discursive and adjustive processes is the self. Such a self is present in all acts undertaken by a human being; conversely all acts present a self. Acts and selves become, then, ongoing accomplishments that incorporate the acts and selves of others.

These encounters between a self and the other are in fact conducted, I argue further, drawing from the work of Mikhail Bakhtin and Kenneth Burke, by deploying language in varying rhetorical modes and reaping the fruits

xi

thereof. With these means a self is given a distinct identity. Identity then becomes a rhetorical achievement, one supported by a logic of signs. Further, insofar as identity is achieved through the use of language, a poetic of identity becomes impossible to avoid. To use signs to construct identity is in fact a poetic enterprise, and I delineate a few strategic examples of such a poetics of identity.

The last two chapters treat the activities of the self in various social encounters. In the first of these, a number of conversational interactions are analyzed to display the nature of the rhetorical processes involved in the constitution and presentation of self. Besides the work of Bakhtin and Burke I use various ideas from Paul Ricoeur and Paul Grice as resources for this discussion.

In the final chapter I argue that selves are not only experienced, felt, and presented but are also put into play by a cognitive and sentient and reflexive actor with varying intentions and are also watched as the play is conducted and consummated. It is possible, I think, for a symbolic and imaginative creature to feel the world and act in it directly or vicariously.

In any case, here it is—a dialogue with various thinkers, often with their own words—the final essay in a quest to understand the relationship between language and existence. Issues raised in my earlier works are given further discussion and elaboration and amendment just as new issues are presented. Those who liked my earlier work may find this, too, of interest. As for the others . . . well, the caravan moves on.

# Acknowledgments

In the production of this work, I have incurred several debts. Professor Doyle McCarthy read several chapters and gave me valuable advice. I am also extremely grateful to members of the East Side Book Club for allowing me to record their proceedings for use in this work. It needed a special kind of openness and generosity to allow a comparative stranger to listen to their dialogue on matters profound and frivolous. I am grateful to my friend Anne Snow for introducing me to the Book Club and helping me to transcribe the tapes. I was also able to obtain the taped records of conversations in an office. These two records of conversational interactions are cited in the text as "Book Club Transcripts" and "Office Transcripts," respectively.

Nalayini Fernando typed the manuscript from my handwritten version and, as usual, did a splendid job. Veronica Manlow gave me exemplary editorial and typographical assistance. I am truly grateful for this. Various skillful editors have worked on this manuscript too and they deserve my thanks. Without their patient and understanding work, the publishing of a book would be more troublesome than it is.

Finally, I must thank the staff at the Hunter College library for the unfailing courtesy and despatch with which they obtained books and articles for me.

## CREDITS

Lines from "Many Happy returns" from *W. H. Auden: Collected Poems* by W. H. Auden. Copyright © 1945 and renewed 1973. Reprinted by permission of Random House, Inc.

Passages from *The Philosophy of the Act* by G. H. Mead. Chicago: University of Chicago Press, Ltd. Copyright 1938.

Lines from *The Bald Soprano* by Eugene Ionesco. Grove/Atlantic Inc. Copyright 1958.

Lines from *The Geographical History of America or the Relation of Human Nature to the Human Mind* by Gerturde Stein. Vintage Books: New York. Copyright 1976.

Lines from *The Invisible Man* by Ralph Ellison. Random House: New York. Copyright 1952.

Passages from *The Grammar of Motives* by Kenneth Burke. Berkeley: University of California Press. Copyright 1969.

# I

# Dialogic Processes

# Chapter 1

# Dialogic Acts

First Gentleman:     Our deeds are fetters that we forge ourselves
Second Gentleman:    Ay, truly: but I think it is the world that brings
                     the iron.

George Eliot, *Middlemarch*

Acts or actions are the basic units with which living phenomena manifest their presence in nature. Suzanne Langer has reviewed the relevant literature and has argued for the centrality of the "act concept" in understanding the behavior of all organisms. To begin with, she notes that "the difficulty of drawing a sharp line between animate and inanimate things reflects a principle which runs through the whole domain of biology; namely, that all categories tend to have imperfect boundaries" (1967: 259). Organisms and plants for Langer have this "imperfect boundary" between them to the extent that they both can be said to be able to act. She describes these acts as follows:

> It is with the concept of act that I am approaching living form in nature, only to find it exemplified there at all levels of simplicity or complexity. . . . The act concept is a fecund and elastic concept. It applies to natural events, of a special form which is very widely represented on the surface of the earth . . . a form characteristic of living things, though not absolutely peculiar to them. . . . An act may subsume another act, or even many other acts. It may also span other acts which go on during its rise and consummation and cadence without becoming part of it. Two acts of separate inception may merge so that they jointly engender a subsequent act. These and many other relations among acts form the intricate dynamism of life which becomes more and more articulated, more and more concentrated and intense, until some of its elements attain the phase of being felt, which I have termed "psychical," and the domain of psychology develops within the wider realm of biology, especially zoology. (1967: 261)

The "act concept" unifies the study of "living forms," argues Langer, and becomes the root of psychology as well. The "act concept" may unify living form in one encompassing category but within it Langer accepts the existence of simple acts and complex acts, or rather, acts of varying degrees of simplicity and complexity, degrees that set apart human acts from those of amoebas or even rats and fruit flies.

G. H. Mead, too, had given primacy to the act and he too included animals and human beings in the same category as acting entities but went on to discuss the special qualities that human acts bear. "The unit of existence," Mead observed,

> is the act, not the moment. And the act stretches beyond the stimulus to the response. While most of our acts stretch into the world that does not yet exist, they inevitably include immediate steps which lie within the existent world, and the synchronizing, with recorded elements in some uniform process of change, of attitudes in the act by means of the indication of these to the self, affords the only approach to the definition of the span of existence. (1938: 65–66)

Mead comes to this conclusion after an exposition of the various "stages of the act" in a rather abstract and at times obscure manner. Nevertheless, it is possible to see a thread running through it connecting the voluntary moves that an organism makes in various sequential stages in the world in which it finds itself.

For Mead the act consists of four stages: impulse, perception, manipulation, and consummation. To begin with, the impulses of the organism lead to the "perception" of the objects in its environment. With this perceptual act, the organism recognizes its color, shape, likely weight, and so on. The organism, that is, takes the role of the object in perception and organizes his or her act accordingly. This idea is further advanced by Mead's claim that the reality of the object in perception is a "distant" one, and it invites us to "action with reference to it" (1938: 12). Once again Mead stresses the relation between the actor and the object. The object is perceived and defined by a series of moves, its character and qualities apprehended and the possibility of acting with reference to it considered.

These various moves in the activity of perception are followed by what Mead calls manipulation. Discussing the manipulative phase of the act, Mead introduces the notion of the social self:

> The "what" of the object is, then, the expression of the whole of which both the environment and organism are essential parts. If the function of perception in its immediacy were that of knowledge, it would be necessary to add to this object as it exists for the organism a capacity for awareness located in the organism. There seem to be two reasons for the assumption of this awareness. One is found in the reflective process in which knowing the perceptual object becomes a definite part of conduct, and the other is found in the identification of the organism with the social self. (1938: 16–17)

In prosecuting an act then, once it reaches the manipulative phase, both a reflective process and a social self become influential in the action that an organism is intending to take toward an object. "Thus," Mead notes, "the object of immediate perception has been placed in consciousness, as the experience of this social self, while the real object is placed outside experience, revealed only by thought" (1938: 17). The object—that is, whatever is seen, heard, or touched—becomes an element of the reflective consciousness and is *refracted* through the socially constituted self. Mead goes on to say, "We approach the distant stimulus with the manipulatory processes already excited. We are ready to grasp the hammer before we reach it, and the attitude of manipulatory response directs the approach" (1938: 24).

The "directionality" of the steps to the act leads Mead to claim that the acts contains a "future." "It is not until this initiated response is carried out [in the manipulative phase] that its reality is assured. The experimental method is imbedded in the simplest process of perception of a physical thing. In this sense the future is already in the act" (1938: 25). But that is not all that is in the act as it is consummated: "And the past is also in the act, for facility and familiarity are products of past reactions" (1938: 25). The consummation of an act also brings in its own dynamism and perhaps pathos. "Every act," Mead writes,

> however, is moving on from its physical objects to some consummation. Within the field of consummation all the adjectives of value obtain immediately. There objects are possessed, are good, bad, and indifferent, beautiful or ugly, and lovable or noxious. In the physical things these characters are only mediately present." (1938: 25)

The act at this stage becomes not only a social act but one capable of introducing an ethical dimension into it. The bland "good" or "bad" of Mead's formulation is really an allusion to the capacity of a human to introduce judgments based on abstract values and ethics into the prosecution and consummation of an act. Acts are then moves in which an individual delays his or her responses, takes the role of the objects in the situation, as of the others in it, and makes a selection of the act he or she is going to present: Whatever other promptings may manifest themselves, at the moment of the act, typically, it is the social one that dominates it. In the manipulatory and consummatory phase of the act, it becomes a social act, and subsumes a reflective social self. In these phases, an individual is able to incorporate his or her knowledge of the world, his or her values and verities, into the act and convert it into a meaningful act. In these "phases of the act" the individual marshals, minimally or maximally, the knowledge that he or she possesses and uses it to construct not only an act that is pragmatic but also expressive. Furthermore, insofar as he or she is able to remember a past and anticipate a future, that also plays a part in the expression of the act. These pasts and futures are assembled as symbols and leaked into the act—or even flooded into it.

The knowledge that the individual uses to construct a social act includes whatever knowledge he or she has acquired as a member of a historically antecedent community. This community, through its various and multitudinous agencies, has provided the individual with what Alfred Schutz calls "recipes" (1964: 73) and "stocks of knowledge" (1964: 29) with which to navigate through the daily grind. They become the stock from which an individual selects various elements that are relevant to the situation to prosecute his or her act, define his or her self. This knowledge and its manifestation in self and act impact on the others with whom he or she has to deal, just as their knowledge impacts on the individual in question. These stocks of knowledge, to the extent that they reach the individual and become accessible to him or her through various intermediaries, will bear their influences and angulations.

Insofar as the knowledge that an individual uses to construct an act and define his or her self is so mediated, it will always be partial knowledge. The individual will not be able to have all the facets of knowledge or even a small segment of it at his or her disposal. The self is no doubt constituted by language, and the "languages" in which the knowledge, the "discursive formations," are manifested to the individual will thus be partial, incomplete, and given to featuring one theme rather than another. For all that, however, the languages are received and interpreted by an active and functioning intelligence, subject to either habitual or delayed responses, and incorporated into the acts by the individual. The individual, subject though he or she may have been in the socialization processes to these same discursive formations, nevertheless has enough independence from them to be able to view them critically and analytically, compare them with other discursive formations and select one over the other or select elements from each and form one's own discursive formation and a discursive self with it. It is this capacity to be socially formed and discursively constituted, and be subject to cultural and historical processes, and at the same time to be a conscious and deliberate agent with the ability to devise new discursive formations, challenge the relevant cultural and historical forces, and reconstitute the self and the world, that is the central paradox of the human condition. Having acquired a more or less steady state of competence, a finite set of items and instrumentations, the human organism is able to generate an infinite number of acts—or is at least capable of doing so—acts which have a connection to earlier acts of others or itself.

An act is a singular and voluntary move made by a conscious agent accountable for the move—at least, it can be attributed to him or her. Such an accountability and attributiveness of the act can be accomplished by the agent himself or herself as well as by others. The act has further consequences for the actor: it activates a completion in the respective responses of the actor as well as in those of others and becomes meaningful to both. The responses of the other or others defines the act for the initiator and gives the act a new character. It is no longer a private event but a public one, its character and quality being subject to evaluation, judgment, and further acts from the initiator and the respondent, each of whom is now encapsulated, to varying degrees, in the act. It is, in other words, a *dialogic act.* They are *addressed* to other and self simultaneously and *answered* by self and other as well. Such acts are produced by deliberative and purposeful agents who orient their acts to others, as well as to the self as an other, and to inanimate objects. Acts are the means by which an individual seeks to influence the world around him or her as well as announce his or her own presence in the world. Acts are the conditionals of an individual as an existent in the phenomenal world of multiple existents and the relationship between such existents is both pragmatic and dialogical. These acts are pragmatic, because they involve the mutual adjustment of each to the other; and dialogical, because they involve the mutual orientations of each existent to the other. An act is undertaken, indeed is possible, only on the basis of conceiving and incorporating the otherness of the world into it. Such a dialogism views the subject-object dualism as a convenient fiction rather than a description of a separateness. The subject of an act performs an act and conceives its subjecthood in terms of the otherness of the world in which it finds itself. In Michael Holquist's description of Mikhail Bakhtin's work,

> In dialogism, the very capacity to have consciousness is based on *otherness*. This otherness is not merely a dialectical alienation on its way to a sublation that will endow it with a unifying identity in higher consciousness. On the contrary: in dialogism consciousness *is* otherness. (1990: 18)

Mead's conception of mind, self, and act is along similar lines: Mind and world, act and other, self and other are not connected after an initial separation but exist simultaneously in dialogic unity. Mead in fact observes, "The self is not something that exists first and then enters into relationship with others, but it is, so to speak, an eddy in the social current and so still a part of the current" (1934: 182).

These dialogues are conducted mainly by constituting and managing discursive acts. Human individuals are inescapably discursive creatures. To begin with, as minded organisms they engage in discursive activity in their inner forums (Mead, 1964: 243). Further, as social organisms they engage in discursive interaction with others, usually real ones, but often with imaginary and fantastic ones. Indeed, whenever one speaks of a human being, he or she is describing an entity that is dialogically situated and discursively active.

The self is not so much immanent in consciousness as it is present, overtly or covertly, in the acts that the individual prosecutes in what may be termed his or her self-otherness. The acts that humans prosecute have this quality to them: they occur as discrete events, often with vague and uncertain boundaries, but are events that are nevertheless connected to other such acts. As Sandra Rosenthal puts it in an analysis of Charles Sanders Peirce's views on time, presence, and continuity,

> The aspects of discreteness and continuity combined allow for the emergence of the present and, with it, the possibility of the emergence of semiotic and temporal creativity; but this is the case only because of the way in which continuity allows for traces of the past as possibilities for present creativity, possibilities that are "there in the present and stretch into the future. (1996: 25–26)

The act then is in the present, but a present that a discursive mind constitutes, a constitution in which the signifying traces and residues of past acts, just as the anticipation of a future, play a part. Following St. Augustine's statements on time, recently examined by Paul Ricoeur, one can conceive the act as occurring in terms of "Expectation," "Attention," and "Memory" (1984: 19). One attends to the moment, anticipates a future, and remembers a past. Ricoeur quotes St. Augustine as follows: "It might be correct say that there are three times, a present of past things, a present of present things, and a present of future things" (1984: 11). These three "times" are indubitably semiotically constituted presences and not empty exercises in pure phenomenology.

The present of the act is richly textured and, to the extent that the actor is neither amnesiac nor autistic, the act will incorporate a constructed past and a construed future. The human typically confronts a situation and produces an act, all the while remembering his or her own past and that of the others. To the extent that he or she remembers the past, however incompletely and selectively, and anticipates a future, however tentatively, a self is involved in the act.

To the extent that all humans are subject to what Charles Sanders Peirce called the "four incapacities," the self cannot emerge in any other way and be sustained in any other way except by the systematic production of acts in an ongoing series and assembling their meanings. Peirce has argued that humans "have no power of Introspection but all knowledge of the internal world is derived by hypothetical reasoning from our knowledge of external facts" ([1868] 1958: 41). In the emergence of the self this Peircian maxim would mean that each individual's knowledge of his or her self could be achieved only by acting in the external world and reflecting on such acting. The second incapacity was described as follows: "We have no power of Intuition, but every cognition is determined logically by previous cognitions" ([1868]1958: 41). The self has a continuity insofar as it is a cognition that is connected to earlier cognitions. These cognitions were of course derived from our contact with the external world as per the first maxim and no doubt it is in the form of the interpretation of acts of the individual and others that the external world becomes available for cognition. The third "incapacity" reads as follows: "We have no power of thinking without signs" ([1868] 1958: 41). The acts and experiences of the "external world" are given interpretations—that is, provided with signs and then made into features of one's consciousness—thematized and made into a more or less coherent definition of the self. The final incapacity that Peirce describes is: "We have no conception of the absolutely incognizable" ([1868] 1958: 41) and this no doubt applies to the self as well. To exist in the world with others, in communities and societies, is to exist as a cognizable phenomenon, to wit, a self, which can be subject to reflection, which can be addressed and referenced with a proper noun and a common noun and pronouns. Such references and addressings issue from the others as well as from the individual himself or herself. It is then not possible to talk of a human or think of him or her and claim that he or she does not exist, that he or she is noncognizable. At a certain point in time, the human individual was without a self (soon after birth and for a while afterwards) and then at another point in time he or she acquired it. Such a self will continue to exist in the interactions and relationships that the individual conducts with others as signs so long as the organism itself and the others address it or refer to it. These acts and the responsive acts the discursive organism mobilizes will create a phenomenon that can be *named, addressed, and described* and therefore, for all practical and social purposes, it exists; to the extent that it can name itself, address itself, and refer to itself and describe itself, too, and even if such exercises are achieved in culturally provided vocabularies, it too exists. This is the self. Once a self is formulated this way, it will certainly influence any action that issues forth.

The self, however, is never complete, never safe and intact. It is always a tentative achievement and forever dependent on the next act or sequences of action. To the extent that such actions and their sequences and the others to whom they are addressed and received are relatively stable, a stable self may be achieved—at least for the time being. Such a self considers and assembles a variety of intentions and sensations, cognitive and emotional, into a more or less coherent gesture, presents it to the world in anticipation of a response, and awaits a response. In the course of the assembling process, however spontaneous and instantaneous and habitual it may be, the author of the move is able to observe the acts and change them. That is to say, he or she will take into account his or her knowledge, recipes, and so on as well as the responses from others while prosecuting an act. The resultant self then is both singular and social, individuated and cultural. It is a feature of the minding process, of the discursive mind, and achieves a presence in the reflexive minding of the individual as well as in his or her interactional minding. To talk then of a self's presence is to give it a causal and signifying role in the acts that an individual, a discursively and interactionally minded organism that he or she is, undertakes.

## BIOLOGY AND SOCIAL ACTS

One cannot, however, say that either the paradox of being simultaneously an individual and an other has not been denied or the mystery of the human predicament of being caught between individuality and sociality has been generally accepted. One of the major challenges to the claim that acts undertaken by humans are subject to the selection and control by a social self comes from biology and its offshoot, sociobiology. For sociobiologists there are other whisperings and promptings, or even louder and more insistent noises, that govern the human actor in the prosecution of his or her acts. Describing the nature of sociobiological explanations David Barash notes that there are four basic ways of employing evolution to study behavior: historical, evaluative, co-relational and predictive. The historical

> involves the attempted reconstruction of behavioral phylogenies. . . . Typically, studies of this sort proceed by describing the behavior of numerous closely related species; historical insight is then gained by assuming that the ancestral condition is most closely reflected in behavior shared by the largest number of extant species, as well as in the simplest and least specialized behaviors. (Barash 1978: 20)

This method, Barash continues has resulted in "excellent and convincing results . . . notably with studies of empid flies (Kessel 1955), sand wasps (Evans 1966), and fiddler crabs (Crane 1943) among invertebrates; and gulls (Tinbergen 1959) and ducks (Lorenz 1958) among vertebrates" (Barash 1978: 20).

This may well be true but its relevance to an explanation of human conduct is somewhat remote. It is no doubt the case that humans evolved from earlier forms into present forms and natural selection played a role in the constitution of the present formation and therefore the human's present condition has an evolutionary history. But at some point in the past the human evolved into a symbolic creature and henceforth, instead of just behaving in accordance with some biological propensity, he or she uses this symbolic capacity and *acts* in full cognizance of self, other, and world in undertaking his or her respective acts.

Barash goes on,

> Instead of asking "What is the history of behavior in a population" . . . we can ask, "What is its adaptive significance?" This approach seeks to evaluate a behavior by how it contributes to the fitness of animals performing it; that is, for

any phenotype (behavior included) to be positively selected, it must carry with it more advantages than disadvantages—or else alternative behaviors, coded by alternative alleles, would be selected. (1978: 21)

Tinbergen's gulls serve as examples here too. This selecting of "behaviors" by these birds may occur one way or another but among human beings such selection occurs as an act that is circumscribed by purely social factors. To begin with it is limited by the *knowledge* that the actor possesses of the consequences of his or her action. This is not a constant or a given, but a systematic variable. Further, the act will be determined by the rules and regulations that a culture has provided for the behavior in question. To say that these rules and regulations were established by the culture in accordance with biological imperatives will not pass muster; such establishment was also made by human actors who exercised a choice and made some rules and did not make certain others. Third, the act will be determined by the significance that the act has for the actor: If it is an act that is forbidden by the rules and is known to be detrimental to his or her group of others, he or she can nevertheless decide to overcome these objections and execute the act because it has a special significance for him or her at that juncture of his or her life; the act has a meaning for his or her self.

Barash is, however, willing to accept the role of the "environment" in adaptive behavior and develops a "co-relational" theory. The co-relational approach to evolutionary explanations of behavior is undertaken by

considering the ecology of each individual and assessing the extent to which the behavior in question contributes to fitness, given the environment in each case. If behavior is specifically adapted to particular environments then different environments should select for different behaviors. (1978: 21)

Blackbirds, weaver-birds, and marmots have been studied to establish this point (1978: 22). Once again, the correlations between macrovariables not withstanding, these behaviors were indubitably behaviors undertaken by individual birds. Translating this into the human realm, we are faced with individual human agents selecting a series of acts that result in being detrimental or adaptive. How could a human undertake such an act? Once again he or she is limited by the knowledge he or she may possess at the time of the action. Needless to say, unless he or she reads the extensive work on weaver birds and is willing to accept the relevance of these findings to his or her own life and circumstance, there is no guaranteeing that his or her conduct would be adaptive. In other words, his or her action to be undertaken in a direction adaptive to his or her group can be undertaken only as a self-conscious and *knowledgeable act.* Such knowledgeability is, however, a variable and all human actors do not have access to the same knowledge. Furthermore, even with the possession of the knowledge that certain acts or series of acts may damage the self, or its group or community, adaptive behavior is not guaranteed; too many humans in the history of the species have undertaken too many acts that were destructive to themselves as well as to the groups of which the actors were members.

The final approach to the study of evolutionary factors in the study of behavior, according to Barash, is the predictive one. The application of this method relies on what Barash calls "the central theorem of sociobiology." This is said to be: "Insofar as the behavior in question is genetically influenced, animals ought to behave so as to maximize their inclusive fitness. Predictive tests of the central theorem have been successfully employed in studies of the chronology of nest defense in alpine accentors . . . variations in paternal behavior in hoary marmots . . . and the male response to apparent female adultery among mountain bluebirds (Barash 1978: 22). The question of whether the male bluebird considers it "adultery," as obviously Barash does, I will leave unasked. These behaviors listed here are described by Barash as "defense," "paternal behavior," and "response," respectively, and in the human realm these behaviors will be considered and thought-full acts, considerations, and thought-fullness that take into account the powers, limitation, and knowledge systems of the actor. The particular others involved in the activities and the specific rules and regulations that govern the conduct in question will also play a crucial role in the execution of the relevant acts. In other words the behaviors would be conscious and situated activities. For example, it is the case that humans defend their "nests"—home, land, and country—but they are defended as culturally and socially defined phenomena. Furthermore, there will be numerous occasions when they are not defended. The "nest" may be gifted to somebody else, abandoned, destroyed, betrayed, or sabotaged by the actor—be it home, homeland, or country. Similarly, while many could view adultery as unacceptable, there are those who participate in adulterous relationships that are consensual.

The conduct in question, in each case, is an act that an individual, choosing one set of rules or another, produces to meet the demands of a life or a situation. These would be acts that an individual undertakes in order to adjust, not to the biological imperatives, but to the socially and culturally defined meanings of situations. In the final analysis an individual organism has to produce a series of moves, more or less in full cognizance of his or her history, experience, strengths, and limitations—in short, an awareness of self. Defending one's nest, appropriate paternal and maternal behavior, and responses to adultery are all made up of acts in which a self is present. Whatever he or she decides to do will certainly not be determined by a biological imperative but by a judgment made on the basis of all the available information and the estimation of the consequences of one line of action rather than another. Even the most ardent proponent of the biological imperative cannot deny that in the final analysis an individual organism has to produce a series of particularized moves that provide particularized solutions to particularized problems. In other words the organism has to act and, if it is a human organism, it has to produce a social and self-conscious act: It has to give expression to his or her intentions, in a defined situation, and to the extent that these moves are subject to delayed action, or the possibility of such action, the social and situational imperative will play an important part.

Barash's inclusion of "environment" as a factor in the evolution of selected "behaviors" is taken one step further by William Durham. He is willing to accommodate culture into the evolutionary-behavioral paradigm and consider human behavior as a function of both genes and culture, of "co-evolution." In a comprehensive work, Durham advances the thesis of coevolution of culture and genes. He recognizes that the fundamental issue to be resolved here is the nature and degree of *independence* that social scientists can reasonably claim for culture—independence from genetic influence, if not determination. Durham puts it very succinctly and follows it with a number of what seem to be rhetorical questions:

> Is cultural evolution also an autonomous force in the shaping of human diversity? The question is all the more necessary because we know that the structures and functions of our "capacity for culture" . . . particularly those of the brain and vocal tract are themselves products of organic evolution. How much freedom from the genes can one expect from such a "derived" information system, that is to say, one whose existence depends so directly upon the products of organic evolution? (1991: 34)

Durham answers this question with statements from Edward Wilson, who asked,

> Can the cultural evolution of higher ethical values gain a direction and momentum of its own and completely replace genetic evolution? I think not. The genes hold culture on a leash. The leash is very long, but inevitably values will be constrained in accordance with their effects on the human gene pool. (1978: 167, quoted in Durham 1991: 34)

Durham comments,

> Contained within the image of genes holding culture on a leash are a number of important questions or groups of questions like: (1) Is the leash of the same length at all times and all places? Why or why not? (2) Are there ever instances when the chain of command is reversed, and culture "drags along" the leash bearers? When does that occur, if ever? (3) Is the leash ever so long as to be ineffective, allowing the "domesticated pet" to run free, in effect? When does this happen? (Durham 1991: 35)

After reviewing a great deal of literature Durham arrives at the conclusion that both cultural and natural selection—that is, genes—influence the emergence of "human diversity." He calls this "the theory of coevolution." He summarizes his position as follows:

> (1) that both systems, separately or in combination, are capable of causing heritable change in the nature of phenotypes; and (2) that neither system exerts its influence in a way that could accurately be described as "deterministic." In both cases, environment and chance effects . . . are also intimately involved. (1991: 420)

This position, actually a compromise, is so general a one that, using one of Durham's expressions, it is, shall I say, "functionally ineffective." No one in the social science community would deny that human beings are biological creatures with an evolutionary history and that they have genes that define their biological natures. The issue that the theory of coevolution evades is the specific nature of the relationship between the biological elements of the human and his or her behavior. And this evasion is accomplished by a holistic sleight of hand. By employing "culture" as an explanatory variable, the issue of human action, which is accomplished by an individual actor in a dialogic process with himself or herself as well as with others, is subject to an epistemological evasion. Culture, a holistic category that describes a multitudinous variety of events and processes, does not do anything. Rather, culture is *present* in the actions of individuals who live in interactions and communities. To show that genes influence or determine human conduct, it is necessary to go one step further and show how genes control actual instances of human conduct, to wit, the acts of given individuals. The issue is not really how genes and "culture" influence each other, but what are the specific modalities by which actors, in concert of one kind or another with each other, make the judgments, decisions and accompanying programs, accounts, and motives that guide and accompany their actions. In other words, the issue is the process by which genes enter the construction and presentation of a social act and not whether genes influence "culture"—as Durham asks. It is surely beyond debate that if one accepts that "culture" is capable of causing heritable change in human populations, one can actually find it in the moment when an individual is reaching a decision to *select* one line of conduct against another. This is not a matter of a philosophical preference for reductionism as opposed to holism, but a stubborn empirical fact that, though indubitably culture affects individual conduct, it does not do so in a mechanistic way; it enables discursively minded organisms to *select* one line of activity over another. If then culture and genes "co-evolve," how do they manifest themselves in the conduct of an individual at the moment of the making of the social act?

One can use Paul Weiss's defense of the holistic position to show what is lost when holism is in fact adopted for explanatory purposes. He writes:

(1) That as our brain scans features of the universe we shift range and jolt back and forth between telescopic and microscopic vision, as it were; (2) that as we move downward on this scale, we mostly gain precision and lose perspective; (3) that as we move upward, new and relevant features, formally unrecognizable and unsuspected, come into view; (4) that this emerging novelty pertains to macro-samples of nature—that is, reflects the properties of collectives—of groups, assemblies, systems and populations composed of micro-samples; (5) that the required additional terms to characterize such collectives must come from rigorous scientific procedures rather than from anthropomorphic and allegorical allusions to mythology. (1967: 802)

These are undoubtedly sound propositions—but the question for my purposes here is that when and under what circumstances is it appropriate to "gain precision and lose perspective," and when is it mandatory to "lose precision and gain perspective?" Weiss defends the holistic position by claiming that often "one plus one does not equal two." Yet, often one plus one *does* equal two. I hold that in the social sciences, it is appropriate when answering certain questions to sacrifice precision for perspective and when answering certain other questions it is necessary to sacrifice perspective and gain precision. When seeking to explain behavior, conduct, and action it is imperative that a commitment to precision be maintained. To use Weiss's own concept, one plus one does not equal two under one set of circumstances: When two humans forgather, for example, they are not just bodies, or for that matter two minds; rather they become a social dyad with emergent properties. They also have a different mass and can collectively achieve something that cannot be done by the mere adaptivity of the two. If, however, one is purchasing two items in a store and each costs a dollar, the total amount that must be surrendered to the storekeeper is one dollar plus another which is two; here precision becomes imperative. In seeking to explain why when John hit Mary and why Mary hit John back, neither a holistically conceived "culture" nor "genes" will prove *adequate*. The respective assaults were situated, personalized, and interactive events, acts in fact, and this must be taken into account. The particular socialization that Mary underwent that bound her to hit back and the specialized training she received in assertiveness and self-expression should be considered in explaining Mary's moves.

A commitment to precision will lead to an examination, not of the near end of the Wilson's leash but the far end, where someone undertakes an act or series of acts with varying degrees of awareness and deliberation. Such a human is equipped with a brain that is no doubt subject to an "evolutionary morphology" and is able to engage in complex functions—the most crucial of which is the ability to use symbols and syntax. Undoubtedly, this ability leads to the emergence of what Mead called the capacity to produce "delayed reaction" (1934: 99). Such a capacity enables a human actor at the moment of conduct—at the edge of producing an act—to consider alternative possibilities, evaluate possible long-term or short-term consequences, examine the ethical, moral, and legal aspects of the act and then produce an act or refrain from producing the act, which is also an act. To be able to claim then that culture and genes "coevolve" to create adaptive behavior it is necessary to show how they both enter the production of a social act in its expressive moments. This is not even minimally done by any of the proponents of either the sociobiological thesis or the cultural-sociobiological thesis. Even a cursory glance at the history of the human species would indicate that individuals engage in maladaptive social acts as frequently as adaptive social acts. They are able to resist not only the whisperings of the gene but often also the promptings of a culture to undertake conduct that is destructive to self, society, and culture.

In other words, the significant feature of human conduct is not only the numerous acts that he or she prosecutes that increase, arguably, his or her "inclusive fitness," activate his or her "selfish gene," and so on, but the numerous occasions in which he or she prosecutes acts that are either irrelevant or decidedly detrimental to such fitnesses and selfishnesses. He or she seems to be obedient to the promptings of genetic forces as much as he or she is rebellious of them. Furthermore, even when individuals give expression to "inclusive fitness" in their conduct, it appears that every human act is always *more* than what is biologically warranted; it is ceremonialized, ritualized, embellished, subject to certain political and social economies, and usually expanded to meet the standards imposed by particular cultures. These processes cannot have any direct relevance to either genetic forces or to biological adaptations. Rather, they are *symbolic constructions and reconstructions* designed for cultural *expressivity* and the construction of social structures. Every act that an individual produces is produced at the far end of Wilson's leash and is inexorably subject to the processes that Suzanne Langer called "symbolic transformation" (Langer [1942] 1970, 44).

Nevertheless, in many ways, Wilson's metaphor of the leash and the questions that Durham poses are brilliant counters to the cultural argument. The answer to his questions, rhetorical though they may be, can be given directly and simply. If we must use the metaphor of the leash, the answer is that indeed the leash is so long and flexible that for *all practical human purposes* it doesn't make a difference whether genes hold culture in their grip or not. Consider this: The culturally constituted minds of humans like Wilson and Durham are able to conceive and present their thesis about evolution and behavior, theories that are distinct from the theories of others, in a style and a language that is different from those of the others, and bring a vigor and a flair that is also different from those of the others. The theories, moreover, are identifiably theirs, theories that they will claim and defend as their own. Insofar as neither they, nor any other sociobiologists, claim that there is a *specific* connection between a particular gene or gene-complex that will lead to the construction of the *particular* theories of Wilson and Durham, it is surely right to insist that the leash from gene to behavior is so long that no meaningful causal connection can be made between them. It is therefore *far-fetched* to claim that the genes cause the behavior. Along the evolutionary process, the leash became longer and slacker as humans evolved as symbolic and syntactic creatures and learned to act from other such humans as well as to create actions of their own, which they in turn passed along to others.

The positing of a genetic basis of behavior, an "innate" propensity, is a futile move if the goal is an *explanatory* thesis about behavior, if one is also willing to concede that other factors, i.e., social ones, also influence behavior. The genes, it is clear, cannot explain the specific acts of humans insofar as the social and the psychological influence them sufficiently to change their character and course. The specificity of acts are controlled by the symbolicity of the mind and the evolved brain that, once it reached the stage of symbolicity, became different from the brains of other species. The position taken here is well described by Terrence Deacon's recent work. He summarized his project as

> a detailed reappraisal of human brain and language evolution that emphasizes the unbroken *continuity* between human and non-human brains, and yet, at the same time, describes a singular *discontinuity* between human and non-human minds, or to be more precise, between brains that use this form in the communication and brains that do not. (1977: 13, my emphasis)

Once the evolutionary change into symbolicity and syntacticity occurred, it was possible for humans to develop conscious knowledge and capacity for a conception of self which will make all the difference. As Mead argued, "The biologic individual lives in an undifferentiated now; the social reflective individual takes this up into a flow of experience within which stands a fixed past and a more or less uncertain future" (1934: 351). Whatever the biological forces may dictate, and however strong the pull on Wilson's leash, at the moment of action it is the presence of a self that will determine the action. This presence will control the action that is to follow. It is then not a denial that humans are biological creatures and subject to an evolutionary process that is claimed by cultural theorists; rather that the quality, quantity, and power of the influence that biology exerts on human action and existence is always shaped by the human's symbolicity. This claim is as true for other gene-based theories of human action as for ones based on "temperament" and "personality structure" and so on that posit an invariant continuity over time of a particular disposition to act. Whatever the glands may dictate or temperament and personality may demand, at the moment of the act, at the fulcrum of action, a human individual refers his or her act to a conception of self and produces a delayed move to meet the exigencies of the exact situation.

## THE CONSTITUTION OF ACTS

At the moment of action then, the indubitably biological human and, equally indubitably, a being with a brain whose morphology has been subject to evolutionary processes, is nevertheless, in Mead's phrase, a "social reflective individual" who is able to remember a past and anticipate a future. *This is the presence of self in an act and in a situation, in the moments in which conduct is selected and articulated.* For example, a man's territory is invaded by another and his response to this will be made not on the dictates of the gene, but by his knowledge of his capacities as a fighter, his understanding of his physical strength, his awareness of his social and political rights and powers vis-à-vis his culturally defined role—all in relation to the one who has invaded his territory. All this is subsumed under what Mead discussed as the "past" (1964: 345–354) that influences his action in the nowness of the moment. In addition, an actor will have to estimate the likely consequences of his action for the future of the individual and his relationship with the one who had insulted him by invading his territory. This estimation will include his conception of his own esteem and reputation, as well as his claim to certain expectations that accompany his assumption of the role of manhood as defined in given cultures. For all anyone knows, the genes may play a part in all this, but it is a self, based on the knowledge of a past and an anticipation of the future, that will parsimoniously describe the variable acts that are produced to meet the situation. In fact, this action cannot be predicted on the basis of the genes that the individual may possess. The action and the situation are themselves indeterminate and even the minimum predictability they may possess is based on the knowledge we can garner about the selves, society, and culture of the individuals in question. It is imperative that we recognize this self as an agent in all its richness, variety, and complexity, and posit him or her as the alternative to a biologistic entity.

These variations in acting are possible only because the human mind is able to undertake various *subtle* and *exquisite* maneuvers. Mead writes, "The essence of the self . . . is cognitive: it lies in the internalized conversation of gestures which constitutes thinking, or in terms of which thought or reflection proceeds" (1934: 173). This conversation occurs between what Mead calls the "I" and "me" aspects of the self. The "I" and "me" as aspects of the self is at the center of the social act for Mead. It is in their interrelationship and in their "conversation" that Mead locates the impulse to action. As Mead writes,

> This process of relating one's own organism to the others in the interactions that are going on, insofar as it is imported into the conduct of the individual with the conversation of the "I" and the "me," constitutes the self. (1934: 179)

It is this conceptualization that gives Mead's approach its dialogical cast: the interplay between the "I" and "me" in the consciousness of an individual is conducted as if they were separate persons having a conversation. It is the locus of what Mead calls the "importation of the social process" (1934: 186). The imported social process is a conversation between "I" and "me" in the mind of the acting individual and, as in ordinary conversations, sometimes one and sometimes the other gains the upper hand. Mead, conscious of the pitfalls of solipsism that was facing him in dealing with the notion of "I," writes, "I do not mean to raise the metaphysical question of how a person can be both 'I' and 'me,' but to ask for the significance of this distinction from the point of view of conduct itself" (1934: 173). It is then not a metaphysical problem at all but a practical one and seeks an answer to the question: How to explain the complex dialogical process by which an act is produced by an individual?

> The simplest way of handling the problem would be in terms of memory. I talk to myself, and I remember what I said and perhaps the emotional content that went with it. The "I" of this moment is present in the "me" of the next moment. There again I cannot turn around quick enough to catch myself. I become a "me" insofar as I remember what I said. . . . *It is as we act that we are aware of ourselves* . . . the "I" in memory is there as the spokesman of the self of the second, or minute, or day ago. (1934: 174, my emphasis)

In the execution of an act, then, the "I" and "me" are both involved in a dialogical and temporal interaction. The "I" and "me" participate in defining each other as well as in *controlling* the act that issues forth from the individual, just as one follows the other at a point and then is followed by the other at another point. Neither is given an a priori sovereignty or dominance. In the terminology of quantum physics, "I" and "me" are commuting variables, or in the terminology of Chinese cosmology they are yang and yin, forever in a moving relationship with each other. Nevertheless, in given moments of a life one can be more dominant than the other. The relationship between "I" and "me" can be diagrammed as follows:

In the first case there is a balance between "I" and "me" with neither achieving dominance and having a commensurate effect on conduct. The second case represents a state in which "I" is dominant and the acts of the individual will be more creative, spontaneous, less sensitive to the influence

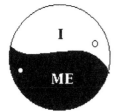 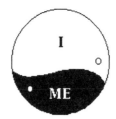 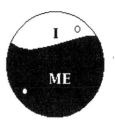

and demands of the other, society, culture. The third case is the reverse of this; creativity and spontaneity are suppressed and a very rigid conformity to social and cultural standards is maintained.

Conduct, Mead shows, is never the easy production of responses; rather it is a consequence of convoluted conversational processes. It is the conversation between "I" and "me" that enables an "organism" to be *both* individuated and social. For centuries, these have been held to be opposed concepts captured in various antinomial codings: individual *versus* society, self *versus* collectivity, microsociology *versus* macrosociology, and so on. The possibility of simultaneity has escaped many, but not Mead. The self is simultaneously individual and social, private and public, closed and open, finished and expectant, oriented to a past and a presumptive future. To the extent that such acts are *simultaneously* objective and subjective, I-centric and me-centric, it takes into account relevant features of "social structure," "history," "economy," and "politics" and the capacity for agency. In undertaking an act, in organizing its contours and parameters, an individual, then, to begin with, takes his or her own role: He or she intimates in such a taking his or her own understanding of his or her value in a hierarchy of class, one's place in a structure of power, in a system of divided labor, in a framework of signs, privileges, and obligations, all of them socially defined and learned. Once having taken his or her own role, he or she takes the role of the other and incorporates into such a taking the class, gender and race, power, place and rights, privileges and obligations of the other. In the dialogue that begins this way and ensures, these factors of the self and others function to define the further development of the respective selves of the participants. It is in these continuing dialogical processes that an action occurs and a presence of self is realized. The grammar of the self, for Mead, is the grammar of *interrelating* an objective and subjective sense of being. Such an interrelating marshals the creative capacities of the "I," the memories from past experiences, the "me" and the situation in which it finds itself and expresses a complex act.

It is possible then to talk of I-centric selves, me-centric selves, and the balanced styling of selves. The actions of Dylan Thomas in the later years of his life may be cited as an example of an I-centric self. The details of his moves are reported by John Malcolm Brinnin's work on Thomas's sojourn in the United States. Nearly everywhere he went he violated one social convention or another and had to have his conduct forgiven by indulgent friends and hosts. He meets Shelley Winters, who was familiar with Thomas's poetry and was keen to discuss it with him. Yet they talked about baseball and the, Brinnin writes, "The conversation changed, becoming centered on Dylan's appreciation of Miss Winters' more obvious physical attractions which he had wanted to measure for himself" (Brinnin 1955: 53). Here is another description of Thomas's moves:

> As the evening wore on, Dylan returned to unabashed dalliance with his hostess while, sprawling on the floor, he spilled liquor over himself and seemed to have retreated into a state of loud drunkenness in which his boyish self-indulgence overtook all his lovable qualities and left him a figure of ridicule to strangers and a figure of despair to friends. (1955: 261)

Lest this behavior be attributed to mere drunkenness, it must be noted that soon after this incident he was able to stop this line of action, get up from the floor, pick up his briefcase and leave the party with Brinnin and his friend. However, there is no doubt that alcohol must be considered the great leveler of the "me" and the liberator of the springs of the "I." Indeed it could be said that one consumes alcohol in order to open the embankment in which "I" is kept and release it to act, sometimes tentatively and at other times more vigorously.

A perfect example of a me-centric self can be found in Robert Merton's description of the "bureaucratic personality." He argues that such a personality displays in Thorstein Veblen's phrase a "trained incapacity" to adjust his or her actions to changing circumstances (Merton 1968: 249–260).

A balanced self, a self in which the I and the me are in control of each other, can be discovered in the actions of most ordinary human beings. They are spontaneous and creative when the situation warrants it and controlled and disciplined when such is the situational exigency.

In Mead's discussion of the phases of the act he assumes the presence of a social self to which the act is referred in its later phases. What in fact is the relationship between the social self and the act in the primary processes by which the social self is constituted? A social self, Mead argues, is constituted through acts in what he terms "general stages." For the early stages of the emergence of the self, Mead argues that "play" and "game" could be used as convenient descriptions. In the play stage children play at various roles. The fundamental feature of these stages is that they are constituted by very particularized acts and they develop in the individual the capacity to construct social acts. Mead describes the process of such playing in a way that calls attention to the process by which a child objectifies himself or herself and develops the capacity to act on the basis of such objectification.

> He plays that he is, for instance, offering himself something, and he buys it; he gives a letter to himself and takes it away; he addresses himself as a parent, as

a teacher; he arrests himself as a policeman. He has a set of stimuli which call out in himself the sort of responses they call out in others. He takes this group of responses and organizes them into a certain whole. (1934: 150–151)

These moves by the one who is engaged in play—"offering," "buying," "giving," "addressing," "arresting"—are *systematized social acts,* and it is in the course of such acting that the self is said to emerge. Das and McCarthy put this very well; "In the acts of children at play one can observe the initial stages in the 'genesis of self.' The self is built up, so to speak, over the course of an individual's life through its engagement in act" (1986: 37).

Once he or she is able to engage in these acts, it is possible to say he or she begins to form a certain rudimentary self. He or she still needs to develop a social self and this is accomplished in the next stage where he or she seeks to play roles vis-à vis others in rather restricted circles—what Mead calls the "game stage." This is followed by learning the roles and expectations that are appropriate to larger social groups. He summarizes this as follows:

> The individual's self is constituted simply by the organization of the particular attitudes of other individuals toward himself and toward one another in the specific social acts in which he participates with them. But at the second stage in the full development of the individual's self that the self is constituted not only by an organization of these particular individual attitudes, but also by an organization of the social attitudes of the generalized other or the social group as a whole to which he belongs. (1934: 158)

The engagements in acts are pragmatic exercises; an individual acts in order to solve various problems. It is when confronted with a problem of some sort that an individual acts, and in the playing and gaming that Mead uses as descriptions of the stages in the constitution of self, plays and games present problems for the individual. In these plays the individual acts to face and solve problems, in maximal or minimal ways, and proceeds to the next step. The problems may be said to offer resistances that the individual handles to the best of his or her ability and reaps the fruits of such labors.

The significant point in descriptions of the stages by which a self emerges is Mead's systematic avoidance of any whiff of either solipsism or mechanistic behaviorism. *It is the act and the social act, the exercise of choice and selectivity among given alternatives, and the recognition of sociality, together that aids in the emergence of the self.* In contract to the Freudian view that a social being (ego) emerges out of the repression of fundamental instinctual forces, Mead develops a theory of the emergence of the human self in which *expression* plays a crucial part. The child expresses itself in the play stage—at least an early version of itself: When the child *acts* the role of a policeman, what does this involve? At a minimum the child has to assume a certain posture, construct a certain demeanor and, if the child is lucky, he or she may even have some special clothing and props to bolster his or her acting. In these doings the child is undoubtedly in an expressive mode and has to produce not only an act, but a series of more or less coordinated acts. Furthermore, in such doings he or she not only acts but *responds* to his or here own acts, and these responses are also acts. In these beginnings, he or she develops the capacity to objectify himself or herself and perhaps experience the ecstasy of imaginatively being someone other than a mere child.

In his conceptualization of the game stage, too, Mead avoids both solipsism and behaviorism: The individual learns to produce his or her acts in *coordination* with the acts of the others. He or she does not just sit there or stand there waiting for stimuli to hit him or her and then proceed to respond to it. Rather, he or she actively participates in the ongoing social process. In the game stage individuals seek to anticipate the acts of the others, stay alert and observant of the attitudes these acts encode and display, respond to their own responses, and organize them all into an image and a concept of the self.

What Mead proposes here is that, instead of proceeding then from inside consciousness, positing a self and explaining it as the source of the springs of action, we proceed from the act itself and then investigate the consequences of the action. It is these consequences that are assembled as they become available as sedimented meanings into a viable self.

At the moment of the act's realization, it can be allowed to proceed to the next moment as defined initially or put on a different course by the responses it mobilized. The act is dialogical then in being unfinished, capable of being transformed as it proceeds, and eliciting a variety of responses from the participants in its evolving moments. The individual is endowed with certain faculties that ensure that his or her actions become indubitably dialogical constructions.

A human, then, undertakes an act and as he or she is in the process of initiating it, carrying it forward and consummating it, he or she is able to observe it, i.e., "measure" it, and thereby give it an entirely different significance. This process will be readily seen when one examines emotional acts: An individual is made angry by the moves of another and he or she is moved to act in response and gives violent expression to his or her anger, and then as he or she is about to manifest the act, the individual observes that the other is a more powerful (socially or physically) individual and suppresses his or her act, controls it or redefines the emotion and smiles weakly and moves on to the next phase. This is the dialectic of the act; it moves along as it is produced, is watched and measured as it emerges, is subjected to evaluation and examination, however momentarily, and then is allowed to proceed on its initial course or is truncated and a new act initiated, one that is subject to the same process all over again. Yet, all acts do not proceed along this course all the time. Some may be so habitual that they may move without reflection and analysis; nevertheless, they, too are potentially available for inspection and redirection.

It is in the temporal development of acts that a self emerges and manifests itself. To recognize the relationship between acts and the self is to recognize two dimensions of its temporality. One is to acknowledge the self's presence as a historical continuity, to conceive it as having had a very particular past, remembering it and allowing such a past to influence the forthcoming acts. To do this is to be able to also accept the self as being in a particular moment in its own history. For example, at the moment of any act, an individual remembers his or her past, recognizes his or her biography as it pertains to the act in question and also understands that he or she is, shall I say, no longer as young as he or she used to be and should not climb this mountain. The second dimension of temporality that an actor typically recognizes is the significance of the moment in an ongoing relationship or transaction in which an act is occurring or forthcoming and uses such recognition perspicuously. In an ongoing relationship there is, for example, a moment when one had just declared his undying love for someone and the acts that succeed such a declaration will have the marks of the declaration, at least for a while. Similarly the self that is present immediately after one had called someone else a liar and a sneak must acknowledge such an act and all ensuing acts must do so, too.

Acts are then dialogical in this sense too: They have a continuity to earlier acts and still earlier acts. In their tendency to exist as an *interconnected* series resides their capacity to define a self and give it not only a presence but a semblance of continuity. The individual, in other words, remembers his or her past acts, minimally or maximally, recollects the emotional, cognitive, and practical results and residues from them, and organizes them into a more or less coherent conception of his or her power, capabilities, and limitations, and so on. This is his or her self. The acts that an individual prosecutes may be accomplished in the here and now, and all reality may be the consequence of such acts, but for all that, an individual—amnesiacs and others similarly impaired excepted—remembers the consequences of his or her earlier acts, and such remembrances of past acts will influence the selection and execution of current acts. Mead writes,

> It is just this combination of the *remembered self* which acts and exists over against other selves with the inner response to his action which is essential to the self-conscious ego—the self in the full meaning of the term. (1964 [1915]: 146, italics added)

The remembered self is really the recollected, stored, and practicalized meanings of earlier acts—indeed, they are habits of the mind and habits of the body, intertwined inextricably in many cases. In other words, the act is dialogical in both the spatial and temporal dimensions: An individual interacts with the other, particularized or generalized, with objects, environment, and ideas, as well as with the remembrances of earlier acts and produces acts that are layered and complexly faceted. As an individual acts he or she is, in the moment-to-moment moves of everyday life, accomplishing interactions, constituting relationships and groups, and realizing social structure as well as formulating a self. Such moves, however, are part of a series that began earlier, and have roots earlier still, a series which is retained in the mind, and according to some recent researchers, in the very tissues of the brain. (Rose 1992; Brothers 1997). In such a conception of the relationship between acts and memory and their manifestation in the tissues of the brain, the self itself may have a presence in the brain too. Insofar as such memories are as cognitive as they are emotional, the positive and negative characteristics of both may remain and affect one's self. Culture, institutions, and history manifest themselves in social acts as remembered and sedimented meanings.[1]

The "structures" of society—caste, class, race, ethnicity, gender, clan, family, organizations, communities, religious orders, and nations manifest themselves as symbolic experiences for the individual and are present in the selves of given individuals as identities that each recognizes and are given recognition by his or her others. Such identities manifest themselves as memories, emotional and cognitive, and as practices, as vocabularies of motives, and as discursive definitions and programs that an individual would use in prosecuting his or her lines of action.

It is in the operation of these dialogical processes between an I and me on the one hand and between an individual and the other, mediated by memory, in any given act, that social structure enters conduct. It does this in two ways: one, as constraints imposed by others who have the power and the inclination to exercise control over the self; two, as meanings that the self knows and acknowledges and accepts as constraints on his or her conduct. It is the latter that is of interest here: Social structure in the sense of larger units of membership—ethnicity, race, and class, religion, for example—are meaning-systems and action-systems in which an individual participates. As such they are available as rules and regulations, constraining principles and enabling ones, that he or she knows and uses in prosecuting his or her acts. To know these rules, regulations, and principles is to remember them from the past, remember them, not only as rules and regulations and principles but as acts that were prosecuted under their aegis and from the responses they elicited from one's significant social circles.

Social structure, then, is known and remembered, however partially or habitually, and it is in that form that it enters conduct. At the point of conduct the multitudinous elements contained in a people's culture, as well as the elements that constitute social structure, enter the acts as unreflected memories, that is, as habits or as conscious memories of past experiences. Indeed they cannot enter conduct, determine its character, influence it, and guide it except as recollections and redefinitions of acts, images, injunctions, recommendations, commandments, stipulations, expositions, and so on to the acting self. Acts are assembled, presented, and executed in the interaction between the situated moment and the memories that an actor bears, and there is no telling which will become dominant and rule the moment and its selves.

The grace and subtlety of Mead's conceptualization of the act and the self lies precisely in the dialectic in which it is framed. Neither the self nor the act is given a temporal priority in the moment of conduct; they involve each other in these moments. The individual produces an act and it bespeaks the self and the individual responds to the act and it becomes a meaning for the self. The self creates the act and is created by the act. The act creates the self and the self creates the act. The self is present in the act and it is present later as a memory that is inextricably intertwined with the act that produced it. In Mead's words:

> The self is not something that exists first and then enters into relationship with others, but it is, so to speak, an eddy in the social current and so still a part of the current. It is a process in which the individual is continually adjusting himself in advance to the situation to which he belongs, and reacting back on it. (1934: 182)

## ACTS AND OTHERS

The elements that function in the dialectic between the I and me, the terms of the "inner conversation" that become the initiatives for action are themselves "imported from the social process" (Mead 1934: 186). This social process enables another dimension of the dialectic of the act to manifest itself. What in detail, then, is this "social process"? It has two fundamental elements. First, the language that an individual uses to conduct this conversation, language in the broadest sense of the word, is such a social process; and second, the system of others that the individual takes into account in executing a social act is another element of the social process. In doing this an individual "orients" his or her acts, to use Max Weber's word, toward three types of others: *interactional others, significant others,* and the *generalized other.* Erving Goffman's work can be considered as a detailed examination of the influence of the interactional other on the conduct of an individual. The roots of his conception are nevertheless contained in Mead's concept of taking the role of the other:

> This taking the role of the other . . . is not simply of passing importance. It is not something that just happens as an incidental result of the gesture, but is of importance in the development of co-operative activity. The immediate effect of such role-taking lies in the control which the individual is able to exercise over his own response." (Mead 1934: 254)

By taking the role of the other, one is able to assert control over his or her own acts and thus also exert control over the other's response by investing the right quality in his or her acts and eliciting the response that is appropriate.

Goffman's work is articulated squarely within these parameters. From his use of the dramaturgical perspective in his first work to the essays on stigma and interaction rituals, role distance, and behavior in public places, there cannot be any doubt that Mead's concept of taking the role of the other is the central organizing principle. Each move, word, and gesture in these studies is organized—in Goffman's estimation—in such a way that it takes account of the other, its role, its attitudes, and the likely responses of the other to whatever move, in word or gesture, one is making at the moment or is about to make. In other words, he or she takes the role as well as the attitude of the other, thus converting him or her into an interactional other; this is accomplished by submitting one's acts to what Goffman calls the "rules of conduct":

> An act that is subject to a rule of conduct is, then, a communication, for it represents a way in which selves are confirmed—both the self for which the rule is an obligation and the self for which it is an expectation. (1967: 51)

In observing these rules of conduct, which insofar as they are rules are public and shared, the participants become the interactional other of each other and each orients his or her conduct by anticipating the responses of the other. "Thus rules of conduct transform," Goffman continues, "both action and inaction into expression, and whether the individual abides by the rules or breaks them, something significant is likely to be communicated" (1967: 51). These moves cannot be undertaken without identifying the other and taking his or her role and making him or her an interactional other.

Further, to the extent that the individual is a minded creature, forever using a discursive mind, he or she is able to recall deliberately or as a habitualized "response" the attitudes of certain others with whom one has had a particular *emotional* relationship, and let such "recollections"—what Harry Stack Sullivan called "dynamisms" (1953: 102–103)—to influence the prosecution of an act. Such *significant others* were first described by Sullivan as follows:

> Out of the social responsibility of the mothering one, which gets involved in the satisfaction of the infant's needs, there comes the organization in the infant of what might be said to be a dynamism directed at how to live with this significant other person. The self-system is thus an organization of educative experience called into being by the necessity to avoid or minimize incidents of anxiety. (1953: 165)

The dynamism of the self-system is organized to forestall rejection by, and disapproval from, significant others. It begins to be formulated in childhood and as the individual develops, he or she keeps the original significant others and adds new ones as his or her life circumstances change. An individual tailors his or her acts in a way that they *subjunctively* meet with their approval. Sullivan conceives a dynamism "with primary reference to the tensions which recurrently disturb the euphoria of the living creature and manifest themselves in interpersonal relations as integrating, disjunctive, or isolative tendencies of a particular sort" (1953: 109).

Finally, to the extent that the acting individual is a member of a community, it is the case that he or she would act in terms of the standards and values of the community. As he or she is socialized in the community by various individuals, he or she soon generalizes the values and standards and uses this generalization to orient his or her conduct. Mead says of this,

> The organized community or social group which gives to the individual his unity of self may be called the "generalized other." The attitude of the generalized other is the attitude of the whole community." (1934: 154)

In the actual prosecution of an act, then, the individual is implicated in three "otherations"*(alteracion)*, to borrow a concept from Ortega y Gasset (1956: 165); an interactional other, a significant other, and a generalized other. The interactional other gives immediate face-to-face control to the act, the significant other provides the emotional basis of the act, and the generalized other guides the act in accordance with the standards of the community. In the concrete emergence of the act all three others may be subsumed into one process just as in other such instances they may be separated and in conflict with each other, thus making the individual choose one over the other and feel shame, anxiety, or guilt. That is, one is shamed and embarrassed when he or she meets with the disapproval of the interactional other, anxiety-ridden when he or she imagines and anticipates rejection by the significant other, and guilty at having violated the norms of the community.

Situating the acts that humans undertake within a dialectic of relationships with others acknowledges the influence and power of others that are attendant features of all interactions and relationships. These features enter into every act and confer influences of two kinds. First, the power and influence that others asserted at one time and were institutionalized as practices become incorporated as constituent elements of the self. These practices, and the power they embody, become coterminus with self-conceptions and operate *implicitly* in the production of acts. They function to inhibit certain kinds of acts and allow only certain other kinds of acts insofar as a reflexive creature one is able to monitor his or her own acts. Second, there is the power and influence that the others, or their agents, can direct at an actor to sanction certain acts and prohibit certain others. The generalized other manifests itself in the form of various social agents: parents, teachers, priests, policemen, judges, jailers, psychiatrists, and various others—all of whom can control the acts of the individual. The significant others, by their capacity to induce anxiety, guilt, and shame also control the acts of an individual. Interactional others, too, can elicit desired responses from an individual by the moral, physical, or institutional power they embody. These responses get organized and systematized and eventually become habitualized acts and give the self a certain stability.[2]

It has been easy enough to recognize that human beings are reflexive actors without specifying what they are being reflexive about. It is of course not possible to be just reflexive; rather, one is reflexive about self in relation to a world of objects and a world of others—interactional, significant, and general, which latter also includes institutions. One puts oneself into presumptive relationships with these objects and others and defines one's acts and self in terms of such relationships.

## FOUCAULT'S SELF

Michel Foucault claims that the "subject" is constituted discursively within given historical frameworks which are realized through the relationships between "power" and "knowledge." He writes,

> These "power-knowledge relations" are to be analysed, therefore, not on the basis of a subject of knowledge who is or is not free in relation to the power system, but, on the contrary, the subject who knows, the objects to be known and the modalities of knowledge must be regarded as so many effects of these fundamental implications of power-knowledge and their historical transformations. (1979: 27–28)

This view of the "subject" has spawned a veritable industry of scholars who have taken the Foucaldian argument, expressed here and elsewhere, and claimed a "vanishing subject," in Vincent Colapietro's phrase (1990), in contemporary social science and philosophy. Jonathan Culler has put these views very succinctly as follows: "As the self is broken down into component systems, deprived of its status as source and master of meaning, it comes to seem more and more like a construct: a result of systems of convention" (1981: 33).

Foucault may be right in every particular in the statement quoted above except for one claim he is making. The self or the subject is constituted as an object, to be sure by the "modalities of knowledge" available to it, and is "so many effects" of the "power-knowledge" and "their historical transformations." The flaw in this argument, however, is the assumption that such knowledge-systems or discursive formations are singular and clear-cut and invariant in the "fundamental implications" they indicate, the implications that are realized as the subjectivity of the individual. *In the semiotic processes by which these "implications" are apprehended and made relevant in the constitution of a subject, they can be interpreted in a variety of ways and used to construct a subject.* At any moment in the career of the individual, after his or her childhood, as a language-speaking entity, he or she is able to choose among various alternative "implicatons" of the available forms of discourse. The "effects" that become the subject are themselves situational variables. These alternative implications may be subject to the same strictures: that they, too, are effects of the regimes of power and knowledge. There can be no doubt, however, that the agent himself or herself, and his or her own associates, including the agents of socialization, are able to exercise at given moments in time, indeed at the moment of performances, a choice among the alternative "implications" of these regimes of power, knowledge, and discourse and use it to constitute a self. Whether they are able to make this choice in such a moment or not is dependent on the concrete empirical circumstances in which the performance was occurring and cannot be settled by a priori fiat from theoreticians. Once again, an analogy suggests itself: The discourses by which the self is constituted are like language no doubt, but *once they are acquired* they become a steady state of competence, a set of instrumentations, with which the discursive organism is able to generate a range of discursive acts and give presence in one moment or another to one type of self or other. In the moment of acting, that is, an individual acts as an agent who is conscious of his or her self—fashioned though it may be by various regimes of power and knowlege.

If one were to obtain descriptions of a self by asking individuals to write statements about themselves, it will be evident that all of them, even if they are members of the same community or social circles, will not issue the same language of description. One may say, "I am a born-again Christian" and may say, second, "I am a mother." Another may say, "I am a Methodist but I haven't been to church for awhile" and "I am single." "I am a Catholic, but I believe that a woman must have the right to choose to have an abortion." It is undoubtedly true that three of these statements are issued from the discourse of religion and that the other from the discourse of marriage, social roles, and gender, but for all practical purposes, i.e., for *everyday interactional purposes* they are different descriptions and can be taken to be descriptions of different conceptions of self.

A key issue here is that given the primacy of language or discourse, a *sufficiently* different description of the individual can emerge and these descriptions are results of a choice. Insofar as we cannot say that these choices were made, not by the "discourses," but by sentient humans with a mind, we are driven to conclude that the choices were made by a minded self or selved mind. This may well elicit the rebuttal that the self making these choices was itself constituted by an earlier regime of discourse—opening up the logical problem of infinite regress. However, this problem is only an apparent one. The constitution of the self, the choice among various available discourses, is not done by an earlier or primordial self as such but by a mind, albeit a social mind, that is capable of making choices among alternatives. In fact the mind is antecedent to the self, and the self is to be considered a feature of the mind. The mind emerges socially, as language emerges, before the self is constructed.

The question that arises is: when does this construction occur? And how does this occur? At what stage in a particular human's life is it possible to say that the "construct" has been made? And what of the nature of the human before such a construct is successfully completed? And what are the processes by which such a construct is made to emerge, appear, and function successfully? Clearly these are *variables*: Selves emerge at a particular moment in the life of the individual by more or less rigorous processes of socialization and are always subject to alteration as the individual is confronted with different experiences, varied others. At one time an individual may be forced to submit to a particular discourse and at other times he or she may choose the discourse to which he or she wants to give allegiance. To dub all these complex and variable factors as intersecting "systems of conventions," is a sophistry that does not account parsimoniously for the human predicament, leaves too much out, and succeeds in only being trivially clever. *To accept this as a limitation on agentic and deliberate control over a human's actions—i.e., self-conscious actions, is to put the same limitation on them that Watsonian and Skinnerian behaviorism did.* In such a perspective once a newly born human is socialized into a "discourse," "conditioned" into it, he or she loses all his or her capacity to choose one line of action rather than another and becomes merely a "servant of the language" as Foucault put it, an operant machine, a printing press! Rather, when an individual is confronted by another and has to deal with the words that he or she utters, he or she has to deal with them as products of an agentic self. Consider this: A man comes up to me, shows a gun and says, "Your money or your life." This utterance is no doubt drawn from various discourses: the discourse of capitalist accumulation and free enterprise—make money by one means or another, on your own effort, even if you have to hurt other people. It may have elements of the discourse of "possessive individualism," which C. B. MacPherson describes as the claim that, "The human essence is freedom from dependence on the wills of others, and freedom is a function of possession"—particularly property (1962: 3). The demand may also speak to the discourse of gun ownership as a fundamental right guaranteed by the United States Constitution and the discourse of "masculinity," of the male role as one of aggrandizement, initiative, assertiveness, courage, and so on and so forth. Nevertheless, when I hear these words, and see the expression on the man's face and the gun in his hand, I will *necessarily* understand this to mean that the other is a self-conscious agent with control and power over his "subjectivity" and its acts which can kill me if I did not accede to the significance of his remarks. The key issue here is that the words that were used as parts of a social act were chosen by an individual and uttered in a selected situation to a particular other.

My responses to this demand from the other for my money or my life will no doubt be based on the particular discourses with which I have already constituted myself, been allowed to constitute myself. Yet, I have a situated choice here: I look at the individual making the demand, see that he is a big, strong, young man with a cocked Magnum revolver in his hand, and I weakly give him my wallet and all the other money I can gather from my pockets. Or else, I look at the individual, see that he is a weak-looking and emaciated youth who is shaking in his boots and is holding what appears to be a toy gun, uncocked. I tell him "Go to hell" and walk away. In each case, I examined my options based on my interpretation of the environment and produced a response, even if the options from which I am making a choice are "systems of conventions" to which I am already subjected. However cravenly dominated by regimes of discourse a human being may be, he or she possesses the capacity to make this situated choice. There are neither philosophical nor practical gains to be made by denying that acts are self-conscious and situated doings. The self may be a servant of the language but only at the given moment of its constitution; at a later moment, as servants are wont to do, the self learns to manage the master, subtly or overtly.

The position I am advancing here is that between the discursive modes that constituted the individual and the moment of action there is the *interregnum* of a self-indicating and discursive mind, or in Jill McCorkel's (1998) felicitous wording "a critical space," from which one is able to make choices and act. In this interregnum the mind is able to integrate various discourses and arrive at a synthesis which is the self. Consider here Jerry Fodor's refutation of the claims of "psychological darwinism." In a review of books on the subject and commenting on their claims of the evolution of modular structures in the brain, Fodor wrote,

> The moon looks bigger when it's on the horizon; but I know perfectly well it's not. My visual perception module gets fooled, but I don't. The question is: who is this I? And by what . . . computational process does it use what I know about astronomical facts to correct the misleading appearances that my visual perception module insists on computing? (1998: 12)

One can substitute the word "discourse" wherever the word "module" appears in this passage and also ask: Who is this I that constitutes a response to the discourses of various regimes? In the actual performance of the act the individual believes that he or she is in charge of the act as do the others involved with him or her in the act: He or she, as well as those others, will hold him or her responsible for the act. No doubt the realization, of the contradictions in Faucault's conception of "subject," as well as the realization, too, that perhaps it is really not possible to deny that the self is the "source and master of meanings," led Foucault to recast some of his ideas on this in his later work. Alex Callinicos (1990) has, in fact, argued that in his description of the "technologies of the self" in the later volumes of his study of sexuality, Foucault accepted the need for the practices of "self-constitution" and "self government." Callinicos quotes Foucault in support of this claim, "Couldn't everyone's life become a work of art? Why should the lamp or the house be a work of art, but not our life?" (1986a: 350) (in Callinicos 1990: 89). For one's life to become a work of art, for it to develop "style," an individual must be able to take control and fashion a self that conformed to the exacting demands of an artistry and an aesthetic.

This commitment to understanding life as a work of art leads Foucault to considering the self itself as a work of art—at least envisaging the possibility of doing so. This is clearly seen in the studies that he published about the history of sexuality (1986b; 1988). The usage of the concept of self in these works, rather different from the one in the works of Mead, is captured in the following words from his commentary on Artemidorus's book on the interpretation of sexual dreams:

> The guiding thread of Artemidorus' interpretation, insofar as it is concerned with the predictive value of sexual dreams, implies the breaking down and ordering of such dreams into elements (personages or acts) that are, by nature, social elements; and that it indicates a certain way of qualifying sexual acts in terms of the manner in which the dreaming subject maintains, as the subject of the dreamed-of act, his position as a social subject. (Foucault 1986b: 33)

If in fact one can constitute one's self as a "social subject," it must also be possible for him or her to cast himself or herself as a social object. This, too, is not outside of Foucault's conception of the self. In another section of the same work cited earlier he writes:

> The interplay of the care of the self and the help of the other blends into pre-existing relations, giving them a new coloration and a greater warmth. The care of the self—or the attention one devotes to the care that others should take care of themselves—appears then as an intensification of social relations. (1986: 53)

Foucault recognizes here that a human being can cast himself or herself simultaneously as a social subject as well as a social object. Indeed, a human being accomplishes the objectification of his or her self by, in Foucault's words,

> testing oneself, examining oneself, monitoring oneself in a series of clearly defined exercises, makes the question of truth—the truth concerning what one is, what one does, and what one is capable of doing—central to the formation of the ethical subject. (1986b: 68)

In spite of the appearance of the word "subject" in the above passage, it is clear that the activities that Foucault is describing cannot be undertaken without considering the self as an object. It would be "psycholinguistically" impossible to test, examine, and monitor one's self without converting it into an object.

Indeed this is what Foucault seems to have done with his own life. An examination of his life would indicate that Foucault was a very self-conscious and individuated actor: he chooses to go to the École Normale Supérieure, he decides to do the preparatory work to ensure that he does get accepted into it, and he chooses various steps in his career that eventually make him a professor in the Collège de France. He may or may not have chosen his homosexuality but he does choose to live his homosexuality in one way rather than another. For instance, he challenges certain established ways of living his life and chooses to live a life of defiance and to even court death by adopting a particular style rather than another, a style with a certain congruence with his own researches into sexuality (Miller 1993). In short, studying his biography one cannot help but come to the conclusion that here was an individual, undertaking various acts by making choices among a variety of available discourses, regimes of power and authority, systems of knowledge, and thereby giving presence to his self as a work of art. It turns out that it is the self of a world-renowned philosopher, and perhaps a world-weary one, an author who died, but whose work can be identified as his, can be attributed to him and will be studied for a long time. One can indeed marvel at the boldness of his conceptualizations and at the panache with which he related his life to his lifework.

## *DIFFÉRANCE* AND THE SELF

The other important challenge to the presence of a self has come from another French quarter. In his deconstructive enterprise, Jacques Derrida has indicated the impossibility of achieving a stable and dependable self as the center of action and meaning insofar as the symbols that are used to construct it are inherently unstable, in a constant flux, and "play." Coining a word, he writes:

> *Différance* is the systematic play of differences, of the traces of differences, of the *spacing* by means of which elements are related to each other. . . . The activity or productivity connoted by the *a* of *différance* refers to the generative movement in the play of differences. The latter are neither fallen from the sky nor inscribed once and for all in a closed system, a static structure that a synchronic and taxonomic operation could exhaust. Differences are the effects of transformations, and from this vantage the theme of *différance* is incompatible with the static, synchronic, taxonomic, ahistoric motifs in the concept of *structure*. (1981: 27)

If this is the case, no stable self nor subject, dependent as it is on stable meanings of signs, is possible because like Heraclitus's river, meanings become perennially commuting variables. Each word that is used to describe and define a self will automatically suggest an absent word or words that can undermine or expand the meaning of the present word, thereby making a definition of self, with the help of these very recalcitrant words, unstable. Each moment a self conceives itself with these unstable references, it has to defer a final position because the meaning of the conception is shifting as it speaks and conceives. "Needless to say," says Edward Sampson, tracing the implications of Derrida's work for a theory of the self, "if 'presence' is already inhabited by absence, then even the apparent presence of the subject to itself becomes suspect" (1989:9).

Insofar as the information that is needed for the reflexive constitution of the self is in one symbolic form or another (verbal, gestural, visual), it cannot have, according to Derrida, a stability of significance: they will always be afflicted with the "play of differences." Indeed it may not be possible to decipher the significance the individual is seeking to convey with his or her words—there will always be "free play" in the interpretation of the words of the other. Jacques Derrida puts it this way:

> There are thus two interpretations of interpretation, of structure, of sign, of freeplay. The one seeks to decipher, dreams of deciphering, a truth or an origin which is free from freeplay and the order of the sign. . . . The other, which is no longer turned towards the origin, affirms freeplay and tries to pass beyond man and humanism, the name man being the name of that being who, throughout the history of metaphysics or ontotheology—in other words, through the history of all his history—had dreamed of full presence, the reassuring foundation, the origin and end of the game. (1972: 264–265)

Novel as this approach to the analysis of meaning may appear at first, it is nevertheless foreshadowed in the work of Charles Sanders Peirce. In his succinct statement on the relationship among a sign, an object, and an interpretant, he leaves open the possibility that the "interpretative structure as a whole can in turn become a sign for a further interpretive structure" (Rosenthal 1969: 176). This "infinite regress" needs to be arrested, however, in the practical affairs of everyday life, and as in the problematics of quantum physics, everything must be subject to ordinary processes of "measurement" so that some action can be taken. John Boler and Sandra Rosenthal, along with other students of Peirce, recognize this problem in Peirce's theory of meaning. For Peirce, the way out of such a *pragmatically* unacceptable "regress" is to posit a "logical interpretant" as the end of one series of interpretive procedures, an interpretant that can become a "habit of response" as George Gentry (1952) puts it in an analysis of Peirce's works. Rosenthal provides a more complex answer to the problem of the infinite regress of interpretations by integrating Peirce's ideas with those of Mead. She writes, quoting Peirce:

> The term "interpretant" refers to an effect produced in the interpreter by a sign (5: 475). Thus, an interpretant is an effect in an interpreter. The logical interpretant is a concept (5: 486) and is the only interpretant "properly denominated a concept" (5: 467). Furthermore, such intellectual concepts (which are, properly speaking, the only kind of concept there is) are "those upon the structure of which arguments concerning objective fact may hinge" (Peirce 5: 467). (Rosenthal 1969: 174–175)

In the notion of the "concept" and "the logic of concepts" as further developed by Mead, she argues that we find an answer to the problem of an infinite continuum of interpretations. For Rosenthal, such a logic of concepts leads to the emergence of the "ultimate logical interpretant." She notes,

> As an intrinsic "part" of any interpretive structure or concept one finds both the logical interpretant (as well as the emotional and energetic interpretants), which *necessarily* requires a further interpretant, and the ultimate logical interpretant. (Rosenthal 1969: 176)

This ultimate interpretant makes it possible, in the form of "concepts" and "imagery" to convert mere "collections" into a "system"—that is, an organized or bounded set—for example, sets of meanings.

> That binding element is the ultimate logical interpretant, the real and living interpretant, habit. The emotional, energetic, and logical interpretants thus require a further interpretant in that they must be *unified or held together* in a triadic relationship by the ultimate logical interpretant. (1969: 183, my emphasis)

In the world of practical affairs the self is *centered,* shall I say, by making it into a *concept,* an ultimate logical interpretant, that summarizes and collates the "play" of interpretations that have gone before, a concept that is bound by structures of habits. Even as they allow the play of differences to operate, interpretations are, after all, acts and can occur as a series. These interpretive acts can eventually become habitual and coalesce into a general concept that can be understood by the individual and his or her others and used to formulate a self. Rosenthal puts this as follows:

> The human being is understood as a process through which occurs the praxis-oriented constitution of time through acts of adjustment. Its present, as the locus of reality, is understood in terms of the dynamics of human activity, or what Mead calls the "act," which incorporates past and future in its process of adjustment. (1993: 254)

The act as a unit of human experience then emerges as the "ultimate logical interpretant" act as defined by Mead as beginning in impulses and perception, the confrontation of a problematic situation and its development into "manipulation" and "consummation" (1938: 3–26). In keeping with the pragmatic program, the act may be called the *practical interpretant*, the translation of a *perceptual interpretive* process into acts that impact the external world. Practice settles the meaning of signs, for the time being. The "time being" may be short or long, but it has a significant enough *durée* and is typically "thick" enough to indicate to the individual himself or herself, and to his or her others, the presence of a self. The presence of self is manifested in the *durée* of the act and insofar as an individual and his or her others engage in a series of acts the self is also present in the series.

For all the flux, for all the deferment that can be accomplished, and for all the arbitrariness of the assembly of discrete moments into larger units, they can be so organized by a sentient intelligence into what Rosenthal calls a "thick now" (1993: 252). Further, if time is to be so conceived as discrete moments these moments must still have stability to be considered at all—as Zeno pointed out long ago. Since time, as a continuous variable and time as a discrete variable are equally metaphysical concepts, one can conceive the self as both discrete, manifested in acts, and as continuous, manifested in the narrative assemblage of these acts with a name to designate it. Rosenthal further argues that Derrida's thesis about the "loss of the self . . . is rooted ultimately in his inadequate understanding of time" (1993: 250). She concludes her study with the observation that the powerful views of time and the self found in Mead can be used to "solve issues, problems, and dilemmas on the cutting edge of philosophy today" and

> to avoid the all too easy backslide into the all too treacherous, often all too elusive, terrain of discreteness and its related self-defeating alternatives that Derrida so cleverly exploits and upon which his own tools of deconstruction so fully depend. (1993: 263)

In the fulcrum of an interaction the words that issue from the participants are subject to "free play," no doubt. Nevertheless for *immediate* purposes, and in order to prosecute an action in response to the issued words, he or she has to *assume* if not an origin, at least an originating presence, a self with which he or she has to maintain an interaction and a relationship. In pursuing this goal, the respondent also produces a text that is subject to the same opportunities for "free play" as the original text. In this orgy of free playing at least a minimum of agreement is reached, and for a given duration, by using the standard significations of the words in question. The participants then can produce texts, maintain interactions, conceive and define selves for themselves and for the others in this *durée*. Neither will wait for an Ur-meaning, one without free play, to emerge before dealing with the world, acting in it or on it. Rather, whatever he or she takes to be the significance of the words that he or she receives and completes in his or her action, whatever is *conceived* as the practical consequences of such interpretations is the meaning of the words. If he or she was to take all the free-playing significations into account before making an interpretive response he or she would suffer what may be termed semantic paralysis. For example, while driving, a motorist often comes across a board on which is written the word "Stop." Since the sign does not say "stop and then go," conceivably the motorist could stop there forever. He or she may or may not interpret the sign as defined by the absent word "go." Interpreting the sign for purposes of practical action, however, the motorist would put a conjunction "and" between the present word and the absent word and act on that basis. Indeed the motorist does not wait to trace the traces of the meaning of the word, all the absences it indicates, its deferrals and contradictions, its poetic allusions and ambiguities, but acts on the basis of a habitual interpretation of the word and faces the consequences. By electing to act on one of the deconstructed elements of the word "stop" and moving forward with the vehicle an actor has defined himself or herself as one who lives, perforce, in a situated and practical world.

Let us consider a man, one who calls himself "General Radko Mladic, commander of the Bosnian Serbs." He confronts a Muslim man in Srebrenica in June 1995. There is no doubt that each of the terms of identification in this sentence are subject to the "play of differences," their respective significations infinitely deferrable and unstable. Will this prevent, or should I say, did it prevent, General Mladic from identifying himself as a Bosnian Serb general whose task it was to kill as many Muslims as possible? David Rohde (1997), in a painfully detailed book, has shown that it did not. General Mladic did not wait to deconstruct himself, or the others, did not bother to check for traces of Christian compassion in it, did not defer his action on a recollection of the United Nations' Declaration of Human Rights, did not wait to deconstruct his enemy by wondering about his or her real Muslimness, but acted a *selected* identity with disastrous consequences to the Muslims of Srebrenica. In other words, he already had at his disposal the material with which he could have dissolved the Christian versus Muslim hierarchic binarism. He could, for example, have deconstructed this religious binarism and concluded that the Christians and Muslims were Slavs together or children of the same God of the Jews, Christians, and Muslims together, or humans together. To believe that with the proper deconstructionist training the result would have been different is to commit what may well be termed the textualist fallacy—believing that changing the structures of a text alone will change the world. The reality is rather that though a human being experiences the world in terms of *différances* of a text, he or she can nevertheless differentiate between the practical consequences of one text and another, shift from one to the another and return to it or abandon one text to choose another.

In these acts and in the acting process, then, the deferment of meaning is *always interrupted* and moves of consequence to the self and the world made. If one denies the possibility of these "interruptions" for object-manipulation, a stopover for the process of meaning-organization and self-constitutions to occur, one also has to deny the existence of anything on the basis of which any action can be taken. From such a proposition, it is but a short step to claim that no action should be taken since all actions are fraught with "unanticipated consequences," in Robert Merton's famous phrase (1968: 73–138). Of course there are unanticipated consequences, but there are also consequences that can be anticipated and steps taken to create them. In fact the political implication of the stance that meanings are indefinitely deferred is that no action can be taken now and one always has to wait for the next moment. Conversely, if any action is not possible since the meaning of the action to which this action is a response is unstable and in free play, the action that is not taken, which is itself an act, will have dangerously anticipated consequences. The cry of "fire" can, for instance, be subject to the free play of interpretations, if one had time enough and sufficient love of words, but in certain other moments one must act quickly and make some moves. Nevertheless, there is no doubt that in giving a presence to a self in interaction the "free play" of meaning provides subtle variations to the self. The self is made available to others, not in gross and undifferentiated forms, but as subtly shaded presences. These shadings will change as the interaction proceeds and the significance of the situation and the quality of the interpersonal transaction changes. These shadings are a result of the "free play" that occurs in discourse, plays that can be undertaken by the speaker as well as by the listener. To the extent that they can, by *mutual agreement,* arrive at a working definition of what was going on, and limit the "free play" to manageable dimensions, interactions and interlocutions can proceed, and a viable self be constituted by the construction and presentation of acts. There is, to be sure, deconstructionist activity occurring in a human's response to the symbolic world but such activity is soon, shall I say, *pragmatized*—that is, becomes mindful of the practical consequences of the response—with the actor proceeding to the next step. It is the way out for the actor from a paralytic indecisiveness just as, perhaps, it is the means of escape for deconstructionism itself from a self-defeating and nihilistic cul-de-sac.

## THE GRAMMAR OF ACTS

Every human being, whatever other imperatives may be present, must typically confront others in a situation and the world in its various situational manifestations, experience their "resistances," and produce acts that are "adjustments" that enable the individual to proceed to the next step in the trajectory of its life. In the course of doing this, he or she will remember his or her own past and that of the relevant others and will exercise a *choice* between alternative lines of action. He or she is not controlled by external forces exclusively or pushed by internal forces to act in a certain way. Rather, he or she acts by selecting the moves he or she wants to make and the ends to which they are to be directed by taking into account whatever internal forces and external ones may be active. These acts are used to make *distinctions* between the individual producing the acts and others. They establish an identity for the actor. The exercise of choice and the definition of an identity implies the assumption of *responsibility* for them. The individual stands by the acts, acknowledges their significance and their consequences, and holds himself or herself answerable for them. *Authority* too is claimed for them—that is, both authorship and a certain power to articulate particular significations and present specialized roles and selected addressivities. To author a self is to selectively arrange one's acts in all their details and specificities to indicate not only a particular self but a specialized quality to the self. In authoring a discursive act, for example, one chooses the phonological, symbolic, syntactic, and structural forms in which it is to be articulated, a selection that carries the significance and authority of the self with it (Perinbanayagam 1991: 28–62). Acts, too, carry varying shades of *emotionality*—strong, overt, weak, subdued, hysterical, controlled, subtle, disciplined, and so forth.

Conversely, the others in one's life—the interactional others, significant and primary others, and the agents of the generalized other—will hold the individual as having exercised a choice and made a distinction and that he or she is responsible for the act in question, and in fact its author, and that the emotionality it carries can be attributed to him or her.

Among these various features of act, the primal one, it seems to me, is the capacity to choose from among a number of alternatives after suitable delays and deliberations. Indeed, the other features derive from this basic capacity: That is, from a field of alternatives he or she selects one line of action rather than another and gives it succor and sustenance and reaps the consequences. The males among Barash's mountain bluebirds (1977), discussed earlier, may respond in only one way to the "adultery" of their mates, but a human can choose to respond in a variety of ways. He or she can pretend that he or she does not know anything about it and continue his or her life with the mate; he or she can resent it, upbraid his or her mate, and feel helpless to do anything else about it; he or she may decide to confront the lover and kill him or her; he or she may encourage it in the belief that it will help his or her career. And this does not exhaust the alternatives that he or she may have. The self then is manifest in the acts that an individual chooses to construct, choices that reflect further meanings on the self and allow it to elaborate its presence. Choosing one path rather than another, one method, one strategy, a particular vocabulary, syntax, phonology, prosody, and imagery, and assembling them in unique ways is the strongest manifestation of self that can be made. It denotes the absence of controls of a biological or mechanistic sort and gives the actor sovereignty over his or her actions.

It is not claimed, however, that the individual has an *absolute* choice in the execution of acts. Free from biological or mechanistic control, the individual nevertheless faces constraints of other kinds. These constraints include those imposed by the memories of the past that are elements of the self of the moment and may be available as discursive memories or as habits, constraints imposed by others and their memories and habits and who may or may not be parties to the acts of the individual—these latter often summarized as "institutions." Two quotations, one famous and the other not, capture these claims nicely. Marx wrote,

> Men make history, but they do not make it just as they please; they do not make it under circumstances chosen by themselves, but under circumstances directly encountered, given and transmitted from the past. ([1869]1963: 15)

The other quotation comes from Thomas Szasz, who wrote, "There is, however, an important limitation to man's freedom—namely the freedom of other men. . . . Often a person can enlarge his range of uncoerced choices only by reducing that of his fellow man" (1970: 1).

Contemplating Marx's statements leads one to wonder what he could have meant by "circumstances directly encountered, given and transmitted from the past." What are these circumstances and how do they manifest themselves? Clearly these are "historical" circumstances that are constituted as "institutions"—that is, patterned and repetitive series of acts that humans undertake. This repetitiveness and patterning give to "institutions" their obdurate character, and such obduracy is the feature that limits humans from "making history" without being "constrained by circumstances."

It is clear then that it is the activities of individuals that are constrained by circumstances and these constraints are of two basic kinds: one that the individual "contains" within his or her self and the other that is "contained" in the selves of those whose actions impinge on the acts of the initial self. In the first case the individual's capacity to "make history," that is, to act, is constrained by his or her knowledge of what he or she can do and cannot do, by what may be called the "habituated horizons" of his or her self and world, while in the second case the capacity to "make history" is limited by what others, with their own knowledge, interest, and habits permit him or her to do—provided they have the power to do so. "History" then may be made by men and women and they may not do it under circumstances of their own choosing, but choose they must out of the available alternatives at the decisive fulcrums of history, personal or societal. It is a self-conscious human that must make one choice rather than another, including choosing not to do anything. Victims of false consciousness will be defined as those who are considered by certain others to be practicing a historically inappropriate universe of discourses. One must accept that there are limits on choice just as there are certain degrees of freedom to these limits.

For the individual, self-constraints are put into place by the circumstances of his or her own past. How does this past manifest itself? Two candidates suggest themselves for the locus of the presence of the past in the act of the individual: One is the unthought-through and unreflected action that can be termed habits and the other are the restrictions and licenses, qualifications, and modifications that the self remembers and uses in executing its acts.

The memory of a self is then a memory of past acts of self and other, memory that is both cognitive and emotive, and presents itself as a factor in the prosecution of current acts. Such memories can be of acts of an immediate past or of a series of acts from the anterior and intermediate pasts. It is in memory, it is as a remembered phenomenon, that the self can in fact exist, and it is as memories that a self is present and manifests itself in acts of an individual. It is this memory that is converted into habit—habits being memory executed as practice.

This certainly would be one circumstance from the past that would constrain action, limit the choices, and control the making of history. Such memories are provided, not by the actor's earlier choices alone, though that may play a part, but by the choices made available by the sedimented and habituated actions of others. Ideology becomes instrumental in conduct by its presence in the memory of the individuals and its manifestation in the acts of the individual.

The same observations apply to the others the self encounters and with whom it lives: They too have memories which affect their acts and habits, cultivated over the years, and these become sedimented into institutions and historical practices shared by a large number of people. Actions, and the making of history, proceed on the basis of the intersection of these different individuals assembled in one social formation or another and acting collectively. Individuals act and thereby make history, but do so under certain constraints they carry in their selves which function to restrain themselves or to restrain others. In the event, once the choices are made, their consummation is decided by a struggle for power and control which can be minor or major confrontations. The self is allowed to make choices, though under circumstances defined by a past and a system of others—but choice does exist for it.

Acts with these features are typically elements of a series. Each act will have a connection to earlier acts and will have consequences as well. That is, the acts that an individual produces are never discrete and isolated happenings, but are related to earlier acts of the individual as well as to imagined future acts. Further, they are also connected to the acts that others in a situation are producing at the moment and the consequences of these acts. In other words, the acts that an individual produces are units in a plot and elements of a narrative. A narrative is a manifestation, in orderly forms, of the interrelationship between temporality and action. Each act, that is, occurs in a given moment, but insofar as the act was perpetrated by a conscious and memoried agent, it would necessarily carry some significance from earlier acts and may even have a causal relationship to it. In addition, the current act is perpetrated in anticipation of further acts that are causally and sequentially related to it. Together these various acts—the retrospectively understood ones, the currently occurring ones, and the anticipated ones—constitute a unity and confer on the acts that a human produces an essential narrativity. That is, one can watch a play or read a novel and participate in its narrativity just as one can watch and interpret the acts of others and interpret their narrative logic. Similarly, one can observe one's own acts and both conceive its narrative logic and narratively apprehend it after the acts have been performed.

The human understanding for which "plot" is an organizing dynamic and which provides the logic of narrative discourse can be applied, certainly, to novels and plays that have been deliberately constructed in accordance with this narrative logic. To the extent, however, that such understanding is not confined to readers of novels but can be undertaken by all and sundry, the activity of plotting can be applied to an individual's act by himself or herself, as well as by others. If a novel can be read for the plot, and the narrative logic discerned, so can the acts that humans produce: They, too, could be seen to have a narrative logic to them, an interconnection with earlier acts and imagined later acts by the individual and by others. Indeed, it would take a particularly idiotic individual not to recognize the narrative implications of his or her moves. In fact a plausible definition of idiocy could well be a state or condition in which an individual is unable to recognize the narrative implication of his or her acts. When one studies small bits of behavior—as in those who observe conduct in an experimental situation, or a small strip of conversation—they are no doubt studying acts, but they are acts that are isolates. They are not part of a plot, and are not acts that are narratively connected to earlier acts and forthcoming acts. They tell no real story and in fact obliterate the life of which it is a part and deny the dialectical relations they have to earlier acts and with forthcoming acts in the individual's imagination. Such perspectives minimize the human being, truncate him or her, and examine a minute segment of his or her life, a life that he or she, without a doubt, conceives as a more or less continuous narrative of which the experimental situation is only a very insignificant part.

The concept of narrativity has been used in a number of recent works in social psychology in the study of the self concept and identity (Sarbin 1986;

Polkinghorne 1991, 1995, Maines 1993) and in work in psychotherapy. Russell, citing Arthur Danto, notes, "In contrast to the rational paradigm, the narrative paradigm assumes that to exist as a human being is to perceive one's life as a story to be told" (1991: 24). *I am suggesting, however, that to exist as a human being is to act in awareness that these acts are units of ongoing narratives.* I am referring here to the reflexivity that informs acts: In conducting himself or herself through the daily routines of a life, an individual understands the sequential significance of the moves he or she is making and their logical and narrative connections to earlier moves and forthcoming moves. In reflexively contemplating one's own life an individual can comprehend the interconnection of the various acts in it—that is, its narrative structure—and live accordingly. The individual himself or herself is able to see the plot of his or her life, sometimes vaguely and uncertainly, sometimes for only short durations, and at other times vividly and with assurance, and for longer durations, thus making acts therein fecund with the future.[3]

The socialization that a human child undergoes, the process by which he or she is rendered capable of living with others in orderly communities, is not one that makes him or her into static condition of "being" or having an identity or a personality. Rather, socialization allows an individual to *cast* himself or herself into one narrative or other, to reflexively apprehend the plot and produce acts accordingly. Such an individual does not pass from one stage of identity into another but learns to act in such a way that the acts that are constructed are narratively coherent: act like a boy or girl, act like a man or act like a woman, act like a Christian, act like a hunter, gunman, pacifist and so on and so forth. The content of each of these action-sets or identities are, of course, cultural and historical variables.

The narrativity of acts can occur in the short or long run, giving the selves implicated in them a narrativity of their own. The selves of given individuals come to be conceived with particular narrative identities. Each individual has a conception not only of his or her self in its situated aspect but as a moment in larger structures of time. A Christian, for example, has a conception of himself that is no doubt derived from the attitudes directed toward him or her by the others in his or her social circles. It is also the case that the attitudes assumed and practiced by these circles will be drawn from the generalized other that included the Christian narrative of identity: a human is born with a soul with a given span of life in this world and then passes into another stage. Between these two moments, the career of the self is punctuated by various religiously defined and sanctioned stages—baptism, confirmation, holy matrimony, parenthood, death. Such narratives may be supplemented or enhanced by secular narratives: passage into adulthood from childhood, earning a living, finding a career, developing in the career, retirement, and eventual death. An individual can conceive his or her other with narrative identities as well: One can place the other as a protagonist in various narrative structures and give presence to these identities in a variety of activities. Without allowing oneself to go to the extremes of James Thurber's Walter Mitty, it is possible for actors to imagine themselves in alternative careers to the ones in which they are currently involved. In all these cases, then, identity is conceived, not as a situated presentation of self in short *durée* but as extended narratives in which the self faces successive situations and deals with them. In confronting such situations, the individual simultaneously *casts* himself or herself into an unfolding story as he or she *casts* the other in it and proceeds to act out the implications.

Every move an individual makes, then, is typically conceived and understood as a unit in an unfolding series with either a definitive or flexible structure to it. These narratives are drawn from the culture: "I am a man and a man has to do what a man has to do." It can also be a different story: "A man who fights and runs away lives to fight another day." These stories can have various sub-themes. The former can lead to one learning to box or use a gun while the latter may induce one to learn the skills of placation and negotiation. In either case the acts of an individual develop an implicit narrative and give presence to a very particularized self.

Narrativity is the instrumentation with which a discursive individual places himself or herself in time—remembered or anticipated or attended. Time is a construction that uses socially given vocabularies to arrive at a sense of temporality. Time is a presence in consciousness, as in interactions, as complex sign-systems. These sign-systems are organized in numerical forms, in linear configurations, or circular ones, in seasonal and diurnal rhythms and so on and so forth. Time is also apprehended in narratives in which acts and events are constructed and presented as sequences and inter-connections that enable an individual to decode them as representations of temporality. Narratives in the form of myths, tales, epic poems, novels, stories etc. are sign-systems that enable an individual to construct and deconstruct time. Before one meets with the myths, tales and stories however he or she meets the narratives of a culture—manhood or womanhood, Christian or Jew, Hindu or Buddhist or Moslem, etc.—and will use them to inform his or her acts in the world and thereby constitute an ongoing self.

The self, it turns out, is not elusive nor is it mysterious, coterminus with mind, soul, or consciousness, and not a residual category; rather, the self is manifest in the acts, the individuated product of a mind, that the actor and others recognize and classify as the issue of an embodied entity. The self is not a static thought-way but a recursive sign or system of signs, constituted by the mind, a process with ups and downs, bumps and grinds, with starts and false starts and retreats, a maxisign that is able to elicit both cognitive and emotional responses. It is the mind's way of organizing the responses it has received, and initiatives that it has taken, into a more or less coherent system, a maxisign. Its texture is given by signs and the structures in which these signs are embedded, signs that are able to elicit further signs, and so on, thus constituting a self-pollinating complex. These acts that lead to the emergence of the self at one moment in the trajectory of an individual's career through life, and what emerges from the self at another moment, are ones that the individual chooses and uses to make distinctions. The acts are ones for which the individual takes responsibility and claims authority and displays emotionality, ones whose connections to earlier signs are recognized and in which the emerging future signs are anticipated.[4]

An individual then *is* a self in semiotically constituted *relations* to others in the world, to his or her own being, as well as in relation to the details of the material world. The others and the world objectify the individual just as the individual objectifies himself or herself in relation to the world. One becomes a self as a result of acting in the world of others and one acts as a result of being a self. As the other changes and as the varied resistance of the world changes, the self changes too, minimally or maximally. As such it is available to the individual, as to others, as mutable signs that the mind uses to relate to the world in the execution of acts.

In the execution of these acts a self is given presence and, to the extent that the acts are always circumscribed by the material and social phenomena of the world, so is the self. The material and social phenomena of the world that sociologists refer to as class, race, caste and gender, not to speak of nation or civilization, with all their ideological distortions, enter into acts and selves as various discourses within which acts are prosecuted and selves maintained and identities presented. In the moments of the act class, race, caste and gender, etc. are inescapably meanings derived from various discourses and assembled variously in the act and richly articulated in the mind and memories of the self.

## NOTES

1. See Steven Rose (1992) for discussion of how the mere activity of moving around can create molecular changes in the tissues of the brain of chickens. Similarly, there is abundant evidence now that words spoken to another affect the structure of the brain of the recipient. The brain is no doubt causally significant in the actions of an individual just as actions are consequential to the organization of the brain. The relation between brain and environment, mind and activity, is a two-way process. See Brothers (1997) for a close examination of the relationship between experience and the structuring of the brain. If memories of both a cognitive and emotional kind remain as traces in the very brain of the individual and affect the conception of his or her self, then "mental illnesses" may be reframed as behavioral manifestations of social experience/brain interactions.

2. There is, without a doubt, an affinity between Pierre Bourdieu's concept of *habitus* and G. H. Mead's concept of the self. In fact, introducing Bourdieu's theory Moishe Postone, Edward Li Puma, and Craig Calhoun say,

Bourdieu characterizes the habitus as a system of general generative schemes that are both durable (inscribed in the social construction of the self) and transposable (from one field to another), function on an unconscious plane, and take place within a structured space of possibilities defined by the intersection of material conditions and fields of operation. (1993: 4)

Vincent Colapietro has also argued against what he calls the "vanishing subject in contemporary discourse." He argues that such subjects are

distinguishable but inseparable aspects of those continuous, though continuously changing, centers of experience and activity. . . . Although the context of their emergence is a social setting inclusive of or (more accurately) constituted by discursive practices, what emerges from such settings is a unique enduring center of action—in short an agent. (1990: 653)

Jill McCorkel (1998) has shown in an excellent study of a rehabilitation center that inmates are able to resist official definitions of self by cultivating a "critical space" between the official versions and their own. See also Doyle McCarthy (1996) for an analysis of the relationship between knowledge-systems and self-conceptions and agency.

3. If one ignores the reflexive capacities of the human individual, the fact that he or she always operates with a discursive mind, it can lead to bizarre research programs. One can see this, for example, in the work of the "structural social psychologists." They claim that they produce scientifically valid conclusion with their experiments. In an article Edward Lawler, Cecilia Ridgeway, and Barry Markovsky (1993), summarizing the claims of structural social psychology, say that it has a "pervasive concern with the emergence and effects of social structure" (1993:269). Second, they claim, "In most approaches the individual is portrayed in a "realistic" way—that is, as possessing a wide variety of capacities, dispositions, opinions, behavioral proclivities, experiences, and so on" (1993:271). In contrast, the structural social psychologists, they say, "eschew realism; they portray the actor for *theoretical purposes* as a relatively simple entity exhibiting a few well-defined properties" (1993:271). In other words, the human beings are conceived as "minimal actors" (1993:271) capable of acting in a limited way. From this conception, experimenters are able to derive theories, i.e. "a set of logically related, abstract, general, and testable claims about a set of phenomena" (1993:269). The methodological constraint that led the researchers to assume "minimal actors" led them also to assume minimalist selves for them, which in fact resulted in findings that are only minimally valuable as sociological explanations. In fact the actors that the researchers posit are actors who have no pasts, have not lived and negotiated a relationship before, and are innocents in the interactional situations in which experimenters chose to put them. *Indeed they are actors with minimal minds.* Mead, commenting on the place of subjective experiences in Watsonian behaviorism, writes,"What was to be done with these? John Watson's attitude was that of the Queen in *Alice in Wonderland*—'Off with their heads'—there were no such things" (1934:2–3). The attitude of the structural social psychologists to their subjects may be summarized as, "Lobotomise them." Minimalizing actions and selves, it appears, exacts a heavy price and the explanatory fruits of such practices are meager. The assumption of minimalist definitions of self and action leads in fact to an

explanatory impoverishment. The researchers claim that they are producing explanatory theory for sociology—which is a study of maximal human beings and their relationships—and give us essentially a miniature model more akin to blueprints in engineering and architecture rather than an empirical social science. Searching for ways to become a rigorous science, the structural social psychologists have become mere caricaturists. In this connection see David Maines and Mari Moliseed (1986) for a searching examination of a related school of social psychology.

4. For a different conception of grammar of the self see Richard Brown (1987). This work is a salutary essay that situates the self in historical and socioeconomic processes. The concept of narratives and stories has been used very successfully by Plummer (1995) in explaining the development of sexual identities.

# Chapter 2

# Rhetoric and the Self

| | |
|---|---|
| Polonius: | My lord, I will use them according to their desert. |
| Hamlet: | God's bodykins, man, better: use every man after his desert, |
| | And who should escape whipping? |
| | Use them after your own honor and dignity: the less |
| | they deserve, the more merit in your bounty. |

Shakespeare, in Hamlet

"I am I because my little dog knows me," Gertrude Stein had a character say in one of her plays and made the chorus respond, "That does not prove anything about you; it only proves something about the dog" (1976). One's dog is, without doubt, the most unquestioned source of definition and appreciation about one's self that it is a human's lot to possess. No other source of validation can give the certainty of appreciation about one's self that a dog's acknowledgment can give—not religion, not one's kith and kin and their verbal and gestural productions. The latter will always induce at least a modicum of doubt and uncertainty just as they will introduce great complexity and subtlety into their acknowledgement of one's presence. Humans may own dogs and other sources of simple and unambiguous validation, but they typically will also have other humans to see them, cognize and recognize them, know them, and speak to them, thereby enabling one to become not only a you, but an I and me and a he or she as well.

It is by appearing and speaking to others that a self is given a presence, a concrete and situated existence, a tangibility and a facticity. However, appearances need to be seen and noticed, and speaking needs to be hearkened and heard. In fact it is not only speaking that is a distinctive human act, but so is seeing and cognizing and recognizing the other, as well as listening, and attending to all the nuances and subtleties carried in the structures of appearance and discourse. These acts of making oneself understood are in fact "rhetorical devices" (Burke 1969b:65) strategies adopted "to form attitudes or to induce action" (Burke 1969b: 41) from the other. The acts of such validation transform the presenter from being an I into a you from the viewpoint of the audience, and in turn into the me of the presenter.

Philosophers and psychologists have been devising methodologies and theories that will enable an individual to know himself or herself—to find answers to the question, "Who am I?" It is no doubt of great importance to know who one is. *However it is equally important to let others know who one is or thinks he or she is.* A sociologist should be particularly interested in discovering the processes and methods with which one allows oneself to be known by the other. Once such knowledge of each other is established, however, tentatively and uncertainly, interactions can proceed. In fact it could be said that the very emergence of relationships and "society" itself is dependent on my letting others know who I am, and how I want to be known and discovering who the others are by interpreting the signs they furnish. Once this is accomplished, then interaction can proceed on the basis of what each knows about the other, or thinks he or she knows about the other, which then permits an informed and more or less well-founded interaction to occur. Needless to say as the interaction proceeds one or the other individual may experience surprise or disappointment and change the knowledge of the other that one began with and thus alter the course of the interaction. Nevertheless there is no gainsaying the claim that one of the irrefutable responsibilities of a social being is to let the others know who one is so that interaction can proceed apace. An individual then appears and speaks so that the others can understand him or her and appreciate his or her particularized presence in the world and respond to it. In short, an individual creates a dialogic presence for himself or herself so that others can address it and participate in the ongoing proceedings.

To be a self, an individual has to appear well enough and speak well enough so that he or she may be recognized and heard and the process of self-constitution accomplished. That is to say, if there is a grammar of the act and the self, then there should also be a rhetoric of the self and the act so that the self can be given presence efficiently and effectively—defining efficiency here as the parsimonious means of reaching a goal and effectiveness as the degree of success with which these goals are reached. In other words, following Kenneth Burke's lead, if the self has a *grammar,* then it needs a *rhetoric* with which it can announce its presence. Describing his work on the rhetoric of motives, Burke writes that it "deals with the possibilities of classification in its *partisan* aspects; it considers the way in which individuals are at odds with one another, or become identified with groups more or less at odds with one another" (1969b: 22). The rhetorical processes that I propose to deal with here call for an amendment to Burke's statement: My essay considers the ways in which individuals, who are *always* at odds with each other, nevertheless manage to construct reciprocal selves and discursive interactions by using various "rhetorical devices." These "devices" that human agents use to give presence to their selves—that is, to persuade themselves and others about the existence of their selves, are manifest in the acts each of them produces and executes. The social nature of the human individual derives from the exercise of rhetorical prowess in successfully integrating with other people, or for that matter in successfully disintegrating from them, too, when the occasion demands it. Men and women may be "rational animals," as it used to be said, and there may even be merit in conceiving an "unconscious man" or an "unconscious woman" but, above all, men and women are *rhetorical animals.*

One of the unique features of the human being is that at any moment of existence he or she is aware of at least two others, generalized and significant, and at times of a third, an interactional other. In addition, he or she is aware of his or her own being in relation to these three others. This condition may be termed the human's fundamental sociality. This sociality is manifest in the mind's capacity to achieve in Mead's words an "objective reality of perspectives," by organizing different perspectives into a coherent relationship with each other (1932: 161–175).

> What is essential to such a mind is that it should be characterized by sociality in both its dimensions, for not only must it be determined by the different elements that go to make it up in the system to which it belongs but it must in passage be able to occupy successive systems so that it realizes itself in each as a member of the other or others. (Mead 1938: 609, my emphasis)

To be oneself he or she must be another. In relating to the three others, a human deals with two "systems," his or her own being and that of the objective others, and this confers on the individual one dimension of sociality. As Mead put it, "The self exists over against other selves. The relation of the individual to the community is one which involves the distinction of the one from the other. The self is defined in terms of the others" (1938: 654). The second dimension of sociality, for Mead, is the capacity to achieve "passage" from one system to another so that it realizes itself in each and prosecutes acts "as a member of the other or others" (1938: 609). *Sociality then is the imaginative construction and reconstruction of one's own presence in the minds of others as well as of others in one's own mind.*

How does a minded organism achieve this feat of being in different "systems" and passing among them and acting in reference to them? Mead answers: "The social organization of perspectives arises through the individual's taking the role of the other within a social act whose varied phases are in some sense present in his organism" (1938: 610). This taking of the role of the other occurs in an individual's relationship to all three types of others, interactional, significant, and generalized, and such "taking"—that is, interpreting the other's words and gestures, conferring a particular significance on them, and gauging the unspoken and implicit significations contained in them—is typically achieved visually and discursively. The individual looks but above all listens and speaks and it is through these activities that the taking of the role of the others proceeds initially. This is not all, however. The individual also remembers the others from past encounters and relationships, the particular social and emotional impact that they had, and he or she takes the roles of these others, general and significant, absent though they may be, and acts on the basis of the memory of these others and their attitudes. "Mind, in short, is persistence of past experience, but as the sense of meanings that appear in the social structure, or mental characters in relation to certain things. It is thus a statement of relationships" (Mead 1938: 658).

A human being, then, lives simultaneously in two "socialities." First, he or she is "determined, by different elements"; that is, constituted, by various social elements; second, one is determined by the various relationships that he or she takes into account in conducting himself or herself through life. These relationships, the attitudes and emotions they are able to indicate, present in the remembrances of the individual producing an act and present in the remembrances of the interactional others, if there are any, receive attention in the organization of the act and its performance. Such exercises in sociality are made possible by the structures of linguistic communication. It is this faculty that enables human beings to be "determined" by the various social elements on the one hand and to "move" from one perspective another. Indeed, the very structures of linguistic communication in which all humans become embedded makes it impossible for him or her to escape the conditions of sociality. The language faculty may have a genetic basis and may well be an "organ" of the brain as Steven Pinker has argued (1994). It, however, needs social stimulation from infancy to manifest itself, and its very occurrence as instances of behavior, even in infancy, and its effective functioning, inextricably imbricates humans with each other.

It has been customary to trace the interdependent nature of human existence to the fact that the human infant is born in such a way that it is totally dependent on adult care for its mere survival. The infant as it is fed, fondled, and nurtured learns to depend on others just as those who do the nurturing develop attachments and loyalties to the infant. The sociability and group-centeredness of humans no doubt arise from this early experience. Nevertheless, there is another feature of human existence that contributes mightily to the sociality of the human and its dependence on others. Such sociality is in fact practiced and achieved by using, interpretively, the rhetorical capacities of the language. Language exists as a living reality only insofar as it is addressed to others and is able to elicit a response from them (Bakhtin 1984:181–194). By the nature of the case a human being, insofar as he or she speaks, speaks in order to be heard, thereby connecting him or her to others and, equally, if he or she thinks, it is presumptively, to address others. The very uses of language inevitably posit a human subject in an addressive and interactional mode, a mode from which the only escape is madness or death.

In fact the very possession of linguisticity as a species characteristic of the human being demands that humans interact with each other and maintain at least a minimum of solidaristic relationships. Linguists have identified many features that are definitional to language as such—grammaticality, structurality, phoneticity—but its fundamental feature is its social nature: Language has to be addressed. Human beings do not just "speak," or produce "utterances" or "process" sentences, but speak to others and produce utterances and process sentences so that they may receive commensurate responses. *It is as it is spoken to an other, as to the self, that it gains its standing, presence, and evolutionary value.* Furthermore, once it is addressed, the very fact of its addressivity demands an *answer.* Language, for it to have presence, then, must be addressed and elicit an answer. It is in this circumstance that the social nature of the human resides. Humans, insofar as they are linguistically competent, must perform this competence in interactions for both the language itself and the practitioners of the language to achieve presence. *In short, there is a dialogic imperative to the existence of the human species.* The social nature of humans and their linguisticity are inseparable features: To be human is to talk (not merely to "have" a language) and to talk is to draw the other into one's own life just as the other faces the same predicament. A selfish gene there may well be, and it may control the life of a human for all anyone knows, but for all that, even one driven by it must talk to the other, and talk to him or her in such a way that he or she responds, and the moment both partners do this, sociality is created and selfishness is diminished. Each party must control his or her selfishness, tailor his or her attitudes, manage his or her emotions, control his or her ambitions and aspirations in order to constitute a dialogue. The interaction order that Goffman described in his many works is achieved dialogically by observing, as faithfully and frequently as possible, various rules and specifications. Saving face, one's own as well as that of the other, maintaining demeanor and observing deference, cooling the mark out when necessary, and behaving decorously and with mandatory civil inattention, or for that matter, civil attention, are really prescriptions for maintaining dialogic interactions and cultivating interactional solidarity. And it is in addressing the other and answering him or her that such solidarity is achieved.

One speaks, then, and addresses another, and this is done in such a way that it may be answered and typically does elicit an answer. Addressivity and answerability are in fact the central *motifs* in Mikhail Bakhtin's dialogic theory (1981; 1986). In addition to these processes a human being also makes references to others and thereby gives them a presence in the discourse and in the world. Paul Ricoeur has recently developed this idea of referentiality and has written that, "It is along this path of identifying reference that we encounter the person for the first time, considering this term in an equally modest sense as globally distinguishing this entity from physical bodies" (1992: 27). Further, the individual is able to address himself or herself, answer himself or herself, and even refer to himself or herself. This faculty has been called reflexivity. Mead makes reflexivity the central process in the constitution of meaning and self.

I will call these four the rhetorical modes of self-constitution and presencing. It is in such rhetorical encounters that the individual as a self can exist: He or she is reflexively present to himself or herself and in such a reflexivity his or her three others find a presence too. As the individual addresses others, and in such addresses he or she takes account of his or her presence and that of the others he or she is addressing. Similarly in referencing others the same *socialities* are involved: In being answerable to one's presence in the social world, he or she is, to begin with, answerable to himself or herself, just as he or she is answerable to the three others. The discursive mind that Harre and Gillett (1994) describe is one that functions to define an "individual" self, but one that is inextricably intertwined with the others through reflexivity, addressivity, referentiality, and answerability. In fact, the answers to the question, "What is an individual?" is that he or she is one who is able to engage in various processes to achieve a presence for a self by reflexive and referential acts, on the one hand, and addressive and answerable ones, on the other.

The self then is not so much owned or possessed as articulated in relation to others and remembered as the articulations and the responses they elicited. In such articulations an individual uses a shared vocabulary and a culture; to the extent that he or she does that and keeps speaking and presenting a self, the traps of solipsism and the travails of social and emotional isolation are avoided. The articulations posit the individual syntactically with others and enable the responsiveness of the external world and the reflexivities of the mind to constitute a self. These articulations—*visual, tactile*, and *verbal*—can be said to address an external world, particularly the world of other individuals in anticipation of responses from it and reflecting on it as the interaction with it proceeds. Once the self is articulated in this way and the responses are forthcoming, it is necessary to listen to the responses, take account of them one way or another, and orient the self accordingly. To the extent that the listening is inattentive and inadequate, the resulting presence of the self and the acts that are issued would be to that extent wanting and incomplete. The typical moment, then, in which selves are present is in the conversions between people, between an I and you, reciprocally changing places as the conversation proceeds and moments when there is both speaking and listening.

While the four rhetorical modes of the self occur together in varying permutations and combinations in actual discursive acts, I will discuss them in detail separately in order to achieve clarity of communication—indeed, to achieve a certain rhetorical efficiency. Insofar as the primary point of the dialogic processes is the individual actor I will begin with the reflexive processes.

## THE REFLEXIVE PROCESS

G. H. Mead makes "reflexivity" a central process in the doing of an act and in the emergence of the self. For him it meant that the individual is able to examine himself or herself from the standpoint of others. Mead writes, "The self has the characteristic that it is an object to itself, and that characteristic distinguishes it from other objects and from the body" (1934: 136). He also asks how can an individual get outside himself experientially in such a way as to become an object to himself and answered by giving primacy to the act: "This is the essential psychological problem of selfhood or of self-consciousness; and its solution is to be found by referring to the process of social conduct or activity in which the given person or individual is implicated" (1934: 138). That is, even the reflexive activity of minding is not a solipsistic exercise: It occurs in a social field in which the individual has been implicated since birth. Mead expands on this argument further and notes:

> For he enters his own experience as a self or individual, not directly or immediately, not by becoming a subject to himself, but only insofar as he first becomes an object to himself just as other individuals are objects to him or in his experience; and he becomes an object to himself only by taking the attitudes of other individuals toward himself within a social environment or context of experience and behavior in which both he and they are involved. (1934: 138)

How does the individual come to *know* the attitudes of the other members of the social group? Or to put it in terms that originated out of another tradition of philosophy, how does the individual gain "knowledge of other minds"? Wittgenstein observes that an individual uses one *criterion* or another to come to conclusions about the mind of the other. "An 'inner' process stands in need of outward criteria," he says (Wittgenstein 1958: epigram 580). Commenting on this, Norman Malcolm writes,

> When [someone's] thinking is freed of the illusion of the priority of his own case, when he is able to look at the familiar facts and to acknowledge that the circumstances, behavior and utterances of others actually are his *criteria* . . . for the existence of their mental states." (1966: 380–381)

It is not the case then that one reads the "mind" of the other as such or that one "enters" the mind of the other in some magical or mysterious way. Rather, it is that one takes their acts as *expressions* and *indices* of the other's attitudes in order to organize one's own self. To do this, however, the other must act and produce the "circumstances, behavior and utterances" that the individual can use as "criteria" for the "inner process" of the other. Conversely, the individual must also produce his or her own "circumstances, behavior, utterances" to give the other the criteria for his or her own uses.

Each participant, that is, produces his or her own "criteria," which also func-tion to elicit "criteria" from the other. It is in the *intertwining* of these mutual acts, it is the responses—that is, meanings—elicited by these acts, which each other is able to use in order to develop a self and keep it going. In developing and presenting these acts each individual is able to reflexively cognize the significations of these acts and their probable consequences and produce them accordingly and then, as a second step, interpret the acts of the other and use them to constitute his or her self.

On this process Mead writes, "The importance of what we term 'communi-cation' lies in the fact that it provides a form of behavior in which the organ-ism or the individual may become an object to himself" (1938: 138). Having said this, Mead describes the process of such communication in such a way that puts conversations as the major instrument of such communication:

> Of course, one may hear without listening; one may see things that he does not realize; do things that he is not really aware of. But it is where one does respond to that which he addresses to another and where that response of his own becomes a part of his conduct, where he not only hears himself but responds to himself, talks and replies to himself as truly as the other person replies to him, that we have behavior in which the individuals become objects to themselves. (1934: 139)

This is a description of an individual's conversation with himself or herself and it is seen as a continuation of the conversation that the individual has or has had with others. There is no essentialist interiority to either Mead's theory of the self or the mind. Reflexivity is not a private and individuated process but the processing of attitudes derived from the external world. As an act it may be private and even secretive, but it perforce will use a shared and pub-lic language, indeed signs from the external world. Nevertheless, there is no claim here that these signs are absorbed into the self in a mechanical manner; rather, they are subject to examination and analysis, distortion and exaggera-tion, deflection and even rejection and are used rhetorically to constitute a self—at least, once infancy and early childhood are transcended satisfactorily.

The reflexive process can be recognized most clearly in the acts of speech produced by each participant in an interaction. While speaking, an individ-ual posits an I at the center of the act, an I that is typically visible in the very structure of the sentence—though sometimes remains implicit. Various struc-tures follow the presentation of this I and carry the features of the self that are relevant to the occasion in which the presentation is made. In making this presentation the individual typically addresses another: The presentation is made to another, a you, and must ensure that the remarks that issue forth are intelligible to the other on the one hand, and take into account all about the other that is relevant on the other hand. One's remarks, as they are spoken, take into account a priori the relevant qualities of the other and incorporate them into the very form and substance of the remark. Conversely, the other receiving and interpreting these same remarks acknowledges the relevant qualities of the initial speaker and uses them for his or her own purposes, and this is true of speaking as of all other performances. The individual then is speaking as a self and listening as an other to the very speech itself and simultaneously listening to the other as a self speaking to him or her. The individual addresses himself or herself, addresses the other, and listens as well even if no one is physically present. Indeed this facility seems to develop very early in life. Consider the following excerpts from the monologue of a two-year-old child reported in a remarkable study (Nelson 1989). A small microphone was attached to the crib of the child, Emily, and recorded both her dialogues with her parents and the talk she produced when she was alone. Here is an example of the latter:

> Emily: Maybe when my go—come
> maybe my go in Daddy's blue big car
> maybe maybe when Carl come (again)
> then go to back home
> go Peabody
> Carl sleeping
> not right now—the baby coming
> and Carl coming
> my house
> Aaaaaaaaaand Emmy Emmy ((everything)) (???) coming
> after my nap
> not right now—cause the baby coming now (Gerhardt 1989: 219).

The child is able to use the pronoun "my" often and use the proper noun Emmy as well to refer to herself. Further, she is also able to formulate a number of substantive relationships of herself to events of the world: going in daddy's car, car coming again, Carl going home to Peabody, Carl sleeping, and the coming of a new baby; and to objects: car, with allusions to size and color, home, and Peabody. These are reflexive activities with which the child Emily is able to place her self in relation to these events and objects and thereby give her same self the semblance of a definition, a place, and a presence. Furthermore, Emily's articulations are couched in such a way that, though they are monologues with no one there to listen to them, they are *intelligible* to others. Talking to herself, Emily is implicitly talking to others as well and is making herself understood by others by using words, phrases, and syntactic structures that are common to the community.

These acts of speaking by Emily contain what Ricoeur had called "the reflexivity of the utterance" (1992: 44). In speaking, one listens closely and anticipates the other's listening. To do this satisfactorily the speaker must anticipate the other's responses to one's speech and tailor it accordingly. And as he or she speaks, the other is able to simultaneously situate the speaker as the one who is speaking and listen to him or her, thereby giving him or her, or rather this self, a presence. In speaking to the other, moreover, one is able to indicate the attitudes and intentions that one has to the other, just as he or she is able to discern them in the speech. Conversely, by responding to the original speech, the other is able to indicate his or her intentions and attitudes—however imperfectly, and at times erroneously.[1]

Ricoeur refers to verbal exchanges as "interlocutions" in which "an exchange of intentionalities, reciprocally aiming at one another" occurs. This circularity of intentions demands that the reflexivity of utterance and otherness implied in the dialogic structure of the intentional exchange be placed on the same level (1992: 44). That is, the interchanges that occur in the reflexive process should be given the same standing as those that occur between two sentient beings. The "inner forum," as Mead (1964: 288) calls it, is very much like the "outer forum."

The I that occurs in such interlocutions, and the me too, are indices of reflexivity and a double consciousness, and they occur readily in utterances. The I, then, that is present in the discourse is presented to the other, the you. During an interaction the I is not a *mere* reference to the nowness of the speaker and not just a shifter that changes as the interaction changes. Rather, as a pronoun it stands for a noun, not only in the simple grammatical sense but also in a substantive sense. For example, when Hamlet says "It is I, Hamlet, the Dane," it is clear what the I stands for. Very conveniently, and for effective dramatic purposes, he is spelling out all that the I stands for. It stands here for Hamlet, the prince, and for one who is unquestionably Danish with all that these identities represented in terms of rights and privileges and perquisites. As such Hamlet will speak and claim also his love for Ophelia, who was being buried when he made this declaration. The various significations of the I are then established by the speaker knowing them, signifying them, and the respondent's recognizing them and giving legitimacy to the claims by accepting them, by not challenging them or refuting them. Typically, one does not have to spell it out in such detail; a simple I would be enough.

In ordinary conversations, an individual uses the I in a similar fashion but the details of the noun and the adjectives that go with it are typically left unspecified and implicit. A voice on the telephone says, "I am coming home on Saturday." The moment a mother hears these words and the opening "I" of the utterance, she identifies him as her son James who has been away at college and is coming home because his Christmas vacation is beginning. This "I," which she identifies as a "you," of course, is a pronoun that stands for nouns such as James and noun-phrases such as "James my son" or "Jimmy-boy," and it also stands for rights that the son enjoys vis-à-vis his mother, his father, his home, his siblings. Conversely when James made the call he was aware of these rights and claims of love and was able to say "I" to a you, the mother, in full cognizance that this you is his mother with whom he has a special relationship as a son and to whom he can address this remark. Such reflexive moves are undertaken, in other words, by incorporating the *perspectives* of the other and that of the self into them.

The assertion of an I occurs in real or presumptive interactional moments and are *simultaneously* reflexive and addressive procedures that elicit *interpretants* from a real or presumptive other, thereby defining the presence of a self. This argument applies to all I-you relationships: *The I and you are representamen of a gamut of identities and relationships, one of which becomes tangible in selves that are present in discursive interactions.* The "I" and "you" are rhetorical devices, used to summarize claims, and are indices of the presence of selves. As the "I" is asserted and used in an utterance, it reflects the user as it reflects the user's relationship to the one addressed. The use of these signs makes claims about its right to use not only the signs but to everything that follows them—the rest of the utterance, its contents, their subtleties and nuances, their shape and form. The reflexive "I" colors the rest of the speech, adds new qualifications to it, and certainly does not stand alone. Similarly, the "you" also is a rhetorical device that summarizes the attributes of the other, his or her various identities for use in discursive interactions. It is then not merely an I and me that are involved in the presences of the self, but I as a you to the other and the other as a you to the I, thereby giving the selves of both participants a dialogic dynamic.

This reflexive rhetoric is defined by the nature of the relationship in which it occurs. It is not everyone who can say, "I order you to shoot the prisoner." The entity that says "I" here is a self that has a history, a history that it remembers and uses to claim the right to say "I" in this context and to append the verb phrase to it. Not only does the self know it and remember it, but it expects the other to know it and remember it and acknowledge it. In the event that the other does not know it, he or she will have to be provided with the knowledge: "I am your new commanding officer," or else he or she may have to be reminded: "I am your superior officer." In the event that the other does not acknowledge the "I" of the first speaker, there are two developments that are possible. One, there is a rebellion and an insubordination afoot and steps have to be taken to establish the rights of the I to have said "I" and the words that followed it. Or else the first speaker would be rendered ridiculous, his claim to authority rejected with the addressee assuming a dominant position. In any case, the I and the you in the transaction become salient not as mere pronouns but as nouns—as names or titles—that encapsulate a history and represent multiple social and interpersonal claims. When asserted, the "I" reflects back on the noun and the proper noun of the asserter and announces all the claims that the individual can make about his or her self and identity. These claims represent the biography of the individual—occupational, social, and interpersonal—that are relevant. If these are not known to the other and cannot be recovered from his or her memory, they have to be made available in the ensuing discourse. Typically, the situation, appearance, and the selected vocabulary of the discourse would suffice to indicate what the "I" of the speaker represents. The self of the speaker can be seen to be present insofar as it is possible for one to say "I" in relation to an act and a verbal articulation; and to the extent others can respond to this "I." The discursive act places the self in various particularities and transfixes it. The reflexivity of the utterance, typically manifested as an I in utterance and a me, invites the individual to consider his or her complex presence in the world and to consider it from the standpoint of others, a you, and then for the other to consider it as a you in return. Reflexivity is then not an interior monologue, but an active rhetorical process by which the other is implicated in one's acts and a self given presence.[2]

One can see this reflexivity of self even among people who are reputed to have a weak sense of self. The Dinka, writes Godfrey Lienhardt, "have no conception which at all closely corresponds to our popular modern conception of the 'mind' as mediating, as it were storing up experiences of the self" (1961: 149). It appears that memories, experiences, and even dreams are taken as part of the external world that acts upon the individual. Commenting on this, Yi-Fi Tuan writes:

> What, then, happen to the feelings—those of guilt and envy for instance—that the Dinka, like all human beings, unavoidably have? The answer is that these feelings are expelled from the experiencing self to the external world. Because a sense of guilty indebtedness can come to the debtor suddenly (as memories often do) he finds it reasonable to interpret that unpleasant feeling as a Power directed at him by the creditor. Likewise an envious man, not recognizing the envy in himself easily transfers his experience of it to another person who thereby assumes the visage of a witch. The outside world, thus loaded with projected moods and passions, comes alive—a dense-textured, vivid, but often also frightening place. (1982: 142–143)

It is clear from this that it is not the case that the Dinka have a weak sense of self or that they have no sense of self, as some would no doubt have it, but rather that each Dinka actor conceives the self as defined, guided, directed and controlled by an external force. Indeed the person would be unable to act at all if he or she did not initially conceive a self, albeit one given shape and presence by witches and powers external to his or her mind and body. Insofar as a Dinka is himself or herself symbolizing and naming with various particulars this external force, and doing so by the exercise of his or her own powers, that is, the power to name and symbolize, he or she is in fact reflexively conceiving a self, albeit one that uses an externalist metaphor to do so. *It is not the witch that is making him envious but that he is conceiving his envious self as witch-induced.* These external elements are *signs* that are given by the culture and are used reflexively as rhetorical devices for the constitution of a self. The irrefutable universal of the human experiencing of the world—be he or she a New England Protestant or a Dinka from the Nile Basin—is that he or she will experience the world through signs and their interpretants and use them rhetorically to constitute selves.

## THE ADDRESSIVE PROCESS

Insofar as the presence of self is typically manifested in conversational interactions, there is always the issue of addressing the other. Each must address the other in some way and the way itself will define immediately the addressee and the addressor. Bakhtin describes addressivity thus:

> An essential (constitutive) marker of the utterance is its quality of being directed to someone, its *addressivity.* As distinct from signifying units of a language—words and sentences—that are impersonal, belonging to nobody and addressed to nobody, the utterance has both an author . . . and an addressee. The addressee can be an immediate participant-interlocutor in an everyday dialogue, a differentiated collective of specialists in some particular area of cultural communication, a more or less differentiated public, ethnic group, contemporaries, like-minded people, opponents and enemies, a subordinate, a superior, someone who is lower, higher, familiar, foreign, and so forth. (Bakhtin 1986: 95)

What Bakhtin calls addressivity, it turns out, is the combination of two processes that Mead called "taking the role of the other" and "taking and attitude of the other" (1934: 360–362). In the first one, an individual identifies the other and identifies with the other and in the second process, one appreciates the other's attitude to the self, for example, that he or she is hostile, and incorporates it into one's acts. Such addressivity is to be found both in the content of the utterances and in the form.

Indeed, one of the markers of such addressivity—an easy empirical index of addressivity, in fact—is the term used by a speaker to address the other. It is typically the opening move in a dialogic interaction. With this move an individual is able to "take," that is, first define and then incorporate, the other into one's own acts. The addressing moves then are rhetorical devices by which the other is both defined and understood and his or her self given a presence.

The dialogic interactions in which an individual presents an I and is addressed as a you by another contains a powerful dynamic: The addressed one is thereby confirmed and validated in it and is expected, if not actually forced, to live within its parameters. Addressed as "You, my son" by a woman fixes the addressee in the identity of the son and forces a reciprocal, "You, my mother," from the addressee—though the last two words are usually left implicit. This applies to all such addressive interactions: The pronouns of address define and confine each other, the addressor and addressee, in the terms by which each is addressed and creates a symbiotic entrapment. Such addressing defines and transfixes the other's self like the eyes of the Ancient Mariner transfixed the Wedding Guest, making it difficult, if not impossible, to escape its gaze. Coleridge wrote of this particular gaze, as follows:

> It is an ancient Mariner,
> And he stoppeth one of three.
> "By thy long grey beard and glittering eye,
> Now wherefore stopp'st thou, me?
>
> The Bridegroom's doors are open'd wide,
> And I am next of kin;
> The guests are met, the feast is set:
> May'st hear the merry din."
> He holds him with his skinny hand,
> "There was a ship," quoth he.
> "Hold off! Unhand me, greybeard loon!
> Eftsoons his hand dropt he.
> He holds him with his glittering eye—
> The Wedding-guest stood still,
> And listens like a three years' child:
> The Mariner hath his will.

Everyone may not have as glittering an eye as the Ancient Mariner and everyone may not listen with the rapt attention of a three-year-old, but there are addresses that are difficult to resist. As Bakhtin puts it, writing, it is thought, under the name of Volosinov,

> Orientation of the word toward the addressee has an extremely high significance. In point of fact, *word is a two-sided act*. It is determined equally by *whose* word it is and *for whom* it is meant. As word, it is precisely the *product of the reciprocal relationship between speaker and listener, addresser and addressee.* (Volosinov [1930]1973: 86)

The addressor can, by employing one rhetorical device or another, transfix the other and elicit the necessary attention—an elicitation that is dependent on the two-sided power of the device used.[3]

In encountering the other in interactions and engaging them in dialogue, one is obliged to name them with proper nouns, common nouns, or pronouns. In this way one gets into the addressive mode and rhetorises a relationship verbally and gesturally. *These are interactions between the richly textured selves of the participants, each of whom is summarized in the terms with which each is addressed—names, nicknames, titles, or pronouns.* They represent the biographies of the individuals, relevant elements of which are summoned to aid in the management of the current interaction. One uses the proper addressive terminology—Your Majesty, Sir, Mr. Peabody, Jack, Jill, Johnny-boy, old man, old girl, Daddy, Mummy, and so on; one bows, curtsies, removes one's hat, kowtows, grins apologetically, smiles arrogantly, looks disdainfully, and so on—and each such move addresses the rich biography of the other as it is known to the speaker.

Commenting on one aspect of this, Goffman puts this issue as follows:

> Certainly our obligation to keep the names of our friends in mind, along with other pertinent social facts concerning them, is more than a means of celebrating and renewing our social relationship to them; it also ensures a shared orientation for reference and hence for talk whenever we come into contact with them. What affirms relationships also organizes talk. (1983b: 42)

Rather, what affirms relationships also announces a self and orientates actions, including talk. I am not talking only of "pronouns of power and solidarity" that Brown and Gilman (1972) discussed, but all forms of address—pronouns, common nouns and proper nouns, collective nouns and singular nouns, epithets, names, nicknames—indeed, the entire system of signs by which actors place the other, and hence the self, in the interactional moment by using one such sign rather than another.

Nevertheless, Brown and Gilman's pioneering work on the subject has a wealth of information and analysis that is useful here. Distinguishing between pronouns of "power" and "solidarity," they argue that the pronouns used in addressing the other indicate whether the ensuing relationship was characterized by power or solidarity—that is, if the addresser was creating a relationship of domination over the other or one of intimacy. They further note the historical changes in the use of these pronouns and their relationship to the types of society in which they flourished. "The non-reciprocal power semantic is associated with a relatively static society in which power is distributed by birthright and is not subject to much redistribution." They cite the feudal and manorial social systems of Europe as examples and argue that, "the reciprocal solidarity semantic has grown with social mobility and an equalitarian ideology" (1972: 265). A major contribution of this work is to the study of language and interpersonal relations; yet one can still use their work to answer further questions.

In interpersonal relations, at the moment of address, the uses of particular terminologies define the self of the other and places him or her in the specific relationship that the addresser is willing to accept. To the extent the addressee accepts the terminology, a particular presence of his or her self has been made available for the dialogue that is to follow. Further, by using a particular form of address—be it a pronoun or noun, titles, last names, first names, or both last name and first name and various combinations thereof—the addresser defines not only the other but his or her self as well as the presence of self that is relevant to the moment. He or she in fact defines a *structural relationship* by using titles and other formal addresses, and an *interpersonal relationship* by using first names, nick-names and so on (Stone 1970). In the dialogic relationship, and in the establishment of a presence for the selves in it, the terms of address are parsimonious instrumentations. Indeed these terms of address, within the interactional moment and situation, are signs of the self of each participant. The availability of these varied terms with their capacity to represent minutely varied significations enable the articulator to presence his or her self and the other's self in exactly the way he or she wants. The degrees of intimacy and distance, familiarity and strangeness, formality and informality, kinship, non-kinship, and pseudo-kinship can all be coded into these usages. The tonation and intonations used in the speech to the other also warrants attention here; they, too, possess particular addressivities and need to be modulated in the interactional moments to place the self of the other vis-à-vis one's own self. These tonations and intonations addressively signify "inferiors," "superiors," adults, children, parents, lunatics, beggars, and so on.

If the terms of address in conversations, the opening moves, so to speak, inscribe the relevant aspects of the other's self into the conversation—what may be termed *formal addressivity*—the rest of the discourse is not exempt from the imperative to be addressive if it is to be effective as a social act. The addressivity of the content of a discourse—what may be called its *substantive addressivity*—is no less important in giving presence to selves. In producing addressivity in the discourse that follows the naming or the pro-naming of the other, one "takes the attitude" of the other. Attitude, Mead argues is "the beginning of the act; it is a part of the act" (1934: 5). In speaking to the other, one displays one's attitude to the other in the content and design of the discursive act. To be able to take the attitude of the other, the attitude must be available in some significant form. In the interactional moments, the individuals present in it must make two moves simultaneously: *take*, that is interpretively attend to, the attitudes of the other and *enable* the other to take one's own attitude. In order to do the latter, an individual *invests* his or her acts with addressivity.

Investing one's speech with addressivity means that the general and the particulars of the resultant discourse contain ideas, concepts, assumptions, allusions, references, values, stylizations, imageries, and so on that define the other and that are accessible to the other. In being addressive, an individual composes his or her discourse in such a way that it becomes rhetorically efficient and effective. An individual who articulates a discursive act, recognizing that the speaker and hearer are at odds with each other—because each has a different self and multiple identities—will seek to reduce the differences as much as possible by arranging the words, tonations, and intonations appropriately. The rhetoric of addressivity, at a minimum, makes it possible for individuals to maintain interactions for a while and at the maximum sustain relationships. One initiates an interaction, thereby giving presence to his or her self by addressing the self as well as that of the other by attending to his or her name, nickname, kin-term, or title. The addressivity of such openings, however, are but the first step: All the subsequent words flow from this opening and carry forward the addressivity. One opens an interaction with "Al, how are you? I haven't seen you in a long time," the words that follow "Al" are contingent on the opening: It is Al who is being addressed, an Al who has not been seen in a long time by the addresser, an Al who is entitled to be addressed in such familiar ways and asked such familiar questions. The rhetoric of addressivity demands that in facing someone an individual produces texts that are trimmed and arranged in such a way that the other's self is properly tended as well as one's own is suitably situated and assembled, both in form and content. Addressivity as a rhetorical mode gives the individuals engaged in interactions and communications the capacity to cognize and recognize the presence of the other's self, attend to it, and give it both its moments and its discursive substantivity. In such discourses, the aim is to give presence to particularized selves and maintaining interactions and relationships. Consider an ordinary conversation:

> *Max: Where have you been these last few days?*
> *David: I have been here every day. Karen came over the weekend so we had a good time. . . . Savvy spoke to me last week so he said to me, he said, he'd like to see me take the SPO position. He knew I wanted CIP work and it, and it, and Larry's got it, it went to Larry.*
> *Max: Really?*
> *David: Yeah, Larry. It's just a line, it's just line job.*
> *Max: Oh.*
> *David: So if I would have taken it, I would have given up my CIP work. We can't risk that.*
> *Max: No, we can't.*
> *David: No.*
> *Max: You got to stay on the CIP.*
> *David: Oh yeah.*
>
> (Office Transcripts)

The opening lines are expressions of friendly interest and exchange of personal information that are very quickly abandoned when David describes Savvy asking him to take on a new job. It turns out that if David had taken the job—a job that Larry got—it would have exposed some operation in which both Max and David stand to face some risk. David is able to speak to Max about this by using various allusions that are substantively addressive: The reference to Savvy without further qualification identified him readily to Max and indicated the addressive use of shared and remembered information; the use of various esoteric acronyms indicated a similar state of affairs between the two; and the allusion to a "risk" was enough to indicate the precise nature of the risk, leading to an agreement that David did the right thing in not taking the job. The use of various diminutives of names also helped in the maintenance of addressivity: They are one of us, we are familiar with them, it said. In using this shared information and putting them into the discourse David can be said to have invested it with a certain necessary addressivity and successfully negotiated a presence for his self and that of the other.

In interaction, then, not only do we *take* "the attitude of the other" as Mead (1934) argued, but we also indicate our own attitudes to the other by our speech—attitudes of friendship and loyalty, aloofness and hostility, and superciliousness and hauteur, and so on. Attitudes are not only received from the other but are also offered to the other.

## THE PROCESS OF ANSWERABILITY

Bakhtin writes about answerability, in a very general sense, as follows:

> What guarantees the inner connection of the constituent elements of a person? Only the unity of answerability. I have to answer with my own life for what I have experienced and understood in art, so that everything I have experienced and understood in art would not remain ineffectual in my life. But answerability entails guilt or liability to blame. . . .Art and life are not one, but they must become united in myself in the unity of answerability. The individual must become answerable through and through: all of his constituent moments must not only fit next to each other in the temporal sequences of his life, but must also interpenetrate each other in the unity of guilt and answerability. (1990: 2)

The "art" that Bakhtin is discussing here includes the art of speech, the production and enactment of utterances in everyday life as much as the creation of novelistic texts and the discourses therein. Indeed Bakhtin seeks to unravel the relation between self and other by examining "the ways in which literary authors mold their relation to characters and the relation of those characters to each other in the fiction of a unified art work," as Clark and Holquist put it (1984: 63). They also elucidate nicely the implications of the notion of answerability:

> What the self is answerable to is the social environment; what the self is answerable for is the authorship of its responses. Self creates itself in crafting an architectonic relation between the unique locus of life activity which the individual human organism constitutes and the constantly changing natural and cultural

environment which surrounds it. This is the meaning of Bakhtin's dictum that the self is an act of grace, a gift of the other. (1984: 68)

Answerability, and the facticity of the answers as such, complete an architectonic relation to addressivity with a self achieved between the two. There is, however, an ambiguity in the concept of answerability that a social psychology must exploit. One is answerable, reflexively, in a "unity of guilt" for ones own acts; that is, one must speak for them, defend them if necessary, and stand by them. One must also answer, however, the acts of the other satisfactorily if the architectonic of the dialogic process is to be sustained. A failure to answer for one's acts, just as a failure to answer the acts of others, will lead to a failure of dialogue.

This gift of a self has to be earned and a reciprocal gift offered. And this reciprocity is achieved by using the rhetorical device of answerability. In giving presence to a self two forms of answerability are involved. First, a self is put forward as answer to the implicit, and at times explicit, demand from the other that one does so. For example, one dresses himself or herself in the manner appropriate to his or her gender, class, office, worth, or mood so that others can respond to it suitably. Such a presentation of a self is a management of the details of a self so that others can respond to them. Second, once such a self had been put forward, one is answerable to the others for that which has been put forward: If one puts forward the self of a policeman he is answerable to the others for such a self. As one puts forward a self that is answerable he or she confers a "gift" on the other, making it an act of grace; the other can thereby understand what has been put forward and resolve— however tentatively—the mystery of the other, appreciate it, and answer it. Further, by answering what had been presented, the other confers the reciprocal grace and gift on the initial presenter.

The significance of answerability becomes clear when one considers the deviant case: When one does not present a self that can be answered on the one hand and when the other does not answer the self that has been presented. Living in a household with others, for example, demands that one presents a self to others: one dresses appropriately, speaks appropriately, responds when spoken to, shows interest in and appreciation of the others in the establishment. By doing this he or she has answered the demand of the others that one presents a self. However, he or she can remain unclothed, indifferent to others, and refuse to either open conversations or respond to them. This is often a first step, in Jules Henry's (1973) phrase, in a "pathway to madness." It refuses the answerability of the individual to others and prevents him or her from receiving corresponding acts of grace and gifts from the other.

A good example of this comes from another analysis of "madness," by R. D. Laing and his collaborator A. Esterson. They describe the performance of Sarah Danzig:

She began to lie in bed all day, getting up only at night and staying up thinking or brooding or reading the Bible. Gradually she lost interest in everyday affairs and became increasingly preoccupied with religious issues. . . . She began to express bizarre ideas, for instance that she heard voices over the telephone and saw people on television talking about her. (1964: 109)

Both her actions and her ideas in fact lacked answerability: if one lies in bed all day, when everyone else in the family is up and about, and is out of bed at night when everyone else is sleeping she cannot very well be recognized, addressed, and answered. Further if one presents "bizarre" ideas, i.e., ideas to which the others cannot give even a minimum of comprehension or credence, one also forestalls answerability. Indeed what an auditor would consider "bizarre" are words that he or she could not answer intelligibly. Not only were her words unanswerable, she was interactionally unavailable and therefore neither addressable or answerable. Laing and Esterson (1964) cite her mother's comment:

Sitting up all night thinking and not telling anyone what she thought. Not that we particularly want to know what Sarah's thinking or doing, although it's only natural that a mother should be curious. . . . Sitting up all night in a blue night dress in the kitchen—just the lights on, nobody making a sound. She is thinking and thinking—goodness knows what the heck she is thinking about. It's enough to twist anybody's mind. (127–128)

If one is unanswerable as well as unaddressable he or she can be considered "mad"—or will become "mad" if he or she is left unaddressed and unanswered.

There is no guarantee, however, that taking the steps to present an answerable self would elicit the appropriate answer. Someone can present himself or herself with sufficient warrant and the others in his or her circle can refuse to answer him or her. This problem has been given fictional presentation in Ralph Ellison's novel *Invisible Man*. Ellison wrote:

I am an invisible man. . . . I am invisible, understand, simply because people refuse to see me. Like the bodiless heads you see sometimes in circus sideshows, it is as though I have been surrounded by mirrors of hard, distorting glass. When they approach me they see only my surroundings, themselves, or figments of their imagination—indeed everything and anything except me. . . . That invisibility to which I refer occurs because of a peculiar disposition of the eyes of those with whom I come in contact. A matter of the construction their *inner* eyes, those eyes with which they look through their physical eyes upon reality. (1952: 7)

Ellison is describing the travails of a black person achieving a presence in a world of white people: They don't answer the black persons's presentation but answer something that they concoct with their inner eyes. Even today, years after Ellison penned those words, a young black man can walk into a store, wearing a new shirt that resembles ones sold by the store, wander around and leave and have the store detective stop and search him and ask for the receipt for the shirt he is wearing. Here is a description by David Stout of an incident:

> Mr. Jackson, now 18, Mr. Plummer, 19, and Mr. Cunningham, who is now 20, were shopping at a Bauer outlet stone in Fort Washington, MD, a largely black and middle-class community, on October 20, 1995, when they were confronted by two uniformed Prince George's County police officers who were moonlighting as security guards.
>
> Testimony revealed that one of the officers, Robert Sheehan, had become suspicious after noticing that Mr. Jackson's shirt looked new. In fact, it was: Mr. Jackson had bought it at the store the previous day.
>
> Mr. Jackson could not immediately produce a receipt, so the shirt was confiscated, despite a cashier's recollection of selling a shirt to him the day before, according to testimony.
>
> Mr. Plummer and Mr. Cunningham were detained about 10 minutes while their friend was being questioned, the jury was told. At one point, Mr. Cunningham was told, "Sit down or I'll lock you up," according to testimony.
>
> Soon after the three were allowed to leave, Mr. Jackson returned to the store with the receipt to retrieve his shirt, but it was too late for the company to avert a major embarrassment. (Stout 1997)

Here we have a stark case of a failure of answerability. The young man has presented a self that sought a particular answer, to wit; "I am an ordinary man, I buy my shirts; I am an honest man." However, this presentation did not elicit the proper answer. Rather, it elicited the answer; "There is a black young man, wearing an expensive shirt that we sell here. He must have switched shirts in the dressing room and is in fact stealing the shirt." Such mis-answers can, without a doubt, lead to rage and resentment and even violence at times.

Answerability, then, faces two issues in interactional relationships. One, an articulator must present statements that are capable of eliciting answers, and two, once they are so presented the respondent must be willing and able to respond to them. The speaker can take the necessary steps to make himself or herself answerable by employing effective rhetorical strategies, by recognizing that the respondent is at least minimally at odds with him or her—that is, differentiated from him or her—and by taking the steps to bridge the gap. Once this responsibility is fulfilled, the individual can only hope that the other will give the gift of an appropriate response with the fateful consequences for the self of the speaker.

Statements made to the other represent one's self, or an element of one's self, and are announcements of a self's presence. Once it is given such a presence, it is answerable to it. And, conversely, once a self is given presence, the other is obliged to answer it, to the extent that he or she lives in the dialogic mode and answers it in terms of the significations of the initial statement. Answerability in its double sense is a rhetorical device in dialogic interactions and is used to give presence to selves in efficient and effective ways. It also has a moral dimension to it: Not to answer someone else is to deny the individual a social existence, just as making it impossible for the others to answer one is to deny them the opportunity to join in a sociality. To escape these moral responsibilities is also to reject the opportunities to make society possible. In engaging in actions that are answerable by others, then, an individual takes steps to enable the others to know his or her self. One can invest one's acts with answerability and allow oneself to be known by the other. Goffman's work in dramaturgical social psychology (1959) can be considered here as a systematic inquiry into the processes of presenting an answerable self to the other, of making oneself available in a *relevant guise* to the other so that a particularized interaction can proceed. Performances, selective and aforethought, props, regions, and teams that Goffman described with such perspicacity (1959) are really semiotic instruments with which one allows the other to know oneself by giving presence to a self that the other can take and answer. In assembling these dramaturgical devises and putting them into practice, an actor is constituting not just a self, but one that the other can read. One must not only know thyself, but insofar as a human life is social and sociable, he or she must allow others to know "thy self" as well so that they may answer it.

## THE REFERENTIAL PROCESS

In talking to others, an individual will often make references to absent others, thereby giving presence to those others in the interaction. This referential process is captured by the uses of the third-person pronouns: he, she, them, they. Such references can also be made by names, nicknames, and diminutives. Such references are not neutral or inconsequential events; rather, they define the self of the referred to the one addressed and give it a social and interactional presence. In mentioning somebody's name in the course of a conversation, various rhetorical maneuvers can be used to define the other: Doctor Brown, Professor Smith, Chicken Charlie, Barber Boris, Lucky Luciano. Derogatory references are often tagged to the name: Sam the shylock, Jim the cutthroat, Ravenal, the riverboat gambler, Mark the malicious. These are *adjectival* characterizations of the other's self. Further, the reference can code the nature of the relationship one has to the one named: To refer to someone named Susan James, as Ms. Susan James or Mrs. Dennis James defines one kind of relationship, just as does referring to her as Susan or Susie or "Miss Susan James, my teacher," "Susan, my friend, or "Susie, my sister." These are *nominative* characterizations of the other's self.

While these are simple instances of the creation of a referential self, there are the more elaborate ones by which a presence for the other as a self that has to be faced is created. These references can take the form of allusions and characterizations of an absent other that *narratively* define him or her and thereby give a description of his or her self. These can be either negative or positive images of the selves of others. Insofar as a human can deal with others only on the basis of a certain *sufficiency* of knowledge about them, it becomes imperative to gather this knowledge in one way or another. It is obviously impossible to always gather this information on the basis of personal inquiry and research. One has, therefore, to depend on the information provided by others. This knowledge an individual acquires and uses, as he or she remembers it, in dealing with the relevant party when he or she meets him or her. The acts that result from such interactions will be colored by the information that one party possesses about the other, which can be addressed to the other, thereby influencing his or her self.

The information that individuals use to form an image or conceptualization of the other, or to add details to the one he or she already knows, can be called *testimony*. C. A. J. Coady (1992), in an exhaustive philosophical study of testimony, defines testimony as "a speech act, or in J. L. Austin's (1975) terminology, an illocutionary act, which may be and standardly is performed under certain conditions and with certain intentions such that we might naturally think of the definition as giving us conventions governing the existence of the act of testifying" (Coady 1992: 25). Testimony, or rather testifying, is no doubt an illocutionary act, which Austin defined as the

> performance of an act *in* saying something as opposed to performance of an act *of* saying something; I shall call the act performed an "illocution" and shall refer to the doctrine of the different types of function of language here in question as the doctrine of "illocutionary forces." (1975: 99–100)

It is then an act with illocutionary force and it has its own conventions by which it is to be judged as a felicitous performance or not. These conventions distinguish between different kinds of testimony—formal, natural, and extended testimonies (Coady 1992: 25–53).

Formal testimony, for example, the one given in courts of law, is characterized by the following conventions of usage "that mark it as formal testimony" according to Coady:

> (a) It is a form of evidence; (b) It is constituted by persons A offering their remarks as evidence so that we are invited to accept p because A says that p; (c) The person offering the remarks is in a position to do so, i.e. he has the relevant authority, competence, or credentials; (d) The testifier has been given a certain

status in the inquiry by being formally acknowledged as a witness and by giving his evidence with due ceremony; (e) As a specification of (c) within English
law and proceedings influenced by it, the testimony is normally required to be
firsthand (i.e. not hearsay); (f) As a corollary of (a) the testifier's remarks should
be relevant to a disputed or unresolved question and should be directed to
those who are in need of evidence on the matter. (1992: 32–33)

In everyday life many of these same processes are in operation. In fact,
there is no doubt that the procedures in formal settings were carried over
from experiences in the interactions of everyday life.

It is, however, not enough to produce a felicitous speech act—for example
a "promise"—with the requisite illocutionary force; it should also be believed,
accepted, at least taken at its face value, and interaction allowed to proceed.
This is often achieved by considering the identity of the person providing the
testimony. The very term "testimony," which is related to *testis,* shall I say,
*attests* to the fact that only those with testicles could be trusted to give evidence: Men being of course "rational" creatures, responsible, and so on were
a priori more reliable as witnesses and indeed had the right to bear witness!

One recent work speaks to some of the issues raised by Coady and introduces an additional element to the formal ones—the identity of the testifier,
his or her social standing. In an extensive study of a "social history of truth"
Steven Shapin has argued that

> what we know of comets, icebergs, and neutrinos irreducibly contains what we
> know of those who speak for and about these things, just as what we know
> about the virtues of people is informed by their speech about things that exist
> in the world. (1994: xxvi)

or, for that matter, even about things that do not exist in the world! We
accepted the discoveries in science reported by these people because they
were "gentlemen" who could be "trusted to speak truth." The "gentleman,"
Shapin argues, was "that culture's paradigm of the type of individual one
could trust to speak truth" (1994: xxvi). The culture in question is that of
early modern England, the period in which many scientific inquiries were
made. In Coady's terms these "gentlemen" were considered to be individuals who had "relevant authority, competence or credentials" to offer testimony. As gentlemen they could be trusted to speak what they believed to be
true. Conversely, these scientists were also speaking to other gentlemen who
could be trusted to be civil about the claims made by other gentlemen and
to accept what they were being told. In either case, the identity of the com-
municants as gentlemen guaranteed the claims of the speaker and enabled
scientific truths to become canonized. The acts of testifying about their discoveries gave presence to the selves of the scientists with a double identification process in operation: scientist and gentleman.

In courts of law testimony is also given in which the identity and self of the witness is defined and described. Once again its dependability becomes an issue. In many courts of law, a witness is made to take an oath before giving testimony that what he is about to say is "the truth and nothing but the truth." These oaths are typically administered by the witness repeating certain words with the right hand on a religious text. This procedure is once again a claim and an affirmation of an identity of the self of the witness: "I am a Christian and as God is my witness, my testimony is the truth." If one cannot take this oath, for one reason or another, he or she can "affirm" that he or she is a truthful witness. In such cases it could be said that the witness's identity is being transformed then and there. From being a neutral as a potential liar or truthteller, he or she is transformed into one whose testimony can be trusted. Even here, however, other identities besides that of "one who had taken the oath" can intrude itself on judgments about the veracity of the testimony. The professional standing of the witness, his or her biography, as it is relevant, the individual's demeanor and decorousness, and, often, his or her class and ethnic identity will have a strong bearing on whether the testimony is likely to be accepted for the construction of the identity of the other.[4]

While at one time class-based identities were adequate not only for testimony in the courts as well as in scientific endeavors, today one needs credentials given by accredited institutions to gain the authority to confer identity on others. In the procedures by which someone is defined as "mentally ill" or "insane," these credentialed identities seem to be in operation. His or her self is subject to these procedures and referentially labeled as insane, with or without his or her active and consented participation. Often the emergence of a referential self of "insanity" begins with a reflexive process and ends with a referential one with the testimonial interference of experts. Susanna Kaysen gives one such example:

> I signed myself in. I had to, because I was of age. It was that or a court order, though they could never have gotten a court order against me. I didn't know that, so I signed myself in.
>
> I wasn't a danger to society. Was I a danger to myself? The fifty aspirin—but I've explained them. They were metaphorical. I wanted to get rid of a certain aspect of my character. I was performing a kind of self-absorption with those aspirin. It worked for a while. Then it stopped; but I had no heart to try again. (1993: 39)

This description of a reflexive self is the beginning of a process by which she surrenders herself to the hands of experts who will now create a referential self for her. Later on in her narrative Kaysen says, "I have to admit though, that I knew I wasn't mad." Nevertheless she is incarcerated and given medications. She describes the process of being referentially constituted as an "insane" and a "patient" thus:

Take it from his point of view. It was 1967. Even in the lives like his, professional lives lived out in the suburbs behind shrubbery, there was a strange undertow, a tug from the other world —drifting, drugged-out, no-last name youth universe —that knocked people off-balance. One could call it "threatening" to use his language. What are these kids *doing?* And then one of them walks into his office wearing a skirt the size of a napkin, with mottled chin and speaking in mono-syllables. Doped up, he figures. (1993:39–40)

Kaysen is admitted to the clinic and elicits a referential self, to wit: "Psy-choneurotic depressive reaction. Personality pattern disturbance, mixed type. R/O Undifferentiated schizophrenia. Borderline Personality" (1993: 4). These terms are put in her "case record folder," along with father's name, mother's name, address, and names of persons to notify in an emergency. Her referential self is, if anything, complete. And provided by one "who has the relevant authority, competence and credentials," in Coady's already cited words, to identify Kaysen's self. While the formal language of this ref-erential self is not made available to Kaysen while she is a patient, she is treated in such a way that she accepts the designation of herself as insane and defines herself with fragments of this diagnosis and the attitudes they conveyed.

Formal testimony as a discursive act is found more frequently in courts of law and in front of committees of inquiry. I will take Elia Kazan's testimony before the House Committee on Un-American Activities for analysis here. He went before the committee that was investigating the influence of the Com-munist Party of the United States of America in the film industry. Kazan had been a member of the party for a while and had left it. In his testimony before the committee, he made two significant claims: (a) he explained the reasons why he left the party and interpreted the meanings of his films in a way that a priori refuted all suspicion that they were critical of American society and civilization; (b) he named the other people who were members of the party, thus creating or confirming a referential self for each of them. Kazan told the committee: "I was instructed by the Communist unit to demand that the group be run 'democratically.' This was a characteristic Communist tactic; they were not interested in democracy; they wanted con-trol" (Navasky 1980: 202).

Kazan sets up a subtle set of categories of opposition here: Communist democracy versus. real democracy; that is, Communists may speak of democracy, but what they really want is centralized control.

Kazan goes on:

This was the specific issue on which I quit the Party. I had enough regimenta-tion, enough of being told what to think and say and do, enough of their habit-ual violation of the daily practices of democracy to which I was accustomed. (Navasky 1980: 202)

Here the opposition is between his own integrity as a person, used to the "daily practices of democracy" as opposed to the "regimentation" of the Communist Party.

In both these passages all the symbolic resonances of "democracy" are given full play. Democracy is the characteristic, defining feature of the ideology of American civilization. It means autonomy for the individual, freedom to resist authority, participatory decision-making, and Kazan's testimony swells with its various representations. Needless to say these features of the testimony gave it force and power—at least to the committee and to various admirers and defenders of Kazan.

In the second aspect of this testimony—the naming of his former comrades in the party—once again he establishes himself as one who was misguided and misled at one time but now had seen the light, while others were still in the darkness and deserved to be exposed. Kazan was able to establish a self for himself just as he was able to referentially create one for the others he named—one that they refused to honor for the rest of their lives. Nevertheless, many members of the public defined the selves of the named with the terms and categories provided by Kazan. Similarly, the named and their friends and admirers constituted a referential self of their own for Kazan: turncoat, betrayer, stooge.

What Coady calls "natural testimony" is encountered

> in such everyday circumstances as exhibit the "social operations of mind": giving someone directions to the post office, reporting what happened in an accident, saying that, yes, you have seen a child answering to that description, telling someone the result of the last race or the latest cricket score. (1992: 38)

To this I would add telling or testifying what sort of person someone is or has been or will be. This kind of testimony includes the kind of talk described as "gossip" but is not exhausted by it. Detailed and systematic descriptions of the other for certain defined purposes constitutes a referential self: For example, letters of recommendation, often also called letters of reference, are good examples of referential selves being constituted by means other than gossip. Reports provided by private detective agencies, espionage organizations, and law enforcement units also constitute referential selves for the objects of their attention. The difference between gossip and the latter kind of referentiality is that the latter is likely to be more systematic and in accord with certain disciplined evidentiary procedures—though these reports may include gossip as well.

In spite of its bad reputation among moralists, gossip has an important function to play in social life. Jorg Bergmann, in a rather thorough examination of gossip, considers it a "communication genre" that has its own regularities, organizational principles, and presentational styles. Further, he argues that gossip has its own relational structure: the subject of the gossip, the producer of the gossip, and recipient (1993: 45–49). With this framework Bergmann develops a sophisticated hermeneutics of this particular genre of communication, paying attention to the situational and interactional imbrication of gossip. This interactive "securing" of gossip, as Bergmann puts it, is what is of interest here: It is in such a relationship between the producer of the story and the recipient that the identity of an absent other is defined or refined. Various stories that define the identity of the other are recounted in such relational structures. This identity will be accepted by the recipient, unless he or she has reasons to challenge the stories, and carried away, to be repeated to the another person. This establishes a chain of gossip, which, when it is sufficiently interconnected, will become the commonly shared identity of the individual in question. The relational structure of gossip extends from an initial dyad into a chain of such dyads and traps the subject of the gossip in it.

In the talk between the two, certain significant meanings for the participants themselves are also created. Patricia Mayer Spacks, in her study of gossip, addresses the latter issue. She distinguishes "idle talk," "malicious and frivolous gossip," and "serious gossip" from each other and notes that the latter

> takes place in private, at leisure, in a context of trust, usually among no more than two or three people. Its participants use talk about others to reflect about themselves, to express wonder and uncertainty and locate certainties, to enlarge their knowledge of one another. (1986: 5)

To enlarge knowledge, not only about themselves, I may add, but of others as well, others who are not parties to the talk, and thereby create an identity for them.

Gossip typically takes a narrative form and uses plots, characterizations not only of the other in question but of the various others involved in the plot. One does not merely say "John the wife-beater," but gives a story with corroborative details that suggest at least a minimum verisimilitude: "I was speaking to Anne and she told me that Susan, John's wife, was all black and blue in the face," or "Victor told me that Jane, Bob's wife, and Carl were having a lovey-dovey lunch yesterday at the Carlton." Not only do these have a semblance of a plot but they bring in the names of others as presumptive witnesses who can attest to the veracity of the story as well as providing significant details: Susan's face was black and blue, Jane was having an intimate lunch at the Carlton with someone other than her husband. Or else the teller of the gossip can present himself or herself as the witness and say "I saw Jane and Victor coming out of the Step Inn, arm-in-arm."

In the first type of gossip the veracity claimed for the tale is dependent on citation: Somebody else is cited as the source of the story, and its capacity to become a constituent element of the referred one's self is dependent on this person's reputation for reliability. In the event of such a reputation being low, the auditor of the story can debate the story, reject it, and refuse to code it as an element of the self of the referenced one. In courts of law that are influenced by Anglo-Saxon jurisprudence, this kind of report—hearsay—is not considered acceptable as evidence. In everyday life we are heavily dependent on such reports to form impressions of the other. Nevertheless, as in the formal settings, the identity of the testifier—his or her reputation as a truth-teller, fabricator, fabulist—will play a part in the acceptance of the testimony. The testifer must be able to elicit "trust" from the auditors of the testimony. This in fact has come full circle—in an etymological sense: The word "truth" comes from the word for trust. One accepts statements as "true" from another because he or she is "trustworthy"—i.e., bears the identity of someone who can be trusted—indeed a matter of interpersonal transactions.

When the tale about the other is reported by the teller as one that he or she witnessed himself or herself, the individual may be believed or not, once again depending on his or her reputation for veracity and reliability and on whether he or she has a special interest in either maligning the referred one or praising him or her. If either of these conditions is suspected, the tale could be subject to various degrees of *discount:* "You know Harry, you can't trust anything he says about Susan—she left him for Charles;" "He is talking about his son. It is his father's pride that's talking."

The rhetoricity of the referential mode—that, is defining a self by attributing qualities to it, sometimes by the mere naming of it—demands, if not veracity, at least plausibility. To say that someone is a thief or that someone is "really a man" it is necessary to go one step further and give necessary details, occasions, and circumstances under which this information became available and the reasons for accepting it as persuasive. Conversely, if the reference is a noncontroversial one, again it must conform to certain forms of verbal and social decorum. If a lowly worker in a corporation is to refer to the president of the corporation by his first name or nickname—except in ironic allusion—he or she is making a claim of familiarity and friendship. In the absence of such a familiarity the referential rhetoric here would be grossly inappropriate and unpersuasive. Indeed it would persuade the others that the speaker is presumptuous and ill-mannered, out of place in the social world. Referentiality that cannot or does not receive the acknowledgment and acceptance by the other is one that has failed rhetorically. In making references to the other and helping in constituting a self for him or her, it is imperative to have a certain rhetorical vigor and effectiveness.

"Natural" testimony, that is, everyday talk, can also lead an individual to be constituted as "mentally ill," indeed made "mentally ill" by referential processes. In a now classic paper Edwin Lemert argued that paranoia can be caused by systematic exclusion from social circles:

Suffering misfortunes of one sort or another in one's professional or domestic life, an individual becomes emotionally overwrought and begins to be seen by his or her social circles and referred to as one who was violating the norms and values of the primary group, revealed by giving priority to verbally definable values over those which are implicit, a lack of loyalty in return for confidences, and victimizing and intimidating persons in positions of weakness. (1970: 656)

As these perceptions get discussed in the chains of interactions in which each member of the organization is involved, in Lemert's words "a new configuration takes place in the perceptions others have of the individual with shifts in figure-ground relations. The individual . . . [becomes] an ambiguous figure. . . . From a normal variant, the person becomes 'unreliable,' 'untrustworthy' 'dangerous' or someone with whom others 'do not wish to be involved'" (1970: 656–657). The adjectival references are made about the person by other members of his or her social circle and become the modalities with which their relationship to the individual so referred would be conducted. They will avoid him or her and exclude him or her from informal social interaction, thereby, of course, making him or her more angry and disturbed. Acts of avoidance or exclusion, starting as referential ones, eventually become ones addressed to the other, nonverbally to begin with but verbally later. The upshot of these interactions is that the referential self of the individual in question eventually becomes an addressive self and leads to the emergence of a paranoid reflexivity by making, "the situation or group image an ambiguous one for ego, much as he is for others" (Lemert 1970: 658).

Testimony, whether it is of the formal kind or "natural" kind, then, is used as a rhetorical device to constitute the self of the absent other. *Such constitution sooner or later affects the reflexive self of the individual in question.* This is done in the interactional situation. Testimony given to the other, addressed to him or her, performs a double rhetorical function: one, it creates the details of the self of the absent other; two, the testimonial rhetoric is used by the testifier to influence the listener in one way or another, to induce his or her cooperation in whatever line he or she is pursuing vis-à-vis the listener and vis-à-vis the absent other. Once such a conception of the absent one is agreed upon, it becomes the stuff of the attitudes that are directed to him or her by both and eventually becomes incorporated as his or her self.

These rhetorical devices then are discursive modes with which an individual is constituted as a subject and object of attention for interactional purposes. Such constitutions are achieved, not by the mere fact that certain discursive formations are available in a general sense but by the active deployment of discursive acts in which these formations are featured. Such deployment takes the form of reflexive, addressive, answerable, and referential moves within situated interactions and ongoing interpersonal transactions. Individuals, in a sense, are always at "odds with one another" (Burke

1969b: 22), find it difficult to fully "know the mind of the other" (Malcolm 1966: 371), and seek, with varying degrees of desperation, to overcome such problems and construct a self, an other, and interactions, relationships, and social order with the help of various rhetorical strategies. In the reflexive process, they seek to overcome their own doubts about their own selves and knowledge of their own minds, while in the addressive, answerable referential modes they seek to overcome their separation from others and seek to know their minds and reveal one's own, as may be necessary and prudent, to others.

## NOTES

1. I have given here only a small segment of the data and analysis contained in this work for any one who is interested in the relationship between narrative and the self. See in particular the insightful essay in this volume by Katherine Nelson on the functions of monologues in the crib as well as the work of Julia Gerhardt (1989) and especially John Dore's (1989) work, which draws on the work of Mikhail Bakhtin (Nelson 1989).

2. See Wiley (1994) for a sound argument that takes the "I" and "Me" of self-presence that one finds in G. H. Mead's work to an "I," "Me," and "You" through a Peircian route. He does not, however, take this discussion beyond the pronouns to examine the nouns they represent and the further significations that these nouns themselves represent. Pronouns, of course, represent nouns and these nouns in turn represent an entire plethora of significations, some of which will influence the current interaction. When the pronoun "I" occurs in a situated utterance, it no doubt represents the one speaking, but anyone uttering it and the others listening to it, will also know *what else* that particular "I" represents insofar as both parties have knowledge, memory, and expectations. There are always further interpretants to the initial interpretant, constituting thereby a chain of signs. The meaning of a sign is not exhausted by merely one transition from a sign to one interpretant. A decisive statement on this can be found in Burke, "What are signs of what?" (1966b: 359–379). Nevertheless Wiley's study is a creative synthesis of Charles Sanders Peirce and G. H. Mead and contains insightful discussions of reflexivity and the conversational placement of the self. Also see Singer (1984) for a probing discussion of the relationship between dialogue and pronouns and identity. He, too, sees only the immediate deixic significance of pronouns and not their embedded significations.

3. It is believed by many that "Volosinov" is a pseudonym under which Mikhail Bakhtin published some of his work. While there are many similarities in the ideas in the books published under these names, the Volosinov books are explicitly committed to a historical-materialist view of language, whereas the Bakhtin books are not.

4. In cultures outside the influence of Anglo-Saxon jurisprudence different strategies to indicate the dependability of the testimony being given had to be devised. For a perceptive study of the practices in Sri Lanka and conflict between the English view of oath-taking and the Sri Lankan view, see Samaraweera (1997). He discusses the

differences between an act of truth, which is used in dealings with God, and other oaths, which are used in everyday relationships. He also describes the introduction of sacred objects other than the Bible that were used in the administering of the oaths in order to elicit dependable testimony from witnesses. They were not, apparently, too successful.

# II

# Identificatory Processes

# Chapter 3

# Identity: The Continuity and Differentiation of Self

| Mrs. Smith: | You know very well that they have a boy and a girl. What are their names? |
|---|---|
| Mr. Smith: | Bobby and Bobby like their parents. Bobby Watson's uncle, old Bobby Watson, is a rich man and very fond of the boy. He might very well pay for Bobby's education. |
| Mrs. Smith: | That would be proper. And Bobby Watson's aunt, old Bobby Watson might pay for the education of Bobby Watson's daughter. That way Bobby, Bobby Watson's mother, could remarry. |

Ionesco,
*The Bald Soprano*

The relationship between identity and self has been an unsettled issue in social psychology for a long time. Some use these terms conjointly, and confusingly, as in "self-identity," while others use them interchangeably. The two concepts, however, have different referents and should not be conflated. Self is reflexive objectification of one's presence in a world of other selves and objects, a process achieved by using signs of various kinds. Such signs of objectification, however, are always elements of complex vocabularies, each of which is able to allow a minded organism to identify itself and be identified by others. This is identity. Identities are embedded in these discursive structures. An individual and his or her social circles use elements from these structures to name a self and be named by it.

One of the earliest scholars in recent times to use the concept of identity in his social psychology was Erik Erikson. He developed what may be termed an enrichment and amendment of some of Freud's ideas and produced the concept of identity to denote an individual as evolving in stages through the life cycle, with each stage being different from the earlier stage while at the same time being connected to it. He describes one such stage, adolescence, as follows:

> The integration now taking place in the form of ego identity is more than the sum of the childhood identifications. It is the inner capital accrued from all those experiences of each successive stage, when successful identification led to successful alignment of the individual's *basic drives* with his *endowment* and his *opportunities*. In psychoanalysis we ascribe such successful alignments to "ego-synthesis." I have tried to demonstrate that the ego values accrued in childhood culminate in what I have called a *sense* of *ego identity*. The sense of ego identity, then, is the accrued confidence that one's ability to maintain inner sameness and continuity (one's ego in the psychological sense) is matched by the sameness and continuity of one's meaning for others. (1950: 89)

At any stage in this "epigenesis" of identity, an individual is able to maintain "an inner sameness and continuity." In other words, identity is a reflexive sense of continuity and sameness and is separable into stages that are culturally defined. An individual has to pass, at a certain chronological age, from one stage to another, assuming the responsibilities that are commensurate with the "basic drives" that are appropriate to the stage, and thereby acquire his or her ego-identity. He or she may pass from one stage to another but he or she would nevertheless maintain an inner sense of continuity with the earlier stages.

Nelson Foote, in a paper that was to define identity more clearly for sociologists, described it as an ongoing activity rather than as an achieved state. Influenced by Freud, Mead, Sullivan and Burke, Foote says,

> We mean by *identification* the appropriation of and commitment to a particular identity or series of identities. As a process, it proceeds by *naming*; its products are ever-evolving self-conceptions—with the emphasis on the *con*, that is, upon ratification by significant others." ([1951] 1970: 484)

He went on to say that the activity of identification "will continue, for what is involved is the necessary activity of every social being, and not merely of social psychologists. Every man must categorize his fellows in order to interact with them" (Foote [1951] 1970: 484).

Foote's paper had a great impact in sociological circles that were working with the ideas of G. H. Mead and Herbert Blumer. Anselm Strauss in an essay on identity—which he happily characterized as consisting of *mirrors* and *masks* (1959)—further developed the connection between naming, language and identity, calling attention to the act of *naming* as the placement of the other in an identity. Such naming classifies the named into various categories that together provide "for directive to action" (Strauss 1959: 22). Such a classification also indicates an evaluation of the object: "Classifications not only carry our anticipation, but also those values that were experienced when we encountered the things, persons or events now classified" (1959: 23). Strauss then appeals to Kenneth Burke and indicates that the struggles for identity are struggles for terminologies that can be used for classifying individuals, and these struggles are really rhetorical moves to establish identity.

Having described his perspective on identity along these lines in his opening chapter, Strauss devotes the rest of the book to their explication and then focuses on "transformation of identity," the changes it undergoes over the life cycle, the continuity it maintains in each individual case, and concludes with a statement on the relationship between identity and membership in given groups. While Strauss's work was full of insights of the interconnections between fields considered disparate, there is a certain vague and underdeveloped quality to this monograph. It cries out for more detail and specification.

This specification, if not more detail, was to come in the work of Gregory Stone, in whose work it is easy to see the influence of both Strauss and Foote. Among the many fruits of Stone's work was the clarification of the relationship between self and identity. He argues:

> Almost all writers using the term imply that identity establishes *what* and *where* the person is in social terms. It is not a substitute word for "self." Instead when one has identity, he is *situated*—that is, cast in the shape of a social object by the acknowledgment of his participation or membership in social relations. One's identity is established when other's *place* him as a social object by assigning him the same words of identity that he appropriates for himself or *announces*. It is in the coincidence of placements and announcements that identity becomes a meaning of the self. (Stone [1962] 1970: 399)

Identity then, according to Stone, depends on the *words* that an individual appropriates, which others acknowledge and accept, thereby placing him or her *in* an identity. These words, as Stone was to show in his study of appearance and clothing and their uses in social interaction, can be transformed into visual imagery as well. In this formulation of identity, an individual is placed and situated as a social object by the use of "words" that are current in the social circles in which the interaction was occurring.

Stone also gives weight to the processes by which identification is accomplished, arguing that there are really two processes involved in identification: *Identification with* and *identification of.* He describes the relationship between the two as follows; "Identifications *with* one another, in whatever mode, cannot be made without identifications *of* one another" (1970: 396). Identification of one another precedes all interpersonal communication processes and is initially accomplished silently or nonverbally. The sighted see the appearance of the other and place him or her in an identity that the other had defined by controlling his or her appearance, indeed *claimed* by the organization of an appearance. The visually impaired, however, have to rely on voice and tone recognition and the recognition of touch and smell to identify the other, and the producer of the voice has less control over it than those who present appearances.

Identity is presented as a system of claims by the self that elicit validation from others, albeit in varying degrees. Further, these claims are also made by the presenting self to that very self in question as part of the "reflective process." If "the self has the characteristic that it is an object to itself" (Mead 1934: 136), then before any given interaction with others it is able to objectify itself and present this objectification to the other, and it is only then that it can be validated. This process of objectification can be accomplished by using clothing and other "apparent symbols" as Stone shows, and/or it can be accomplished afterward in and through conversations that ensue after the appearance has been presented. Stone, in fact, refers punningly to appearance as *pretext*, i.e., the identity that appears before the text and which can be used to deceive the other as well. Nevertheless, identities are established more securely and with greater subtlety and with more delicate nuances by discourse than by clothing and demands analysis in its own terms.

Recently, Harrison White has offered a theory of identity as the source of action and situates it in networks of social relations. He observes,

> Identity here does not mean the common sense notion of self, nor does it mean presupposing consciousness and integration or presupposing personality. Rather, identity is any source of action not explicable from biophysical regularities, and to which observers can attribute meaning. An employer, a community, a crowd, oneself, all may be identities. An identity is perceived by others as having an unproblematic continuity. Identities add through contentions to the contingencies faced by other identities. (1992: 6 my emphasis)

Such an identity is essentially social; it is a variable to which *observers* attribute meaning, an attribution that results, cumulatively, in the emergence of social organization. Identity here becomes the keystone with which social organization is constituted. However, if observers define identity, it is safe to say that sooner or later it becomes subjectively acknowledged as well.[1]

Fruitful as these studies and essays are, they can stand further specifications and descriptions. This is true of Erikson's depiction of what may be termed reflexively achieved identities, and Foote's, Stone's and Strauss's depiction of what may be termed addressively achieved identities. Erikson, for example, speaks of the "accrual of inner capital," leaving the shape, form, and character of this capital unspecified. Strauss and Foote describe naming as a key process in identification, whereas Stone describes the identification process as occurring with the "assignment" and "appropriation" of words by interacting individuals. For White identity is a meaning conferred by an observing intelligence. The "capital" that an individual acquires, whether it is inner or outer, the "names" that are used in the identifying process, the "words" that are appropriated and assigned during the same activity, and observer's "attribution of meaning" can be achieved only with the operation of semiotic processes. They need to be articulated as signs and read as signs. These signs may be called *signs of identity*. These signs are deployed within various discursive formations and through a variety of discursive strategies. They can be further specified into two broad categories: Verbal signs, which may be termed *vocabularies of identity,* and tactile and visual signs, which may be termed *materials of identity.*

These signs are used by human agents to *objectify* their respective selves to others, as to themselves, so that they may be readily identified. Identities, in other words, are not possible without a specified process of identification and such a process of identification is not possible without signs to represent them. These signs of identity are used in all four rhetorical modes of self-presencing. They are used reflexively to identify the individual to himself or herself as well as to others: "It is I, Hamlet the Dane." They are used to address the other and thereby identify the "you": "How fares our cousin, Hamlet?" Referentially they occur to establish an identity too: "Something you have heard of Hamlet's transformation, so call it, since nor th' exterior nor the inward man resembles what it was." Answerability, too, involves signs of identity: "I am glad to see you well: Horatio—or I do forget myself." These signs of reflection, reference, address, and answer are forms of objectification, and processes in the objectifications of self or the other. They are in fact used in everyday life to identify self and other through *acts of identity.* Such acts are deliberate moves made by an individual to classify himself or herself, or an other, in culturally given categories.

Once the self has been identified in this manner, the particular signs of identification become a meaning for the self and are used to achieve his or her presence in the world through these vocabularies. Such a presence enables the individual to establish a *continuity* as well as *claim* a substantiative *sameness* over time for self or for other. Further, in claiming and being conferred an identity by using concurrent vocabularies, he or she is also *differentiated* from relevant others and given a shape and a substance that is sufficient unto itself for all practical purposes. *An identified person is not only the same individual who was similarly identified, by self and others, at an earlier occasion, but is also different from other individuals who are so identified by self and other.* Identities indubitably exist only within the discursive processes of the mind and those between minds, and in these discursive processes given signs of identity are used to define a narrative continuity for an embodied and social entity and to differentiate the same entity from others. Each such identity will have a separate, *addressively conferred* and *reflexively appreciated*, trajectory through life. The key process, then, the fundamental activity that occurs when an individual identifies himself or herself and is identified by others, is the claim of continuity of the individual over time and a differentiation from others. Such claims, made in the reflexive and addressive modes of discourse, as well as in the referential and answerable modes of discourse, are possible only with a particular logic of classification.[2]

## THE LOGIC OF IDENTITY

Processes of identification are essentially exercises in classification. Classificatory exercises that lead to identifications of objects in the world are ways of organizing the perceptual world and bringing an *intelligible* and *communicable* order to it. Such exercises are coded into the very language that we use, and they eventually become habits of action. Classificatory processes are an essential part of the adaptation that an organism makes to the environment, and insofar as the human is a discursive organism *par excellence* his or her adaptations are discursive ones, too. One parsimonious instrument with which the perceptual world—or the elements thereof—can be given an "intentional unity" (Rosenthal 1977: 208) is to give it a logical character. Rosenthal writes,

> Man is also that being in the world which perceives his world through an intentional unity with it; man is that organism in the world which is conscious of its own ends. Thus, pragmatism approaches the perceptual situation in terms of a second type of analysis which emphasizes the "logical character" or intentional character of the relationship. (1977: 208)

The intentional character of this relationship with the perceptual world begins with the identification of the elements that are perceived. Abraham Kaplan puts this issue as follows;

> Knowledge begins with discrimination of differences, but every difference presupposes an identity. A differential response becomes a cognition—as Aristotle, Kant and Peirce all emphasized—insofar as a habit of response is engendered, which confers on the stimulus a meaning embodied at last in a symbol. There is no cognition without recognition, that is without a constancy of some kind by which what is being known is recognized for what it is. (1964: 85)

The intentional organization of the world, then, involves identifying the objects in the world. And such identifications, to be *practicable* and *talkable,* must separate the objects on some basis or other and ensure that a particular identified object is not confused for another or taken for another or is indistinguishable from another. In other words they must follow schemes or conceptual systems that enable a discursive mind to achieve this conceptual clarity and practical validity. Such conceptual systems are, a fortiori, semiotic systems. If one examines Peirce's seminal paper on logic as a semiotic, it will be clear that he proposes not only definitions of a sign and its attendant elements but a logic based on the classification of signs. The point and purpose of these complex systems of signs is indubitably to enable an individual to intentionally organize the perceptual world, to put into practice a logic of inquiry, and to achieve the necessary abductions with which he or she can "adjust" to living in the said world. Peirce wrote: "The first starting of a hypothesis and the entertaining of it, whether as a simple interrogation or with any degree of confidence, is an inferential step which I propose to call *abduction*" (1955: 151). This is applicable not only to the conduct of inquiry in scientific endeavors but also in the conduct of everyday life, which also proceeds as a series of inquiries. Consider in this instance Peirce's distinction between a *qualisign, sinsign,* and a *legisign:*

> A *Qualisign* is a quality which is a Sign. It cannot actually act as a sign until it is embodied; but the embodiment has nothing to do with its character as a sign.
> A *Sinsign* (where the syllable *sin* is taken as meaning "being only once" . . .) is an actual existent thing or event which is a sign. It can only be so through its qualities; so that it involves a qualisign, or rather several qualisigns.
> A *Legisign* is a law that is a Sign. This law is usually established by men. Every conventional sign is a legisign. . . . It is not a single object, but a general type which, it has been agreed, shall be significant. (1955: 101–102)

Insofar as various kinds of signs are put to use to indicate an object and elicit an interpretant, they enable the sign-user (who is himself or herself a sign) to organize the world—by abductive processes, as *qualisigns, sinsigns,* and *legisigns* as the situation warranted. In such organizational activities, the sign-user, insofar as he or she is also an element of the perceptual and intentionally unified world, has perforce to organize himself or herself as a qualisign, sinsign, and legisign as well. In less cumbersome words, what an individual does is to organize the world in terms of identities that are subtly or grossly signed into differences and similarities given by their respective qualities, uniqueness, and their applicable "laws." Everyday life, in such a conceptualization, becomes then a "conduct of inquiry," indeed the conduct of semiotic inquiry, in which a "social logic" is put into operation. In conducting such inquiries in everyday life, an individual discovers the signs of his or her own identity as that of the others that he or she encounters and arrives at a working relationship with them. The identity of the self as that of the others is apprehended as logically distributed signs.

The intentional organization of the perceptual world and the assembling of them into a "unity" must perforce use an already established instrumentation, one that is known to the organism in question, so as to "sign," that is, identify, the objects in the world with its own logic. Such a logic is, no doubt, put into practice in given contexts and situations but not invented by the actor, then and there. Far from being endogenous to the occasion, it is an essential element of the conceptual system and what Mead called the "imagery" (1904:2; 1964: 274) of the organized world that an actor has learned and "remembers," and puts into practice. Volosinov puts this very well, as "consciousness takes shape and being in the material of signs created by an organized group in the process of its social intercourse. The individual consciousness is nurtured on signs; it derives its growth from them; it reflects their logic and laws" (1973: 13). The actor, far from being an *immaculate conceiver*, is subject to a logico-linguistic socialization, which affects his or her interpretation of the world. The language that he or she acquires is in fact structured, at the simplest level, into binary systems and it is this logic that he or she would use to code identity as well. This system of codification will manifest itself as the basis of an individual's "stock of knowledge"(Schutz 1964: 283) and would become useful in the management of both the continuity and differentiation of identity.

This logic of classifications—expressed in *significant signs*—may be available in concrete forms as well as in abstract ones. Indeed the symbols themselves, to be able to signify anything at all, need to be organized in accordance with a logic. No doubt for Mead acts were practical accomplishments in an unfolding of experience but even such practices need a logical system with which individuals can achieve precision and clarity for their acts. Without a minimum of such precision and clarity no meaning can emerge because no one will be able to separate one act from another or one meaning from another.[3]

In the course of constructing an act an individual needs perforce to identify the external objects in some fashion or another in the ongoing imagination that accompanies the act, place them concretely or abstractly in categories and proceed to complete the act. Insofar as Dorothy Lee's (1959: 131) claim that identification of selves is dependent on the "law of contradiction" seems indisputable, one can say that one of the "images" or "conceptual systems" that an individual, a discursive organism that it is, will use to organize identities is Aristotle's systematization of logic—not as an a priori stencil—but as a semiotic in the pragmatic organization of experience. Again I resort to Sandra Rosenthal's perceptive analysis of the issue:

> The world, as the "outermost" content, encompassing frame of reference, or implicit categorical contours within which the independently real reveals itself within experience, provides the context for the propositions that can delineate experience. . . . The world answers to the laws of the excluded middle and non-contradiction because it is the regulative ideal of that which can be conceptually articulated and made precise to an ideal limit. (1988: 314)

Identities may be fluid, moving, imprecise at the boundaries, and may indeed be characterized by the same "play of differences" that Derrida finds in words, but for all that, a *conceptualizing intelligence* and an *acting self* will define boundaries that are relevant for the purposes at hand, separating one from another into semiotically realized categories, and conduct his or her life with their help. Just as engineers who build bridges do not pause to consider the implication of the developments in quantum physics in their work, discursive individuals in everyday life do not pause to deconstruct identities and play with differences in their acting moves: They perform the acts of identity and expect them to be either confirmed or corrected.[4]

In Aristotle's logical system these three "laws"—the law of identity, the law of contradiction, and the law of the excluded middle—are used as *socially shared* rules of thought for the conduct of inquiry. The laws seek to establish that A = A—that is, a phenomenon remains identical to itself for all *discursive and practical purposes*. Whatever the importance of this law in other fields of endeavor, it is of paramount importance in undertaking discursive activities. During the course of a discussion, debate, or argument, or, for that matter, reflection and thought, a phenomenon that occurs in it must maintain its integrity. Without such integrity, without the phenomenon in fact being equal to itself, at least for all discursive processes—which can, of course, be long or short—no *intelligible* activity can occur. If one is referring to Abe, he must remain Abe during the course of the discussion. If X is speaking to Abe and Y understands X to be speaking of Ave, then intelligible exchange cannot occur. Similarly if Sam thinks that he is Napoleon and Josephine thinks that he is only Sam no fruitful discussion can emerge. Similarly if X believes that he is Anton at one point in the conversation (or in a larger duration for that matter) and Antonia at another moment, neither successful conversations nor stable relationships can emerge.

For discourse between actors to proceed efficiently and pragmatically, and for that matter within each actor himself or herself, the use of a categorical logic is unavoidable. Insofar as one has perforce to engage in speech acts that are intelligible to self and other, then one must perforce use the logic of categories. Anton and Antonia may be "really" the same or be "really" different—but at the discursive level and practical level they are classified as separate and different—a classification that may be changed later by mutually agreed rules of transformation.

The law of identity as an operational principle within discursive processes means that in the activities of every day life, an individual treats himself or herself as having a *continuity* with earlier manifestations of his or her self and a *separation* from other such individuals. The others treat him or her with the same consideration: He or she (or it) is what he or she was earlier for all practical purposes and different from me, him, her, them, or it. It is of course not the case that humans read Aristotle or learn Aristotle's system and put it into operation; rather Aristotle systematized practices that were in use by humans who were in the business of communicating with each other and seeking to do so with parsimonious methods. To be able to operate in the social world, an individual must be able to maintain a sameness and continuity over time—that is, to be able to claim, and allow others to claim, that Abe=Abe. Second, he or she must be able to claim and allow others to claim that simultaneously he or she is not someone else: that he is Abe and not Ave at the same time, thus affirming the validity of Aristotle's law of noncontradiction. And finally, Aristotle's third law states that a phenomenon cannot be a member of two opposing classes: Abe cannot be Abe and not-Abe.

There is, however, no claim here that the differences between identified objects—between A and B for example, as between Anton and Antonia—are "real" or "essential" in any meaning of these terms or can always be "empirically" substantiated. There is no need to insist that identities are forever fixed and unchangeable or that they have an obdurateness and quiddity outside discursive processes. These moves of identification truly arrest ongoing and evolving identities into easy categories so that discourse can proceed. The names of identity—the categorization of reality—are "measurements" achieved by means of a commonly agreed system: They capture commuting variables into a coherent stability. It is not, then, that the world and its contents, including human beings, have fixed identities, forever stable; rather by one means or another, individuals fix and stabilize them so that they can handle the world at the practical level of action, interaction, and discourse. As instruments of measurement these categories of identity run into the same conundrum that quantum physics faces: to measure something is to arrest it in its onward movement thereby changing its character; without measuring it, its existence cannot be gauged or discussed. This difficulty gives rise to what Werner Heisenberg calls the "principle of uncertainty"—which applies not only in physics but has a general application. Commenting on the generality of the Heisenberg principle, Burke writes:

> One may well take it for granted that statements about the nature of the world's substance can never be established any more firmly by instruments than they can be by words. At least, since instruments themselves are so fundamentally implicated in language, deriving both their formation and their interpretation from this source, one might well expect in advance that they would be as beset by ultimate dialectical embarrassments as language itself. For though they contrive to eliminate pressures that beset language at the Rhetorical and Symbolic level, they are profoundly Grammatical. . . . We might glimpse the full paradox in stating the Heisenberg principle thus: A margin of *indeterminacy is inevitable* in measurement. That the determination of a particle's speed would interfere with the determination of a particle's position and vice versa seems simply an ultimate refinement, in precision instruments, of the old paradox considered by Zeno, just as in mathematics there is, finally, the principle of discreteness pitted against that of continuity. (Burke 1969a: 260)

These moves by which an acting individual classifies the objects in the world, including himself or herself and other human beings, by using the law of identity and its derivatives are devices for *measuring* the objects in the world. *Indeed without such measurements no human being would be able to deal with any object in the world—be it a human or nonhuman one.* The issue really is not whether a dialectical and processual logic that is needed in quantum theory, or for that matter in Jacques Derrida's grammatology, is "better" or "worse" than a logic using stable categories; it is rather that both logical systems are, if I may use the term, *complementary* systems. "Either we make a good measurement and obtain an accurate knowledge of the speed of a particle without being able to tell exactly where it is, or else we can make an accurate measurement of the position at the cost of interfering with the velocity," as Silva and Lochak (1969), summarizing the conundrum in microphysics, put it. The sacrifice of velocity, i.e., process, needs to be made in order to even discover the existence of the particle. In the world of meaning—in fact, the physicist John Wheeler (1984) called the new physics "the child of meaning"—in everyday life the same principle is applicable. No doubt identities are evanescent, changing, in process, and categories of identity are arbitrary impositions in the social and interpersonal life of the individual. Nevertheless, stable units need to be produced so that dependable discourse and interaction can proceed. An individual reflexively and the others addressively and referentially define, "measure," and label a self with an identity—labels, names, nicknames, and so on, which are constituted in accordance with the law of identity.[5]

## IDENTITY AND INDIVIDUALISM

While many have argued for the universality of some form of the conception of self and identity for the *linguistically minded* species, this has recently been challenged by some scholars. This challenge focuses, on the one hand, on the *historicity* of the concept of self, arguing that it emerged only recently and only in Western civilization, and, on the other hand, that it is a *culturally* specific conceptualization. This view has been put forth by Clifford Geertz as follows:

> The Western conception of the person as a bounded, unique, more or less integrated motivational and cognitive universe, a dynamic whole, the center of awareness, emotion, judgement and action, organized into a distinctive whole and set contrastively against other such wholes and against a social and natural background is, however incorrigible as it may seem to us, a rather peculiar idea within the context of the world's cultures. (1976: 229)

Geertz draws, with his characteristic rhetorical vigor, too sweeping a contrast here. In fact the polar opposites he depicts between a "western conception of the person" and other such conceptions confounds the particularized notion of the "individual" resuscitated during the period of the Renaissance after its first appearance in classical Greece (Dumont 1983; Barbu 1960) and the conception of a *self-conscious* human who can initiate acts as a "bounded, unique, more or less integrated motivational and cognitive universe." An "individual" in the former sense is a term in political and religious discourse and literary studies. In political discourse it manifests itself in the definition of the individual as one who is endowed with certain inalienable rights and duties. In religion the doctrine of individualism finds its perfect expression in Protestantism: the individual as the "master of my fate;. . .captain of my soul," in the words of the poet Ernest Henley. In literary studies when characters in various works of the imagination are given "inner" feelings and desires as the "cause" of their actions one can see the presence of such an individualism.

These doctrines of individualism found in various political, religious, and literary texts may very well be reflective of the way in which the people who produced these texts sought to live their lives. But that is a far cry from the claim that all the humans who lived in cultures that did not create these texts were not self-conscious agents of their action. A human acts with a consciousness of self regardless of whether his or her culture produced texts of the individuation of the person. *This is a characteristic of the human being, not merely as a subcultural-being, but as species-being.* To the extent that all humans are born into an ongoing linguistic community and learn both language and being from other humans, he or she also learns to be a self.[6]

Consider here the Greek case. Barbu has argued that the conception of "individualism" emerged in the Hellenistic period of Greek history, but that in Homer's time such a conception was unknown: "The people described by Homer did not feel that the "motives" of their behaviour lay in themselves; on the contrary, they believed that their behaviour was determined from the outside, by the gods" (Barbu 1960: 75). However, by the time of Sappho these beliefs had changed in such a way that "the inner world of emotions is exalted so much that it dominates the life of the individual" (79). Nevertheless, there can be no doubt that the Homeric hero, after telling himself that it is Athena who is responsible for his action, must yet tell himself again to act, to take the next step. To take the example that Barbu uses: Achilles is in a predicament in the beginning of the *Iliad* as to what to do next, and "Athena stepped behind him, caught him by his golden hair" and helped him to make his decision (Barbu 1960: 75). Of course there is no such goddess as Athena, outside the discursive process, engaging in such actions, either to an exalted figure like Achilles or to an ordinary person. Rather, Homer and Achilles, and other human beings at certain points in history, *used* the rhetoric of divine causation to propel their selves into action. Even Achilles on this momentous occasion had to *recognize* the push from the divine Athena and then take various mental and physical steps and act on his own, recognize himself as a "dynamic whole," a "center of awareness," in order to execute the next step.

This claim cannot be challenged by arguing that "individualism" as a doctrine emerged only in Western civilization and emerged only recently. This may or may not be true, but is quite irrelevant to the claim that human conduct is self-conscious activity. This claim can be refuted only by showing the existence of humans who have no linguisticity, no minding capacities, and no capacity for what Mead calls "delayed reaction" (1934: 99). Long before Mead developed these notions, it was Marx who put this very eloquently—almost poetically:

> A spider conducts operations that resemble those of a weaver, and a bee puts to shame many an architect in the construction of her cells. But what distinguishes the worst of architects from the best of bees is this: *that the architect raises his structure in imagination before he erects it in reality.* At the end of every labor process, we get a result that already existed in the imagination of the laborer at its commencement. He not only effects a change of form on the material on which he works, but he also realizes a purpose of his own that gives the law to his *modus operandi,* and to which he must subordinate his will. ([1865] 1965: 179)

If one is an architect and achieves a design of a projected work in his or her imagination, he or she is doing that indubitably as a self—that is, as one who can observe his or her actions and projections as objects, consider them, delay executing them, and perform accordingly. It is, however, not only the architect who raises his or her structures in imagination before he or she erects them in reality, but all humans who erect the structure of their acts in their imaginations. Such imaginations are conscious of the place of the actor in the world of others, things, space, situation, context, time, and biography. In other words, a human erects the structure of his or her acts in either a maximal or minimal awareness of self and its place in the world. This is not subcultural peculiarity but an evolutionary universal of the human species (Franks 1985; Bickerton 1990).

Even if there are cultures in which the person is not conceived as a "bounded and integrated motivational and cognitive universe," in their own ethno-theories of the person and the world, the individual is, to begin with, at least bodily separate from others and has a name that separates him or her from others; surely there are no cultures in which someone, say a man, is denied his physical integrity and told that his body is constantly disintegrating and coalescing with that of others. At least in this respect, he is bounded and integrated. When he declares, "I have a headache," I am sure his significant others don't tell him, "No you cannot possibly have a headache and make this claim because you are not a bounded and integrated spring of action. *You* do not have a headache; it's *your brother and you* together who have a headache." He does have, at least at this level, a motivational and cognitive dynamism and unity. When the same individual claims that he is bleeding from a wound and that he is in pain, his others will surely not refuse to attend to him on the premise that since he cannot be a center of awareness, emotion, judgment, and action, neither his pain nor his bleeding, or for that matter, he himself, can exist. Once this is granted, it is easy to take the next step: With these separate bodies and names, he or she at least can be considered "individuated." If he or she can be thus individuated, he or she can identify a self, but the self may be defined, at times, as being coterminus with dyads, triads, or a whole group. Consider the case of the Wintu. Dorothy Lee has argued:

> The Wintu Indians of northern California have a conception of self which is markedly different from our own. . . . The definition of self in our own culture rests on our law of contradiction. The self cannot be both self and not self, both self and other; the self excludes the other. The Wintu philosophy in general has no law of contradiction. Where we have mutually exclusive dualistic categories, the Wintu have categories which are inclusive, but not mutually so; that is, object A will be included in object B, but not vice versa. (1959: 131)

Yet there is no doubt, according to Lee's own version, that the Wintu are able to conceive of A and B as separate categories, even though A may include B, because without such a categorization it would not be possible to include B in A. Lee continues, however, to derive an inference from this want of a law of contradiction among the Wintu:

> A study of the grammatical expression of identity, relationship and otherness, shows that the Wintu conceive of the self not as strictly delimited or defined, but as a concentration, at most, which gradually fades and gives place to the other. (1959: 134)

As an example of this she writes,

> The Wintu do not use *and* when referring to individuals who are, or live or act together. Instead of analyzing the *we* into: *John and I*, they say *John we* using John as a specification. Only when individuals who are not already in relatedness are brought together is the word *and* used. (134)

This does not mean, as far as I can see, that the Wintu do not have a law of contradiction in their thoughtways or that they have no conception of the self as a bounded unit. It rather means that the Wintu use conceptions that are collective rather than singular nouns to identify their selves: "John we" is still spoken by one individual about a unit that is different from other units of identity—"Mark they," "Luke they," "Matthew they," "Simon they." The Wintu seem to identify the self with vocabularies that are different from Western ones, to be sure, but identify they do and they do also separate one entity from another—"John-we" from "Mark-we," for instance. In other words, the vocabulary of identity a Wintu man would use to identify the self may be a collective noun and Wintu may very well attribute the "spring of his motivation" to this collective entity—but for all that he is doing exactly what others, say in "Western civilization," are doing: naming his self, identifying it with a culturally specified vocabulary, and claiming it as his essential being and motive for action. The Wintu man in this example is able to use certain vocabularies to identify himself and define a continuity for himself just as he is able to distinguish himself from others. A Wintu man will no doubt identify his self in specific circumstances as "John we," which really means that he would consider this vocabulary as defining himself as a "bounded unique and more or less integrated motivational unity," and predicate his bodily actions on such an identification. There is no ethnographic record that the Wintu speaking and doing their acts always do so in unison. When a Wintu man says "John we," he does not have others standing with him harmonizing their speech to his; nor are they standing with him when he eats, fights his enemy, copulates with his mate, or defecates. *The locution "John we" is rather another sign for identifying the self.* It identifies the self in all its social complexities, as does the I and me, and functions as the description of an individuated entity in his relations with the world. Such different metaphorisations for identifying the self would no doubt have different consequences for the kind of morality, industry, and social organization that would emerge. Nevertheless, it is a far cry from claiming that the basis of action among people like the Wintu is radically different from the Western one. "John we" is really an *interpretant* of the self of John, a concept of self formulated within the cultural logic of the Wintu.[7]

Buddhism, too, is said to present a challenge to conceiving the self as a continuity of identity over time and a source of action and meaning in the world. Indeed, one can see in the Buddhist texts dealing with self, identity, and time one of the earliest attempts at the practice of deconstruction. The *Milinadapanha* text describes a conversation between a Buddhist monk, a *Bhante*, and a king in which this thesis is examined. This discussion and the examples that are used were developed to validate the Buddhist claim that there was no continuous personal identity: The seeming continuity is an illusion, Buddhism claimed, and at each moment an individual is a unique "instantaneous being." Nevertheless, when this argument given by the monk in the following excerpt is examined, one can see the paradoxical nature of this claim. An individual at a given point in time has an instantaneous being, to be sure, but his or her continuity with earlier such identities is also recognized:

> "Bhante Nagasena," said the king, "is a person when just born that person himself, or is he some one else?"
>   "He is neither that person," said the elder, "Nor is he someone else."

"Give an illustration."

"What do you say to this, your majesty? When you were a young, tender, weakly infant lying on your back, was that your present grown-up self?"

"Nay verily Bhante. The young, tender, weakly infant lying on its back was one person, and my present grown-up self is another person."

"If that is the case, your majesty, there can be no such thing as a mother, or a father, or a teacher, or an educated man, or a righteous man, or a wise man. Pray, your majesty, is the mother of the *kalala* one person, the mother of the *abbuda* another person, the mother of the *pesi* another person, the mother of the *ghana* another person, the mother of the little child another person, and the mother of the grown-up man another person? Is it one person who is a student, another person who has finished his education? Is it one person who commits a crime, another person whose hands and feet are cut off?"

"Nay, verily, Bhante. But what, Bhante, would you reply to these questions?"

Said the elder, "It was I, your majesty, who was young tender weakly infant lying on my back and it is I who am now grown up. It is through their connection with the embryonic body that all these different periods are unified."

"Give an illustration."

"It is as if, your majesty, a man were to light a light;—would it shine all night?"

"Assuredly, Bhante, it would shine all night."

"Pray, your majesty, is the flame of the first watch the same as a flame of the middle watch?"

"Is the flame of the middle watch the same as the flame of the last watch?"

"Nay, verily Bhante."

"Pray, then, your majesty, was there one light in the first watch, another in the middle watch and a third in the last watch?"

"Nay, verily, Bhante. Through connection with that first light there was light all night."

"In exactly the same way, your majesty, do the elements of being join one another in serial succession: one element perishes, another arises, succeeding each other, as it were instantaneously. Therefore neither as the same nor as a different person do you arrive at your latest aggregation of consciousness." (Warren [1896] 1987: 148)

What does the Bhante Nagasena's explication leave us with? "Neither as the same person nor as a different person do you arrive at your latest aggregation of consciousness," the Bhante says. The individual, at any given moment, is neither the same person as he or she was at an earlier moment, nor is he or she a different person. *He or she is the same person under the auspices of one set of conditions and another person under a different set of conditions.* What are these conditions? If the issue is whether there are any sort of connections between the person at a given moment and another at an earlier moment, then Nagasena's Buddhist answer is, yes, there are these connections, and therefore for these purposes one can consider this person, having varying presences in varying moments, the same person. The answer to another question, "Are there differences, substantial or otherwise, between this person at this moment and at an earlier moment?" is also in the affirmative. An individual at any moment maintains a continuity with earlier moments of his or her existence, just as he or she is different from the one who inhabited the earlier moments.

The Buddhist version of the problem of identity, it turns out, is not able to dispense with what may be called the paradox of measurement: it understands consciousness and consciousness of identity as an ongoing and changing process, but to be able to discuss such evolving identities it has to name static stages so that intelligible discourse can occur. It calls attention to the complex implications of the processes of identification demanding in turn complex solutions as well. *An individual then is the same as he or she was at one time and a later time in certain respects and different in certain other respects.* The social-psychologically relevant question at this stage is how does an individual operate this double consciousness of sameness and difference? This question cannot be answered in any abstract logical way but by attending to the way an individual—Buddhist or Christian, Jew or Hindu—operates in the world of everyday life. Such an individual will be one who talks to others and talks to himself or herself. He or she, that is, lives and dies in a discursive community and operates with a discursive mind. One way of attending to the problem of identity of such an individual with a given continuity and a certain difference is to investigate how he or she attends to the problem of his or her identity. The discussion between the king and Bhante Nagasena provides a fruitful starting point. The Bhante asks the king: When you were a young tender weakly infant lying on your back, was that your present grown-up self? In this conversational gambit, the Bhante introduces various concepts that implicates a theory of continuous identity: "tender, weakly infant" is *contrasted and connected* with the "grown-up self." When the king denies a sameness between the infant and the grown-up, the Bhante introduces the various stages of the embryo. These are *named and sorted* stages of the embryo: *kalala, abbuda, pesi, ghana.* Each named stage is identical unto itself and remains stable at least for a time. These names were devised and used in discourse to identify the changes that were occurring to the same *presumptive* entity. Indeed, then, one can say that in the talk the king and the Bhante recognize both the existence of difference and sameness in the embryo. The embryo at an earlier stage is called *kalala* and the same embryo is called *abbuda* at a later stage. That is to say, the embryo has sameness under one set of conditions and difference under another set of conditions—conditions that are culturally available to the discursants.

These identities, the way they are conceived and "discoursed," imply a continuity: It is the *kalala* that "becomes" the *abbuda,* and it is this that "becomes" *pesi* and then "becomes" a *ghana* and so on to become a little child and adult person. As the discourse separates and identifies these entities, it also recognizes their continuity by articulating them in the very for-

mulation of this sentence. This discourse from the Bhante Nagasena also recognizes the importance of the interactional process in the establishment of
identity: He brings the mother into the discourse. It is from the standpoint of
the mother that the embryonic child and the little child and the adult individual achieve their continuity. These various moments of the evolving individual are unified into a coherent identity: He is the son of this one, mother.
She can identity him, however many changes he may have undergone since
sperm met egg and constituted the entity. And she can identify the stages
through which he has passed and what he is now by employing very distinct
terminologies, which have their own logic to them.

One can envisage a slightly different discussion between the king and the
Bhante. Are you now the king of this land? Yes, the king can answer, I am king
of this land. Were you king yesterday, last month, last year? Yes, I was because
I remember discursively that I was king at those particular times. That is to say,
I was able to refer to myself as a king yesterday, last month and last year, treat
myself as such and have various relevant others refer to me, address me, and
treat me as a king. Are you the same person, the king now, as you were when
you were five years old, or when you were a *kalala?* No I am not the same person, but I have "grown" from the *kalala*, to a five-year-old and so on to the
present kinghood. How do you know? So have I been *told* along the way by all
and sundry and I remember being told. In other words, the continuity of identity and its difference from earlier shapes of such identities are *discursively
established* and used by participants in ongoing relationships. So to the extent
that vocabularies are made available to describe these continuities and differences then an individual as a discursant will use them to claim the reality of the
paradox: I am the same person and I am a different person. These vocabularies may be finely differentiated—as in the Buddhist one about embryo, or more
grossly differentiated—but one uses what one and his or her others, know,
understand, accept and are willing to validate.

If there are distinctions made along the temporal dimension of existence,
the same distinctions are made between different individuals. One has a continuity and a difference simultaneously from earlier moments in the discursive process of the individual just as one can claim a separateness and a connection with others by similar processes. The king and the Bhante, for
example, have separate identities and the descriptive titles they bear—that is,
accept and use—confirm the respective identities of each of them.

Even as continuous identity is being denied, the monk addresses his interlocutor as "Your Majesty," which is equal to "King," and the king in return
addresses the monk as "Bhante"—honorific title for a monk. "King" and
"Bhante" are *concepts* that summarize a long series of "incidents" into a coherent usage. In other words, each participant takes these various experiences of
the past and treats them as an interpretant. The particulars of kingliness and
bhanteness are collapsed into a universal and subject to a logic of classification;

it becomes a concept. Neither the king nor the monk can address each other, relate to each other, or treat the other as an object without remembering who the other was a moment ago, a day earlier, or months before that. The same can be said of the mother mentioned in the Bhante's discourse: She is able to recognize her "son," a concept that cannot be used without it being a continuous identity. Indeed, as the good king and the equally good Bhante seek in their debate to question the existence of a continuous identity, they are forced to *talk* as if there are such identities. In such talkings an individual is forced to semiotize the concept of identity, thereby giving it a discursive presence. In the moments of referential and reflexive discourse it has a static existence, as is apparent in the exchange between the king and the Bhante, as a discreet identity. A Buddhist must yet use it as a sign to conceive the nonexistence of his or her presence in the world as in his or her relationship with others.

Buddhism, seeking to deny the validity of the notion of a continuous personal identity, has succeeded in providing a theory of *successive identities* that nevertheless constitute a logical series of separated identities which can be unified into a coherence when seen from a particular perspective. An embryo may have these separate but successive identities but from the mother's standpoint it still bears the identity of her son. In the absence of these vocabularies of identity there cannot be an identity or memory or consciousness of a continuing or separate existence. It is the continuity *indicated* by given and available vocabularies that gives an identity that can be simultaneously continued and differentiated. There cannot, however, be any doubt that an individual who claims to be *anatta*, and is both same as he or she was at an earlier time and different from it as well, will be able to function as a "motivational unity" in the everyday activities of this world.

However hard some theories may strive to obliterate or underplay the individual "as an integrated motivational unity," and whatever metaphors of collective identification that they may fashion, at the fulcrum of the act the embodied entity must produce moves and countermoves against or with another such entity and against the material world. This is, one may say, a limitation put on humans by the fact that they are physically separated from each other and can face the body and feel it and command it with their discursive minds. Without such differentiation, there is nothing to either see in the world or conceive in the mind; without differentiation there is no world that the discursive mind can discuss and such differentiations are constituted by the use of systems of classification and identification.[8]

## ACTS OF IDENTITY

The differentiation of self and the interactive claiming of a continuity of self is accomplished by moves that may be termed acts of identity. David Snow and Leon Anderson describe the various means by which these acts—what they call "identity work"— are accomplished. Identity work, they aver,

> is the range of activities individuals engage in to create, present and sustain personal identities that are congruent with and supportive of the self-concept. So defined, identity work may involve a number of complementary activities: a) arrangement of physical settings or props; b) cosmetic face-work or the arrangement of personal appearance; c) selective association with other individuals and groups; d) verbal constructions and assertion of personal identities. (1987: 1348)

These four instrumentations for the claiming of identity may be reconsidered as *materialistic identification, associative identification,* and *vocabularic identification.* These acts of identification are simultaneously acts of classification. Acts of identity are undertaken then by selecting one vocabulary or another for use in the identification process or set of associates or objects and materials to do so. In such forms of action, an individual uses modes of identification either to define his or her own identity just as to read the identity of the other. The verbal form of identification and the material form manifest themselves as claims and assertions on the one hand and as acceptance and validations on the other—unless, of course, the claims are refuted and rejected and a new identity demanded or conferred on the other. In any case identificatory processes are social acts that are fundamentally moves with which actors seek to separate their selves and that of others from other selves and facilitate the emergence of reflexive and discursive interactions.

Such naming processes practiced by an individual, the acts of identification, are redolent with purpose. Such acts are not just empty logical activities but are indubitably pragmatic exercises and as the purposes change, the systems of classification used may also change. The purposiveness of the process of identification introduces a fundamental *selectivity* to it as well: An individual and his or her social circles, the cultural group in which he or she lives and acts, chooses among many options, which particular identity that he or she is to have. Societies, for example, can select "adolescence" as an identity for individuals conforming to certain boundaries marked by age and the nature of the responsibilities that he or she has to accept and this can be distinguished from "childhood" and "adulthood." Other societies may choose to skip adolescence altogether and move from childhood to adulthood and expect the person in the latter category to undertake commensurate responsibilities.

Narrower identities, the more personal ones, are also subject to pragmatic selectivities. A man may have had conferred on him a patrilineal name that also coded his ethnicity and religion. He may choose to change his gender and become a woman—by one means or another. Or else he may seek to alter his ethnic and religious identity: He changes his name from Franco Rosenweig to Francis Roberts. Indeed, changes of names always accompany nearly all conversion experiences: When a heathen becomes a Christian he or she gets a new name that connects him or her to the source of the new religion in the Bible, when one changes from an ordinary civilian into a revolutionary, he or she would receive a *nom de guerre*, and so on. Further, an individual himself or herself can selectively construct an identity and project it as the salient one in given social circles. A talented and accomplished woman may allow herself to be identified as a talented and accomplished woman in her professional life and seek to diminish or obliterate it at home and become a submissive wife in order to keep her marriage to a traditional husband going. Or else a man who is a successful gambler at certain times of the week may choose to submerge it at other times when he is a successful schoolmaster.

In each of these cases the complex and evolving, multifaceted and kaleidoscopic reality of an individual is submitted to the available logic of categories and thereby identified and classified, so that he or she can conduct relationships with their respective others. The discourse that subverts that relationship in fact demands this seeming coherence to be effective and efficient. One can be many things to many people but it is easier to be one thing at a time to relevant people. The identification or naming process, that is, can be self-referential as other-referential and the "properties" that an individual can attribute to himself or herself, just as those that he or she can attribute to others, are provided by the discourse of the community in which such operations are being performed. Indeed, the very purpose of naming and delineating an identity for the self is to facilitate the interactions and relationships that are fundamental to the society.

In addition to a strictly defined vocabulary of identity one can also use things and territory to define his or her identity, that is, use them in acts of identity. Such a view of the relationship between objects and the identification of self was discussed by G. H. Mead himself. Doyle McCarthy (1984: 105–121) has elicited the relevant discussion in Mead's work. This can be summarily put as follows:

(a) Objects play a central role in the constitution and maintenance of social identities.
(b) Objects serve to provide the self with a stable and familiar environment.
(c) The acts of touching and grasping play a central role in reality construction and reality maintenance.
(d) The self's relation with the physical world is a social one.

The use of space and its contents—props and the arrangement of settings and other materials of identity—have been extensively described by Goffman (1959). Space and its contents are the arenas in which identities are situated but they are used purposively to identity the self—that is, show its continuity in other identities and separation from still others. In Goffman's work places and things are used to represent the self and identify it for others. It is full of rich examples of identity work. I will call attention to merely one such case and recast it in terms of the logic of identity. In setting up what Goffman calls "barriers to perception," an individual arranges the various objects in his or her domain in such a way that there is a "backstage" and a "frontstage." The essential process here is the establishment of certain categories by the use of space and to give them social significance. I, and certain others, bear the identity of those who can enter the backstage; we represent a particular structure of relationships, and "you" or "they" do not. "Backstage" then becomes an identifying tag that separates one set of individuals from others—for example, family and close friends, or teammates. In this way not only does the arrangement of the barriers enable identities to be defined and claimed, they can be actively used whenever others enter the scene: Certain people I will allow inside, while others will remain outside, thereby defining the identities of insiders and outsiders, intimates and strangers, and so on. Further, the identities can be transformed by one asking the other to transcend the barrier and enter the inner space; one is thus made an intimate. Conversely one can transform an intimate into an outsider by ordering him or her out of particular territories, temporarily or permanently. A spouse, for example, who separates from the other has to leave the space they occupied together and relinquish rights to it—essentially redefining the identity he or she bore before. The use of space to define identity extends to larger spheres and arenas: concepts of neighborhood and region and so on are signs that individuals use to claim identity. I belong here and the "here" enables me to put myself into one category and excludes certain others from this category. These places do not then symbolize a self so much as enable an identity denoting a continuity and a difference to be claimed by self and other. The self is particularized as one who belongs to this household, as an insider, backstager, as a West-sider, as a New Yorker, as an American—all words with distinct spatial referents and counterreferents: I am not an outsider, I am not a frontstager, an East-sider, not a Jerseyite, not a Canadian.

Objects also play an important part in Goffman's thesis about the presentation of self. From the standpoint adopted here, these objects—called props by Goffman—may indeed be used to present a self, but as such a self is presented through these objects, it is particularized as bearing a given identity because it is registered with the help of these objects as being one kind of self rather than another, as well as a self that is continuous with an earlier manifestation. If one exhibits the tennis trophies he or she has won in high school in the living room, he or she is claiming the identity of champion, albeit a past champion, and to the extent the trophies remain on display the individual is claiming a continuous identity to himself or herself as to a real and presumptive audience. Similarly, he or she is also establishing a difference between himself and herself and other slobs and nonathletes, nerds and bookworms, and so on.

The relationship between objects and identity goes deeper than the examples given by Goffman. Objects, or objectified things, after all, have their own identity. That is to say, they have a continuity over time, though they may not recognize it and they are differentiable from other things as particularized objects. A diamond has a continuity as an object of value just as it is differentiated from other diamonds by the fact that it is bigger, more expensive, a better grade, but most significantly for our purposes that it is owned by X rather than Y. To the extent it is owned by X, he or she can use it to present a self. This particular diamond confers an identity on the owner: He or she is the one who owns and wears the diamond, he or she is the one who can afford to own this particular diamond. Objects and identities in fact are participants in a dialectic in which the individual uses the object to present a self and claim an identity as the object in turn elicits an identity from the owner: the Sultan's diamond.

The objects then in one's particularized world are not merely signs that are extensions of the self in which the "psychic energy" of meaning and attention are conferred by an individual as Mihail Czikszentmihalyi and Eugene Rochberg-Halton (1981) have argued. They may certainly do that, but they also exist as signs in themselves and as signs in relation to other signs. A diamond has sign-power of its own and such power is augmented by the fact that it is not a sapphire, is not a tiny diamond, and is not dull of color and water. That is, this object exits in a world of other objects and other's objects, and in its unique claim to belong to me it has an identity that it confers on me. The object, of course, can be a diamond, a car, a house, or even a trophy wife or trophy husband, for that matter. These things in the world, objectified as they are by the attention of individuals, have their own identities and in a symbiotic dance of being and becoming, a human confers an identity on the thing and the thing in turn confers an identity on the human: "It is my Rolls Royce, the steel gray one," a man may say reflexively. "It is Mr. Wilson's Rolls Royce," someone else may say, or, "It is your Rolls Royce, isn't it?" These processes allow individuals to convert neutral things into objectified vocabularies and make them into relational indices of identity.[9]

These signs of identity, with their logical structures, are put into practice in everyday life to organize the world in which an individual has to live. The signs become elements of acts, the meaning and significance of which may change as they proceed. Further, with these acts of identity an individual casts himself or herself into a role and a character in the strictly dramaturgical or narrative significance of these terms. To claim an identity by an act is also to claim a place in an evolving narrative. Proposing marriage may be said to be an act that identifies a man as one who is a heterosexual, interested in a continuous social, emotional, and sexual relationship with a woman that is legally and/or religiously sanctioned. Once this act of identification has been announced, the man becomes committed to playing the role of husband and perhaps father. Or else, in a shorter time span, a woman may wear the uniform of a police officer and will find herself cast into the narrative of being a police officer in the acts that are subsequent to the donning of the uniform. That is to say, an individual can appropriate certain objects and acts in order to cast himself or herself in a selected narrative of identity. Guns, for example, are assembled and used in acts that cast an individual in narratives of masculinity and self-aggrandizement. A boy growing up in circles in which a close identification of acts with guns and masculinity, with aggression and violence, is the accepted norm may choose to shoot someone because he or she has offended him in some way. Such moves may be considered not as indices of underlying psychological pathologies but as subculturally recommended ways of producing masculinity.

Identity is not a mysteriously immanent process nor is it a mechanical and static act of naming. Rather, once individuals are identified with one or many forms, they are subject to a variety of uses by self and others. Indeed they are used *improvisationally* to suit the situation and align it with other participants in the situation in all the four rhetorical modes discussed earlier: reflexively an individual is a self to himself only in terms of the logical and nameable categories of identity: "I am what I am; I am Hamlet the Dane," or "I am a Christian, a Southern Baptist," or "I am a paranoid-schizophrenic of the hebephrenic type." In the addressive mode the categories of identity manifest themselves in the initiating moves of conversations. The very form in which this address is presented has an impact on the nature of the interaction that emerges, and such addresses define and elicit the particular identity that is relevant to the interaction. Brown and Gilman's (1972) study of the use of intimate as opposed to formal modes of address, what they called T and V forms, are surely acts of identity. As one addresses the other in a T form he or she automatically classifies him or her and establishes an identity for the other. In American usage, the pronominal distinction between the formal and the intimate styles are not available, but the need to make this distinction in social relationships nevertheless remains. It is handled by an elaborate system of conventions for the use of first names and nicknames: John becomes Jack, Jacqueline becomes Jackie, and so on, or Jackie and Jack sometimes become "Honey" or "Sweetheart" or "Darling." In American society today, one cannot copulate with a woman, have children with her, and live in the same household for a certain period of time and continue to call her "Mrs. Bennet" as Jane Austen allowed Mr. Bennet to do in *Pride and Prejudice*. These forms of address are substituted for the intimate pronouns that the French have thoughtfully allowed to remain in their language. In the initiation of conversation and in greeting the other, the intimate mode can be established by this instrumentation. This is to be contrasted with a number of formalistic variations:

(a) Mr. John Smith, Doctor, Professor, or President John Smith, Mr. Smith. In these usages the other is defined as a superordinate in a system of hierarchical relationships in which Mr. Smith bears the identity of a superior to the one doing the addressing.

(b) Smith without titles will be used to address one in a subordinate position—except, of course, in England it will be used by those of equal standing who have not yet become familiar.

(c) John, without surname and title is used to address friends or those of subordinate rank.

In each of these addressive interactions with their reciprocal answerable modes, the other is identified for purposes of immediate conversation and an identity conferred on him or her. However, such conferral procedures are reflexive on the addressee as well: As he or she confers an identity on the other, he or she is conferring an identity on himself or herself as well, both of which acts need the support of the other to proceed to the next step. The same observations can be made about kin-terms: Each time somebody calls another "Dad," he identifies not only a father but a son—whether the relationship is legally sanctioned or merely fictive. They too are reflexive exercises, for as one identifies the other by kin-term, one also places oneself in a *reciprocal identity*. Some reciprocal identities reflect the unequal status relationships between the partners, while others reflect their equal statuses.

Referential modes of discourse must perforce proceed on the systematic use of the logic of nameable categories—or else one would be faced with the situation described in Ionesco's elaborate joke on identity presented at the beginning of this chapter. Referential identification of the other's self also allows one to introduce various qualifications to the relevant identity: That's Sam the carpenter; It is Max the spy, and so on.[10]

Differentiation of identity, with whatever cultural vocabulary that is available, is not something that a functioning human consciousness can avoid; rather it is an ontological condition of the beingness of itself and of the others it encounters. Such processes of the construction of the self of an individual, as of the other, is not a matter of choice but a semiotic imperative that cannot be dissolved or undone by deconstructive fiat and will. Culler's claim that "deconstruction seeks to undo oppositions that in the name of unity, purity, order, and hierarchy, try to eliminate difference" (1989: 783) is merely a literary conceit rather than a practically useful proposition. To eliminate, dissolve, undo one pair of binarisms is to automatically create another—for instance, those who accept the new "undone" oppositions and those who cling to the old ones. Insofar as humans have perforce to live with others in organized relationships, differentiations will be semiotically impossible to avoid—though no doubt certain obnoxious and invidious and ahistorical ones can be eliminated in favor of others.

## FIELDS OF IDENTITY

The differentiation of identities is not achieved solipsistically in the practical world. Rather, they are culturally constituted and collectively shared discursive representations. Each such representation—or field of identity—gives both *depth* to the entity being identified as well as *range*. Each such field of identity will have a number of features that are specific to it. To be a Christian is to have a rich variety of identifying features that separates the bearer of the identity from Jews and Muslims and Hindus, thereby giving the identity depth. Some fields of identity, for example, that of "East-sider of New York," are shallow. To the extent that this identity is shared with others—members of small social circles or world religions or nations—identities may be said to have a range, small or large.

The fields of identity use the logic of categories to establish terminologies that can be put into practice in the identification of individuals. They embody the logic and give it a practical reality on the basis of which an individual can organize his or her world, act in it, live in it with a minimum of confusion. They provide what E. J. Lowe called the "sortal terms" with which an individual can name and act in the world in such a way that his or her others, interlocutors, fellow-participants, will be able to accept his or her actions as valid. A sortal term, says Lowe, drawing from Aristotle, Locke, and various other philosophers, is a term used to sort individuals from each other: "for any sort of individuals, there is a *criterion of identity* for individuals of that sort" (1989: 9). Lowe further notes, "Individuals are only recognizable *as individuals of a sort*, while sorts are only intelligible as *sorts of individuals*" (1989: 11). Fields of identity are theories or schemes that provide individuals with the terms for sorting the objects in the world, including the individual himself or herself and other such individuals, as objects of a certain sort, rather than another sort for immediate purposes. For example, a racist in an airplane may sort the man seated next to him as an unacceptable outsider and may not even speak to him, but if the plane crashes on a deserted island and they are the only two survivors he may now sort him as a fellow survivor with whom a working relationship can be constituted. Here the racist has to abandon one field of identity—"non-Aryan," say—and adopt another—"survivors together"—who will need each other to survive further. Sorting draws from one field or another to identify the self or the other and is always fitted to an immediate purpose. Typically they name the identities on the basis of contrasting sets. Religion, for example, as a field of identity orders its membership in terms of, say, Christian or Jew, Hindu or Muslim, my religion or your religion.

While there are many fields and subfields of identity I will examine four here: therapeutic, familial, national, and racial. These too are to be taken as "representative anecdotes;" that is, I am not dealing with all the possible fields of identity.[11]

## THERAPEUTIC IDENTITY

The varied processes of identification, dependent as they are on a variety of discourses of separation and continuity, create their own institutional complexes in order to confer identity on those subject to them. In modern Western society what may be broadly termed the psychological field—in which I will include all the institutionalized programs that deal with the individual as a unit for either academic study or therapeutic intervention—has become very powerful and influential. For example, a number of Freudian concepts have become the normal currency of therapy in many circles. Erikson's concept of "identity" and "identity crisis," not to mention the countless idioms of popular psychology, have also achieved a decisive place in the culture. Most of these therapeutic vocabularies have their roots in Freud's monumental work and should be given prominence in any discussion of the psychologistic field.

To begin with, Freud initiated one of the most effective ways in which identities are transformed and confirmed—the therapeutic interview. This came with precise instructions on how a patient should be treated, how he or she should comport himself or herself, how the interview should begin and end, and how he or she should be charged. The very architectonic of this situation sets up a definition of a relationship: the patient as a supplicant, lying down, helpless, with the therapist dominating him or her and presenting authority and control. Any words that come from the patient are issues in this supplicatory mode needing completion in the commentary by the therapist—a commentary that will give the patient an identity. In such a situation, the patient engages in "free association" and displays to the therapist, conversationally and addressively, whatever comes into his or her "mind." This method was discovered "gradually" says Ernest Jones, "becoming steadily refined and purified from the adjuvants—hypnosis, suggestion, pressing, and questioning—that accompanied it at its inception." (1963: 153) Once it was discovered, it became the standard method for the field. Jones describes it well:

> The patient, lying down with closed eyes, was asked to concentrate her attention on a particular symptom and try to recall any memories that might throw some light on its origin. When no progress was being made Freud would press her forehead with his hand and assure her that then some thoughts or memories would indubitably come to her. Sometimes in spite of that nothing would seem to happen even when the pressure of the hand was repeated. Then, perhaps on the fourth attempt, the patient would bring out what had occurred to her mind, but with the comment: "I could have told you that the first time, but I didn't think it was what you wanted." (Jones 1963: 154)

Jones also notes that Freud gave his patients "the strict injunction to ignore all censorship and to express every thought even if they considered it to be irrelevant, unimportant, or too unpleasant" (1963: 154).

Once these thoughts, even the "unimportant" and "irrelevant" and "unpleasant" ones, are vocalized within the confines and architectonic of the interview, it was possible for the therapist to *interpret* them and make the new meanings available to the patient. This process of interpretation is inescapably a substitution of a new metaphor, a new poetics, for the one in which the patient expressed himself or herself initially.

The social and interactional process by which dreams come to be interpreted by the therapist can serve as a representative case here. Freud writes,

> My patients were pledged to communicate to me every idea or thought that occurred to them in connection with some particular subject; amongst other things they told me their dreams and so taught me that a dream can be inserted into the psychical chain that has to be traced backwards in the memory from a pathological idea. (1965: 133).

The process involved in these activities can be summarized as follows:

(a) There is a patient who, recognizing some problem in her or his life, mind, relationships, submits herself or himself to the therapist.

(b) He or she has dreams, which are remembered sufficiently and articulated; that is, the dreams are put in the shape of discursive acts and narratives and presented to the therapist.

(c) In recalling and in recounting the dreams, the patient is able to interpret/respond to them on his or her own.

(d) The therapist receives the articulated dreams and interprets them for the patient.

Consider here, then, a dream that Freud reports and then analyzes. In the interpretation one finds the twin elements of Freud's interpretational theory nicely blended: The daily empirical experiences of the patient manifesting themselves in a different form in the dream and the details of the dream as indices to the unconscious wishes, accumulated from childhood onward. Here is the dream:

> A man dreamt that he had a secret liaison with a lady whom someone else wanted to marry. He was worried in case this other man might discover the liaison and the proposed marriage come to nothing. He therefore behaved in a very affectionate way to the man. He embraced him and kissed him. (Freud 1965: 434)

This is of course Freud's report of the dream. The actual words, their arrangement and imagery, are lost to us; however here is Freud's interpretation of this dream:

> There was only one point of contact between the content of this dream and the facts of the dreamer's life. He had a secret *liaison* with a married woman; and an ambiguous remark made by her husband, who was a friend of his, led him

to suspect that the husband might have noticed something. *But in reality there was something else involved, all mention of which was avoided in the dream but which alone provided a key to its understanding.* The husband's life was threatened by an organic illness. His wife was prepared for the possibility of his dying suddenly, and the dreamer was consciously occupied with an intention to marry the young widow after her husband's death. This external situation placed the dreamer in the constellation of the Oedipus dream. His wish was capable of killing the man in order to get the woman as his wife. The dream expressed this wish in a hypocritically distorted form. Instead of her being married already, he made out that someone else wanted to marry her, which corresponded to his own secret intentions; and his hostile wishes towards her husband were concealed behind demonstrations of affection which were derived from his memory of his relations with his own father in childhood. (Freud 1965: 434, my emphasis)

A dream, *remembered* and *reported* to the therapist, has now become, besides a therapeutic tool, a poetics of identification for the hapless patient. To begin with, he is being given the "Oedipus constellation" as a primal metaphor not only for all family relationships, but for others as well. Then he is identified, from being merely an adulterer and seducer, perhaps a sexual adventurer, into a potential murderer, a murderer who is capable of killing his friend in order to obtain his wife, of being a hypocrite in having disguised this in his dream, and finally he is also identified as reproducing in his dream his father and mother. The dream, as well as his liaison with the married woman, was a reproduction of his "Oedipal constellation": The married woman was *really* his mother, and her husband was *really* his father.

The therapeutic situation had essentially functioned as a ceremony of identification, a rite by which an old identity is refurbished. Once this dream has been presented by the dreamer and the interpretation received from an authoritative scientist and accepted, the dreamer has to place himself and define and identify himself as a potential murderer, hypocritical, recalcitrant to certain social standards and certainly needing a thorough reevaluation of his life—i.e., his identity. Freud had successfully translated the bare outlines of the dreamer's account into his own more intricate poetic: the "married woman" is really "his mother"; i.e., she is a metaphor for his mother; the friend is really his father; the dreamer behaving in a friendly manner to his metaphorical father was a distorted metaphor for killing him. The dreamer's liaison with a married woman is also a metaphor for mother, who was of course a married woman, and with whom love was forbidden.

Freud was able to convince many of his patients that the discourse they presented him were really disguised versions of Oedipal languages. In other words, Freud was able to take one version of a reported story, say, a dream, convert it into another, and use it to confer on the hapless subject the identity of Oedipus: father-killer and mother-fucker! Freud writes:

When I insist to one of my patients on the frequency of Oedipal dreams, in which the dreamer has sexual intercourse with his own mother, he often replies: "I have no recollection of having had any such dream." Immediately afterwards, however, a memory will emerge of some other inconspicuous and indifferent dream which the patient has dreamt repeatedly. Analysis then showed that this is in fact a dream with the same content—once more an Oedipus dream. I can say with certainty that *disguised* dreams of sexual intercourse with the dreamer's mother are many times more frequent than straightforward ones. (1965: 433, my emphasis)

The disguise is in fact removed by Freud himself, by analysis, according to a theory of symbolism that he himself had devised. Interactionally speaking, a patient submits a discourse that includes dreams which the therapist recasts into different vocabularies and uses to confer an identity on the patient. Given the fact that the patient voluntarily submitted himself or herself to these procedures and that the therapist had institutional authority and cultural/intellectual power, whatever identity that is conferred, Oedipal, neurotic, and so on would become one facet, if not the dominating one, of the identity of the patient. Therapeutic sessions are in fact *identity forums* where particular identities drawn from the psychotherapeutic field are foisted on a more or less hapless and helpless self. From being a member of a civilian community with an appropriate identity, the patient by submitting himself to analysis becomes identified as a character in a replay of a Theban tragedy.

## FAMILIAL IDENTITY

The family, and the kinship system of which it is the central unit, is the most ubiquitous source of identifying vocabularies in the world. He or she is given a name (or a set of names) and soon thereafter it is used to address him or her as well as to refer to him or her. In all cultures these names have certain properties: they separate boys from girls and each sibling from the other. They in fact code an identity and a difference: John is John and is sometimes John-John, John Jr., and Jack, but they identify the same individual, one who is different from Susan and Robert, which identifies some other individual. In being systematically and persistently addressed and told that he is in fact John he learns to identify himself as John and may even address himself as John in his earlier discursive exercises. He soon learns that he is differentiated from Susan and Robert, not to speak of Mom and Dad and any others who may be hanging around. John has an identity only because Robert and Susan have their separate and continuous identities. Indeed, without others having identities, one cannot have his or her own identity either. He or she is continuous and separate because relevant others exist who are also continuous in different trajectories and separate in varying realms. In addition, he or she learns that the world of objects around him or her also confers an identity on him or her: John's teddy bear, John's shirt, not Susan's, John's diamond. These locutions confer an identity on the object in question, of course, but they also reciprocally identify John as one who possesses a teddy bear, a shirt or the Hope diamond. Objects in the world become endowed with possessive significations thereby becoming signs of identification. Needless to say, in cultures in which objects like toys or shirts or chairs are not identified as belonging to named individuals, they cannot be used for purposes of identity-formation and other signs have to be devised. Conversely, if there is a systematic rejection of the aggrandizing of objects to self, shall I say, personalization of objects, then the nature of the identities of separation that emerge may also be different. If objects are collectively owned by the siblings and shared by them on a rough-and-ready basis then a sense of a shared sibling-identity, or sense of shared male-sibling identity, or female-sibling identity, "brotherhood," "sisterhood," and so on may well emerge.

In any case, sooner or later the child John—in cultures of a particular sort—learns that he does share with Robert and Susan another type of identity, one that is articulated in a surname: He is no longer John or Jack, but John Wilson and he has an identity as the "one of the Wilsons" that he can claim along with his brother and sister and father and mother and paternal ancestors. This may be termed the second level of the familial identification process, and it is made possible by the availability of another set of culturally devised codes: patrilineal systems of descent signed in "surnames." John then becomes John Wilson of the Wilson family and the Wilson line of descent.

Such proper-naming vocabularies of identity exist in conjunction with kin-terms. These terms have been studied as elements in the structure of relations by many anthropologists from A. Radcliff-Brown onward. No doubt they are units in a social structure, but primarily they are elements in a vocabulary of identity: They identify an individual by means of his or her relationship to others and these terms are used for reference, reflection, address, and answer. In addressings and answerings every time the one says "Dad" to someone he expects an answer that defines as a son. The same claims can be made about other kin-terms: uncle, aunt, nephew, niece, grandfather, grandmother, and so on.

In addition to these vocabularies, one can consider nicknames as bearers of identity. Nicknames too have their discursive regimen. Some diminutives are standard alternatives to proper names and indicate special rights: Bob for Robert represents an identity that can be addressed and referenced by familiars and intimates; Jack for John is an alternative that also indicates familiarity. Further, there are very personal nicknames that members of families develop that code the special standing that each has with the other and identifies each to the other accordingly such as "Tiger," "Princess." Conversely, as Morgan, O'Neill, and Harre (1979) have argued, nicknames can be used to indicate negative designations of the self of the other. Accidental events, irrelevant attributes, and arbitrary categorizations of the self of the other are selected and given force and substance in discourse and used to identify the self of the other.

The vocabularies of proper-naming and kin-naming and the consequent acts of identity are derived from the discourse of patriarchy. The examples used earlier are of course derived from the European model of patriarchy as it underwent changes along the way. In Europe itself there were some variants: In Iceland daughters are identified as mother's daughters and in Spain, the mother's maiden name becomes a part of the child's own name along with that of the patrilineal surname. Indeed when the holds of the patriarchal discourse begin to weaken, naming practices, or the processes by which identity is bestowed, also begin to change. Zhigang Wang and Michael Micklin report for example that "the declining influence of patriarchy" among certain members of the Chinese community has resulted in changes in the naming practices for newborn children: Even the family name is a matter for debate and often it is abandoned in favor of a new name. "These microsocial conflicts," they aver, "are consistent with observed structural discontinuities in family organization, illustrating the reciprocal relationship between institutional conditions and behaviors" (1996: 187). Indeed, they describe conflicts within families over these naming practices suggesting really a debate between patriarchal discourses and other such discourses.

In any case, the construction of identities, the schemes by which selves are identified and given particular characteristics, is an exercise in the logic of classification. The family, of the extended sort or the nuclear one, can be described as an institution where units are created in such a way that they achieve a differentiation from each other. Each unit becomes equal to itself and separate from the others and on it is conferred a descriptive label, a name, a title to indicate it. It is the existence of the names or vocabularies of identity that enables anyone, or anything, for that matter, to have identity. In addition the vocabularies of identity also specify certain rules of combination, such as the incest rules for example. These rules in turn protect the law of identity from disintegrating: They ensure that one's son remains a son and one's daughter remains a daughter and does not also become one's stepsister and stepbrother.[12]

## NATIONAL IDENTITY

This field of identity emerged comparatively recently—indeed, with the emergence of the nation-state. Once such states emerged, local and regional, ethnic and religious identities were also subordinated to national ones. Romans became Italians, Jews became Germans, Saxons became Englishmen and Englishwomen. In a penetrating study of the emergence of England as a nation—and Englishness as an identity (which can be used here as "a representative anecdote")—Richard Helgerson has examined how it began to take shape in the reign of Elizabeth I and the variety of instrumentations that was used to occasion it. He considers language as the central and unifying feature of the emergence of Englishness and describes various projects in the middle years of the sixteenth century as having contributed to it. He quotes as his opening gambit a sentence from a letter that the poet Edmund Spenser wrote to Gabriel Harvey in 1580: "Why a God's name, may not we, as else the Greeks, have the kingdom of our own language?" (Helgerson, 1992:1). These words, Helgerson, argues, "carry us from an essentially dynastic conception of communal identity ('the kingdom') to an assertion of what we recognize as one of the bases of post dynastic nationalism ('our own language')" (1992: 2). Nevertheless, Helgerson argues, "Nor are the possible competitors for representational attention exhausted by the extremes of 'kingdom' and 'language,' for between them comes that first-person plural 'our' with its suggestion of shared participation and possession" (1992: 2). The century following the one in which these words were written by Spenser was characterized by conflicts that attempted to resolve the contradiction implied by "language" and "kingdom."

> Even a small acquaintance with the history of England in the next century or so will remind us that conflict was to develop along precisely the lines suggested by those few words: between royal prerogative, subjects' rights and the cultural system. (1992: 2)

The aim of one side in this conflict, and of Spenser and this cohort, too, was "To have the kingdom of their own language. To govern the very linguistic system, and perhaps more generally the whole cultural system, by which their own identity and their own consciousness was constituted" (1992: 3).

Helgerson, having set the terms of his argument then describes the various modalities by which Englishness as an identity, distinguished from a monarchically based one, was devised by various authors. He begins by showing how the forms of Elizabethan poetry and the composition of the most "ambitious single Elizabethan poem, Spenser's *Faerie Queen*," contributed to this. The analysis of English verse is followed by a discussion of the emergence of English law, as distinct from Norman law. He quotes Thomas Starkey who in 1529 wrote, "Who is so blind that seeth not the great shame to our nation, the great infamy and rot that remaineth in us, to be governed by laws given to us of such a barbarous nation as the Normans be?" (Helgerson 1992: 65). Yet Starkey's pleas were not heard by anyone at that time and he did not produce his own work on the subject. It was left to Edward Coke nearly seventy-five years later to produce works on English laws. Coke, it appears, was not very learned in Roman law, which had become the dominant mode in the rest of Europe, and it was this ignorance that enabled him to produce treatises suitable for the newly emerging Englishness.

> Yet I would contend that Coke's very insularity, his myopic insistence on the uninterrupted Englishness of English law, was the product of a constant sense of legal and national difference, a persistent awareness of a rival system of law against which English law had to defend and define itself. (Helgerson 1992: 71)

Helgerson describes also the map makers who defined the nation cartographically, the description of overseas voyages by returning travelers who helped define English differentness and the institutions of the theater and newly reformed church.

> But as poets, lawyers, chorographers, propagandists for overseas expansion, playwrights and churchmen, they all belonged to different discursive communities and, as a result, wrote England differently. . . . But unexpected similarities nevertheless link the divided communities, suggesting that the walls between them were less solid than they sometimes seem. (1992: 5).

These various discursive communities, participated unwittingly in the narrative construction of Englishness, a construction that was to give both the language and metaphor for the construction by men and women born in England in later years of their identity as Englishmen and Englishwomen.

Helgerson's work, then, describes in great detail how the field of national identity was created for England. Similar exercises were undertaken—are being undertaken now—to create fields of identity in every part of the globe. The coming of the nation-state coincided with the creation of discursive fields in which national identities can be maintained. Once such identities were constructed, they became potent sources of action that were creative and sustaining of life but were also often murderous and genocidal.


## RACE AND IDENTITY

The most perfect representative anecdote with which race can be examined as a field of identity is without doubt the emergence of what may be termed the Aryan mode of discourse in nineteenth-century Europe. By the beginning of the eighteenth century the close affinity between most of the European languages and certain languages in India and Iran had been recognized. James Parsons was one of the earlier scholars to make this discovery. After detailed work in comparative philology, he concluded that the "languages of Europe and Iran and India were all derived from a common ancestor, the language of Japhet and his offspring who had migrated out of Armenia, the final resting place of the Ark" (Mallory 1989: 1). In spite of these biblical claims, Parsons is credited with having discovered the group of languages called the "Indo-European family." Later in the century (1796) the Chief Justice of India, William Jones, a trained philologist himself, gave a lecture on Indian culture, in the course of which he spoke the words that have become famous to students of historical linguistics:

> The Sanskrit language, whatever may be its antiquity, is of wonderful structure; more perfect than the Greek, more copious than the Latin, and more exquisitely refined than either; yet bearing to both of them a stronger affinity, both in roots of verbs and in forms of grammar, than could have been produced by accident; so strong that no philologer could examine all the three without believing them to have sprung from some common source, which, perhaps no longer exists. (quoted in Mallory 1989: 12)

Once the affinity between the languages of Europe and certain languages of India was discovered and the Indo-Persian word "Aryan" was applied to them, the search for an Aryan race, an Aryan language, and an Aryan homeland was begun in earnest. One early writer begins his book on the "Aryan Race" with these striking words:

> Somewhere, no man can say just where, at sometime, it is equally impossible to say when—there dwelt in Europe or Asia a most remarkable tribe or family of mankind where or when this was we shall never clearly know. No history mentions their name or gives a hint of their existence; no legend or tradition had floated down to us from that vanished realm of life. (Morris 1888: 1)

This is Charles Morris's description of the prehistory of the Aryan. Morris continues:

> And yet from the earliest date of which we can trace them, the Caucasian exhibited the qualities they still possess—those of superior intellectuality, enterprise and migratory vigor. When we first gaze upon the race—or rather at its Xanthochromic section—it is everywhere spreading and swelling, forcing its way to the East and the West with restless energy. Before its energetic outflow, the aborigines vanish or are absorbed. In the continent of Europe no trace of them is left, with the exception of the Basques, pushed back into a mountain corner of Spain, and the Finns and Lapps, driven into the Arctic regions of the North. A similar fate has befallen them in Southern Asia. During the whole historical era this migratory spirit has continued active. The separate branches of, and the Aryans as a whole, have been persistently seeking to extend this border. They are still doing so with all the old energy driving the wedge of invasions deep into the domain of Mongoloid and Negroid life until the Caucasian of today number one fourth of all mankind, and bid fair in many countries to reduce the other race to mere fragments like the Basques or the North American Indians of the present day. (Morris 1888: 108)

A recent scholar of the Indo-Aryan puzzle, J. P. Mallory, describes Morris's work as one that provided "comic relief." Nevertheless, there is no doubt that it presents the main elements of what was to emerge as the themes of a popular discourse. Morris was no doubt influenced by the works that were being produced in Germany at this time. Indeed, if Morris's work was comic and expressed in the optative mode, serious scholars themselves were not immune to the seductions of the Aryan discourse. Gordon Childe was to write his own book on the subject, making substantially the same claims as Morris, though he dismissed it as a "childish" exercise later (Mallory 1989: 143). Nevertheless, Childe's work is a sober examination of the available evidence and is of a different genre than those of Morris's ilk. He dismisses the theory of "the Asian cradle of the Aryans" with a number of well-grounded arguments and opts for a north European cradle for them. He further rejects the idealization of the Aryan past. He writes,

> They were not the inaugurators of the neolithic civilization even in Europe nor were they as a whole the pioneers in the use of bronze and iron. The makers of the widens on the Danish coasts have been justly termed "disgusting savages." Even stranger epithets might be applied to the other claimants to the title of proto-Aryans, for a suspicion of cannibalism clings to the ochre-grave peoples. (Childe [1926] 1970:206)

In his later work he even acknowledged the relationship between the usage of the concept of Aryanism in more recent years, after the work of Houston Stuart Chamberlain in England, to racist doctrines and to "pogroms" ([1926] 1970:164).

Nevertheless, the search for a homeland and for a linguistically defined race is the substratum of Childe's work as well. The roots of this search, however, lie in certain structures of German intellectual and political life. Max Muller, in his "Biographies of Words" and the "Home of the Aryan," raised certain issues that others were to take up as well. One was the "original home" of the Aryans, as Muller calls it, who were subject to the "Great Separation" (1905). This quest carries its own pathos. Here were these heroic people who were "scattered" by some force or another to many parts of the world and no one seems to know their home! This theme of a lost and scattered people driven from paradise looms large in the writing of the Aryan theorists. There were those who thought it was Germany, but Muller comes down to "somewhere in Asia." Muller writes,

> The actual site of the Aryan paradise, however, will probably never be discovered because it left no traces in the memory of the children of the Aryan emigrants partly because imagination would readily supply whatever memory had lost." (1905: 127)

In the late eighteenth century itself Johann Herder gave an initial impetus to an association between India and the Aryans. He, having evidently never met a brahmin, wrote rhapsodically:

> The brahmins have formed their people to such a degree of gentleness, courtesy, temperance and chastity, or at least have so confirmed them in these virtues, that Europeans frequently appear, on comparison with them, as beastly, drunken or mad. In their air and language they are unconstrainedly elegant; in their behaviour, friendly; in their persons clean; in their way of life, simple and harmless . . . they are not destitute of knowledge, still less of quiet industry or nicely imitative art; even the lowest castes learn reading, writing and arithmetic. (Herder 1803, vol. II; 34, in Poliakov 1974: 186–187)

Here, then, one faces the earliest example of a confusion, so common in later expressions of the Aryan mode of discourse, between race and language that was to find acceptance in the work of many others. The essential elements of this mode of discourse was to become themes in the discursive culture of both literary and political institutions of European and particularly German society. This is nicely satirized in Mallory's words. Some nineteenth-century and even twentieth-century writers, he notes, portrayed "Proto-Indo-Europeans or Aryans as a single people constrained within their homeland, perfecting their language and then bursting out all over the earth waving swords and spreading paradigms" (1989: 22).

This identification between language and cultural and psychological endowments was to blossom further into one about a whole race of people and their unique personal and cultural characteristics found in many continents and become the foundation of various political movements and historiographical studies. The German and German-speaking nationalism that it engendered was to find its fruition in Nazism and became also the foundation of other nationalist movements.

The basic epistemes of the Aryan mode of discourse can be summarized as follows:

(a) A language, loosely defined, can be used as the criterion by which a peoples' identity as a homogeneous unit can be defined.
(b) There was an ancient people who lived somewhere in India or in the Caucasus Mountains who created and spoke a pristine language that was beyond compare in every way.
(c) These people not only spoke this pristine language but they possessed distinct moral and psychological characteristics that were exemplary in every way.

(d) These people, for one reason or another, had a habit of leaving their homeland and wandering into Europe, taking with them their language, culture, and genes.

(e) What is glorious, noble, and unique in European culture is derived from these people who came from India, or somewhere else, in successive waves of immigration.

One of those who built modern race theories on these assumptions was Joseph Arthur, Counte de Gobineau. His "principal criterion for judging the superiority of a '*race*' was its capacity to originate a great civilization," writes John Barker, summarizing Gobineau's views.

> In his opinion there were ten such civilizations in the course of history, seven in the Old World and three in America. The seven were those of the Indians, Egyptians, Assyrians, Greeks, Chinese, Romans, and finally "*les races germaniques. . . .*" The Germanics were, for Gobineau, a branch of the 'Aryan race', to which he ascribed, in part at least, no fewer than six of the great civilizations of the Old World. (1974: 37)

Gobineau's rather tentative conclusions on the racial basis of civilization were soon followed by a large number of others. Francis Galton in England sought to show that "Negroids" were of systematically lower "intelligence" than English people, and Vacher de Lapogue did the same for the French. Lapogue divided the French into *endemics* and *immigrants*, the former tall, blond, blue-eyed dolichocephalic (Nordic), and the latter, short, brown-haired brachycephalic (Alpinids). He claimed the "former as superior, and gave a list of eminent Frenchmen who appeared, from their portraits or other evidence, to belong to this subrace" (Barker 1974: 47).

Two kinds of logical operations are being performed by these various authors. One was a continuity for a large structure of members—continuity of character, disposition, talent, capacity for hard work, discipline, leadership, intelligence, creativity, idealism, bodily stamina, industry, foresight, and so on. *Strikingly, all the members of the taxon of race, or at least the males, were, more or less, equally endowed with these characteristics.* This continuity of identification was then both across time and across whole populations: They inherited these characteristics ancestrally, mongrelization having been avoided, and shared it with all others similarly appointed. Two, these characteristics separated them from the other races or "species," as they were sometime labeled, who of course did not possess these characteristics and did possess other repulsive ones. Continuity of the people over time and space provided a wide-ranging and encompassing terminology that could be used to identify with such a large group. Further, the meanest member of the relevant population, however insignificant his or her own personal achievement may be and however ignorant, inartistic, nonscientific, and intellectually backward one may be, could nevertheless identify with the highest achievement of individual members of the population and derive satisfaction. I once heard a member of the "Aryan Nations of America," barely able to speak a literate sentence, and unable to contain his anger and resentment, explain his political views to a television audience: "All the great achievements in the history of the world were made by white people." In one clear stroke this poor embittered illiterate young man has become one with Aristotle, Plato, Leonardo da Vinci, Beethoven, Michelangelo, Shakespeare, Isaac Newton, Charles Darwin, and so on: "It is my people who made these contributions; I am one of them." Such an identification with a larger structure of members enables the author of his own identity to *disidentify* himself or herself from others—non-Aryans, Jews, Africans, Asians. "They did not create great civilizations or great art and science; my *volk* did and I can claim to be part of it." Such claims are essentially continuations of statements made in white supremacist literature. Jessie Daniels has argued that such statements are really assertions of male identity and describes an illustration that carries a picture of a working-class white male with the legend "white men built this nation." She argues,

> The image points to a connection between white masculinity and class position; the white men to which the illustration presumably refers are those materially involved in "building" an infrastructure, those who literally "built" the bridges, airplanes and skyscrapers featured in the background. (1997: 34–35)

Not only does this claim exclude the contributions made by nonwhite people, it also enables any and every white man to claim participation in the enterprise without having contributed anything to the buildings and the inventions and the technology.[13]

Racism, then, is a field of identity that provides richly textured vocabularies of identity. These vocabularies conformed to a very particular logic: Populations of people with certain physical characteristics could be classified into a discrete structure where each member was logically equal to another. Insofar as each member was logically equal, it follows that they were equal in every other way—for instance, in social and intellectual characteristics, as well as in the entitlement to preference, power, and authority. If one belonged to a particular population, one had claims to all its achievements and if one did not belong to it, one did not have claims to it. This is a reverse of the conventional stereotyping: Stereotyping is a form of addressive and referential identification of the other's self by generalizing a particular to cover the whole population. One criminal or duplicitous member of the population is taken as evidence that the entire population is similarly distinguished. In identifying the self with the achievements of given individual members of a population, one reflexively assigns to himself or herself the same achievements and an inherent and potential capacity to obtain the same achievements. Stereotyping then has two forms: stereotyping of the other and stereotyping of self. Such acts produce an automatic identity that elevates a doubtful and lowly self to a secure and exalted position: I am one with them, an incarnate of greatness by affiliation.

Such self-stereotyping and restrictive identifications is not necessarily the domain of the feeble-minded or the unimaginative. Rather, this logic of classification and identification has been practiced by anyone—indeed has been practiced systematically over the centuries, and the Aryan mode of discourse is a mere variation on a general theme. Various religious discourses are based on this logic: the people of the book versus the people of the heath; the people chosen by god versus the others; Christians versus the pagans and infidels, Buddhists versus Hindus, Hindus versus Muslims, and so on. The mere membership in these categories confers moral qualities on the individuals and excludes the others from such qualities: All are equally the children of god, the chosen, the heathen, the pagan, and so on. This logic of classification has its analogue in the gender sphere as well: Males have moral qualities that women lack and therefore are not entitled to the same privileges. As in the Aryan mode of discourse, the claim is that mere membership in a category confers on each member of the category, however different in other respects each may be, moral and ethical qualities that members of other categories lack, confers on them in fact a particular identity.

### IDENTITY AND EMOTION

These structural elements of the fields of identity, however, are manifest in the everyday lives of the relevant peoples. They in fact serve to identify these people to themselves and derive their strength from the emotional bonds that they can create and sustain. When someone identifies himself as "John Watson" it automatically embeds him in a number of real and presumptive interpersonal relationships: his father and mother, his brothers and sisters, and perhaps his cousins and certainly some of his ancestors and descendants. John Watson is not alone: he is connected laterally as well as vertically. His identity has breadth and depth. Similarly, when someone identifies himself as an Englishman, he embeds himself not only in some or all of the aforementioned structures but in a structure of other interpersonal relationships as well: me, my family, my ancestors and descendants, my neighbors and friends are all English together. I am not alone: there are so many of us who are English, who can talk in the shared language about shared phenomena.

When one identifies oneself as an Englishman or American, as a Christian or Jew, as an Aryan or a Semite, then one invokes not merely arid texts and lifeless monuments, but interpersonal relations and emotional ties and loyalties that define a self. The texts and the monuments may have an independent existence but they also function as signs by which communities are created and sustained and interpersonal ties given significance. They provide the symbolic medium in which selective ties—as Watson to Watson, as Englishman to Englishman, as Christian to Christian, as Jew to Jew, as Aryan to Aryan—are cultivated. *Once such a vocabulary of identity is made available to an individual and sustained by continuous usage in interactions and relationships it becomes a ready answer to the ever-present sense of uncertainty and anxiety that bedevils humans.* These answers situate him or her in interactions, societies, and histories and at times in cosmologies and eschatologies. One's being gets defined, then, by interpersonally and structurally embedded vocabularies that identify the self. The claimed, presented, and acknowledged identities also become *felt* identities and it is as felt identities that they elicit commitment, loyalty, and passion. Such feelings for identities, however, can emerge only on the basis of their being continuous, differentiated, and nameable and *interactionally viable* phenomena. If one cannot separate one's identity from that of others, if one cannot comprehend its continuity over time, however segmented into fragments it may be, and if it cannot be reflected upon, referred to, and addressed, it cannot possibly elicit any emotional commitment.

Emotions may be "sensations," "feelings," or "bodily reactions," but for all that they must also be cognitions. For a while cognition was considered free of emotionality, and complex theories of action and behavior were formulated as exclusively cognitive acts. Now it is believed by some that emotions are sensations and bodily reactions. These disjunctive contrasts should be abandoned and cognition should be considered as carrying degrees of emotionality all the time. Emotions are indubitably felt sensations, but to be felt and experienced they must be about "something": Emotions occur within cognition of situations, self, and objects. Peirce wrote,

> Now every emotion has a subject. If a man is angry he is saying to himself that this or that is vile and outrageous. If he is in joy, he is saying "this is delicious." If he is wondering he is saying, "this is strange." In short, whenever a man feels he is thinking of *something* (Peirce 1960: 292).

For Peirce emotions are inconceivable without there being also thoughts or cognitions. It is then a conceiving and cognizing individual who also feels the emotions. The conceptions occur to individuals who are situated in interactions, real or presumptive, and one of the foundations of such a conceiving and experiencing of emotions is the identity of the conceiver. One of the "something" that a person thinks of whenever he or she "feels," besides the relevant emotion, is his or her own identity and that of the identity of the other or others with whom he or she is dealing. To be able to do this, the individual must be able to identify his or her own self and the other, be it person or thing, and use such identifications as the "subject" of the emotions. Such emotional resonances cannot typically be done in a general or vague and uncertain way; rather, a more or less precise subject of the feelings must be made available. One such subject about which an individual can experience feelings is the differential identity of the self and the other in given scenes and situations.[14]

The relationship between emotion and identity can be profitably examined by considering occasions in which someone's identity has been challenged. Such challenges can occur when one is subjected to an insult that questions one's chosen identity or when an event, public or private, makes one re-examine one's identity and affirm one's solidarity with others who share the identity.

What is to insult someone? It is to answer the other's presence with an inappropriate address, to challenge his or her presumptive identity and to substitute another one implicitly or explicitly. Insults can be considered as modes in which the selves of individuals are diminished by introducing negative descriptions of one or another specific identity of the other. In tune with the earlier representative discussion of family, nationality, and race, I will consider the *familial insult* and the *ethnic or racial insult.*

Familial insult can take two forms. First, the family as a whole is denigrated with various tags: "White trash," "Trailer park trash," "Soup-kitcheners," "Welfare family;" second, individuals may be described with various tags that question central aspects of their identity: "bastard," "son of a bitch," "whoreson," or "son of a whore," "motherfucker." The second set of insults are typically capable of eliciting strong emotional reactions and are in fact widely used throughout the world. These are insults that can be addressed only to male members of the family. The female members of the family are addressed insultingly as: "bitch," "whore," and with various allusion to bodily parts. Each of these insults speak to central elements of patriarchy. Indeed in the insults addressed to male members of the family, the identity of each as a legitimate member of the family is challenged and refuted by using "woman" as the signifier. When a male is called a "bastard" it is his mother's fidelity and chastity that is being used to denigrate him. Because a mother was unfaithful to her husband or produced the child out of wedlock his identity as a member of the family is unacceptable. And if he is not a legitimate member of the family, he is also not a legitimate member of society. The same observations apply to "bitch." The allusion to the female of the dog family is based on the belief that it is incapable of loyalty and is an unreliable and flighty partner to the male. A son of a bitch, then, is once again defined from the standpoint of male rights: Males are entitled to loyalty and disciplined commitments from female members of the family, and anyone who is a son of a bitch is likely to be of questionable character. Again, the phrase strikes at the heart of a familial identity of the male as member of a disciplined patriarchal and patrilineal household. "Whoreson" and "son of a whore" have similar significations as insults.

"Motherfucker," however, is in a class by itself. Its ubiquity in the world is itself noteworthy as is the absence of the parallel "fatherfucker." To suggest that a male is having intercourse with one's mother is to charge him with violating one of the central features of the patriarchal and patrilineal system and question two of its cherished identities: son of his mother and father and brother to his siblings. The most famous violator of the rules that lead to the primal confusion of identities put it in Sophocles' version of it as follows:

> My own blood, spilled by my own hand: can you remember
> The unspeakable things I did there, and the things I went on from there to do?
> O marriage, marriage!
> The act that engendered me, and again the act
> Performed by the son in the same bed—
> Ah, the net
> Of incest, mingling fathers, brothers, sons,
> With brides, wives, mothers: the last evil
> That can be known to men: no tongue can say
> How evil!

> (Sophocles: *Oedipus Rex,* trans, by Fitts and Fitzgerald 1977: 72).

Oedipus's offense may have been against religion and may have been the one to which "no tongue" can be given, certainly in his own consciousness. The "mingling" that Oedipus mentions here is not merely the mingling of kin alone but the mingling of the identities of "fathers, brothers, sons," and "brides, wives, and mothers," and is not so much the last evil as the first one—the confusion of categories. As a result of his actions, it was not possible to identify his children Antigone, Ismene, and Haimon as his sons and daughters because they were also his siblings as children of his mother. *His offense was against the logic of identity.* It was no longer possible to identify the kin with clear and noncontradictory labels, making interactional life and discursive activity difficult.

In everyday life when someone is addressed as a motherfucker he is being charged with violating the central organizing principle of the family, the rule of incest. The rule of incest in fact permits the construction of stable familial identities: it enables what may be termed colateral identities such as brother and sister to have clear boundaries but also enables the constitution of identities of descent: Son, daughter, grandson, and granddaughter. In the familial field, then, the strongest condemnation seems reserved for those who presumptively violate one of the principles on which the family is founded.

However, this leaves unexplained why no woman is ever charged with being a fatherfucker. When a male is being charged with copulating with his mother, he is also being charged with violating one of the sacred rights of the father: the exclusive sexual rights to the mother. The converse does not of course obtain: if a man copulated with his daughter, he is merely exercising his rights to the "fruits of his garden," as one man expressed it in a court of law. In other words, it is not considered a serious offense in patriarchal and patrilineal societies, though modern law considers it so. Hence there is no insulting term that one can find in any culture that uses father/daughter incest as a signifier.[15]

Similar arguments can be made about other types of insults. One of the most pervasive forms of insult in Western society is the ethnic insult. Some of the insults are issued by using single words that have over the years achieved so much special negative connotations that the mere uttering of it is enough to evoke anger—"nigger," "kike," "wog," "paki," "wop," "spick," "dago," and so on. These words can be used to address someone or refer to someone in everyday life. Wherein lies the insult? Among other valences that these words may possess, the insulting power of these words arises from the fact that they constitute identification and the *placement* of the individual into a *generalized* structure of persons. To call someone a nigger is to reject the other identification of himself or herself and put him or her into the category of a large group. The response of the person so addressed is to get angry on the ground that he is not a nigger but Frank Robinson, accountant, husband, father, and American citizen. In other words, such name-calling advances a particular identity into the forefront and provokes resentment because the individual himself is committed to the other identities. Not only does this form of address project an irrelevant identity into the forefront but it also obliterates the individual's unique identity and submerges it into a group. Furthermore, the historicity of this term and the others listed above carries its own emotional weight: It had been used again and again precisely as a word of belittlement of the other's identity, even an effacement, in acts of power and domination, so that its further use can evoke complex feelings in response. Indeed, all ethnic insults have been selected and invested with meaning as an instrument for the management of relations with people of varying ethnic identities. Consider the following incident:

> Three days after Nets coach John Calipari called the reporter a "Mexican Idiot," the team publicly apologized today. Calipari declined to discuss the incident but his agent acknowledged that Calipari had made the comment to Dan Garcia of the Star Ledger of Newark as Garcia stood 30 to 40 feet away in Ramapo College parking lot on Thursday afternoon. (Roberts 1997: B9)

This remark was not addressed directly to the recipient but he was no doubt meant to hear it. It was defined as an ethnic insult rather than an insult to Mr. Garcia's intelligence. That is, the adjective "Mexican" was the focus of the hurt feelings, rather than the attribution of idiocy. The thrust of the insult, therefore, is the invocation of an identity that was irrelevant to the situation and interaction. Mr. Garcia is of Mexican ancestry but in the situation in which the abuse occurred he was a reporter for a newspaper. The issue was that his Mexican identity was not *salient* to his present occupation and the nature of the interaction he was conducting with the coach. In a sense he had transcended that identity and become a sportswriter belonging to the mainstream of journalists. By calling him a Mexican and using it as an adjective to qualify "idiot" the coach compounded three categories into one phrase—his identity as a Mexican, the intelligence of the sportswriter, and the intelligence of Mexicans in general—and produced a phrase pregnant with insult.

Another incident, this too from the world of sports, was also considered offensive and required an apology. Tiger Woods, the golfing champion, was told by Fuzzy Zoeller how he should disport himself at the champion's dinner of the professional golfers. Here is Dave Anderson's description of this incident:

> "So you know what you guys do when he gets in here?" continued Zoeller, surrounded by at least one CNN camera and several microphones.
> "You pat him on the back and say congratulations and tell him not to serve fried chicken next year."
> Snapping his fingers Zoeller turned to walk away and added, "or collard greens or whatever the hell they serve." (Anderson 1997:8:2)

Earlier in the same interview Zoeller had described Woods as "that little boy who was driving well and putting well, he is doing everything it takes to win" (Anderson 1997:8:2).

Strikingly, this insult—though it was dismissed as a joke—did not use any of the standard epithets of racial identification, but contained what may be considered a "racial slur." It was in fact insult by sly allusion and indirection. Nevertheless, here, too, there was a process of insult by identification: The "little boy" is the use of an identification label by which white men and women systematically diminished the social presence of black men, whatever their status or age, by referring to them and addressing them as "boy." The allusion to the items of food was used to reinforce the identification of Mr. Woods as not only a diminished man but as an unsophisticated backwoodsman who would not be able to choose from the *haute cuisine.* Collard greens and fried chicken is, of course, the habitual fare of the black masses in the southern United States. Golf has always been the sport and pastime of the courtly and cosmopolitan gentlemen and gentlewomen, and here was Mr. Woods, the son of a working-class black man, usurping an identity to which he is not entitled. In one fell swoop Mr. Zoeller has thrust back Mr. Woods to his ancestral identity: both race and class were neatly captured in his remarks and Mr. Woods stood identified, irrelevantly, as a black working-class usurper.[16]

If one insults the other by placing him or her in an unwanted identity, often individuals forcefully claim a desired identity by a variety of other means. One such method is to use certain public events to place oneself in a definite category and thereby claim an identify for oneself as a member of that category. If insults generated negative feelings of anger and resentment and were meant to forestall the emergence of interactional solidarity, the latter process of identification was meant to announce solidarity. While this can occur with any public event that becomes available for partisan posturings, racially charged events seem to elicit a great deal of identificatory activity. They often get transformed into what Victor Turner calls "social dramas." He writes, "Social dramas are units of aharmonic or disharmonic process, arising in conflict situations. Typically, they have four main phases of public action, accessible to observation" (1974: 37–38). These phases were identified as: *breach,* where normal relations between persons or groups are disrupted; *crisis,* where the breach widens unless it was repaired soon after it occurred; *redressive* action, in which steps are taken to prevent the crisis from developing further. Eventually, these various stages lead to *reintegration,* the final stage. While this is a useful model there is, of course, no necessary guarantee that in every social drama the stages will follow this order or that a final reintegration will in fact take place. Social dramas nevertheless present individuals a fertile opportunity to claim and display identities and be emotionally drawn into them. The occurrence of breach by definition creates two sides, enabling individuals to select one side and identify with it. Once the identification is made and commitment created, it is possible for the individual to participate, *either directly or vicariously,* in the subsequent stages: He or she can either contribute to the healing of the breach or participate in widening it, all the while reaping the emotional benefits of identification. The same can be said for the next two stages or redressive action and reintegration: An individual can participate, directly or vicariously, and feel the relevant emotions and identities.

Such social dramas are ubiquitous in social life. Sporting encounters between teams, for example, are social dramas of this sort, as are more serious cases of riots and other forms of social conflict. Electronic media have made some of these conflicts national events and indeed made it possible to convert them into social dramas. Long years ago W. E. B. DuBois understood this clearly when he wrote:

> When, now, the real Negro criminal appeared, instead of petty stealing and vagrancy we began to have highway robbery, burglary, murder, and rape, there was a curious effect on both sides of the color line: the Negroes refused to believe the evidence of white witnesses or the fairness of white juries, so that the greatest deterrent to crime, the public opinion of one's own caste, was lost, and the criminal was looked upon as crucified rather than hanged. On the other hand, the whites, used to being careless as to the guilt or innocence of accused Negroes, were swept away in moments of passion beyond law, reason and decency. ([1903] 1982: 201)

Cases in the courts of law have often become such social dramas. One can take one such case and examine it as a source of emotional identification—

the trial and subsequent vindication of O. J. Simpson for murdering his wife and her companion.

Mr. Simpson, a football player of renown in his youth, had continued to be in the public eye as a commentator on televised football as well as an actor in movies and advertisements. He was an African American and was married to a white woman. They were divorced after a stormy relationship but he had not given up his interest in her. She and her male friend were found dead one morning in July 1994, and soon after that Mr. Simpson was arrested and charged with the murder. With this move we have an example of Turner's breach occurring: The public was divided into those who believed he was guilty and others who believed he was innocent. Once the trial started the breach really became a crisis because it was claimed one of the policemen, who investigated the crime and was a witness, was a racist who had in fact used standard derogatory epithets to describe black people. The trial went on, and eventually the jury rendered a "not guilty" verdict. No redressive action was taken, and no reintegration took place after the trial—though most people seem to have forgotten about it. During the course of the trial and soon after the verdict, it was possible for a large number of the members of the public to proclaim Mr. Simpson guilty or innocent. If indeed we had justice by plebiscitary processes of adjudication in the country Mr. Simpson probably would have been found guilty! However, it was not justice that was involved here, on either side, but the claiming and proclamation of identity by using the vocabulary of justice.

Arriving at a judgment of guilt or innocence by a jury is a complex process in which its members have to weigh every piece of evidence that is submitted by attending to its significance as it emerges in the proceedings in the court itself. It is not that they do not come to serve on the jury without a knowledge of a common culture of what is just, what is unjust, what is acceptable evidence and what is not, and what is the correct procedure to follow in the presentation of evidence. Everyone on the jury, however, will not have the same expertise on these matters. Further, they will also have varying identities with varying intensities of commitment. Nevertheless, there is the dynamics of the jury deliberation: the interactional system, power plays by individual jurors, and their rhetorical skill also play a part in arriving at a final judgment. Yet, without the benefit of most of these circumstances, the public at large judged Simpson guilty or not guilty on the basis of what they saw on television. These judgments, however, were distributed generally along racial lines: Most of the black people accepted the verdict of "not guilty" as the only correct verdict, whereas most of the white people thought it a travesty of justice. These people were not, however, passing a judgment on the evidence as such and were not even saying that Simpson was guilty or innocent; rather, they were announcing their identity as "black people" or "white people." Or else as "people committed to justice," or as "people who believed in the American system of justice," or as "feminist," or as "masculinist," and so on. Polls conducted over several weeks in the United States showed that 80 percent of white people said that the charges were true and 15 percent said that they were not true, compared to 34 percent of blacks who said the charges were true and 58 percent who said that they were not true, reported Frank Newport. He noted further, "The recent polling shows little sympathy for Simpson as a person." Nevertheless, there is once again a striking difference in the attitudes of black and white respondents: "79 percent of whites interviewed in May 1996 said they were unsympathetic toward Simpson as a person, while 18 percent said they were sympathetic. Among blacks, 36 percent were unsympathetic while 56 percent were sympathetic" (Newport: 1996). On a more personal level Diana Beard-Williams, a black talk show host, describes various processes by which the verdict in the trial of O. J. Simpson was used to make claims of identity: "The verdicts had wounded the psyche of white America in a way that was unprecedented in American history and vengeance was the key to white America's healing—there could be no other acceptable antidote," she writes and introduces the interpersonal dimension of the reactions to the verdict. "But I knew I wasn't alone in my frustration and growing fear of how out of control white America was at that time. Any black person who spoke up in defense of O. J. Simpson or the verdicts was looked at with a jaundiced eye." She uses the verdict herself to make identity claims of her own as well as describes the selective exercises by which such claims are made:

> African-Americans have had to become adept at politely and skillfully sidestepping all O .J. conversations if they wanted to keep their white relationships intact, much the same way they sidestep comments with racist subtleties in the office, in corporate boardrooms, on the golf course or at the gym. (Beard-Williams 1996)

That is, one cannot discuss this issue with white colleagues and can do so only with one's kith and kin who now become one's identity forum. The white people, presumably, could discuss it easily with their kith and kin and have one or more of their identities—as white people, as law-abiding and law-respecting citizens, for instance, validated and sustained in their social circles.

These moves were then *identity claims*, affirmations of memberships in one category or another, and not a studied and responsible judgment of the evidence. They are acts by which identities are manifested, made public, defined for relevant audiences, and can be taken as indices of emotional commitment to them. In primary relationships, and in secondary ones as well, it was possible for an individual to take a position on the verdict in the Simpson case both to experience the emotions of identification as well as to display loyalty to one's ethnic taxa. As one did so, he or she showed loyalty and commitment not only to this abstract category but simultaneously to one's own kith and kin and received their support and validation in the flesh. The trial and the verdict became, then, a social drama in which both cognitive and felt identities were given play and the consequences thereof experienced.

To conclude, these cases of patriarchy, psychology, nationalism, and racism can be taken as exemplary anecdotes that describe different fields of identity. Needless to say, these fields also construct opposing fields: the family as a field establishes outsiders to the family who become contraries for selected purposes. Clans and other kinds of familial organizations do the same. Nationalism as a field creates enemies and outsiders as does race. Englishness as a national identity creates non-Englishness, "Frenchmen," "Frogs," "Wogs," and so forth, as alternative fields against which Englishness learns to define itself and act. Aryans too establish non-Aryans as the contraries. These identities too—"non-Aryans," "Africans," "Asians," and so forth—will construct themselves as fields with their own texts and narratives and use them to exclude the other.

The fundamental feature of fields of identity is their systematic embeddedness in a variety of structures: verbal texts, artifacts, architectural and monumental forms. Such an embeddedness enables and facilitates the formation of interpersonal and communal relationships—cognitive and emotional. The family certainly has its hallowed texts in the scriptural writings of all religions, and in the legal codes, property, and the literary and poetic compositions of the culture. Nationalism, too, has the same forms. Englishness, for instance, can be discovered in literature, historical writings, legal codes, travelers' tales, religious doctrines and their practices, churches, cathedrals, statues of national heroes, and a shared language. These various structures can be said to be integrated into a more or less coherent whole providing the discursive font for the construction of an English identity. Similarly, the field of race has its scholarly texts, its arithmetic—measurements of intelligence, skulls—a presumptively common language, theories of the relationship between biology, language, and mentality, and myths and rituals that bind them together.

If indeed a human is constantly faced with having to encounter *nothingness*, or contemplate the possibility of such encounters, the availability of embedded familial, racial, ethnic identities, and religious and political ones, can be used to diminish the nausea that would ensue and convert such encounters into those with a *somethingness*. A reliable way to overcome the feeling of nothingness is to be an Englishman or American, an Aryan or an African, a neurotic with unresolved Oedipus conflicts, a Christian or Jew or Hindu, or perhaps even an agnostic. It is easy enough to conclude that in life a human being confronts a nothingness and sooner or later discovers that life is absurd. The sociologically interesting task, however, is to discover how human beings nevertheless construct meaningful identities and sustaining relationships and carry on with their lives.

## NOTES

1. The concept of identity has been widely used in the social sciences since Erikson published his work in the 1950s. Structural social psychologists, Freudian theorists, critical theorists, and macrosociologists, as well as interactionists, have all seen it as a valuable concept, either to depict the unique subjectivity of the human, or as a source of action. For a comprehensive examination of the concept as used in sociology and social psychology, see Andrew Weigert, J. Smith Tietge, and Dennis Tietge (1986).

2. Philosophers have been seeking to clarify the meaning of the term identity but a perusal of many such essays leaves one with the impression that anyone with the least bit of philosophical sophistication will have no warrant to use the word at all! See the essays in the collections edited by Amelie Rorty (1976) and John Perry (1975). Elvi Whittaker (1992: 191–219) has discussed the importance of the concepts of self and identity in recent anthropological work.

3. I am indebted to Karl-Otto Apel (1981: 84–135) for a discussion of Peirce's defense of the "principle of the social nature of logic" in an essay that Peirce wrote in his early years. Peter Mills, however, concludes in a review of the relationship between Pierce's view of logic and Mead's reaction to it:

> Social pragmatism [Mead's]. . . forms a coherent base for symbolic interactionist sociology in its Blumerian formulation. Logical pragmatism [Pierce's] is by contrast, antithetical not only to symbolic interactionist sociology but also any examination of naturally situated social order considered as an on-going accomplishment. (1982: 130)

This may well be true in a strictly textual examination of Mead's work and that of Pierce, but is *empirically* indefensible. The "on-going accomplishment" of "situated social order" is, after all, undertaken by using signs that an actor has already mastered and such signs carry a logic with them. Milton Singer has also provided a sketch of Peirce's attempt to deal with the idea of self and identity and its relationship to dialogic processes (1984: 74–104).

4. The recent work on a social logic by Bourdieu (1980) can be fruitfully compared to pragmatic work in the field. Indeed, I would say that Bourdieu's entire opus, innocent though it is of any reference to the work of American pragmatists, is a thoroughly pragmatic social theory. Consider, for example, Bourdieu's position on the relationship between "mental structures" and the objective structures of society. Summarizing Bourdieu's argument, drawn from the work of Durkheim and Mauss, Wacquant notes, "Bourdieu proposes that social divisions and mental schemata are strictly homologous because they are genetically linked: the latter are nothing other than the embodiment of the former" (1992: 13). Peirce had argued the same position with the claim, "All knowledge of the internal world is derived by hypothetical reasoning from our knowledge of the external facts"(1955: 230).

5. See Heisenberg's (1958) discussion of these issues in connection with physics, particularly the section on "Language and Reality in Modern Physics." A lucid examination of the relationship between quantum physics and certain issues in philosophy can be found in Vladmir Fok (1971). See also my essay on the relationship between Meadian social psychology and the new physics (Perinbanayagam 1986).

6. One of the more extreme challenges to the practice of categorization in sociology, as in everyday life, comes from Steven Seidman (1994), who has called for a

rejection of all categories. The inescapability of categorization in *conceiving* and *communicating* about objects in the world becomes apparent when one examines Seidman's own argument. Guy Oakes in fact shows that what Seidman calls "queer theory," the "overarching alternative" to "modernist theory," is replete with binary categorizations. Oakes writes,

> On the one hand queer theory exhibits a peculiar loathing for binary oppositions and . . . damns them all by subjecting them to the implacable logic of radical constructionism. On the other hand . . . queer theory is possible only on the basis of the binaries queer/conventional. Without these or equivalent dichotomies queer theory would have no redoubt from which to criticize and transgress rules. . . . Queer theory is either self-contradictory or reflexively self-defeating. (Oakes 1995: 379–388).

But then of course postmodernists may claim that the demand for noncontradiction and consistency are themselves evidence of a modernist neuroses! For an informed and sober examination of the place of logic in the deconstructionist enterprise—from which Seidman's thesis is derived—see John Ellis (1989). He notes that deconstructionism's "new logic," as some of its advocates (for instance, Barbara Johnson 1980) call it, is the old mysticism. He cites Johnson and other deconstructionists as claiming that the way to pin down the "unclear" logic of deconstruction was to proceed by *distinguishing* it from traditional logic (1989:8). In other words binary logic is needed to characterize, with *due clarity*, deconstructive logic itself.

7. See Rosenthal (1969) for a discussion of the relationship between "interpretant" and "concept."

8. The claim has also been advanced by some sociologists who have worked in India that

> individualism is devalued in India . . . [and] that personal autonomy is subordinated to familism . . . and that explanations of motivation for behavior are expressed in the logic of caste rules and kinship ideologies or in terms of extrinsic factors such as astrological considerations or beliefs about the actions of demons, deities and supernatural forces,

notes Mattison Milnes, and he provides a convincing refutation of these views using personal narratives from informants who displayed an abundance of self, autonomy, and individualism (1988: 568–579).

9. See in this connection a study by Carmen Luke (1994) on the manner in which toys are used by the adult world and the world of consumer industry to confer particular race-related, gender-related, and family-related identities on children in Australia. Needless to say, her conclusions can be extrapolated to all cultures.

10. Gregory Stone (1970) referred to identities based on formal categories as structural identities and those based on informal ones as interpersonal identities.

11. My use of "field" here is to be differentiated from Pierre Bourdieu's usage. For me, "fields" are primarily conceptually organized meaning-systems and not arenas of contention, or conflict, for the manifestations of power. Nevertheless, to the extent that such meaning systems are often issues in conflict and contention, there is, no doubt, an affinity between his usage and mine.

12. Susan Ervin-Trip (1969) has provided a thorough linguistic analysis of these terms of address by examining titles, last names and titles, last names, first names, and multiple names as forms of addressing others. As one addresses the other, one is indicating

the identity of the other vis-à-vis self and claiming that their subsequent relationship is going to be based on these respective identities. Roland Barthes has discussed the significance of proper names in the novels of Marcel Proust. A proper name, he writes, "is a voluminous sign, a sign always pregnant with a dense texture of meaning, which no amount of wear can reduce, can flatten, contrary to a common noun which releases only one of its meanings by syntagm" (Barthes 1980: 59–60). The dense texture, of course, allows them to become markers of varied and complex identities.

13. Were only males conferred with these identities? Some of the terms used in these descriptions seem to apply only to those associated with male identities. Nevertheless, it is clear that the racial identity was conferred on both males and females, leading also to the claims of protecting the females, the mothers of future members of the race, from contamination by alien impregnations.

14. See Lynn Stephens (1981) for a perceptive discussion of the relationship between cognition and emotion in the work of Charles Peirce.

15. In matriarchal and matrilineal societies, one would expect insults indicating copulation with a father to occur. I have been unable to check this out, however.

16. Items of food that are typical to a group are used as objects of identification and are also used as summarizing terms to identify the group in question. The availability of these summaries also makes them potent terms for insults: "kraut," "meatball," and so on.

# Chapter 4

# The Poetics of Identity

Since by nature we are given to representation, melody and rhythm . . .
from the beginning, those by nature most disposed to these, generated
poetry from their improvisations.

Aristotle

One is a self when one is able to look upon one's actions and being as an
object, and such conceiving of oneself as an object is made possible by the
use of linguistic categories. In Mead's words, "I know of no other form of
behavior than the linguistic in which the individual is an object to himself,
and so far as I can see, the individual is not a self in the reflexive sense unless
he is an object to himself" (1934: 142). More recently Derek Bickerton, after
surveying a variety of anthropological and neurological studies, observes,
"For, more than any other factor, language created our species, and created
too the world that our species sees" (1990: 255).

However, there is no such thing as "language"; rather, all languages are constituted by various structures and tropic mannerisms: paradigmatic and syntagmatic structures, deep and surface structures, tropic structures and phonological structures. Every usage of a word manifests itself in paradigmatic and
syntagmatic embeddedness and in grammatical forms, and in phonological
voicedness and as metaphors or metonymies, synecdoches, oxymorons, or
ironies. If the meaning of a word is its usage in language, as Wittgenstein
argues (1958), then insofar as the usages are always structured and troped, it
follows that the meaning of a word is its usage as it is manifested in structures
and tropes. In such purposive use of structures and tropes the special qualities
of cultural systems as well as specific interests of given individuals may be realized—perhaps even their very destinies. *The moment one acknowledges that
language is necessary to constitute oneself and objectify it, the structured and
tropic nature of language itself must be accepted as significant in constituting the self and objectifying it.* These intrinsic characteristics of language ren-

135

ders its usages, in everyday life, as in other forms of life, inescapably poetic. After examining a variety of studies, Raymond Gibbs observes,

> Recent advances in cognitive linguistics, philosophy, anthropology, and psychology show that not only is much of our language metaphorically structured, but so is much of our cognition. People conceptualize their experiences in figurative terms via a metaphor, metonymy, irony, oxymoron and so on, and these principles underlie the way we think, reason and imagine. (1994: 5)

That is, we "conceptualize experience," and the world itself, poetically. It is this feature of language—that it is always available in poetic forms—that is also used in the construction of identifying vocabularies for the self.

In order to achieve a differentiation of self from others and a continuity over time, thereby constituting an identity for the individual, a poetics of identity becomes imperative. Poetics is the use of all the resources of language to rhetorically constitute a social object. In an early paper Burke writes:

> Indeed, beginning with such a word as *composition* to designate the architectonic nature of either a poem, a social construct, or a method of practical action, we can take over the whole vocabulary of tropes (as formulated by rhetoricians) to describe the specific patterns of human behavior. Since social life, like art, is a *problem of appeal*, the poetic metaphor could give us invaluable hints for describing modes of practical action, which are too often measured by simple tests of utility and too seldom with reference to the communicative, sympathetic, *propitiatory* factors that are clearly present in the procedures of formal art and must be as truly present in those informal arts of living we do not happen to call arts. (Burke [1935] 1965: 264)

One of the "social constructs" to which Burke's procedures of analysis can be applied is the poetic processes by which identities are constituted. It is a process infused with "communicative, sympathetic, proprietary" factors and are truly one of the "informal arts" by which individuals and their others manage to live in the social and material world. By poetics of identity, then, I will signify the use of various resources of the language, such as the tropes, to constitute and announce identities, and I will argue that these resources make a difference in the particular identity that emerges. In talking of the poetics of identity, I am addressing the *art* and the *artfulness* with which social identities are constituted in given cultures and subcultures. This artfulness depends on using the tropic features of language with varying degrees of deliberateness—sometimes with total willfulness and at other times unwittingly, to depict the self and delineate an identity. Recognizing that literally countless treatises have been written on the four major tropes—metaphor, metonymy, synecdoche, and irony—from Aristotle in the West and to Abhinavagupta in ancient India to modern times, I will confine my discussion of the tropes to Burke's own work on the topic.[1]

Among other attractions of Burke's work—for example clarity and economy—his is also the most sociologically relevant because his examples are nearly always social and political ones. He identifies metaphor, metonymy, synecdoche, and irony as the four "master tropes" of rhetorical communication. His primary concern with these tropes is not in "their purely figurative usage, but in their role in the discovery and description of 'the truth'" (1969a: 503). Burke admits that these four tropes are not self-contained and readily bounded in their actual usages:

> It is an evanescent moment that we shall deal with—for not only does the dividing line between the figurative and literal usages shift, but also the four tropes shade into one another. Give a man but one of them, tell him to exploit its possibilities, and if he is thorough in doing so, he will come upon the other three. (Burke 1969a: 503)

Summarizing his ideas on the four tropes, Burke observed that metaphor is equal to *perspective,* metonymy to *reduction,* synecdoche to *representation,* and irony to *dialectic.* The dividing line among the tropes may shift, just as the identification of everything in the world will, but one can nevertheless use them categorically to order the constitution of identity in everyday discourse.

The choice of the tropes with which particular identities are to be constituted is, however, not a matter of whimsy; rather the choice is dictated by the aims that the theory is meant to serve. For example, a Buddhist poetics of the self functions to fulfill a Buddhist theory of knowledge and world and individual, just as a Freudian poetics of the self serves to support a psychobiological view of humans. In each case a theory of knowledge and world accompanies the poetics selected to define the self. Nevertheless, any theory about the beingness of the discursively minded organism and its propensity to act in nondeterministic ways demand one poetic or another, and it is not possible to claim that one theory is empirically more defensible than another. They are all poetry composed by that being who, in Kenneth Burke's words, faces "a staggering disproportion between man and no-man" and finds that

> there is no place for purely human boasts of grandeur, or for forgetting that men build their cultures by huddling together, nervously loquacious, at the edge of an abyss. ([1935]1965: 272)

One product of such nervous loquacity are theories of the human subject that such a subject uses to construct its presence and being in the world. Harry Stack Sullivan, in fact, argues that a human constitutes a "self-system" in order to obviate the feeling of anxiety that the significant other would reject him or her if he or she violated its expectations (1953). The self-system becomes a "security operation." I am suggesting something larger here: One formulates an identity and has it ratified as an answer to a more existential anxiety than the fear of rejection by a significant other who is one, after all, at large in the world at hand. It is psychologically safer to be something rather than nothing, to be anything rather than nothing.

Such theories, patently rhetorical in their construction, enable a linguistically minded organism to construct an identity by using one of many available theories. These theories deploy within them the various tropes of the language in varying ways. Nevertheless, it is possible to identify certain tropes as dominant in one theory as opposed to another. In some theories, metaphorical tropes may be featured while in others metonymies, synechdoches, or ironies may be the mainstay of the rhetoric of identity. I will select certain of these rhetorics of identity and show how tropic figurations are featured in them. These tropes are the instrumentations with which the logic of identity is given shape, form, concrete expression. These poetic devices at once separate an individual from another as join him or her with another and work to separate a structure of individuals from another. A man is separated from a woman, for example, but joined to each other by their kinship as siblings and they, as well as various others, are joined as, say, Christians, and separated from Hindus.

## METAPHORS OF IDENTITY

Burke defines metaphor

> as a device for seeing something *in terms* of something else. It brings out the thisness of a that or the thatness of a this. . . . If we employ the word "character" as a general term for whatever can be thought of as distinct then we could say that metaphor tells us something about one character as considered from the point of view of another character. And to consider A from the point of view of B is, of course, to use B as a *perspective* upon A. (1969a: 503–504)

In seeing something in terms of another, in delineating its shape and contour, its thisness, one may see it from several perspectives.

> If we are in doubt as to what an object is, for instance, we deliberately try to consider it in as many different terms as its nature permits: lifting, tasting, tapping, holding it in different lights, subjecting it to different pressures, dividing, matching, contrasting etc. (1969a: 504)

If we are in doubt about identity, our own or identity in general, then we have to view it from different perspectives in order to arrive at some definition of it. Given cultures, however, typically do not put this burden on individuals but provide them with the perspective with which to view their respective identities. These perspectives are then metaphors of identification and they are used to achieve rhetorical effects. Or, in other words, the process of identification involves acts of composition, both individual and collective, and identities of individuals are results of such poetic exercises. In these exercises perspectives are clarified, metaphors put into action, by verbal and practical means and identities constituted.

Different cultures of knowledge and belief use different poetics to constitute identity. I will take Christianity, Hinduism, Buddhism, and Freudianism and expose their respective poetics of identity. Such a discussion will focus on the particulars and details of the "language" used in the construction of identities and their function in the structures of the respective narratives in which they occur and makes no claim at all about their theological validity or philosophical acumen. Furthermore, the discussion does not purport to be a comprehensive analysis of various religious and secular theories but draws selectively from each of them as they pertain to the construction of differentiated identities.

## Christian Identifications

Christianity as a religious and cultural field has perhaps provided the most pervasive poetics of identity in the world today. The texts in which this poetry is articulated, their variations and subtleties, are rich and narratively complex, and have produced a plethora of commentaries. I will select four "representative anecdotes" (Burke 1969a: 59–61) and examine their uses in the constitution of a Christian identity. These four are the myths of creation and Eden, the story of Jesus' birth, his baptism by John, and his death and resurrection. Each of these "anecdotes" presents a perspective on man, woman, and world by embodying them in a narrative in which each episode becomes a metaphor for identification of "man," "woman," and "world" and the interrelations thereof.[2]

The poetics of Christian identity may be said to begin in the pre-Christian myth of creation described in the Old Testament. It first describes the place where this identity was to be given play and then sets the stage where it was to continue to play: God creates heaven and earth and lights the place and establishes a division between the "firmament" and the "waters" and so on and so forth. Having done this, God creates "water and such things" and then the "cattle and creeping things" come forth. Having done all this, he comes to the main character, the protagonist: "Let us make man in our image, after our likeness: and let them have dominion over the fish of the sea and over the fowl of the air, and over the cattle, and over all the earth, and over every creeping thing that creepeth upon the earth" (Gen. 1:26). But how did he create man? "And the Lord God formed man of the dust of the ground, and breathed into his nostrils the breath of life; and man became a living soul" (Gen. 2:7). He then creates a "garden eastward of Eden; and there he put the man whom he had formed" (Gen. 2:8). Here "grow every tree that is pleasant to the sight, and good for food; the tree of life also in the midst of the garden, and the tree of knowledge of good and evil" (Gen. 2:9). He then creates rivers, gold and bdellium and onyx stone. "Then the Lord God took the man, and put him in the garden of Eden to dress it and keep it" (Gen. 2:15). Having done all this, including making rivers that "compasseth the whole of Ethiopia," and another one that "goeth toward Assyria," and another that is the Euphrates, not to speak of bdellium and onyx stone, he makes a momentous discovery: "And the Lord God said: It is not good that man should be alone; and I will make a help meet for him" (Gen. 2:18). Then "out of the ground the Lord God formed every beast of the field and every fowl of the air and brought them unto Adam to see what he would call them: and whatever Adam called every living creature, that was the name thereof" (Gen. 2:19).

Everything is in place now: the protagonist, the environment, the lighting, and the other characters who now have names. The plot now needs a co-protagonist—a woman.

> And the Lord God caused a deep sleep to fall upon Adam, and he slept: and he took one of his ribs, and closed up the flesh instead thereof; And the rib, which the Lord God had taken from man, made he a woman, and brought her unto the man. And Adam said, "This is now bone of my bones, and flesh of my flesh: she shall be called Woman because she was taken out of Man. (Gen. 2:21,22)[3]

Several poetic devices are involved in this version of the creation of humans. To begin with, there is the narrative sequencing: Space and time are created, then nonhuman living phenomena and water and so on, and then man is created out of the dust. And woman is created after all this is accomplished. This sequencing by itself establishes Adam as the central figure in the narrative and invests him and all his putative male descendants with the identity of chief protagonists in the world. God made the world and the plants and creatures including "woman" for him. Further, he gets to name the plants and creatures—an act of identification that is an exercise of power. The woman herself is created to be his helper and she came out of him, out of his ribs, forever indebted to him for having given the gift of life. These poetics then establish the following identity for Adam and men, and Eve and women: Adam, dominator, center of the earth, he who named the creatures in it, he who was created first in God's image, he who gave life to woman in order to help him—do what? Run the world? The generic identity of man as the lord of all that he surveyed was established poetically and narratively and was to be reproduced in numerous narratives henceforth.

However, the author also used another poetic device here: He sought to create a difference between Adam and the other creatures by breathing "into his nostrils the breath of life, and making him into a living soul." The human identity is separate from that of other living creatures, because humans have a living soul. There is no record of the woman receiving the breath of life, but interpreters of the Bible, for the most past, have assumed that women have souls. From the account in Genesis it is not possible to infer that animals and plants had this distinguishing feature: There is no record of God breathing into their nostrils. However, later theologians have indicated "animal souls" and "vegetative souls" for their respective categories, reserving "rational soul" for the human. Here again a distinctive identity was maintained for humans, for it was argued that humans alone were immortal and capable of union with God. The metaphor of "soul" is one of the most pervasive identifications of humans in many religious traditions. They are endowed with this "vital essence," this "spirit," this "substance," that is different from the body and transcends it. Unlike the Hindu and Buddhist notions of *atman* and *atta* (or *anatta*), the Christian obtains his or her soul either at conception or at birth. Once it comes into being it goes on forever, each soul unique unto itself.

What, then, is the soul? Thomas Aquinas, in a statement preliminary to his discussion of the soul, notes almost in a Wittgensteinian manner,

> Of no thing whatever can a perfect knowledge be obtained unless its operation is known, because the measure and quality of a thing's power is judged from the manner and trope of its operation, and its power, in turn, manifests its nature; for a thing's natural aptitude for operation follows upon its possession of a certain kind of nature. ([1258]1975: 29)

One can obtain knowledge of a thing, that is, its meaning, by understanding its usage, just as a meaning of a word is its actual usage in a language. What, then, is the meaning of "soul"? To answer this question, Aquinas addresses the whole thesis on creation. He deals with three problems, notes James Anderson, a commentator on Aquinas's work. These are "the act of bringing things into being; the distinction of things from one another; the nature of the things which were brought into being and made distinct from one another, was relevant to the truth of the faith" (1975: 13).

The first problem is answered by the claim "that God is the very source or cause of the being of other things" (1975: 13). The second problem is concerned with "the distinction of things—their multiplication and diversification," as James Anderson, puts it (1975: 15).

Insofar as God by his act of creation brought things into being, he also brought them as *different* things, things different from each other. But "why," continues Anderson, "are these things many and distinct?" (1975: 15). Why, in other words, do they have an identity? Anderson summarizes Aquinas's answer:

> The multiplicity and variety of things in the created universe did not, as the ancient Greek cosmologists supposed, result from chance movements or convergence of material principles; that, on the contrary, matters were created diverse and mutually distinct and exist *in order that* they might be suitable

recipients for various forms. . . . There is this distinction—multiplicity and variety and diversity—among created things primarily for this reason, that they may
more adequately represent the perfection of God. (1975: 15)

It was the intention of God to create diversity and inequality in things and it
is "God Himself, who wills to give the creature such perfection as it is possible for it to have" (1975: 16). The third problem is answered with the
"*nature* of the distinct and diversified creatures *as far as this concerns faith*"
and these creatures are endowed with "intellectual substance," notes Anderson as he concludes, "The perfection of the universe required the existence
of some intellectual creatures in order that creatures might perfectly . . . represent divine goodness" (Anderson 1975: 16).

The world created by God needed an intellectual creature (read symbolic
creature) so that he or she could be a *witness* to God's goodness. Such a
creature is

possessed of will and free will; that they are incorporeal and immaterial; that
there is in them, as in all creatures, a composition of essence and being, of
potency and act (though not of course of matter and form); and that they are
therefore by nature incorruptible. (Anderson 1975: 16)

This is the soul. Having argued this, the problem that is left is the union of
these qualities of incorporeality, essentiality, beingness, potency, actionality,
and incorruptibility with a body. Rejecting the arguments of Plato, Avicenna,
Averroes, and many others, Aquinas concludes that each human possesses
not three souls—nutritive, sensitive, and intellective that move the body—
but one cohesive soul. There cannot be two separate souls, or three, because
it faces a logical problem. In Aquinas's words:

One cannot be made from two or more, without something to unite them,
unless one of them be related to the other as act to potentiality; for thus matter
and form become one, without anything outside uniting them. Now, if there are
several souls in man, they are not related to one another, but they are all, by
hypothesis, acts and principles of action. So, if they are united in order to form
one thing, say, man or animal, there must be something to unite them. But this
cannot be the body, since it is precisely the body which is united by the soul; a
sign of which is the fact that, when the soul departs, the body is dissolved. . . .
Since then it is impossible to go on to indefinity, it is necessary to come to a
thing that is one itself. And the soul, especially, is such a thing. Therefore there
must be one soul in one man or one animal. (Aquinas [1258] 1975: 175)

God's creations, then, are diverse and multiple, each of them differentiated from the other on a number of dimensions. There are to begin with distinctions between classes of phenomena: animals, humans, the latter being
"intellectual creatures." Further, there is the distinction between humans

themselves: there is but "one soul in one man." Each human's soul, then, is distinct from that of another and therefore has a separate destiny. Conversely, since each human has a separate soul he or she, in all his or her composite essences, is also distinct from other such humans. This distinctive soul can "depart" from the body, having been united with it for some earthly years, and presumably go elsewhere. This soul has continuity and participates in giving continuity to the body, because when it departs, the body becomes action-less and soon decays.

In every way, "soul" is a very serviceable metaphor with which a sense of continuity and differentiation can be achieved. It encompasses duration: The soul remains constant over time as the body changes from infancy to childhood to adulthood. It remains so, somewhat qualified, no doubt, by its experiences, after the demise of the body and escapes into the great unknown, to be disposed of in one way or another and remain eternally. Further, each soul had a unique destiny: It is different from all other souls and is assured of a unique dispensation after death, though some Christian sects promise that families of souls would reassemble in the hereafter. In the latter case, in addition to a Christian identity, the identity by descent and kinship are assured by the Church of Latter-day Saints. The soul, then, is a metaphor for identity that allows an individual to objectify his or her self and confer on it a sense of continuity and difference.

The second "anecdote" that we can use to investigate the poetics of Christian identity is the incident in the garden and Eve's encounter with the duplicitous serpent. The serpent, representing the Devil, is God's counter. Though there is no record of God having created him, he is dramaturgically necessary, as Judas is in a later anecdote. Thus certain contrasting themes can be made to act against each other and the grand narrative of human existence on earth given its substantive form and shape in various actions and interactions. In Burke's words: "If *action* is to be our key term, then *drama;* for drama is the culminative form of action. . . . But if *drama* then *conflict.* And if *conflict* then *victimage*" (1966b: 54–55).The anecdote of the garden sets up then two victims: Adam and Eve and their putative descendants on the one hand and the Devil himself on the other. On the instruction of the serpent, "the woman saw that the tree was good for food, and that it was pleasant to the eyes, and a tree to be desired to make one wise, she took of the fruit thereof, and did eat, and gave also unto her husband with her; and he did eat" (Gen. 3:6). This leads to a curious consequence: "And the eyes of them both were opened, and they knew that they were naked; and they sewed fig leaves together and made themselves aprons." Unclothed and uncovered they were at the beginning when they were innocent, but after eating from the tree of knowledge, they lost their "innocence" and felt shame and had to cover themselves. Clothing, albeit an apron of fig leaves, becomes recognized as a marker of identity here, the genitals having now become "shameful." What did Adam and Eve learn from the "tree of knowledge"? Here what we have is an elaborate metaphor for the act of identification of self and other, in that they can feel shame in each other's presence and know themselves and the other. From the tree of knowledge each learned the knowledge of his or her self and of the other. Adam entered Eve and they both discovered the difference between them and, since they were different in essential ways, they sought to hide the differentiating member under fig-leaved aprons. The knowledge they acquired after feasting on the forbidden fruit was the knowledge of their selves, which they now are able to identify, in their differences, as man and woman. This is the final act in the identification of men and women that began with the narrative of Creation.

The woman's identity is once again being defined with these rhetorical moves. She has, along with the serpent, become a metaphor for disobedience and duplicity, while the man is honest and noble and is a victim of woman's treachery. The myth in fact contributes a metaphor for the identification of women as well as dialectically for men: Men are dupes, easily led astray into sin and disobedience by women, though some modern theologians have discounted this interpretation of the myth. Nevertheless, Mary Daly opines, "The fact is however that the myth had projected a malignant image of the female-male relationship and of the 'nature' of women that is deeply embedded in the modern psyche" (1973: 45). It is not so much the psyche that it influences as the discourse of identification—not only of the more fundamentalist churches but also the general discursive culture of Judeo-Christian civilization. Long ago Tertullian could say of women, "You are the devil's gateway . . . . How easily you destroyed man, the image of God, because of the death you brought upon us even the son of God had to die" (In Daly 1973: 44). Tertullian is of course punning: gateway=woman. Bringing sinful humans into the world through vaginal copulation and birthing, as well as by Eve's original actions, opened the gateway for human suffering.

Though it is Eve, the woman, who is tempted by Lucifer and is the primary cause, Adam, having acquiesced on the breaking of the covenant with God, is also held responsible. As a result both "man" and "woman" are expelled from Eden and they and their descendants are alienated from God. Every man and woman, then, everyone irrespective of personal experiences, of class, caste, creed, age, and wit, is guilty of the primal sin and will not be redeemed until God sends a messenger. In one metaphorical swoop all humankind is equalized into one logical class, one identity: original sinner. Each human has a separate soul, but each soul shares with other souls the sin of the primal disobedience and will be collectively redeemed by God through his Messiah. In Burke's words, "the conditions for such a doctrine of 'original sin' are set up when our 'first' parent who commits the crucial sin has a name at once individual and generic, a name that can be translated either as 'Adam' or 'man.' Thus, in his sin as Adam, he can personate mankind in general" (1961: 176).

The identity of a Christian is taking shape now. He was created by a creator who gave him dominion over a territory with all its contents; she was created to be his assistant in exerting this dominion and to be the subject of his dominion; each was also given an "inner essence," or a "vital principle" that was independent of the body, which was created from the dust or from the bone, a soul which was immortal. Second, a hierarchy of identities was also established: man and woman over the animate and inanimate environment, and man over woman who was further degraded as being particularly evil and untrustworthy. Beings that by nature respond to symbols can use these metaphors to constitute identities for their particular selves to the extent they come to know them, either directly or indirectly, and the vast majority of people in the Christian world did come directly into contact with them, or indirectly in their manifestation in other narratives (secular or religious), sermons, and exhortations of other kinds.[4]

Man and woman, thus created and put to trials, punished, and promised redemption sometime in the future, are enforced to go forth and create more men and women on their own. These new men and women go forth and do as they are told to, pass through numerous other trials, and in the third great moment of a Christian identification, discover the redeemer. The third event that provided the poetics for a Christian identity is the birth, rebirth in baptism, crucifixion, and resurrection of Jesus.

This is no doubt the most central event that provides the rhetoric of Christian identity. The other two "anecdotes" described earlier are ones that are shared with the Jews and the Muslims. The advent of Jesus, initially given to us by Matthew, sets an ancestral justification for his special status "the generation of Jesus Christ, the son of David, the son of Abraham. Abraham begat Isaac; and Isaac begat Jacob; and Jacob begat Judas and his brethren" (Matt. 1: 1,2). The line is traced in detail, connecting Jesus to the founders of the ancestral religion. Jesus is the son of David, a son of Joseph, too, in a manner of speaking, and "the only begotten son of God" as well: "Now the birth of Jesus Christ was on this wise: When as his mother Mary was espoused to Joseph, before they came together, she was fecund with child by the Holy Ghost" (Matt. 1:18). Being a patriarch, Joseph is upset at this development and secludes her from others but an angel appears to Joseph in a dream and announces "Joseph, thou son of David, fear not to take unto thee Mary, thy wife: For that which is conceived in her is of the Holy Ghost. And she shall bring forth a son and thou shalt call his name Jesus: For he shall save his people from their sins" (Matt. 1:20,21). Jesus comes to save "his people," and he is also the son of God. A believer is thus given a double metaphor of identification: He or she is already a child of God and can identify himself or herself as such because he or she is descended from Adam. Now there is also another child of more awesome bearing because he is born of woman, but fathered by God and he has sent him especially to save "his people." Being already a child of God, a believer can add a new dimension to his or her identity by accepting Jesus by an act of will, no less.

Jesus grows up and has to face another transformation: baptism. To enable this to happen, the gospels give us a precursor, since Christ cannot have himself validated by baptizing himself, and so came "John the Baptist, preaching in the wilderness of Judea" (Matt. 3:1). In his early baptisms, John announces, "I indeed baptize you with water unto repentance: but he that cometh after me is mightier than I, whose shoes I am not worthy to bear: he shall baptize you with the Holy Ghost and with fire" (Matt. 3:11). John, however, baptizes Jesus after a narrative episode that captures the contradiction that this act represents: Jesus is the son of God and without sin or impurity and does not need to be cleansed by water and reborn. Nevertheless, says Matthew,

> Then cometh Jesus from Galilee to Jordan unto John, to be baptized by him. But John forbad him saying, I have need to be baptized of thee, and comes thou to me? And Jesus answering said unto him, Suffer it to be so now: For thus it becometh us to fulfill all righteousness. Then he suffered him. (Matt. 3:13, 14,15).

Suffer it to be so *now*, Jesus said; that is, let it be for the time being; it is true that I am mightier than you, and I am without sin; but baptize me for now. Once John baptizes Jesus, "the heavens were opened unto him and he saw the spirit of God descending like a dove, and lighting upon him: and lo a voice from heaven, saying 'This is my beloved Son, with whom I am well pleased'" (Matt. 3:16).

Jesus is surely reborn here in a double sense: He is born out of the waters of Jordan and is born again to the multitudes assembled on the banks of the Jordan by the announcement from heaven with God claiming him publicly as his son. The first announcement was private; now it is public made by God himself about an adult Jesus. The primal event in the construction of a Christian identity is in fact the ceremony of baptism. In this ceremony all the sacerdotal and mythological claims of Christianity as a distinct religion and one that is radically differentiated from its ancestors are affirmed just as the beginnings of the individual in a Christian identity is confirmed. One may say that the very notion of a Christian identity begins with a baptism—the baptism of Jesus by John. John the Baptist was a dramaturgical necessity: He had to come before Jesus not only to announce publicly Jesus' imminent arrival, but also to publicly baptize him and make him a Christian with God as a witness. Jesus was the Messiah and he was to found a new religion, or at least make a break with the old one, and indeed say: "Ye have heard that it was said by them of old time . . . but I say unto you . . ." (Matt. 5:21, 22). Nevertheless, he too needs a beginning—a biological one and a sociological one. This is handled by the theory of "unpolluted" birth: He is "born without sin," i.e., without the benefit of copulation with an earthly being. This story assures his break from the patriliny of Joseph, the husband of his mother Mary. *On the patriliny, the important line, he has a new beginning.* Once he grows up and is ready for his mission, he is given another beginning as a spiritual being. To achieve this one needs a telling ritual and the ceremony of cleansing by water accomplishes this. He is born again from the waters of the sacred river Jordan.

Joachim Jeremias, writing on this topic, notes, quoting from the gospels of Matthew, Mark, and Luke, "These claims diminish Jesus' stature because they imply that he was himself with sin and needed to be cleansed and that Jesus was subordinate to John the Baptist. This was hard for the early church to accept" (Jeremias 1971: 45). This conundrum, however, was a necessary one for the creation of a specifically Christian identity: It provided a potent metaphor for it, in fact. The baptism of Jesus was not a mere purification but a symbolic separation, or break between the old religion and the new. The ceremony of baptism initiates one, including Jesus himself, into a new identity. He is now the one who was not so much purified as separated from earlier identities by the immersion in the waters and by being born anew to a new identity. Baptism is a handy and dramaturgically effective ceremony by which new Christians could be identified to themselves as to others. It was easily reproducible and can be readily and parsimoniously enacted with all the relevant metaphors of identity given play.

And every time it is reenacted, it endows the supplicant with an identification with one who was baptized first. The newly baptized becomes a kin of Christ, a brother or a sister, and joins the holy family, the church, the brotherhood of believers, and those born again into a new identity. It is after the immersion in the water by John that God publicly claims his son and indeed announces that he is well pleased with him. Every time a human is baptized this event is symbolically reenacted and the baptized becomes a putative son or daughter of God, *a metaphor for Christ.* The ceremony of baptism becomes a rite with which an individual is given a new identity, one by which he or she is *identified with* others who have undergone similar ceremonies as well as to the one who was baptized by John the Baptist.

In some sects of Christianity, children are "Christened" in the presence of a "godfather" and "godmother" for the young child who could not very well consent to being identified as a Christian. The child is also given a name that connects him to the biblical tradition and simultaneously connects it to the current membership of the church through the godparents. They become "sponsor" of the new Christian and ostensibly are standbys promising to raise the new Christian in the traditions of the religion if the parents are unable to do so. However, they are also witnesses to the new identity of the baptized child (or adult) and, as members in good standing of the functioning church, communal *validators* of the new identity. Of course it must be said that if an individual is baptized as a child, as happens in some denominations, an identity is being thrust upon him or her, whereas if it is done as an adult (as among those calling themselves the Anabaptists) identity was being acquired.

The new name, the new membership in a more or less institutionalized community of believers, the new witnesses and validators, and the fresh attitudes mobilized by these activities and the symbolism of water (always used for cleaning in the secular world) then marks the termination of an old identity and the emergence of a new one. Scriptural allusions and justifications and parallels and the communal and institutional participation ensure that it is above all a social identity that is being constituted. The scriptures, it can be seen, provide the necessary poetics, the needed metaphors, with which this identity was to be constituted.

Once Jesus is baptized and his identity is announced by the sound from heaven, he goes forward to preach, gather his disciples, and undertake a series of mass conversions as well as various dramatic demonstrations of his extraordinary power. The miracles that he performs are rhetorical moves guaranteed to elicit respect and devotion from the multitudes and affirm his status as the son of God. All these activities and the eloquent words from the sermons were to provide rich poetics of identity to generations of believers.

However, it is the ending of Jesus' life that was to provide the most potent and abiding set of metaphors for Christian identification: Christ the persecuted, Christ the sufferer, Christ the victim and scapegoat. The following themes can be extracted as features of this phase of the religion:

(a) There is the son of God who came among his people to save them.
(b) He undertook various good deeds and spoke loving, compassionate, and forgiving words.
(c) He showed both his love and compassion, as well as his divinity, by performing deeds that no one else could do.
(d  He gathered a dozen close disciples.
(e) One of them betrayed him to the state, another denied him, and yet another doubted him.
(f) He was arrested, tried, tortured, humiliated, and then hanged on a cross.
(g) He was buried in an open grave.
(h) Three days later his disciples went to the grave and found it empty.
(i) The disciples took this as confirmation of his prophecy that he would be resurrected from the dead, go to heaven, and return to God his father.

This is not just another anecdote from the vast corpus of such anecdotes about Jesus but one that, in its narrative richness and complexity, can function as an extended metaphor for all individuals in the mundane world. It is primarily a tale of suffering, suffering with great forbearance, suffering the

betrayal by friends, suffering misunderstanding and persecution from enemies, suffering mockery from the ignorant, and finally suffering an unjust and
cruel demise, end, and denouement. As such it provides the most complete
instrument for the fashioning of an identity for humans as can be imagined.
Every human being, however successful he or she may be in the mundane
world, can experience one or more of the events that befall Jesus in the end.
He or she could suffer betrayal, denial, and doubt from significant others, he
or she could be justly or unjustly persecuted or mocked, and he or she could
be subject to extreme forms of punishment. To a human facing any or all of
these eventualities Jesus, as a metaphor, suggests humility and acceptance:
Do as he did and you too will be resurrected and find a place in heaven, "the
last shall be first." The tribulations that Jesus experienced in his later life, "the
time on the cross," then, could become a fertile source of metaphors for the
constitution of identity. Some parts of it may be selected and used to define a
particular experience in one's life with the claim: It happened to Jesus, the
son of God, the risen Lord, why would it not happen to me?

The last days of Christ's life also function as a generalized metaphor for the
construction of an equally generalized identity. To quote the lines attributed
by Shakespeare to a non-Christian: "Sufferance is the badge of all our tribe."
For Shylock, suffering is the badge of his Jewishness as well as his lot as a
descendant of Adam and Eve driven from Eden. For the Christian, there is
double source of suffering as a badge of his or her tribe: alienation from God
on account of Adam and Eve and from Jesus who suffered for "our sins." To
rejoice, to enjoy the secular world, to submit oneself totally to epicurean or
dionysian, or for that matter tantric, joys would be to betray Christ again. The
believing Christian, the true believer, should cultivate an identity of denial,
rectitude, patience, a thriftiness of emotions, a commitment to the idea that
life is suffering. The narrative of Jesus Christ, in the end, reinforces the *rou-
tinization of alienation and suffering*, a state from which there is no escape
in the immediate moment. For the Christians in general the theme of the persecution of Jesus provided the poetics of Christian identity and it also provided a reward for those who used these poetics with conviction: resurrection and life everlasting, an identity that transcends the earthly body and
earthly environments. The entire poetics of Christian identity in fact is a play
on the metaphor of birth: Humans are born with a soul, are reborn in baptism, and even death is transformed into a rebirth into life everlasting. Jesus
himself, who is born to woman, then is reborn in baptism, is crucified, enters
the tomb, is reborn from the womb of the tomb to life everlasting, and
becomes the paradigm for Christian identity.

The cycle of metaphors with which a Christian identity could be constructed
is now available. God creates man, breathes his soul into him, and then creates
woman as his helpmate. He also creates other creatures and the environment
as aids and scenes for man and his helpmate to function. He then arrives at a

covenant with both man and woman. Man and woman break this covenant and experience the primal alienation from God. Later God sends his son to save man and woman, and he comes and provides further metaphors of identity, but he is betrayed and made to suffer and this too provides metaphors for identity. The Christian, then, is all of the following: As a human being, he or she is endowed with an immortal soul; he or she is alienated from God; he or she is to be saved by Jesus Christ, if he or she accepts him and allows himself or herself to be baptized and identified with Jesus himself; and he or she conducts his life as far as is praticable, in the way in which Jesus conducted his.

The soul is not a substitute word for self, it is clear; rather the "soul" is a metaphor with which the continuity of self and its separation from others is identified in given eschatologies. It denotes an entity that exists independently of the body and continues to exist after it leaves the body. In the Christian poetics, it is able to achieve a complex of meanings with which a discursive individual is able to conceive both this worldly presence for the self as well as other-worldly ones.

## Hindu Identifications

One can best begin an analysis of the Hindu poetics of identity by examining its creation myth. The Hindu version of a creation myth occurs in many early texts with some variation, but with certain central themes that are consistent. Stanley Tambiah summarizes them as follows:

> The universe first existed in the "shape of darkness;" then the divine self-existent *Svayambhu* appeared as "creative power." He created the waters by his thought and placed his own seed in them; and in that golden egg (*hiranyagarbha*) he was born as *Brahman*, the progenitor of the whole world. Thus was formed the first male *Purusha* famed under the name of *Brahman*.
>
> The divine one divided the egg into two halves, the heaven and earth, together with the middle of space and the waters and so on. And from himself he created the mind and organs of sensation, the elementary particles, out of which again, by joining with particles himself, he created all beings: gods, the eternal sacrificial fire, wind and sun, time and divisions and seasons, mountains and rivers, speech, merit and demerit, pleasure and pain, and so on, and the four *varnas* from his own mouth, arms, thighs, and feet. (1976: 20)[5]

He then not only creates the natural world and its essential features, and does not create a man and a woman as in Judeo-Christianity, but creates the four segments that constitute the Hindu social order—the four *varnas*. The *Brahmins*, who were to teach and study the scriptures "sprang" from his mouth; the *Kshatriyas*, who were to protect the people, "sprang" from his arms; the *Vaisyas*, those who were to tend cattle, "sprang" from his thighs; and the *Sudras*, those who were to serve others, "sprang" from his feet.

The physical body, insofar as it was the body of the original human *Purusha,* becomes the basic metaphor for conceiving the social order itself as hierarchy and a division of labor. In anticipation of Emile Durkheim's argument, the Hindu theory of a division of labor adduces an integrated social order in which each segment is connected to the others as parts of a body that are connected and create a harmonious whole. What can be more perfect a functioning whole than a human body? And, therefore, what can be questioned about a social order that is similarly organized? Each individual member of this order is also able to derive an identity from his membership in the order and accept the society that results as divinely ordained and unchangeable. It provides the basic metaphor for Hindu identity because every Hindu, as a matter of course, has a *varnic* terminology of identification. One does not really become a Hindu; rather one is born into being a Hindu. Such birth, defined as a continuation from earlier lives, always delivers an individual into an already existing social structure with a definite identity: He or she has a gender, he or she has a place in a birth order, and he or she has a place in a status hierarchy, caste (*varna* or *jati*). Each of these various identities are determined by one's conduct in earlier lives; one is born a woman, younger sister, or brother of lowly status because one had accumulated negative *karma.*

Each member of these *varnas* has in him an *atman* that is eternal, a "transcendental immanent principle" as Agehananda Bharati calls it (1985: 189). It is also often called *brahaman* and is really a representation of the original creative principle in each individual's body. It is this *atman* or *brahaman* that undergoes experiences in this world, accumulates merit or demerit (*karma*), and is reborn in new forms and statuses. The animating principle of the created being is this *atman–brahaman,* which experiences the world in many incarnations and eventually returns to its roost in the godhead. This transformation from one manifestation in one lifetime to another occurs to this *atman*: It is this phenomenon that abandons one body at death and sooner or later enters another and begins a new life. *Atman* is a code for an entity that transcends time and body and is said to be returned to the godhead after a cycle of births and deaths.

One is in fact born with an *atman* whose worth or value is also given to it at birth: If it is born into a higher *varna* or as a male, it has a higher karmic value, and if it is not it has a low *karmic* value. The *varna* scheme is in fact a measure—one invented and disseminated by a patriarchal and *braminic* culture—of the karmic status of the *atman,* but a measure that can be changed by the manner in which he or she comports himself or herself in the current incarnation. It is also a measure of each individual's separation from others and continuity with his or her self. During its sojourn in this world in its present *varna* status, the *atman* is enjoined, above all, to maintain the integrity of its identity. The most vivid and poetically distinguished version of this recommendation can be found in the *Bhagavatgita.* This text occurs at a critical moment in the narrative of the *Mahabaratha*, one of the two Hindu epics that enshrines fundamental Hindu themes. In this epic, two great armies are poised for battle and the leader of the good side, variously called Arjuna, Partha, and so on, hesitates, is filled with doubt about the morality of the conflict, and refuses to fight. In refusing to engage in battle Arjuna had given expression to thoughts that were dangerous to social order:

> It were better that without slaying my gurus I went begging instead for alms in this land
> Than by slaying my covetous gurus
> Indulge in the joys that are dipped in their blood. (van Buitenen 1981: 73)

God, in his incarnation as Krishna, tries to change Arjuna's pacifist posture on the battlefield:

> Look to your Law and do not waver, for there is nothing more salutary for a baron than a war that is lawful. It is an open door to heaven, happily happened upon, blessed are the warriors, Partha, who find a war like that!
> Or suppose you will not engage in this lawful war: then you give up your Law and honor, and incur guilt. (van Buitenen 1981: 77)

The contrast between two polar identities in Hindu thought is thus set: The *Kshatriya*, the warrior or "baron" in van Buitenen's translation, and the renouncer, who abandons his varnic identity and becomes a mendicant. Krishna advises Arjuna against such a step that not only must the barons maintain the integrity of the society by maintaining the "law,"—that is, the laws of *varna* and *karma*, just as the barons must maintain their identities by following the law: "Either you are killed and will then attain heaven, or you triumph and will enjoy the earth. Therefore, rise up [*Arjuna*], resolved upon battle! Holding alike happiness and unhappiness, gain and loss, victory and defeat, yoke yourself to the battle, and so do not incur evil" (in van Buitenen 1981: 77). Such an identification of their selves becomes the basis of their respective actions. The *atman* is manifest in action, albeit actions that are *varna*-specific. Krishna tells Arjuna,

> a person does not avoid incurring *karman* just by not performing acts, nor does he achieve success by giving up acts. For no one lives even for a moment without doing some act, for the three forces of nature cause everyone to act willy-nilly. He who, while curbing the faculties of action, yet in his mind indulges his memories of sense objects is called a self-deceiving hypocrite. (van Buitenen 1981: 8–83)

This advice—indeed an exhortation—is ostensibly meant for Arjuna but is really meant for everyone. It is repeated in other texts of the religion and orally disseminated in countless proverbs, religious discourses in temples, and in fictional and dramatic presentations. It is not only Arjuna and the *kshatriya* barons who must follow this advice, but everyone who claims to be Hindu must do so. Everyone—be he or she a *Brahmin*, a *Kshatriya*, a *Vaisya*, or a *Sudra*—has a *varnic* identity that is really an index of his or her karmic identity.

There is only one way in which a Hindu can escape his identity as *varnic* self and that is by renouncing the worldly life and becoming a *sanyasin*, i.e., a mendicant. Indeed to become a *sanyasin* is to abdicate *varna* as an identifying feature of one's self, and be reborn as a "dead" person. To renounce one's self as a *varnic* identity is also to renounce all other identities that were accepted along with the *varnic* one: householder, sexual being, domestic partner, breadwinner, father, brother, son, and so on, all of which are contingent on one having a *varnic* identity.

The details of the act of renunciation—a "poetics of action" in Burke's phrase ([1935]1965: 247–255)—makes this clear. This act of renunciation is a staging of an elaborate ceremony in which the "death" of the man in question is enacted and then a renouncer is "born." Such a transformation of identity involves three features: fire, water, and clothes. Fire is an important element in the rituals of the Vedic Hindus. All the sacrifices are offered to the fire and a head of a household, when he establishes his home, creates a domestic hearth as a sacred place. Olivelle writes in a study of the Hindu texts that deal with renunciation and asceticism.

> The abandonment of that ritual religion by the renouncer is symbolized by renunciation of, or more exactly his 'depositing within himself' of the sacred fires, which is clearly the central and the most important part of the renunciatory rite. . . . The theology of renunciation that underlies this rite, however, considers the abandonment of fire not as a rejection but as an internalization. The external fires are deposited within the renouncer, who continues to carry them internally and, therefore, in a more perfect and more permanent manner. (1992: 86)

The "abandonment of fire and its internalization" in the body are really the means of abandoning "home and hearth" ritually or poetically. Olivelle notes that the "domestic fire was the focal point of domestic religiosity." It was not only a ritual center of the domestic life, but was also the practical center of such a life: Food was prepared here according to ritually prescribed ways by ritually clean women and in the commensality that followed such a rite the domestic unit as a sacred one was affirmed and reaffirmed. In abandoning such uses of fire and "internalizing" it, the *sanyasin* is using the fire as a metaphor of *domesticity* and *sociability* and renouncing both. The fire is not to be used for domestic purposes anymore, and having contained it within himself he does not have to depend on "woman" to tend it and use it for his bodily needs. The act of renunciation is taken to mean the death of the original individual and the "rebirth" of another. Olivelle writes, "Renunciation was considered the ritual death of the renouncer; that the renouncer is a ritually dead person, even though he is physically alive, is a significant aspect of Brahminical theology of renunciation" (1992: 89–90). In the act of renunciation, the would-be-renouncer participates ritually in his own funeral. "Several elements of the rite of renunciation bear a striking resemblance to Brahminical rites associated with dying and death," says Olivelle. One of the rites that a male householder is expected to perform on a regular basis is to offer oblations to his great-grandfather, grandfather, and father, thus affirming his identity as a descendent of a patriline. In the rite of renunciation, however, the would-be renouncer offers these oblations for the last time, to his grandfather and to his father, dropping his great-grandfather, whose place is now taken by himself. He is now counted among the deceased relatives (Olivelle 1992: 90). This rite by itself becomes a poetic of transformation: By including himself in the ritual of oblations to dead ancestors, he is able to define himself as one of the dead. Even his legal and social status is redefined. As Olivelle puts it, "As at a man's death, so at his renunciation his marriage is dissolved and, according to some sources, his wife is permitted to remarry; he is freed from contractual debts and his property is partitioned among his heirs" (1992: 90).

Once he is thus ritually "killed" he is born again into a new identity. Writes Olivelle,

> As the earlier part of the rite symbolically expresses the death of the renouncer, so several elements of the second part expresses the new birth of the renouncer. At the conclusion of the first part, the new renouncer takes off all his clothes and becomes naked. The Sanskrit term is *jātarūpadhara*, which literally means "having the form one had at birth." The renouncer now becomes a new born infant. (1992: 96)

In some sects at this stage the renouncer enters a body of water and after immersing himself returns to the shore and is given a new set of clothes, a new name, and a set of objects that define the life of the *sanyasin*. Olivelle comments,

> The later documents of our collection expect the new renouncer to place himself under the control of an experienced renouncer, who becomes his teacher and father. It is the teacher who gives him a new name and hands over to him the articles that are emblems of his new state. (1992: 96)

These new objects that define his new identity are staff, waterpot, waistband, loincloth, and garment. Each of these is accepted by chanting the following ritual formulas:

Staff:  Protect me, friend,
You who are my strength and my friend.
You are the bolt of Indra, slaying obstructions.
Be my refuge and banish all that is evil.

| Waterpot: | You are the life of the world! |
|---|---|
| | You are the vessel of life! |
| | Like a mother, you who are all gentle, |
| | Always give me counsel. |
| Waistband: | Waistband the support of the loincloth, Om. |
| Loincloth: | Loincloth, cover of my private parts, Om. |
| Garment: | Garment, the sole guardian of the body, protecting against cold, wind, and heat, Om. |
| | (Olivelle 1992: 97) |

The poetic transformation of identity is now complete. Having abandoned real human associates, these objects now take their place: the staff has now become his friend, the waterpot has become his mother, and the garment has become the "sole guardian." One individual is metaphorically killed and is reborn and given new metaphorical kin.[6]

Once he has been made into a *sanyasin,* he gives up all earthly desires and possessions as a result of which he is now qualified to be released from the "cycle of rebirths." He will not be born again to this world, which itself is defined as an abode of suffering and pain. The *atman* is released from its *karmic* causation and it will reach the godhead without further difficulty or interruption, because the act of renunciation has achieved a break in the *karmic* cycle. The assumption here is that the *atman* has a continuous existence over several incarnations, and that at each such incarnation it achieves certain merits and demerits that are tallied and used to determine the next moments in the soul's destiny. What, then, is the *atman?* What in fact is its use in the language? There is no doubt that it is a metaphor for a *presumptive continuity of identity over time.* When a child is born, it is identifiable with an earlier state of its *atman.* As it continues in this life, this same *atman* acquires qualifications to it which accumulate and are balanced off against each other, which balance is now featured in the next moment of the *atman,* that is, its next birth. Furthermore, to the extent that each *atman* has a separate and karmically differentiated past, present, and future, it is differentiated from all other *atmans,* the ones of those with whom an individual is living with at the moment or from the future ones. *Atman* then, to the extent that the individual accepts it and his or her social circles validate it, is a perspective on identity, a metaphor with which to constitute a continuity of self over time and to differentiate it from other selves. *Atman* is a poetic device of identification.

Once these theories of the continuous and differentiated identity represented in the *atman* are inculcated into an individual, accepted by his or her social circles, become elements in the discursive acts of everyday interactions, and are periodically enacted in ceremonies—weddings, funerals of kin, astrological consultations, rites at temples, and so on, they assume the proportions of an encompassing perspective and become the basis of actions and responses in everyday life.[7]

## Buddhist Identifications

The poetic functions of *atman* become clear when one examines its uses in Buddhism. One of Buddhism's fundamental theses is the denial of the existence of any entity or process the Hindus called *atman*—a concept that is also described, in Pali, the language of Buddhism, as *atta*. Hence Buddhism is said to be founded on the doctrine of *antatta*—loosely translated as "soullessness" and sometimes confusingly as "self-lessness." Buddhism in fact emerged as a countertheory to that of Hinduism and very correctly the Buddha perceived that the heart of Hinduism was the assumption that there was a continuous and differentiated *atman* that moved into this world from a past existence and would then move into another existence after death, and perhaps into further existences through rebirths. As the *atman* made these transformations it carried the weight—*karma*—of its antecedent earthly existence so that its next stage was determined by this weight. The *atman* was the instrumentation with which this weight of one's past life was carried, the sign that represented it—as argued earlier. In other words, the merits as well as the demerits achieved by living "correctly" or "incorrectly" needed a vehicle in which it could be vested and the *atman* was that vehicle.[8]

Hinduism's central social structure was the caste system and it functioned on the basis of this continuity of *atman*: one is born a Brahmin and fulfills his or her role as a Brahmin and his *atman* achieves nirvana; one is born a Sudra, and fulfills the duties appropriate to his or her *varna*, and in the next incarnation, his or her *atman* may be elevated to that of a Vaisya. This theory can function logically only if there is a transcendental *atman*, and unless this theory can be logically defended, the entire Hindu system would collapse.

The Buddha sought to challenge these doctrines. In fact, he sought understanding first among the Hindu mystics and did not find it. They believed that the *atman* was immortal, bore the marks of a previous existence, and would continue into the further incarnations, bearing marks from the earlier lives. *If one accepts this theory of* atman, *there is no immediate end to suffering; it is merely recycled until one final moment of liberation.* Further, from the Hindu standpoint, the degree of distance from such liberation is represented and articulated in the *varnic scheme:* The higher one's position in the *varna*, e.g., *Brahmin*, the closer one was to liberation. This means that a substantial portion of the populace, at least their *atmans*, must go through several incarnations, before they see the end of their suffering. It was clear, therefore, that not only is the belief in the *atman* the source of selfishness, desire, hatred and so forth, but that the idea of *atman* promotes continuous suffering. Furthermore, it defended the hierarchic *varna* system and placed the Brahmin not only on top in the earthly domain but also in their closeness to redemption from suffering. Clearly a religious path that sought to eliminate suffering immediately had no use for the metaphor of the *atman*.

The Buddha could challenge and refute this system by denying the continuous existence of an *atman* and he did it with logical rigor. There is no continuous existence of an *atta or atman*; there is only a succession of "instantaneous being." Scherbatsky quotes the Buddhist logician Kamalasila on this:

We indeed are perfectly aware that by proving the instantaneous character of Being in general, these (metaphysical) entities would have been *aeo ispo* repudiated. We therefore will proceed to expatiate upon the arguments in proof of this theory in order to (once more) repudiate those entities . . . viz God, Matter, Nature, the Soul, as it is established in different schools. (1962: 80)

The Buddha, however, accepts the *varna* scheme as a description of the organization of society but adds an important proviso that enlarges on the Buddhist metaphor of an ongoing changing phenomenon. "Both bad and good qualities, blamed and praised respectively by the wise . . . are distributed among each of the four classes," quotes Tambiah from the *Agganna Suttanta* and observes "that is, *varna* status does not determine the ethical achievements of individuals" (1976: 10). Individuals in the Buddhist conceptualizations are "free standing" entities whose ethical status is not defined by membership in a *varnic* strata. He or she can alter whatever ethical status he or she was born with by undertaking his or her own steps.

The rejection of *atman* by Buddhism is then ultimately related to its rejection of the Hindu social system of which the concept was the foundation. In other words, it was a rejection of *varna* (caste) hierarchy as related to salvation. "The whole enterprise" of the Buddhist rejection of *atman,* says Mus,

definitely rested on the Brahminical use of the theory of the atman in its sociological and constructive, rather than just psychological and philosophical aspect. This will make it easier to understand why and how Ancient Buddhism, which has substituted its own Moral code and Cosmic Law (dharma) for the abstract *brahman* of the Brahmins and the personal *Isvara (god)* of the Hindus, denounced so radically the practices of the established religion as an instance of the Fallacy of the Self. (1964: 21, quoted in Tambiah 1976: 34)

Buddhism then sought to reject both caste and ritual—the "sociological aspect" as Mus calls it. Max Weber gives an admirable summary of this sociological aspect of Buddhism:

Buddhism, as well as Jainism, first ascended with the support of the city nobles and, above all, the bourgeois patricians. The refusal of priestly knowledge and the intolerable ceremonious rules and regulations for living, the substitutions of the folk language for the incomprehensible dead Sanskrit language, the religious devaluation of caste relations for connubium and social intercourse, bound up with the replacement of the unholy secular priesthood and its power of the keys by strata of holy seekers pursuing an earnest holy life—these were all features which must have gone far to meet lay culture halfway. (1958: 234)

Rejecting ritual, caste, and the dominance of Brahmin priests, Buddhism had to reject the doctrine of the *atman* as well, because the ritual, caste, and Brahminical dominance depended on the existence of an *atman* that continued from one incarnation into another. If there was no *atman* there would be no *varna* because *varna* measured the ethical status of the *atman*; if there was no *atman*, there was no need for rituals and priests because they catered to the *atman*; if there was no *atman* there is also an end to Brahminical dominance, since Brahmins achieve and maintain their dominance by performing rituals.

In fact, a close examination of the doctrine of *anatta* in Buddhism would reveal that this doctrine is systematically expressed in a vocabulary that is a contrast to the ones that define the Hindu *atman*. Since the Hindu *atman* was a metaphor for representing the individual and his or her relationship to a particular social order, the Buddha creates the metaphor of *anatta* or *anatman* by adding a negativising prefix to the Hindu word, to represent an individual and his or her relationship to a different social order. In the presumptive Hindu social order, the *atman* lives continually and carries the social order with it. In the presumptive Buddhist social order the individual experiences a succession of "instantaneous being" and, compared to the Hindu, is able to achieve a comparatively instantaneous salvation as well.

One Buddhist text, the *Visuddhimagga*, gives a striking image to contain this very complex, seemingly contradictory presence of a continuous and changing phenomena:

> While the flame of a lamp does not move over from one wick to another, yet the flame does not, because of that, fail to be produced; so too, while nothing whatever moves over from the past life to this life, nevertheless aggregates, bases, and elements do not fail to be produced here, with aggregates, bases, and elements in the past life as their condition, or in the future life with [those] here as their condition. (quoted in Steven Collins 1982: 187)

Nothing moves over from the past life, nothing that can be defined as *atta* or *atman*, but, nevertheless, "aggregates" of the meaning of the actions in one's life passes into another. Identity in Buddhism is conceived as a flame that flares from moment to moment, bearing both a connection to an earlier moment as well as a uniqueness in a new moment. It is truly the most perfect image of a dialectical approach to the apprehension of self and world that can be conceived.

The "not-soul," i.e., not-*atman* or not-*atta*, is then a system of signs that are defined by opposing them to those that denote "soul," i.e., *atman* or *atta* and are as semiotical as the latter. They are both given expression in the forms available to the culture and are equally trapped in the structure that all human conceiving has to take—that is, according to Peircian rules of thought. Insofar as the self is a product of the discursive practices of the society, these practices are used to identify a self for the acting individual, i.e., a set of *terminologies* by which he or she can make an object of himself or herself. Such an identification can be done at the first level in opposition to other objects that are tangibly concrete and easily defined; at the second level, it can even be done with imaginary but nevertheless *semiotically realized* objects like devils, demons, spirits, and souls. In the Buddhist case, *anatta*, it turns out, is a metaphor for identity, a poetics for conceiving a special kind of identity. The concept with which self is identified in the language game of the Buddhists. *The existence of "self" may be denied doctrinally, yet the denial must be accomplished discursively, thereby achieving a semiotic self.* Annatta in Buddhism is like the zero in mathematics: It represents both a "nothing" and the semiotic presence of the "nothing," the presence of an absence, as it were.

The concept *anatta,* or *anatman* in other words, denying as it does the existence, presence, availability of a continuous entity that transcends time, nevertheless becomes a description of the social self of a believing Buddhist, albeit a self that is in a process of constant formulation and reformulation. It is a metaphor for the identity of the Buddhist as one who repudiates *karma*-based hierarchies of caste and gender and implies a capacity to achieve liberation by one's own efforts in this world. It is a metaphor that represents the view that the human individual is inescapably an ongoing process in which the will of the individual determines his or her destiny. In contrast then to the Hindu view of a settled soul that carries karma and is defined by it, the Buddha uses *anatta* to represent a constantly moving and originating facility.[9]

## Psychoanalytic Identifications

In modern times, the psychological mode of identifying the self and accounting for its presumptive continuity over time and differentiation from others has become dominant. Among these, the Freudian poetics has been very influential—either in its pristine form or in various revisionist versions. Even in the revisions, while some details have been changed or recast, the poetics remain essentially unaltered. They are really variations on central Freudian themes. What, then, are the elements of a Freudian poetics of identity? Here is a representative vignette from Freud:

> We have arrived at our knowledge of this psychical apparatus by studying the individual development of human beings. To the oldest of these mental provinces or agencies we give the name of *id*. It contains everything that is inherited, that is present at birth, that is fixed in the constitution—above all, therefore, the instincts which originate in the somatic organization and which find their first mental expression in the id in forms unknown to us. (1949: 14)

In Freud's thesis the mind is, from the beginning itself, described as consisting of "provinces or agencies": The latter term, not denoting the capacity of an individual to initiate action, but an organization that manages the provinces—perhaps like the "Indian Agency" that used to manage the affairs of Native Americans at one time. By designating the mind as consisting of "provinces," Freud has given a spacious but subdivided territory with which an individual is constituted as an identity. Furthermore, this territoriality is present at birth—i.e., it is inherited like property. The spatial organization is reinforced by the claim that the id "contains" everything that is inherited. The individual now has at his or her disposal the image of a spacious province in which the instincts are contained. This metaphor of a "container" and the phenomenon that is "contained" has already been defined as a "psychical apparatus." The Freudian believer becomes a container or a spatial arena with other inner areas, all of which constitute an item in the apparatus of his or her mind. This province of id, however, is subject to a certain, shall I say, governance, because of another item in the apparatus. Here is the original version:

> Under the influence of the real external world which surrounds us, one portion of the id has undergone a special development. From what was originally a cortical layer, provided with organs for receiving stimuli and with apparatus for protection against excessive stimulation, a special organization has arisen which henceforward acts as an intermediary between the id and the external world. This region of our mental life has been given the name of *ego*. (Freud 1949: 15)

The id is a special "portion" and "region" that, has been transformed into the ego, and will now act as an "intermediary" between the id and the external world. The spatial metaphor reasserts itself here only to give way to that of a diplomat. The id and "the world" are in a state of conflict and the ego emerges as a mediator who will, if not actually eliminate the conflict, serve to contain it. The poetics of containment, of suppression, and of a state of tension between differing forces is carried further in the description of the activities of the ego:

> It has a task of self-preservation. As regards *external* events, it performs the task by becoming aware of the stimuli from without, by storing up experiences of them (in the memory), by avoiding excessive stimuli (through flight), by dealing with moderate stimuli (through adaptation) and, finally by learning to bring about appropriate modifications in the external world to its own advantage (through activity). (Freud 1949: 15)

The imagery of conflict and of territorial invasion is systematically embellished in this description of the ego: One stores up experiences in the memory, but for Freud after that one has to flee from excessive stimuli and *adapt* to moderate stimuli. The stimuli from the external world, then, are not essentially friendly because they demand either flight or adaptation. Even the third alternative—bringing about appropriate modification—implies an a priori unfriendly world that has to be changed to one's own advantage.

The "internal" processes of the ego are no less driven with conflicts and constraints. Here is Freud on the subject:

> As regards internal events, in relation to the id, it performs that task by gaining control over the demands of the instincts, by deciding whether they shall be allowed to obtain satisfaction, by postponing that satisfaction to times and circumstances favorable in the external world or by suppressing their excitations completely. Its activities are governed by consideration of the tensions produced by the stimuli present within it or introduced into it. The raising of these tensions is in general felt as *unpleasure* and their lowering as *pleasure*. (1949: 15–16)

The id and the ego are in conflict once again and experience "tension" in their relationship with the ego endeavoring to suppress the id—a revolt of the instinctual forces, so to speak.

The id gives up a portion of its province to the ego, which in turn, gives a part of its province to the superego. Here is Freud's description of this:

> The long period of childhood, during which the growing human being lives in dependence upon his parents leaves behind a precipitate, which forms within his ego a special agency in which his parental influence is prolonged. It has received the name of superego. Insofar as the superego is differentiated from the ego or opposed to it, it constitutes a fluid force which the ego must take into account.
>
> Thus an action by the ego is as it should be if it satisfies simultaneously the demands of the id, of the superego and of reality, that is to say, if it is able to reconcile their demands with one another. (1949: 16–17)

The superego is a "third force" that is both differentiated from the ego and opposed to it. It is also a precipitate, a residue of the social experiences of the individual that is deposited in the ego. The superego is, in this way, part of the province of the ego but acts as a force within to control and oppose the ego as well. Once again we have an imperious id and superego making *demands,* acting like a creditor or rent collector and being essentially unforgiving. The provinces of the individual's mind are in a state of perpetual conflict, one making demands on the others, often needing diplomatic intermediaries.

The imagery of a primordial id and its relationship to the ego and superego is a dynamic one as well as one that evokes containment and suppression. The superego controls and manages the other two, suppressing them whenever necessary. One has here a system of provincial administrative units—the id supervised by the superego as the supreme legislative council or a monarch. It suppresses rebellions and insurrections but is always aware that these rebellious forces are lurking in the provinces and that they would periodically erupt into public attention. Internally, then, there is this series of containers and the contained, all of them of course being contained in the individual, and insofar as the contained are dynamic and contentious "agencies," the individual must feel jostled a lot.

It is with these images that Freud depicts the socialized human being, and it is these images that become metaphors for the identification of self for adherents of Freudianism. These images constitute—their empirical validity or invalidity notwithstanding—the metaphorical structure of the Freudian identity. Once they accept these poetics of identity, it is an easy next step to constructing identity for self and perhaps for any other hapless individual who may inhabit their social circles. Once this topography of the mind is semiotically constructed it can be readily used to describe and explain the beingness of humans and their actions. Nevertheless, this particular topography of regions and provinces, of segments and enclosures, it appears, needs additional forces to make them move and act. Once a spatial metaphor has been constructed, it must be followed through and filled with a content that will make it full of something. Here Freud delivers the notion of "wishes"—conscious and unconscious—with which these "agencies" were to act. Literate and imaginative as Freud undoubtedly was, his poetics of identity produce a reconfiguration of Greek myths as an elaborate metaphor on which these wishes are hoisted. The Freudian poetics of identity now takes a decidedly romantic turn. Freud writes:

> In my experience, which is already extensive, the chief part in the mental lives of all children who later become psychoneurotics is played by their parents. Being in love with one parent and hating the other are among the essential constituents of the stock of psychical impulses which is formed at that time and which is of such importance in determining the symptoms of the later neuroses. It is not my belief, however, that psychoneurotics differ sharply in this respect from other human beings who remain normal. (1965: 294)

Freud first discusses this discovery in a letter to Fliess. It is described by Ernest Jones "as more than incidental to the theory of dreams since it vividly illustrates the infantile roots of the unconscious wishes animating all dreams" (1965: 226). Freud himself writes that the discovery of the Oedipus complex is "*confirmed* by a legend that came down to us from classical antiquity: a legend whose profound and universal power to move can only be understood if the hypothesis I have put forward in regard to the psychology of children has any validity" (1965: 294, my italics). He then recounts the Oedipus myth as it is rendered in Sophocles' plays.

> The action of the play consist in nothing other than the process of revealing, with cunning delays and ever-mounting excitement—a process that can be likened to the work of psychoanalysis—that Oedipus himself is the murdered of Laius, but further that he is the son of the murdered man and of Jocasta. Appalled at the abomination which he has unwittingly perpetrated, Oedipus blinds himself and forsakes his home. (1965: 295)

The legend is said to "confirm" the "discovery" of the love of one parent and hatred of the other parent and the play itself becomes a metaphor for psychoanalysis. However these various theories are inescapably metaphors with which a therapist and his or her patient, a layman or laywoman who reads these theories and is convinced by them, a social scientist doing field work, or a mythographer analyzing myths and even literary critics, can construct an identity for the individuals in whom they are interested. The theories of Freud, with their rich mythological underpinnings, become then an inexhaustible source for the poetics of identity that any imaginative theorist can use to explain any one's life, times, and the acts thereof.

Many observers of Freud's work have examined the theory of the unconscious and its Oedipal character and rejected it on the grounds that it was unscientific (see von Eckart 1982, McIntyre 1958, Grunbaum 1984). The scientific validity of his interpretation is quite irrelevant in understanding its use in the constitution of identities. Rather, its mythic power, its poetic complexity, and the institutional power that the therapist is able to bear over the patient are enough to elicit a transformation of identity. Consider the essential features of this poetics: (a) It has a very concrete conceptual framework: The story of Oedipus, Jocasta, and Laius, a story whose essential elements others have been able to discover in other narratives as well, not to speak of Freud's own discussion of Hamlet; (b) It contains strong emotive elements—even if an individual has no romance with one parent, unconsciously or consciously, and does not hate the other, to be *told* so by someone in authority, learned and certified, is enough to create strong emotions of many sorts. These features of the theory and the fact that anything one does or says—accidental moves, "slips of the tongue,"—can be given an Oedipal twist, carrying both narrative complexity and emotional leverage as it does, allow it to become as complete and thoroughgoing poetics of identity as one can fashion. For anyone sitting on the edge of Burke's abyss and facing a discursive nothingness, Freudian poetics provides a richly textured and deeply "feelable" identity. Further, to people already disenchanted with religious sources of identity, Freudian poetics is particularly appealing, because it also provides an effective instrumentation for debunking religious poetics. Nevertheless, what Freud achieved was a replacement of one poetic with another.

## METONYMIES OF IDENTITY

Burke describes metonymy as follows:

> the basic "strategy" in metonymy is this: to convey some incorporeal or intangible state in terms of the corporeal or tangible. E.g. to speak of "the heart" rather

than the "emotions." If you trail language back far enough, of course you will find that all our terms for "spiritual" states were metonymic in origin. (Burke 1969a: 506)

In metonymy something that is convoluted, or evanescent and unsubstantial, is transformed into something simpler and substantial. One can find the uses of metonymy in the constructions of identity, in the organization of kinship relations, and in the naming of individuals. Just as each kin-term of address and reference are identifying vocabularies, so are the names given to individuals and each such usage transforms intangible and complex theories into concrete forms. Anthropologists have studied kinship relations as systems that represented structures of relationships that encoded patterns of rights, duties, and obligations and used the prohibition of marriage between certain selected kin as the key to the maintenance of the system. However, one can also consider the kinship system as a source of tropes with which identity is constructed by members of a society.

Take for instance the fact of siblinghood: some people can trace their generation to the same set of parents. These people grow up and get married to those outside the immediate family and generate children of their own. This development demands the use of various tropic strategies to construct an identity: Children of siblings are rendered as "cousins" to each other. In some societies, however, these cousins are further divided into those who are "brothers" and "sisters" and cousins who are not "brothers" and "sisters." This means that cousins who are children of siblings of the opposite sex are said to be marriageable to each other while children of the siblings of the same sex are said to be unmarriageable to each other because they are brothers and sisters. Anthropologists refer to the former as cross-cousins and the latter as parallel-cousins. This arrangement has important consequences to the structure of social relations in communities that practice it as well as to the transfer of property (Fortes 1969: 13–15). It also confers differential identities on the selves of those who are brotherly cousins and sisterly cousins and those who are cousinly cousins. To achieve this, cousins who are brothers and sisters would treat each other as in fact siblings. The terminologies of address as those of reference and reflexivity and answerability will reflect these principles. In this delineation of cross-cousins and parallel-cousins, the idea of "shared blood" will not differentiate their identities; both kinds of cousins have the same "blood" because they have the same ancestors. It is possible, however, to metonymically depict each of them as sharing "blood" from only one parent, the male one. This would mean that children of the siblings of the same sex would have one type of "blood" and children of siblings of the opposite sex would have a different type of "blood." In the first case they would be said to have similar "blood" while in the second case they would be different "blood." Ergo, the latter can get married to each only while the former cannot without violating the rules of incest.

In other words a brother and sister have the same "blood," but once the latter gets married and leaves the ancestral home and lineage, she ceases to share in this "blood" and begins to share the "blood" of her husband's lineage. Hence her children can get married to her brother's children insofar as they no longer share the same "blood." Kenneth David, in a study of the marriage customs of the people of Jaffna, Sri Lanka, discusses this issue thoroughly and quotes an informant thus: "With my sister I share natural substance until marriage do us part." David observes, "Before marriage she is identical in natural bodily substance with her natal family; during the ceremony, she becomes physically identical with her husband and his kinsmen" (1973: 52). If what the sister shares with her brother can be transubstantiated by the wedding ceremony, it was not a natural substance at all, but a symbolic one. Indeed the notion of "bodily substance" or "blood" was being used metonymically to indicate structural relationships and alternating identities. Among the Kabyle of Algeria, as described by Pierre Bourdieu, parallel-cousin marriage—that is, in this case between children of brothers—is officially "preferred" and justified by using "blood" once again metonymically:

> There is praise for the result peculiar to marriage between parallel-cousins, the fact that resulting children ("those whose extraction is unmixed, whose blood is pure") can be attached to the same lineage through their father or their mother. (1972: 44)

A complex structural principle of the kinship system that determined the transfer of property while at the same time constructing communities united and divided by marriage is converted metonymically into a "corporeal and tangible" phenomenon: differentiated blood. The concept of blood becomes a metonymy with which cross-cousins are given separated identities in their relationships to each other while parallel cousins are united. It is not necessarily the case that people literally believe that there is a difference in *blood* between the people in question. Indeed, at the time these rules of marriage were made there was no theory of genetics or hematology available to the people who constructed these theories. And to all appearances the blood and other bodily fluids of these people, however related to each other, would have looked similar. It was not really the physical substance of blood that was the referent in this discourse of kinship, marriage, and incest; rather, blood becomes a trope with which structurally necessary distinctions are made.

Kinship systems, then, are social constructions of structures of relations that given cultures make, but they manifest themselves in the life of individuals as identities on the basis of which they select the various acts with which they conduct themselves through a lifetime. The kinship theory of each such culture, in other words, provides a poetics of identification, a poetics that the individual ignores at his or her peril.[10]

The names given to individuals as they start their passage through life are typically not chosen arbitrarily; rather, they delineate a poetics of identity and are collapsed representations of elaborate theories of self and world. Often these are religious theories, but secular ones abound too. Theories about beginnings of a self, its "rebirth" in this world, ideas about spirituality and continuity of the soul from one life into another life, or, for that matter from a previous life into this life, are all symbolized in the names given to individuals, thus conferring on them by poetic means a selected identity.

The naming process, and the indications of a connection to a genitor or genitrix, indicates a particular representation of descent: This is the son of X. The metaphoricality of paternity can be easily gauged by the fact that the son could have been bought, stolen, or simply adopted and given the identity of the son of this particular father. Or else, for all he knows the biological genitor may have been the gamekeeper. But for all that, the son will bear the father's name in a patrilineal society and inherit his property. The son's identity will be constituted by the *tropicalization* of a relationship, with biology rendered irrelevant. Not yet knowing who he or she is, even what it is, a human child is told who he or she is and this knowledge is a poetical construction. In a nicely emblematic study for this argument, Michael Mbabuike has described the naming practices of the Igbo of Africa as making "philosophical statements" to society. He summarizes his thesis as follows:

> Igbo personal names can consist of words, phrases, wishes, and prayers. They not only signify individuals, but also place the bearer in a particular family lineage and mark a relation to the gods, ancestors and cosmos. Names show dedication to a god or goddess and reflect the achievements of the family. (1996: 47)

From knowing one person's name alone he or she, or an other, can identify him or her with all these details.

Similarly in Hindu societies, names represent not only gender and caste identity but also allusions to particular religious sects and to local gods or goddesses. In a particularly striking instance of metonymic identification, a cobra-worshiping cult in India names children, under certain special circumstances, after the cobra. In communities that practice snake worship, a childless couple will take a vow to install a serpent shrine in their garden if they are given an offspring. This ceremony, "consists in having a figure of a serpent cut in a stone slate, placing it in a cell for six months, giving it life . . . by reciting *mantras* over it and then setting it up under a pipal tree," writes William Francis (1906: 102). Overlooking the Freudian poetics involved in this worship of a snake so as to have children, it appears that if a child is born after these efforts, the child is given a name that alludes to its connection to the cobra—*naga* or *sesha*. The male child will be called for instance, Nagappa, Nageswara, or Seshachalam. The names using *sesha* are double allusions: to the cobra that was worshiped as well as to the myth of the god Vishnu who sits on the head of a serpent called, in fact, *adi-sesha,* the primal serpent. A name like Nageswara or Sheshachalam becomes a reduction of both myth and practice.

Further, among the Tamil Hindus of Sri Lanka and among the Tamils of southern India, the grandson is given the name of the grandfather. Metonymically the grandfather's identity is being recycled and a sense of patrilineal continuity is being registered. In fact grandfather and grandson are referred to as *peran*—a word derived from the Tamil word for name—*peyar,* or *per.* Grandson and grandfather are both referred to as *peran*—a reciprocal identification, signifying that each bears the other's name and is a continuation of the other.

National and ethnic identities can also be seen to be dependent on metonymic processes. One of the commonest forms of identity is that conferred by ethnicity and nationalism. Some of these types of identities evolved over time and manufactured poetics crescively over the years, while others had to be "invented" more deliberately. Hugh Trevor-Roper has shown, for example, how the identity of a "Highlander" was constructed as part of the construction of Scottish nationalism. The "Highland tradition" was an "invented tradition," as Hobsbawn and Ranger (1983) oxymoronically put it, and the invention included a poetics of identity.

This poetics, it appears, defined the Scots as a distinct ethnic group with the custom of wearing distinct kilts that define a clan, with a bardic literature, and with defined territorial limits. This was accomplished in three stages, argues Trevor-Roper:

> First there was the cultural revolt against Ireland: the usurpation of the Irish culture and the rewriting of early Scottish history, culminating in the insolent claim that Scotland—Celtic Scotland—was the "mother nation" and Ireland the cultural dependency. Secondly, there was the artificial creation of new highland traditions, presented as ancient, original and distinctive. Thirdly, there was the process by which these new traditions were offered to, and adopted by, historic Lowland Scotland: the Eastern Scotland of the Picts, the Saxons and the Normans. (1983: 16)

The inventors of the Scottish tradition seemed to have constituted a past for the Scots, a romantic identity as "noble savages" in the years after the suppression of the rebellion of 1745 when they were denigrated as recalcitrant barbarians, as well as constituting a political and military history. Perhaps the most interesting example of the procedures by which an artifact of identity was constituted is Trevor-Roper's account of the emergence of the kilt or "philibeg" as the traditional costume of the Scots. It appears that it was in no way connected to a Highland past. Trevor-Roper observed,

> unknown in 1726, it suddenly appeared a few years later; and by 1746 it was sufficiently well established to be explicitly named in the act of Parliament which then forbade the Highland dress. Its inventor was an English Quaker from Lancashire, Thomas Rawlinson. (1983: 21)

Once it was thus "invented," it was given a general status by being adopted by the newly formed Highland regiments, a move initiated and encouraged by the elder Pitt, Prime Minister of England. Trevor-Roper writes, "Having been invented by an English quaker industrialist, it was saved from extinction by an English imperialist statesman. The next stage was the invention of a Scottish pedigree. This stage was at least undertaken by the Scots" (1983: 26).

The Scottish "inventors," John McPherson and James McPherson, the Quaker Rawlinson and the elder Pitt—the former two wittingly and the latter two unwittingly—metonymically constituted the identity of the "Highlander Scots." One, they created a past and a pedigree: The Highlanders were descended from an ancient and savage, but noble, people fiercely independent and proud. A large and complex and contradictory past was reduced to the "noble Highlanders." Two, they were given a physical presence and a collective self by the invention and use of a special form of appearance through clothing: the philibeg henceforth would stand for the noble Highlander Scots. Three, a demarcated territory was constituted as Scotland by overlooking—i.e. reducing—various recalcitrant elements of the past and connecting this land to the new identity.

## SYNECDOCHES OF IDENTITY

Synecdoche, Burke notes, encompasses

> such meanings as: part for the whole, whole for the part, container for the thing contained, sign for the thing signified, material for the thing made . . . cause for effect, effect for cause, genus for species, species for genus, etc. All such conversions imply an integral relationship, relationship of convertibility, between the two terms. . . . "The noblest synecdoche," the perfect paradigm or prototype for all lesser usages is found in metaphysical doctrines proclaiming the identity of "microcosm" and "macrocosm." In such doctrines, where the individual is treated as a replica of the universe and vice-versa we have the ideal synecdoche. (1969a: 507–508)

Among the many synecdochic identificatory processes, I will discuss the acts by which the whole is represented by a part or, to put it differently, a single term that summarizes a complex whole is used to identify an individual.

This kind of identification occurs routinely in everyday speech. Claims to being a "Christian" or "Buddhist" or "Jew" are really synecdochic forms of identification. In these single terms and simple words, an individual's religious life, ritual life, values, the food he or she may eat, whom he or she is likely to marry or eat with, when he or she may eat, perhaps where he or she lives in some cases, and various other characteristics are denoted and an identity conferred on him or her. Conversely, insulting and belittling terms use synecdochic processes to identify individuals. One of the most widely used synecdoches of identity in this regard is in the abusive terminologies of everyday life. In denoting another either in anger or contempt, individuals often resort to calling him or her by allusions to sexual organs. Ethnic insults too often reduce an individual's complexity to particular racial characteristics. Stigmatizing identities of every kind are in fact synechdochic identifications: homosexuality, criminal acts from the past, or insane episodes confer an identity on an individual that obliterates all other attributes of his or her self, and he or she becomes reduced to being a "queer," a "con," or a "nut." *The essential quality of this process of identification is the use of a selected singular aspect of the individual to overshadow the rest of his or her self.* A man may be convicted of embezzlement once in his life; he may serve a period of time in jail and may even make good on the money he had embezzled. Nevertheless, he will be identified for relevant purposes as an embezzler and convict. Goffman expresses this with his usual flair:

> In all of these various instances of stigma . . . the same sociological features are found: an individual who might have been received easily in ordinary social intercourse possesses a trait that can obtrude itself upon attention and turn those of us whom he meets away from him, breaking the claim that his other attributes have on us. . . . We construct a stigma-theory, an ideology to explain his inferiority and account for the danger he represents sometimes rationalizing an animosity based on other differences such as social class. (1963: 4–5)

The trait is first isolated and then used to cover his or her entire self: i.e., a part of the individual is used to cover the whole. This is apparently in stark contrast to the identificatory process among the Chinook Indians. If a man kills a child in most civilizations, he will be referred to as "a murderer," a "bad man" who killed the "poor child." The Chinook, however, would render this identification as follows: "The man's badness killed the child's poverty," Boas reports (1911: 657). Levi-Strauss uses this example to support his claim that "primitive people" are, after all, capable of abstract thought (1966: 1). However, this case from Boas illustrates something else as well: The Chinook way for identifying a man who has committed what would be considered murder in certain other societies is by attributing its causation *not to his whole self* but to some element in it called "badness." The Chinook attribute his act to a part of him, his "badness" implying that there are other aspects to his self, even perhaps some "goodness." The act of murdering a child, a violation of the norms of the society, is not overlooked or forgiven but the causal source is found, not in the total individual, but discovered in a reduced aspect of this totality. A complex phenomenon—the murder—is attributed to a simple source—badness. His self would not be coterminus with this act. Hence condemning the person to death—that is the whole person to die—would be unthinkable for the Chinook. In the synecdochic identificationary process in Western society, the one act will be allowed to define his whole self—indeed his "personality." The single act will be taken as representing his whole person and he will be conferred an identity with its help. He may be executed on the basis of this act. If he is not executed he will be imprisoned and every aspect of his life henceforth will be affected by this act. His social circles will remember this act and use it in their relationship with him. In Chinook society, the whole is broken into casually significant parts, whereas in modern Western society the part is taken to represent the whole. Synecdochic identification often occurs in individuals diagnosed as being mentally ill. Here is a succinct description of this reported by Kaysen:

> The patient suffered an episode of depersonalization on Saturday for about six hours at which time she felt she wasn't a real person, *nothing but skin*. She talked about wanting to cut herself to see whether she would bleed to prove to herself that she was a real person. She mentioned she would like to see an X-ray of herself to see if she had any bones or anything inside. The precipitating event for this episode of depersonalization is still not clear. (1993: 105; emphasis added)

This an excerpt from the doctor's report on Susanna Kaysen that she reproduces in her wonderfully observed and stylishly recounted description of the months she spent in a mental institution. The report talks of her "depersonalization." It should also have mentioned her "repersonalization" as merely skin, of her reduction of her whole self and body to "nothing but skin."

If this patient experienced this synecdochic depersonalization and repersonalization unwittingly, occasioned by an unrecognized precipitating event, there are others who reduce their identities more deliberately. In certain religious discourses one can find claims that the human is "only" a soul, the rest as irrelevant or unnecessary or illusory. Here is Appar, a medieval Hindu saint and poet giving us two versions of his identity:

1

When I consider this vile human life,
Wasted in filling up the stomach
Which is like a bottomless pit of the sea,
I cry out in pain.

2

Five fools dwell inside me,
driving me to despair—
I, your servant, cannot live with these,
Oh, lord of the Mūlaṭṭam shrine in Ārur.

(Peterson 1989: 253)

Here, a devotee of Siva, the deity at the Mūlaṭṭam shrine, is appealing to him for release from the earthly cycle of existence. He describes his self, identifies it, as a "body," and the body itself is defined by the appetite for food so that he is really only a "stomach," a "bottomless pit." He then expands the description of his self to include the "five fools"—that is, the five senses. He describes himself reductively as consisting of the five senses that dwell inside him and drive him to despair. Here is another such verse of identification from Appar:

> There is nothing to hold together
> This worm-infested frame
> Covered with skin, with nine leaky holes.
> Five rogues sit within
> And torment me.
> Utterly ruined, I cannot live with them any more,
> Oh Lord of the Mūlattam shrine in Ārur!
> (Peterson 1989: 253)

Here again the poet is identifying himself with only the five senses and alludes also to a claim that his body is nothing but "skin" and "frame" with nothing inside them but the five hated senses. The irrelevance of the body in the cosmic scheme of identification in Saivite Hinduism is rendered synecdochically in these verses. Self, consciousness, the passions, and existence, are all reduced to the five senses from which the devotee seeks an escape for his eternal *atman*.

## IRONY AND IDENTITY

Burke writes about irony as follows:

> Irony arises when one tries, by the interaction of terms upon one another, to produce a *development* which uses all the terms. Hence from the standpoint of this total term (this "perspective of perspectives") none of the participating sub-perspectives can be treated as either precisely right or precisely wrong. They are all voices, or personalities, or positions, integrally affecting one another. When the dialectic is properly formed, they are the number of characters needed to produce the total development. (1969a: 512)

In the formation of identity, too, this ironic relationship of one voice, one position, or personality is used poetically to establish a dialectic with other voices, positions, and personalities. The relevant identity emerges as a contrast and displacement of another identity, a challenge, and a refutation that criticizes the other as it defines itself in opposition to it.

While the construction of such identities can occur in everyday life, I will use examples from three different but connected arenas: the carnival, the circus, and the medieval court. In carnivals one will often find a performer who can be identified as the "fool," in circuses one invariably finds "clowns," and in the medieval court one would encounter a "jester." Though these terms—the fool, the clown, and the jester have been often used interchangeably, I will use them here to refer to ironic performers in each of these arenas. The comments about one, however, may apply to the others as well in many instances.

## Fools

Carnivals were mass participatory events in which all sectors of society participated. "Carnival is not a spectacle seen by people; they live in it and everyone participates because its very idea embraces all the people," wrote Mikhail Bahktin in a pioneering study of the phenomenon (1984: 7). For him the carnival was part of a larger structure of folk culture that included the following:

(a) Ritual spectacles—carnival pageants, comic shows of the marketplace.
(b) Comic verbal compositions—parodies, both oral and written, in Latin and in the vernacular.
(c) Various genres of billingsgate—curses, oaths, popular blazons. (1984:5)

All of these elements of the folk culture challenge, by ironic means, the official culture. Bakhtin continues,

> As opposed to the official feast one might say that carnival celebrated temporary liberation from the prevailing truth and from the established order; it marked the suspension of all hierarchical ranks, privileges, norms and prohibitions. (1984: 10)

One of the ways in which the established order was put in ironic perspective was in the pageants that were presented. One standard figure in these pageants was the fool. Who is a fool? A fool is one who systematically, in verbal and visual presentations, makes comments on the established order. In fact, he represents disorder, refutation, parody, and unseriousness to a world of seriousness and orderliness. Among the many manifestations of the fool in carnivalesque pageants, the one that has elicited the greatest attention is the "Lord of Misrule."

One characteristic of the Lord of Misrule was that he was expected to challenge standard roles and conventions. One easy approach to handle this reversal of rules and roles was to dress up as a woman and act like one or adopt clothes that were unusual and striking in comparison to the clothes usually worn by the people of the community. The appearance of people and the types of clothes that they were expected to wear was not a matter over which an individual had too much freedom of choice in the medieval period. In medieval European society a person was expected to wear clothes appropriate to his or her rank. This was defined by what were known as "sumptuary laws" and strict punishment was meted out to those who disobeyed them (Baldwin 1926).

To defy these laws and customs and wear the costumes of the bishop or the pope or that of king, as many did during carnivals, constituted a parody, an ironic comment on the real institutions of the church and the monarchy. The costuming and the words and the general performance of the "Lord of Misrule" was a parody of the real lords and bishops and in fact succeeded in defining their roles and rules more vividly for the masses. The ironic reversals emphasized the real roles and implied the consequences of the absence of these roles: misrule, anarchy, disorder.

## Clowns

The clowns in a circus again are ironic identities that define an antithesis by managing and seemingly mismanaging words, gestures, and moves. The very world and structure of the circus represents a circle, the endless line, the cosmic circle, the container of the things of the world. Within this circle one finds represented a multitude of phenomena from the real world. To begin with, there are the animal acts: Animals are displayed but always under varying degrees of submission to humans. There are the elephants: huge but docile and obedient, and performing picturesque tricks on command from keepers. Then there are the tigers and lions, baring their teeth, snarling in anger but still under the control of a human being.

Second, there are the acrobats and high-wire artists. They display great balance and coordination and seeming indifference to the dangers of falling and getting maimed or killed. The very existence of the bipedal human is a triumph of balance and coordination and the acrobats and high-wire performers display this and celebrate it with wonderful impudence.

In fact, in the circle of the circus one finds represented the human mastery of the world, a synecdoche of the dominion that the Judeo-Christian God gave to man. It also represents the evolutionary emergence of the human as the captain of the world, the triumph of culture over nature, the celebration of willful acts of balance, and even control and defiance of the pull of gravity, by adroit manipulations and coordinated moves.

It is in the midst of these manifestations of control, management and mastery, and order and decorum, that the clowns make their appearance. They represent the *grotesque,* the presence of which in cultures has been noticed by many scholars. Sowers has identified three basic forms of the grotesque: the monster, the orifice, and the maelstrom. It is the maelstrom that the clown represents, a representation manifest in his clothing. Nelson quotes Sowers's description of the maelstrom as a condition or situation, full of chaos, claustrophobic jamming, nightmarish atmosphere, dark background, all sorts of contrary, extremely unpleasant, disordered conditions which suggest a world of *depravity* and *disorder*. (Nelson 1981: 202)

Whereas all these adjectives may not apply to the clown, some of them do—for example, chaos, jamming, disorder. These words describe the activities of the clown and this is represented, to begin with, in his costume. The clown represents the grotesque antithesis of the man and woman on the high-wire. He does tricks that are reversals of the organized world. He is lewd and indecorous at times, and he keeps falling down often, showing that is he is unable to keep his balance. And he looks disordered, disproportionate, violating the ratio of color and design and shape. In fact, everything about his presence is exaggerated and out of kilter.

The artists on the high-wire are different from this: Their acts are not magical or mysterious and do not defy conventional logic. They are decorous, orderly, never lewd, often romantic, and above all, they keep their balance. They are triumphant and orderly human beings, arrogant in their various masteries, always in control. This is recreated in their attire: light leotards, chest-hugging and form-fitting vests. They are simple, efficient, parsimonious, and in harmony with the contours of the human form.

The clown and the acrobat in the circus are presentations that challenge and refute the other and manifest in their respective acts and appearances, disorder and order respectively. The ironic challenge and refutation posed by the clowns to order and its refutation is, however, merely superficial: At a structural level they help define order and bring it into relief.

Clowning, however, is not confined to circuses: It is found in the theater and cinema as well. Among modern clowns, the supreme ironist is Charlie Chaplin. He claimed to have represented the average man who does not cut a

dashing figure as he blunders through a drab and commonplace existence. . . . Then he sees me shuffling along in my baffled and aimless manner and a spark of hope rekindles. Here is a man like himself, only more pathetic and miserable, with ludicrously impossible clothes—in every sense a social misfit,

wrote Chaplin about his own art (in Bowman 1931). Charlie Chaplin may well appeal to the masses because he represents the vicissitudes that such a man faces in everyday life, but Chaplin's theme in the movies he made were ironic critiques and satirical comments on the society of his times and his very appearance was made to indicate this. To begin with, his jacket is always too small for him and his trousers are always too large. He wore a tie and carried a cane. In using these items Chaplin on the screen is not an average man but one aspiring to be a gentleman, perhaps even a dandy. His ill-fitting clothes and his aspirations establish the first set of ironic contrasts, an internal one in respect to his clothes and an external one in respect to the accouterments of a well-dressed gentleman: His clothes are disproportionate, but "correct." Second, he sets up another violation of ratios by presenting himself as one with courtly manners and graceful and elegant mannerisms—a tramp with grace and courtliness. This again sets up a dialectic with his appearance internally and with manners and mannerisms of a gentleman externally. His shuffle is often in contrast to his dancelike movements at other times: Here is an elegant gentleman who is at odds with a society that spurns him, denies him his fulfillment as a father, lover, adventurer, and machine-worker.

The ironic representation of the identity in effect "speaks" to the other identity, by the "interaction of the terms" of the two identities—the clownish one and the serious one, to produce a "development," to use Burke's words (1969a: 512). The difference between the clown—down and out, seedy, pathetic—Chaplin seems to be saying, and the real gentleman dandy is after all a small one. The dignified tramp was truly the tramp as a dandy, conveying the emergent signification that a tramp was perhaps only recently a dandy and that the dandy may well become a tramp soon.

## Jesters

The work of Norbert Elias has demonstrated the inner structure of medieval and early modern European courts. Such households, for example the one of Louis XIV, was grand in every sense of the term. The Chateau of Versailles contained 10,000 persons, including servants and soldiers. The nobility lived in apartments close to the king's chambers and insofar as the nobility itself was organized on the principle of hierarchy the relations among them were carried on the basis of elaborate etiquette and ceremony. Elias considers such etiquette and ceremony themselves as functions of the power structure of society. One feature of this etiquette was the costuming of the members of the court in terms of such power and status. A good description of the manner of costuming and its connection to decorum comes from the chronicles of another court—that of Henry IV. A would-be-courtier is told:

> You require a doublet made of four or five layers of different taffetas; stocking, such as you see, frieze and scarlet, accounting I assure you for eight ells of cloth at least; then you need boots, the flesh side outermost, the heel very high and the spur slippers also high. . . . The spurs must be gilded. . . . When thus attired you have arrived in the Louvre courtyard—one alights between the guards you understand— you begin to laugh at the first person you meet, you salute one and say a word to another. . . (Elias 1983: 231)

The costuming at court was an essential move in the choreography of status and honor that was essential for it to function smoothly. This elaborate visual dance of status and honor achieved a number of significations: It recreated in miniature a social order that was based on hierarchical differentiations; it mimified the nuances and subtleties of differences in status and honor among the members of the court, and it functioned to maintain the interaction order.

In this society of people with orchestrated appearances there were a few, usually one or two, who were dressed in strikingly different styles. These were the jesters and in Enid Welsford's words, they were apparelled in a way that

> emphasized folly. In the manner of clothing there was great variety; red and green seem to have been favorite colors and were frequently arranged in checks and it is possible that Haincelin was sometimes dressed in conventional motley suits. ([1935]1966: 119)

This suit, a long petticoat-like garment that came to be called "the jesters coat," was adopted widely, and is mentioned in the journal of another famous medieval jester in the Stuart King James's court—Archibald Armstrong, also called "Count Archie." A writer of the period described Archie as follows: "The bright eye-dazzling mirror of mirth, pump of pastimes, spurt of sport, regent of ridiculous confabulations" (Welsford 1966: 174). It is clear that a coat of many colors is being described and the term "jesting coat" identifies the liberties that the wearing of the garment confers on the wearer. If in his verbal thrusts he engages in a "licensed impudence" (Welsford 1966: 173), in appearance, too, he displays the same impudence. In addition to this motley coat, the jesters also wore "eared caps" and caps with a cockscomb, also known as the foolscap, and carried bells and other such objects with them. Nevertheless, the jester's role was essentially a discursive one. He was adept in the manipulation and management of words to good effect. His style was in fact discursive impudence, a systematic violation of the rules of decorum, civility, face values, honor, role, while the courtiers were defined by the observance of these very rules. The correspondence between rules of speech and rules of costuming become clear: Impudence in speech is paralleled by impudence in clothing and accessories. Here too, the differentiation between the orderly and decorous on the one hand and that of the disorderly and impudent on the other enables a hierarchy to emerge with orderliness defined and established as a high value for the society. The jesters participate as the other, the differentiating feature, that establishes a hierarchy between the king and the subject.

In everyday life today, as in earlier times, these poetic devices are systematically used to constitute ironic and rebellious identities. Perhaps the most striking use of such poetics of identification to reject and satirize established societies in recent times was undertaken by the "peace movement" of the 1960s, which soon crystallized into lifestyle under the rubric of "hippies." Their lifestyle was characterized by passionate commitment to be different from the people of the established order, and one of the ways in which they sought to do this was to look different and talk differently. A poetics of identity was used systematically to *ironize* the members of the established order and define a self by the management of clothing, hairstyles and language.

The established order they were challenging and repudiating was one that still bore the marks of American Protestantism and the ethic of efficiency and parsimony, of restraint and discipline, that successful business demanded. The women's clothes were of somber colors, trimly cut, and not given to extravagant frills and bounces. The men wore "business" suits that used dark colors, thin ties and, more often than not, button-down shirts—all representing a decorous restraint and emotional control. These were in fact the poetics of Protestant identity, features of what John Murray Cuddihy (1978) has called "Protestant Taste." While the appearance of these people was a far cry from the one that Robert Motherwell painted in "Homely Protestant," there were vestiges of this Protestant plainness and simplicity in the business attire of the dominant Americans. While many in the society flouted it, the dominant value-system or rather the value-system of those who dominated government, business and academia, accepted it.[11]

For the peace movement and the hippies it was these values that took the United States into the war; it was these people who were urging them to go and fight, kill, and die overseas; it was the institutions that these people created and ran that discriminated against black people, exterminated Native Americans, and so on. The life style, appearance, and identity were all equated with oppression, warmongering, greed and self-aggrandizement.

The need of the hour then was for a new set of values and a new identity that demanded a new poetics of identification. Does the establishment preach restraint? Let us have profligacy, licentiousness, lasciviousness, freedom. Does the establishment practice sobriety in everyday life? Let us drink, get stoned, turn on, tune out. Does the establishment wear somber clothes, neutrally shaded, disciplined, corsetted, and buttoned-down? Let us have a mad rush of colors, shapes, and designs that are eye-catching and sexually suggestive and inviting, loosely structured, and flamboyant. Does the establishment indicate control and restraint by cutting the hair short, often to a military shortness, to a crew cut, keeping it "groomed" and "orderly"? Let us have long hair, luxuriant and seductive, representing mad passions and wild ecstasies. Does the bourgeoisie live controlled and disciplined lives? Let us then live without control and restraint; let us live orgiastically. Does the establishment use "decorous" language, avoid allusions to bodily functions and sexuality? Let us make allusions to them as adjectives, adverbs, and nouns as often as we can. Orgiastic living was paralleled by orgiastic language.

These strategies of identification, then, represented a critique and a rejection of the established order by a visual and verbal poetry and the production of an ironic alternative. The everyday speech of the rebels in fact constituted a rejection of the standards of "decorum" and "good taste" that the establishment had prescribed and used to define itself. The rebels, now liberated from these constraints, were free to use obscenities and scatologies in their everyday discourse in public and private. Political and religious blasphemy were also now accepted as part of the discourse. For instance, a radical weekly published a cartoon of a number of policemen pulling down the Statue of Liberty and raping it. The flag of the United States was demeaned in many ways: It was burned, made into underwear, and thereby desecrated. In rendering the flag into underwear, the poets of identity were using an ancient technique. Bakhtin calls this practice "grotesque realism," whose

> essential principle is degradation, that is the lowering of all that is high, spiritual, ideal, abstract. . . . To degrade is to bury, to sow, and to kill simultaneously in order to bring forth something more and better. To degrade also means to concern oneself with the lower stratum of the body, the life of the belly and the reproductive organs, it therefore relates to acts of defecation and copulation, conception and pregnancy and birth. (1984: 19; 21)

Wearing the flag of the United States as underwear and displaying it to an audience constituted an ironic challenge to the sanctity of the flag. It also defined the wearer as an outsider and a critic, as the costumes of the fools of the carnival did.

These verbal infelicities and blasphemies have earlier parallels, too. During the upheavals associated with the Protestant Reformation, anti-Catholics would go into churches and perform various acts that were meant to repudiate religious doctrines. Robert Scribner reports one telling incident that occurred on the eve of Ash Wednesday in 1560:

> During Mass, the local innkeeper had run into the church dressed in a fool's costume. He took up the holy-water vessel, placed it on the altar and "made his offering in it," perhaps a euphemism for urinating in it. As each person approached to take communion, as was customary, he struck them on the buttock with a whip. (1988: 122)

Similarly during the English Reformation, cults known as the "ranters" emerged who used blasphemy and sexual liberties to reject the established system. Jerome Friedman summarizes their views:

> Religious institutions were a sham and God was within you. There was no heaven, no hell, and hence no need to live as if there were. All governance and property were theft, corruption and extortion. All institutions emanated from and fostered class dominance and were thus of no significance to the poor Englishman. There was neither licit or illicit forms of behaviors, just deeds. (1987: xi)

Rejecting established practices of worship and domestic life, Richard Coppin preached against all institutionalized forms of worship and domesticity. Abiezer Coppe, another ranter, advocated sexual libertarianism and denied that anyone has a right to practice "sexual exclusivity" as in marriage and monogamy (Friedman 1987: 75–96). The challenge to the established order was complete. Nevertheless, the new identities being cultivated by these practices were dependent on the established ones and were essentially ironic reversals of them. The ranting and blasphemies were ironic reversals of the sanctity and awe with which certain words and practices of the church were treated by the faithful.

These, then, were strategies of identification of self, achieved verbally and materially. The hippies in this country, as others in earlier epochs, sought to constitute themselves by establishing a dialectic of irony with established values and practices. In medieval pageants and courts and circuses, the fools, jesters, and clowns were one, or a few, among many. The hippies, however, constituted a *social movement of jesters*, encompassing masses of people who made ironic and dialectical rejection of a society's established values into a style of living. The establishment, however, had the last, no doubt ironic, laugh: it co-opted many of the features of the movement into a style and bourgeoisiefied it.

Ironic constitution of identities then bears a dialectical relationship to an other and speaks in many voices simultaneously. It speaks the voice of rejection of the other while simultaneously helping to define the other in sharper contours by offering a contrast. It speaks the voice of excess and arbitrariness while also exposing the value of restraint and discipline that the other represents. It also voices approbation and exultation in its excesses while implicitly and explicitly criticizing the other. The styles adopted by the ironists for their clothing and hair and the stylization of the diction used in everyday conversations provided the poetics by which complex attitudes and emotions could be articulated.

## NOTES

1. For a discussion of Sanskritic theories of meaning, see Kunjunni Raja (1963). Tzvetan Todorov has discussed Abhinavagupta's work in his examination of symbolism and interpretation (1982). For a contemporary study of the "rule of metaphor" see Ricoeur (1981). Richard Harvey Brown has also argued very forcefully that sociology itself was entrapped in its own "poetics" (1977).

2. In using "representative anecdotes," Burke observes "Men seek vocabularies that will be faithful reflections of reality. To this end, they must develop vocabularies that are selections of reality. And any selection of reality must, in certain circumstances, function as a deflection of reality" (1969a: 59). Nevertheless, he explains, "One should seek to select, as representative anecdotes something sufficiently demarcated in character to make analysis possible, yet sufficiently complex in character to prevent the use of too few terms in one's description" (1969a: 324). I think the creation myth, the story of Jesus' birth, his baptism, and his death meet these criteria for being representative anecdotes.

3. All quotations from the Bible are from the Authorized King James version, published by the New American Library.

4. Perhaps all narratives in the Christian world, major ones or trivial ones, that feature an interaction between men and women represent a version of the Eve and Adam and serpent myth: from Samson and Delilah to *Anna Karenina*, to *Madame Bovary*, to *Rebecca* and to various movies and sitcoms. It was certainly not a fit of absentmindedness that made the writer of a Hollywood movie about a scheming and manipulative protagonist name her "Eve" in a movie that was called "All about Eve." See Daly (1973) for a trenchant analysis of the implications of this myth.

5. "Hindu" and Hinduism are of course broad summarizing terms for what is really an array of beliefs and practices, some of them complementary with each other and some not, accepted and used by people living in India. The words brahaman and brahmin refer to different entities, the former to the progenitor in the creation myth and the latter to the highest caste among the Hindus. Often certain authors spell these words in the same way.

6. Many contemporary sects do not perform these rituals of renunciation today in all their completeness. Swami Yogananda, in his autobiography, reports that the last two stages were not practiced in his renunciatory process. The guru accepted him, gave him a new name, and a new set of yogic garments (1977).

7. One place where this poetic of identification is displayed vividly, or one may say is enacted, is in the consultation that a devout Hindu periodically undertakes with an astrologer. The astrologer will ask for his time and place of birth and sometimes he would study his palm as well. From this information, the astrologer will produce a document that was originally inscribed on palm leaves but is now available in print, a record of the *atman's* past lives, his present one and how it is going to unfold in the immediate future, and its destiny after death. The *atman* is the continuous factor in this transmigration. One's body changes from one's birth to death but *atman* remains the same and participates in experiencing a continuous identity. See Perinbanayagam (1982) for a study of astrology and its relationship to the karmic destiny of the *atman*.

8. The Sanskrit term for this entity is *atman* and Sanskrit is the language in which Hindu texts were composed. Pali is the language of Buddhism and, though it is a derivative of Sanskrit, it contains many variations in terminology. The word that is equivalent to *atman* is *atta*. Putting a negativising prefix to these two words will give us *anatman* and *anatta*. In my discussion of Buddhist identity I have chosen to use both in order to avoid confusion and to suggest that they are related concepts.

Buddhist logicians would no doubt hold this semiotization of *anatta* as evidence of "avidya"—ignorance. For Buddhism there is an absolute separation between language and reality. Fabio Rambelli notes, "According to a well established traditional doctrine, quoted in some Buddhist *sutras*, the words of ordinary language are i) related to superficial aspects of phenomena. ii) uttered in dreams. iii) conditioned by fallacious attachment to wrong ideas. iv) forever conditioned by the seeds of suffering" (1995: 11). Logically, such an understanding of ordinary language would have to exclude the discourses of the Buddha. It was claimed that "the Buddha does not speak, and conveyed his experience in a non-linguistic way," and "that the Buddha, on the basis of his states of consciousness, uses a peculiar language consisting in special systems of signs, which is possible to know and understand" (Rambelli 1995: 11).

This exclusion of the Buddha's words from semiotic imperatives is but another example of the casuistry in which Indian mystics and logicians were very adept.

9. There is a certain similarity between the Buddhist view of the self as an ongoing process and those of the American pragmatists. Kalupahana (1987) has investigated this connection but he focuses exclusively on the work of William James, whereas the work of G. H. Mead would have proved more fruitful. Sue Hamilton has examined the textual material of early Buddhism and concluded that the constitution of the human being "is understood and thought by the Buddha in terms of processes and events" (1996: 194). She also notes, "I would like to suggest here that the doctrine of *anatta* is not intended to be a denial of being as implied in the English, 'There is no self'" (1996: 195). For an account of the beginnings of Buddhism that situates its emergence in a sociohistorical context, see Kogen Mizuno (1982).

10. Pierre Bourdieu (1980: 143–209) has also shown how different transformations are involved in organizing marriages between parallel-cousins and the varied and complex *social uses* to which these "poetics" can be put.

11. See John Murray Cuddihy (1978) for further discussions of what he calls "Protestant Taste" and "Protestant Etiquette" and comments on the Motherwell painting itself.

# III

## The Self in Action

# Chapter 5

# Speaking of the Self

May my speech be one with my mind, and may my mind be one with my speech, O, thou my self-luminous, Brahman.

*The Upanishads*

Human individuals who enter into interactions with others have a history and complex memories and are, typically, neither amnesiacs nor aphasics. They are able to identify, not only others but themselves as well, and enter into conversations as selves. Individuals, on the basis of this knowledge of their selves and whatever knowledge they have of the others with whom they are interacting, make what are usually well-founded assumptions and open and conduct conversations on that basis. Not only are they able to identify the other, but are able to assess the *relative standing* they have vis-à-vis the other and conduct the opening and the subsequent business accordingly. By "standing" I refer here to two features of interaction. First is, the relative social, economic, and political status of the participants, the "social space" they happen to be occupying (Clark 1990). In every human encounter, one participant is of higher status—stands bigger, taller, stronger, more articulate, more powerful politically, richer, prettier, older, younger, and so on than the other. Further, in each encounter one may know the other very well, only slightly, or be totally unacquainted with him or her. If the speaker ignores these factors as he or she opens the conversation and fails to incorporate them into his or her opening gambits and keep faith with them during the ensuing proceedings, he or she would not be able to conduct a successful conversation. Indeed, to ignore them blatantly one would receive negative sanctions—including the label of insanity. One can say that such statements would lack the requisite addressivity and would not be able to elicit the commensurate answers. This knowledge that one has of the other is also typically colored by emotionality: The earlier encounters may have been pleasant and warm and fulfilling, in which case the opening may

185

be easier, or else it may have been unpleasant, insulting, or cold, and the opening becomes more problematic.

Further, in opening a conversation there is always the issue of who is to make the first move. While this poses no difficulty with people who know each other well, when individuals of slight acquaintance come together this problem does arise. In some societies this is settled by rules based on gender and social status—women, servants, or lower-class people have to wait for the higher-status person to open the conversation. If these rules do not dictate the opening move, it can be made by either party. Once the conversation is opened, the one who opened it faces certain risks. He or she may be ignored, rebutted, openly insulted, or even assaulted. On the other hand, the opening gambit may elicit validating responses, but they may be either "barren" ones or "fertile" ones. In the former, the response is lukewarm, conceptually impoverished, and discouraging of further conversational moves, while in the latter the response invites further conversation (Perinbanayagam 1991:83– 84). In other words, when one opens a conversation he or she puts a self into play and the manner in which it is received has consequences to it. Every move in a conversation is aimed at allowing the other to enter the perspective of the initiator and inviting the other to allow the initiator to enter the other's perspective. *This creates the conditions for the emergence of the objective reality of perspectives—including the objective reality of the selves involved.* Such a reality is remembered and shared with others, who remember it too, and used to conduct the affairs of everyday life.[1]

Once an individual has opened a conversation and put his or her self on the line the implications of the ensuing talk to the self are magnified—the self can be diminished or enhanced (Goffman 1967:37–38). It is in such encounters where talk is exchanged that a human lives and dies. "Talk," as Boden and Zimmerman put it unchallengeably, "is at the heart of everyday existence. It is pervasive and central to human history, in every setting of human affairs, at all levels of society, in virtually every social context" (1991: 3). An individual is present in the world in fact in and through conversations—though not all such conversations are dialogical. It is in such conversations that an individual becomes and continues to remain a self. It is the talk that he or she makes and receives, the conversation to which he or she is a party, that gives a presence to an individual's self. When one speaks, he or she is speaking a self and when one listens, he or she is listening as a self and to a self. In such speakings, one gives "voice" to the self, and a dialogic voice at that, since the discursive acts that an individual produces will take account of the other and anticipatorily and reflexively incorporate the other into the acts. He or she does not, indeed cannot, speak as an unmemoried and isolated individual insofar as that the very words that he or she would be obliged to use are already socially and culturally constituted ones (Bakhtin 1981: 294).

To be present in the world of others, to be socially and interactionally alive and to be a self in a community of others, one must present discursive acts and receive them, listen to them, attend to them, and, sooner or later, provide a returning act. If he or she is unable to do this, then it can be said that he or she is socially and interactionally absent, *unselfed,* socially dead. If he or she is allowed to present only a minimal number of such acts, he or she is only minimally present and, conversely, those who dominate conversations are present in a maximal way. An individual can then be said to be able to speak a self into presence, have it validated, listen to others, validate the selves of the others, and feel the presence of self in varying saliences and outspokennesses and emotionalities, obtaining thereby a place for itself in the world. Such a presence can be discovered by examining the semiotic import of the verbal productions that are carried in the syntactic, structural, and, wherever possible, phonological arrangements.

Such a place for the self is obtained by using conversational moves—the initiation of conversations, their conduct and continuation, and their termination—to form interactions, groups, and communities. Interactions, groups, and communities can be discovered as existents by an observer but, for all that, they have to be systematically constituted and conducted by their various participants. Such associational forms are *strategies* that an individual uses to get through the day and get through a life, *adjustive instrumentations* for these purposes. Indeed an individual may have as many such associations as the life-purposes he or she wants to pursue and in each association he or she must act to first construct it and then maintain it. This is accomplished by speaking to the others, by entering and sustaining and terminating conversations. An individual does not, needless to say, open conversations, introduce a topic, interrupt the other or allow him or her to have his or her turn, overlap with it, and close a conversation for any other purpose than to construct interactions, relationships, and communities. These features of a conversation—what may be termed its armature—discovered and analyzed by conversation analysts over the years can be shown to readily have such a purpose. Every conversation is rooted in a relationship: One presumes a relationship that already exists or anticipates creating a new one. Further, the very act of opening a conversation—its character, style, form, intonation—*aeo ipso* defines a relationship, one that is either validated or rejected.[2]

One opens a conversation, it can safely be said, in order to enter into a relationship, fleeting or otherwise, with the other, and opens it in one manner rather than another to ensure that the other does respond in a manner that is agreeable to the initiator. Once the opening has been made, one introduces a topic so that the other and the initiator can continue the interaction. If no topic is available, the interaction will wither and each participant will have to go his or her separate way or remain silent, thwarting or truncating the emergence of intersubjectivity. If they do find a topic on which each could disquisition, they can continue the interaction. As the interaction proceeds each will have opportunities to interrupt the other or overlap the other's remarks. If one does interrupt the other more frequently than the other does, and the other allows this to happen, then one party has established himself or herself as the dominant one. If, on the other hand, one of them protests the other's interruptions, the other may acquiesce and join in establishing a more egalitarian relationship. If he or she continues to interrupt, a quarrel may ensue and the interaction may be sundered. In closing a conversation again there are prescribed ways to do it: If one is closing it after an interaction in which there was no quarrel, one articulates standard phrases, the implications of which are that there will be further interactions. If one closes a conversation after a quarrel, the issue of resuming further interactions is left open. If one does close a conversation in the culturally prescribed manner, interactions will be resumed on later occasions.[3]

It is a series of such interactions that constitute relationships of the one with the many and of the many with the one that become communities. In the conversations that are conducted in standard, routine, everyday interactions, it may be said that participants *harmonize* their remarks with those of the others: Each participant typically understands his or her "instrument" and makes his or her contribution, verbally and gesturally, to the emerging music. This is not a mere mechanical role-playing so much as the nuanced *hermeneutic coordination* of sounds, gestures, timing, and response to each other and to either the implicit or explicit leaders of the interaction. The coordination of these activities leads to the emergence of "social solidarity" in the interactional order. In fact, as Randall Collins (1988) has noted, the analysis of conversations has taken us back to Emile Durkheim. The taking and allocation of turns is truly the practice of the division of labor in the organization of interactions. The warranted practice of turn-taking in conversation leads to the creation of solidarity, as does the invocation of an interactionally efficient topic and the practice of decorous openings and closings and construction of relevant addressivities and answerabilities—not to speak of the maintenance of the proper demeanor and deference. The practice of unwarranted interruptions, the failure to generate topics of mutual interest, indecorous openings and closings, and the failure to invest proper addressivities and answerabilities in one's talk will surely create anomie—as anyone who systematically breaches these rules of conversations will soon discover.

The conversational transactions are, however, conducted with instrumentations that are notoriously unstable and unfinished in their signifying capabilities. This instability has led some to the extremes of nihilistic ecstasy and others to despair. One can, however, approach these instabilities of signification as practical problems in everyday interactions with practical solutions. That is, however imperfect the medium and however subject to uncertainty it is, individuals go about the business of everyday life, using it to construct acts by addressing remarks to each other, eliciting answers, and constructing workable meanings out of them, and using such meanings to constitute selves interactions and relationships.

## THE ANSWERED SELF

A dialogic self in fact is allowed to emerge by the interlocutions that are constructed by the participants. Interlocutions reflect already constituted selves of the participants as well as create new dimensions to them. *Each such interlocution enables the individual to objectify himself or herself as well as enables the other to objectify himself or herself.* When people assemble together and conversation flows, opportunities are provided both to give presence to the self and locate oneself more or less firmly within the interactions that occur, to find a place for the self in the ongoing flow. It follows, of course, that if one doesn't say anything—or is not allowed to say anything—his or her self is either absent or is present in only a minimal way. One finds a place and anchors his or herself in the interlocutory flow that is defined by addressivity and answerability. Such anchoring of the self by processes of addressing and answering involves many moves and countermoves each of them oriented to the other. Such orientations may occur as opening remarks, ongoing discourses, interruptions of such discourses, and as additions to them—leading to the orchestration of the interactions and the emergence of opportunities for the selves to play together.

In the following excerpt from a recorded discussion of a meeting of a book club, one can see this process of presenting and anchoring occurring. The assembly of people, ostensibly to discuss a book they have all been assigned to read, produces ready-made topics on which selves can be hoisted. The assembly consisted of four women: Ann, Mary, Judy, and Susan. They would meet every two weeks in the home of one of them and spend the evening talking, drinking a little, and munching on various snacks.[4]

The book they had decided to read and on which the following disquisition developed was Barbara Kingsolver's *Animal Dreams:*

> Mary:   *A kid in the Southwest, uh, in the Southwest, um, who, um, and I'm not sure when it takes place. I think it's not contemporary. It seems more like the '50s but maybe I could be wrong about that and he, uh, just leaves home and like travels into Mexico and then out of Mexico and a lot of things happen to him. It's, uh, what, what makes it a nice book is it's kind of very perceptive and, uh, and you get a real, yet again real feel for place and time.*
>
> Anne:   *It's in the Southwest?*
>
> Mary:   *Yeah, and Mexico.*
>
> Judy:   *Another rediscovering the heartland book?*

| *Mary:* | Well, rediscovering the Southwest. . . |
|---|---|
| | Moving away time and again. But it, but it's similar, but it's also, you know the . . . about seventeen, eighteen years old so its also kind, kind of coming of age. |
| *Judy:* | A, uh,. . . . |
| *Mary:* | But I liked it. |
| *Judy:* | Um, do we need a contrast? Something terribly witty and brittle, civilized. |
| *Susan:* | Do you know any books like (laughing). |
| *Judy:* | Well, we can always read Emma or something (laughing). |
| *Mary:* | The last one I read was Outcast of the Islands *by Joe Conrad which is . . . which I have to tell you was difficult to get into but it was fabulous. I loved reading it, because it was just the language and everything. It's just, I think that really. . . .* |
| *Susan:* | Is it very long? |
| *Mary:* | No, it's a little pocket book about that big. Let's do it. It would be interesting. Also because it's about this man who's really a loner and an outsider and then he meets this woman and it is one part of the book and like they've stuck and it's like it's sort of a disastrous feeling but it's very good. It's interesting and the most fabulous part of the book is the language. |
| *Judy:* | Outcast of the Islands. |
| *Mary:* | Yeah. |
| *Susan:* | What is it again, Mary? |
| *Mary:* | Outcast of the Islands. |
| *Judy:* | It's by Joseph Conrad. |
| *Mary:* | And you get it, I got it in the library and it's, it would take you maybe like two days to read it. It's really not long. |
| *Judy:* | If it is short enough, maybe we should read that and the Heart of Darkness. |
| *Mary:* | I never read that. |
| *Judy:* | Maybe we should. |
| *Susan:* | I never read it either. |
| *Judy:* | You can read that for extra credit. |
| *Susan:* | Right, OK. |
| *Judy:* | had, I think, I had to, I read it in school. I don't remember it. Which is the film that . . . Vietnam . . . that's Heart of Darkness where the one that had Marlon Brando. |
| *Mary:* | That's Apocalypse Now. |
| *Judy:* | Uh, Apocalypse Now. That was . . . but in this Outcast of the Islands. |
| *Anne:* | Is that right? |
| *Mary:* | It's yeah, yeah, yeah, it's very interesting. |
| *Anne:* | I never knew that it was based on that? |
| *Mary:* | Yeah, yeah. Well in Outcast of the Islands . . . the island you can see that the way they described the natives, did we all see Apocalypse, it's just that feeling of oppressive like heat and jungle and people and it's-sort of like something that you know, never encounter. It's also inter- |

*esting that. . . . I think it's interesting to hear nineteenth-century, to
read anything where nineteenth-century people talk about other cultures with that kind of unconscious white man's burden stuff, that is.
. . .*

Judy:      *Right.*
Mary:      *Extraordinarily offensive now. You know there are no such things as
           primitive cultures. I mean these are stupid people talking, you know
           there are cultures that are different, it's like language. There are no
           impoverished languages—they just have, they're just different.*
Susan:     *Would Conrad be stupid like that?*
Mary:      *Yes, they are all stupid. They refer to these people as really not devel-
           oped at all, um, you know, along the evolutionary chain.*

(Book Club Transcripts)

It is Mary who begins the proceedings by providing a summary of the
book. She chooses to use the word "kid" as a description of a character who
is young and is about seventeen or eighteen years old. This is a colloquialism
that is typically used to indicate younger children but by extending its range
Mary had chosen to suggest a nonrigid, indeed informal, colloquial character
to her self. The "I" that she deploys here is not a mere shifter: It comes to the
others as qualified and enriched, even from the beginning. It also assumes
that the audience would understand her specialized use of the word "kid."
Further, it places Mary's age relative to the character: Compared to her the
young man of seventeen is a kid. She then asserts her authority: "I think it's
not contemporary." She is presenting her ability to understand periodization
of novelistic materials. Yet, she adds a qualification to this claim of authority:
"I could be wrong about that." Once again she claims a fluid self—nondog-
matic as well as nonpedantic. She also makes a judgment and claims responsibility for it and for having fulfilled her assignment to read the novel and
make a valid comment about it. In the course of the short statement she is also
able to indicate that she is distinct from others: She spoke in a particular voice
and the details of her discourse establish herself as unique and individuated.
Mary uses "I" explicitly in this passage a few times and it is implicit in a number of other instances. When she uses it, it is an "I" that the others would recognize as Mary's "I," the Mary who is a student of literature, who is known to
be well read. Mary's presentation of the I of her discourse stands for this distinctive Mary: She knows that she is a student of literature and that she has
read widely, and she also knows that the audience knows that she has.

When Anne interposes a question, "It's in the Southwest?" the "I" does not
begin the utterance—overtly. The full sentence that Anne implied, however,
was really: "I would like to know whether you said that the novel was set in
the Southwest." And Mary answers, "Yeah and Mexico." In this exchange a
new element of Mary's biography had entered the "you" that Anne
addressed: the one who spoke earlier, the one who has read the novel, the

one who has spoken about the provenance of the novel, the one who is knowledgeable about literature. Once again, then, it is not an empty pronoun, but a detailed and developed self that Anne addressed as "you." Mary continues and is able to define the locale of the novel more precisely; she underlines her earlier statement, "What makes it a nice book is it's kind of very perceptive and you get a real, a real feel for the place and time."

Judy asserts herself at this stage: "Another rediscovering the heartland book?" She claims her self as the one who knows the field of literature or novels and is able to classify this one readily. She achieves her own distinction by choosing to present herself in this fashion and indicating also a cultivated weariness in saying, "It is another one of those novels." Mary is now able to distinguish herself from Judy with minor irony: not the "heartland," just the Southwest. She also adds a detail to show, as different from Judy's characterization of it, it is also a novel about a seventeen- or eighteen-year-old "coming of age." This is of course an allusion to another genre of writing and stands opposed to Judy's "rediscovering the heartland" genre. Judy seems to enter a mild demurral indicated by the sound "A, uh," but Mary is firm: "But I liked it."

Judy faces the need to save herself from this mild defeat. She announces once again a broader claim for her self: "Do we need a contrast? Something terribly witty and brittle, civilized?" Susan responds to this inquiry, with mild laughter, and Judy is able to display her breadth of perspective: "We can always read *Emma* or something." Judy also laughs, but she had introduced a contrast with the novel of the evening, a work by one of the leading novelists in the English language.

It is evident here that if one had certain information, knowledge, and competence, in areas that are relevant to the topic of the ongoing conversation, it could be used to create a stronger presence for the self. If this knowledge is authentic the others in the interaction will be forced to acknowledge it and grant the other's claim to this self. Of course Judy is not merely talking about *Emma* and Jane Austen but is achieving a distinction for herself, and the mild sparring with Mary has accomplished that.

Mary interposes herself here and is not going to allow Judy to run with the telling literary allusion: "The last one I read was *Outcast of the Islands* by Joe Conrad which is . . . which I have to tell you was difficult to get into but it was fabulous. I loved reading it, because of the language and everything. It is just, I think that really. . . ." She is interrupted by Susan: "Is it very long?" This interruption is not really an assertion of power but a recognition that Mary had her turn and had imparted sufficient information. It in fact is a contribution to the collective objective of the group—finding a book to read and reading it in time for the next meeting. Further, it enables the conversation to move along and contributes to the maintenance of its tempo. Susan is making a distinction here: I have not read Conrad, while the two of you have, and I don't even know whether it is a long novel or short one. Mary is willing to oblige her with an answer, further distinguishing herself as the one who knows about Conrad.

"No it's a little pocket book about that big." And she continues presenting herself:

> Let's do it. It would be interesting. Also because it's about this man who's really a loner and an outsider and then he meets this woman and it is one part of the book and like they've stuck and it's like, it's sort of a disastrous feeling but it's very good. It's interesting and the most fabulous part of the book is the language.

She confirms her claims to distinction as the one who knows her Conrad, is able to author a statement about it and take responsibility for this knowledge and for making suggestions that would affect the lives, however minimally, of those she is addressing, and shows both commitment as well as passion. The emotivity is evident even without the sounds of her speech: "Let's do it," she commands, "It would be interesting," she continues, and gives her justification for thinking that the novel would be interesting. Besides, the story, she says, had a "fabulous" aspect, the "language." The use of the hyperbole and the metaphor in the adjective "fabulous" defines the emotionality of the address.

Once Mary's speech is done, Judy produces a noncommittal line: "*Outcast of the Islands.*"

The repetition of the title of the book indicates a lack of enthusiasm but not an outright rejection. Mary says, "yeah," and Susan who is still a little lost asks:

"What is it again Mary?" And Mary answers her. Judy displays her knowledge and has her own input:

"It's by Joseph Conrad."

Mary is not done with the presentation of her self: "And you can get it, I got it in the library and it's, it would take you maybe like two days to read it. It's really not long."

Judy makes a suggestion that is an implicit challenge to Mary: "If it is short enough, maybe we should read that and the *Heart of Darkness.*"

This is a subtle move to undermine the ascendancy that Mary had acquired thus far: You may know your Conrad and the *Outcast of the Islands*, but I am not totally ignorant either. I know about another Conrad work.

Mary concedes that she is not familiar with all of Conrad's works: "I never read that." Mary's position of ascendance is somewhat diminished now, and Judy continues to assert herself: "Maybe we should."

Susan once again announces unwittingly that she is a little out of this league: "I never read it either."

This also expresses solidarity with Mary and puts Judy alone there wanting the second novel included in the reading assignment. Judy introduces a joke and blunts the edge off the sparring: "You can read that for extra credit."

Susan acknowledges the joke: "Right, OK."

Judy presses her advantage and authors new details—about her relation to it and the novel's relation to current events and popular culture:

"I had, I think, I had to, I read it in school. I don't remember it." She then jumbles her words, but the significance is clear: "Which is the film that . . . Vietnam . . . that's *Heart of Darkness* where the one that had Marlon Brando. . . ."

Mary intervenes with her: "That's *Apocalypse Now*." This interruption aids Judy's discourse and once again helps the conversation to proceed apace. Judy acknowledges the aid to her recollection:

"Uh, *Apocalypse Now*. That was ... but in this *Outcast of the Islands*. . . ."

She is interrupted by Anne who wants confirmation of the point about *Apocalypse Now*:

"Is that right?"

This is followed by a number of overlapping observations and Anne announces her outsider status anew:

"I never knew that it was based on that?"

The pronouns here have no antecedents in the sentences she has produced but they are clear enough nevertheless: Was *Apocalypse Now* based on *Heart of Darkness*?

This is followed by a long discourse by Mary. She answers Anne's questions about *Heart of Darkness* and recaptures her role by reverting to the topic of an *An Outcast of the Islands*: "Yeah, yeah. Well in *Outcast of the Islands* you can see that the way they described the natives, did we all see *Apocalypse*, it's just that feeling of oppressive-like heat and jungle and people and it's sort of like something that you know, never encounter. It's also interesting . . . that I think it's interesting to hear nineteenth-century, to read anything where nineteenth-century people talk about other cultures with that kind of unconscious white man's burden stuff, that is. . . ."

Judy encourages her along with an interjection:

"Right."

This provides a dramaturgically effective break in Mary's rambling statement. Mary resumes:

> Extraordinarily offensive now. You know there are no such things as primitive cultures. I mean, these are stupid people talking, you know there are cultures that are different, it's like language. There are no impoverished languages—they just have, they're just different.

Susan intervenes with a question, "Would Conrad be stupid like that?"

And Mary has an answer, "Yes, they are all stupid. They refer to these people as really not developed at all, um you know along the evolutionary chain."

Mary's long statement once again displays very clearly aspects of her self. To begin with, she brings the conversation back to *An Outcast of the Islands* and provides another description of its contents. The description of the heat and the oppressive vegetation that Conrad uses, both as a metaphor and as an instrument to create a location, are recalled by Mary and then, using the earlier discussion, she provides her own metaphor: If you have seen *Apocalypse Now*, you would have seen the same thing. This is an aid to her audience to enable them to visualize what she is describing now, what Conrad created in his novel. She then introduces a sociopolitical theme: This novel, like other nineteenth-century novels, contains dated and scientifically unacceptable views about cultures. A strong, well-informed, and literate self is presented and reaffirmed by Mary. Distinctions are indeed made, responsibility claimed, authority asserted, and emotivity displayed, and all are done by making various choices along the way. Mary's presentation of the new novel to read, and her disquisition on Conrad's other novel having begun as a casual introduction of something to read next, however, soon elicits the commitment of her self to it. She is loath to let it go, meets all challenges to its selection, however muted, and becomes identified with the position. Even on matters that are not central to one's self at the beginning of an interaction, an individual can get drawn into a commitment and an investment of self as the interaction proceeds and others react to the initial positions and the individual in question reacts to it in turn.

The most striking impression of the conversational inputs by the various characters in the foregoing discussion is that, after certain initial sallies, the novel that they were set to discuss was forgotten and an entirely new series of topics was introduced. It really did not matter, it seemed, what novel they talked about, so long as they, trusted and interdependent selves that they were, gathered and discussed something and gave presence to their selves. The discussion, the discursive acts in them, announced and validated the various selves and gave them each a presence in a social arena. Each articulation by an individual was addressed generally to the other members of the group and was answered. Indeed, the entire proceeding was a series of moves that complemented each other. In giving presence to their selves, the various individuals started speeches and often completed them, but often they were also not allowed to finish their turns. Others cut in and finished the speaker's remarks or started a new utterance of their own. These should be considered, not so much as interruptions, but as elements of an *orchestration* of the conversational process so that a general *motif* could be constituted. Each individual in the group was contributing her own element, her own noise, to the emergence of a harmony. No doubt some degree of domination was sought by one individual or other but, overall, the mood of the conversation was to get ahead with the topic at hand and get along with each other and experience the presence of their own selves and that of the others.

An examination of a different set of conversational transcripts reveals further information about the addressive and answerable presence of self in speech. This is a recording of a conversation between two people made remotely with the help of a hidden microphone.

| | |
|---|---|
| *Alex:* | *You're going out in the field.* |
| *Bertie:* | *Yeah, always.* |
| *Alex:* | *Good. It's going to be a good day today.* |
| *Bertie:* | *Oh really.* |
| *Alex:* | *Beautiful day.* |
| *Bertie:* | *Oh beautiful, beautiful.* |
| *Alex:* | *Beautiful day.* |
| *Bertie:* | *So you have everything under control?* |
| *Alex:* | *Yeah . . . all right. Bertie, all right.* |
| *Alex:* | *See you later on or what?* |
| *Bertie:* | *No I won't come. . . . I will come later. . . . Please don't.* |
| *Alex:* | *Yeah.* |
| *Bertie:* | *Oh wait, wait, I came to you. . . . All kidding aside. . . . This guy I called . . . he doesn't have the experience, he doesn't have it.* |
| *Alex:* | *Okay.* |
| *Bertie:* | *I don't know what these fuckers are asking. They gave me insurance before . . . what.* |
| *Alex:* | *Okay, okay.* |
| *Bertie:* | *That's why I gave a copy.* |
| *Alex:* | *Good. I'll send it back saying he has no ratings.* |
| *Bertie:* | *Good he understands that I didn't do anything extraordinary? He mustn't think that.* |
| *Alex:* | *Woe.* |

(Office Transcripts)

This exchange, between Alex and Bertie, is conducted on a substratum of knowledge of who each is by the person himself as well as by the other. Alex comes into the conversation knowing who he is in all its relevant details as well as who he is in relation to Bertie. He knows the role that he has to play with Bertie, how he is to present his self and with what shadings and colorings such a presence is to be made available. The same could be said of Bertie: He, too, is a remembered self that is projected into the interaction and defined and redefined in the course of it.

The opening gambit itself captures this nicely: "You're going out in the field." For Alex to address Bertie as "you" he must know him and his own relationship to him; to be able to assume what Bertie was going to be doing that day and claim the right to ask this question Alex must remember at least one aspect of his self, just as he must know that Bertie is the relevant self to which this question can be addressed.

And what does Bertie do? He provides an immediate answer: "Yeah, always." He does not challenge Alex, he does not reject the question or repudiate its implications. Rather, he acknowledges Alex's self by implicitly accepting Alex's right to ask the question as well as the relationship such a question subsumes. Alex in fact assumes, gently but clearly enough, his role and his self as someone who is in a superior position in the hierarchy of the bureaucracy from the opening gambit itself, a presence that is developed as the conversation proceeds. He comments on the quality of the day with Bertie. It's going to be a good day today. This again can be considered as an affirmation of his higher position in the bureaucracy: It is a person in such a position who is given the right to make observations about the weather—the right to bring irrelevant matters into the conversation.

Bertie, however, is not keen to let his official subordination be given more underlining here than was absolutely necessary. He produces an irony: "Oh really?" Insofar as that he has to go out in the field whether it was a good day or not, it matters little to him that his supervisor thinks that it was going to be a good day. The phrase "beautiful day" is repeated like a motif in a musical piece in the next few exchanges, one of them using it to maintain domination, and the other subtly undermining it. Bertie abandons the beautiful day theme and asks, "So you have everything under control?" Alex may be hierarchically dominant, but Bertie's work depends on Alex doing his bit well. Hence, Bertie asks this question and once again it is only knowledge and recollection of Alex's responsibilities that can allow this question to be asked. The "you" in this encounter is a remembered self of the other, a memory that not only captures the other's relevances but also one's own vis-à-vis the other. The conversation could not have proceeded along these lines otherwise. This impression is reinforced as the interaction moves along. Bertie acknowledges Alex's "all right" with his own "all right" and then Alex says, "See you later on or what?" On the face of it this is an innocuous enough question. "See you later" is in fact a conventional parting gambit in American society. The added conjunction "or" changes the significance: It is not a conventional closing of the interaction but suggests a time when a new meeting was to take place. The "or what?" reinforces the impression and gives a slight edge to the interaction by implying that Bertie may not honor the expectation of the later encounter. Bertie rejects Alex's request and adds a plea, "Please don't." The emotionality of the interaction has changed and suddenly there is an element of threat in Alex's "see you later."

In the opening moments of the encounter between Alex and Bertie, Alex's domination over Bertie was maintained by subtle moves. This domination increases perceptibly in the later moves, where, with a series of masterly interjections and phrasings, Alex is able to bring Bertie to a state of a certain abjectness. Indeed, the economy with which Alex was able to induce a fearful state in Bertie is noteworthy. The "or what" phrase and the preposition "on" before that are able to impart extraordinary significance to Bertie. The one word "Yeah" from Alex is enough to induce a slight panic in Bertie as well: he goes into the "Oh wait, wait" move. The "yeah" from Alex that induced this response from Bertie is not just a colloquial form of "yes": it carries with it, in the usage here, suspicion, doubt, the suggestion of disbelief. Bertie pleads, "Wait, wait" and goes into an explanation: "I came to you." This is offered as a testament to his dependability. The broken sentences and the self-interruptions of the onward flow of the discourse displays some agitation just as does the repetition of the word "wait." The implied threat from Alex is dismissed: "All kidding aside." Nevertheless, Alex has in fact subtly undermined Bertie's self with these moves: from being a mere subordinate in the earlier stages of the interaction, he has now become an abject, supplicatory one.

The "you" that Alex is dealing with now is slightly different from the one with which the exchange began, just as is the "me" of Bertie. Bertie's next move is to recover some of his lost honor. To another ominous "okay" from Alex, Bertie proffers, "I don't know what these fuckers are asking. They gave me insurance before." This claim contains a factual statement and an obscenity. Obscenities are typically used by those of equal status, as an index of the camaraderie that exists between them or by a superordinate to indicate his disdain for conventional standards in the company of his subordinates. Using the noun "fuckers" to describe his contacts, Bertie seeks to regain some honor but is not spared. He receives a patronizing "Okay, okay" from Alex—a patronization achieved by repetition, a strategy that recalls a mother pacifying a child. To further explanations from Bertie, Alex finally produces a fuller response and seemingly accepts the explanation: "Good. I'll send it back saying he has no ratings." Bertie produces further explanations and Alex produces, surprisingly, the single word "Woe."

The interlocution between Alex and Bertie is a carefully orchestrated one that resonates with the relative status and power of the participants. Nearly every addressive statement that Alex directs at Bertie speaks of power and status, and Bertie's answers define his subordination and even at times a note of seeming panic. This micropolitics of everyday life, as Clark (1990) calls it, is managed by managing the addressivity in one's conversational inputs and their answerability and putting given emotionalities into them.

## THE UNANSWERED SELF

In the presencing and validation of a self through interlocution, often one of the participants must reject the other's proffered self, either subtly or crudely, and seek to elicit, with grace or force, a different one. He or she can refuse, that is, to answer the proffered self and guide the other in such a way that he or she produces an alternative self, one that can be more readily answered. While this can occur in everyday relationships, it is more vividly seen in therapeutic ones, police interrogations and examinations, and cross examination by advocates in courts of law.

In the following episode, the selves of the participants are constituted and given presence by rather complicated maneuvers: The selves of the interactants are constantly moving and shifting as they talk and get finally defined in the last stages of the episode. The conversation is between a patient and her therapist, with the patient resisting one address and granting another to the therapist and the therapist refusing to acknowledge the presence of a particular self of the patient in the first part and collaboratively constructing another in the second part.

| Doctor: | *Dona Jurema!* |
| --- | --- |
| Patient: | *Mama. (whining)* |
| Doctor: | *Dona Jurema!* |
| Patient: | *Mama, what is it my child?* |
| Doctor: | *Dona Jurema, let's talk a little bit.* |
| Patient: | *What is it you wish to know?* |
| Doctor: | *O.K.?* |
| Patient: | *Madam, my mother, don't you already know everything?* |
| Doctor: | *mmm.* |
| Patient: | *Has she not shown you everything?* |
| Doctor: | *Tell me your full name.* |
| Patient: | *(baby talk) There is no need to cause the doc, doc, doc, the doc papa papa papa papa papa papa P-a-u-l-o de A-z-e-e-v-d-o Mu-ti-nho (chanting and baby talk) you yourself know quite well, better than I, better than anyone, when I get to my ward I'm gonna tell, I'm gonna tell, this was, this was, this was my secret, this was my secret, this was, this was, and this was.* |
| Doctor: | *Dona Jurema!* |
| Patient: | *My secret.* |
| Doctor: | *DONA JUREMA (Forcefully)!* |
| Patient: | *(Singing and baby talk) My dear husband knew very well, he did not come to help, his dear, dear wife but it does not matter, his good luck will not last that is all I can wish on him with all my heart.* |
| Doctor: | *Dona Jurema, how long have you been in the hospital?* |
| Patient: | *[New tune: church hymn] All dressed in white she appeared bearing round her waist, the colors of the sky (whining) Hail, Hail, Hail Mary, Hail, Hail, Hail Mary. What more do you want umh?* |
| Doctor: | *Dona Jurema (half smiling).* |
| Patient: | *Umh? You know that I can't.* |

(Ribeiro 1994: 3–5)

Branca Telles Ribeiro, from whose study the excerpt is taken, discusses these exchanges between the doctor and Dona Jurema in terms of the rule of turn-taking and the processes of Goffman's "framing" (1974). One can also see these words from Dona Jurema as a presentation of a self. In this case, an adult had presented a child self to the doctor, because it can safely be claimed, her usual adult self had become, for one reason or another, unbearable. The anxiety and panic that the adult self induced—perhaps because of the failure of her husband to "support" her—has made her adopt the self of her childhood. She is singing and chanting and doing baby talk and hailing Mary and the addressing to papa and mama as a way of handling the anxiety. In classical psychoanalytic terms this would be called a regression. Harry Stack Sullivan's reconfiguration of it, however, seems a more fitting explanation. He argues that in the developmental history of an individual he or she passes through three basic stages: the prototaxic, when the newborn is able to communicate only with its body and the sounds it can make with its mouth; the parataxic, when it uses a rudimentary language of phrases; and the final syntactic stage, when it is able to use the full language. In some forms of mental disorder, an adult will often present his or her self by using the chronologically inappropriate form: He or she will refuse to speak, but crawl and gesticulate and use other forms of nonverbal techniques of communication. This would be a presentation of self in which the adult individual adopts the role of an infant: He or she indicates this self by the performances he or she presents. When the individual uses words, phrases, verbal mannerisms and gestures that are appropriate to a child, we have a case of "parataxic distortion" (Sullivan 1956: 200–202). When a patient has a series of disasters following the major one, they manifest, Sullivan observes, "a more or less characteristic distortion of personality, distortion of communication, distortion of observation of the other fellow and so on" (1956: 202). Such performances are in fact the presentation of the self of a child and an invitation to validate it. In Dona Jurema's case this is exactly what was occurring: She presents the words and mannerisms of a child and even when she is talking about her husband, she chants the words and uses "baby talk."

The discourse that Dona Jurema presents here and the self that she defines and for which she claims a presence is that of a child, a self that the psychiatrist steadfastly refuses to acknowledge and validate. A self is presented verbally and gesturally, but it is not answered. Dona Jurema's discourse is a manifestation of a reflexive self. She does not actually use a noun or a pronoun; she does not say I at the beginning of a sentence, but her discursive allusion and the use of childlike locutions and mannerism are presentations of the self, are indeed extended nouns and pronouns. She does not say "I am a child" or "I, Dona Jurema, is a child" but by using various verbal techniques and strategies she has in effect made such a claim.

The therapist refuses to accept this definition of self that Dona Jurema had proffered and proceeds to treat her as an adult patient. This apparently succeeds because she is soon facing the discharge interview:

*Doctor:*   *You were born on what date?*
*Patient:*   *On January 11. (nods)*
*Doctor:*   *Of what year?*
*Patient:*   *Of 1921. (nods) I am sixty-one. (nods, smiles)*
*Doctor:*   *You have a son, don't you?*
*Patient:*   *I have a son.*
*Doctor:*   *What is his name?*
*Patient:*   *Francisco Ferreira de Souza.*

| | |
|---|---|
| *Doctor:* | *And he is how old now?* |
| *Patient:* | *He's about forty-two. (looks away, looks at Doctor and smiles)* |
| *Doctor:* | *Mmm, you also have a granddaughter, don't you?* |
| *Patient:* | *I have a little sixteen-year-old granddaughter. (raises head; smiles)* |
| *Doctor:* | *Ummm.* |
| *Patient:* | *She's my life.* |

(Ribeiro 1994: 13)

This is a conventional "discharge interview." In it the doctor recites the facts about the patient that are known to him and patient and seeks to discover whether the patient remembers them and acknowledges the facts of her biography. In the interview, however, more than that is being accomplished. Dona Jurema is being recalled to her identity as well as being given significant details of such an identity: she was born on such and such a day, has a son, was married, has a granddaughter. In other words, she is being allowed to identify and classify her self as an adult, wife, mother, and grandmother. She acknowledges them all, often with a touching alacrity, and introduces a certain emotionality to the details of her life. She smiles when she tells her age—perhaps recalling her childlike behavior in the earlier phase—and smiles when she acknowledges her son and recalls her granddaughter; with magnificent economy she gives her emotional response to the child: "She is my life."

She had rediscovered her self, abandoned the one she created when she was admitted to the hospital, and has now acknowledged all the details that went with her old being. She now chooses to be the grandmother and mother, Dona Jurema, taking responsibility for the words she produces by providing coherence to them, authoritatively claiming her son and her granddaughter, and using these details to claim distinction from others: she is now Dona Jurema, sixty-one years old, born on January 11, 1921, mother to no less a person than Francisco Ferreira de Souza and has, as "her life," a sixteen-year-old granddaughter. The psychiatrist has achieved here for Dona Jurema a return to her former identity and made her abandon the acts and moves of the child self that she had assumed. She is now in charge of the details of her self, addressively charted for her by the therapist, an extended you that encapsulated her age, date of birth, motherhood, grandmotherhood, and a special relationship to her grandchild.

In summary, one can say that these conversational interactions proceeded under the following parameters: (a) Each participant presented a string of words, with a presumptive or actual "I" in it and addressed it to the other; (b) These strings of words contained within them, explicitly or implicitly, indicators that functioned to define the self of the other so that interactions could proceed further; (c) Each string of words was uttered by an individual who was responsible for them and answerable to them; (d) Each speaker was able to assume knowledge of his or her relationship to the other in order to address him or her as a you; (e) The reflexive self, the I, and the addressive self, you, kept changing as the interactions proceeded, indicating that these pronouns are really summaries of complex and evolving selves; (f) Each string of words was a product of choices made of the particularized self that was to be presented, distinctions made in the course of the interaction as to which particular of the self was present, responsibility and authority claimed for the significance and effects of the words, and a certain emotivity indicated by them, too.

## THE IMPLICATED SELF

Commenting on his work on the emergence of "mind," G. H. Mead writes that he was concerned with "cooperative conduct" as it occurred in the "conversation with others, in conversation with one's self, and in the significant symbol and in the appearance of substantive meanings" (1938: 150). More recently Paul Grice has developed the idea that conversations as such proceed apace as each participant accepts and practices "the cooperative principle." He writes,

> Our talk exchanges do not normally consist of a succession of disconnected remarks, and would not be rational if they did. They are characteristically, to some degree at least, cooperative efforts; and each participant recognizes in them, to some extent, a common purpose or set of purposes, or at least a mutually accepted direction. (1989: 26)

Grice goes forward with this "cooperative principle" and develops certain "maxims" by which it is put into practice. The maxims that establish and advance cooperation in conversations are arranged by Grice into four categories: *quantity, quality, relation,* and *manner.* These maxims, he argues, have certain "logical implicatures" and, after a discussion of these, Grice considers the implications of deliberately violating these maxims. If these maxims are followed when participants in a conversation talk to each other a certain cooperation between them will occur and the conversation will move smoothly and efficiently, if perhaps a little uninterestingly. A participant may, however, refuse to accept one or other of the maxims and opt out of the cooperative principle. He or she may violate one of them, experience a clash between one maxim and another, choose one rather than another, flout a maxim, and, finally, may exploit one or another of the maxims and use such moves to announce or imply a self that fulfill his or her own purposes.

In addition to the logical implicatures of following or violating the maxims of conversation, and in spite of Goffman's dismissive treatment of them for being "culture and context free" (1983b: 25), one can find uses for them by supplying the context and the necessary culture. Indeed these logical implicatures, when supplied with context and culture, seem to have social and interactional implications.

To the extent that selves are constituted and maintained by conversational interactions, a certain minimum of cooperation, and, as Goffman showed in his studies of face work, deference and demeanor (1967), an *interactional contract*, seems necessary. There certainly is a social contract to be found in the workings of a social order and it is most vividly present in the micro-processes of everyday life. In such cooperative activities, selves are given presence and sustained. Conversely a participant can refuse to cooperate, fully or partially, and reject the contract and thereby create consequences for the selves of the participants. If each of the maxims is considered with sufficient context and culture, it will be seen that by either fulfilling the demands of the maxim or by violating them, selves of a particular character are given presence, overtly or by implication, and a particular kind of interaction is constituted and conducted.

## The Maxim of Quantity

For this maxim, Grice provides two submaxims:

(a) Make your contribution as informative as is required (for the current the purposes of the exchange).
(b) Do not make your contribution more informative than is required.

(1989: 26)

A question that arises is: Why? Or rather what are the consequences of violating these maxims? Grice gives an example in which one of the submaxims is violated:

A: Where does C live?
B: Somewhere in the South of France.

(1983: 32)

The answer from B is less informative than is required. If A wants to go and visit C or write to him, of course further questions can be asked and this vagueness rectified. However, consider the following exchange:

Ardyth:     I called your office several times today and couldn't get you. Where were you?
Brendon:    Out.

Brendon has certainly violated the maxim of quantity. Ardyth's statement and the subsequent question had the following implication: Ardyth had the right to call the office and good reason to expect Brendon to be at the office and furthermore had the right to ask this question now because she is his wife. The response from Brendon, while violating Grice's maxim, also violates Ardyth's rights that she can justifiably claim in mainstream American culture. His laconism is a rejection of Ardyth's claims to know where he is at a given moment during his working day and also a challenge to her right to ask questions about his whereabouts. In other words, the violation of the maxim of quantity here is deliberate, purposive, and socially significant: It denies Ardyth's addressive presence here and indicates that her claim to a self based on the right to address a husband in this manner is being refuted. It defines the self of the respondent very clearly: You are not to ask these questions and if you do, I will not give you satisfactory answers.

Brendon could have answered his wife's inquiry with the following locution: "I was in the warehouse all morning, and I went out to lunch with Mr. Simpson and then in the afternoon I went to the bank at the instruction of Mr. Simpson and later I went to the gym and then back to the office at three."

Is this a violation of the second principle of the maxim of quantity? It is certainly a more detailed answer with a particular attention to time, and it could be said that Brendon has been "more informative than was required." However, that is only part of the story. Brendon had in fact produced an ingratiating self here, one that is rather afraid of any imputation that his wife might be inclined to make about his absence from the office. His answer establishes a particular self for him in the interaction and defines a relationship with his wife in a particular way. This may be a violation of the maxim of quantity, but it is a purposeful and consequential violation, designed to produce narrative verisimilitude to his answer.

In the first laconic response, Brendon undermined and redefined Ardyth's self while in a more voluble response he defined his self in rather abject terms. In everyday interactions, the effective control of the information given and the management of one's own verbal productions are used to define the selves of the participants and the nature and destiny of the interaction. In the following episode Michael, by giving away as little information as possible and providing as little discourse as was necessary, is able to addressively define the self of the other in the interaction. Indeed Michael achieves a certain invalidation of the self of the other, a positive undermining of it in the interactional encounter. George is speaking to Michael. They both work in the same office but Michael is of higher rank. George begins with an account of his movements.

> George:   *I am on my way down there now, in a little while, to check out to see*
> *what he is doing with my jobs.*
> Michael:  *What brings you in today?*
>
> (Office Transcripts)

George has in fact anticipated one of the implications of Michael's question, which in fact comes after the account is given: why are you here rather than at the other place, checking? He is here, George says, "to see what he is doing with my jobs." And George personalizes the relationship immediately:

*George: I just came by to say hello. . . . you know, I haven't seen you for awhile,*
*you know I figure we go for coffee one of these days.*

(Office Transcripts)

George sounds like a supplicant with the phrases "you know" interjected
here and there. He also did not just "come" to the office, he "came by." The sub-
junctive phrasing, the use of the preposition "by" after "came" all indicate a certain degree of deference and diffidence. To say "I came to see you" would indicate a directness and an expectation that Michael would indeed see him. The
addition of the preposition "by" indicates here that George came in the hope of
seeing Alex without the latter having an obligation to see him. It is indeed a subdued and deferential self that is present here. But Michael does not give any
quarter to George:

*Michael: Yeah . . . Give me a call. This week's difficult.*

Michael in fact shows no enthusiasm for this coffee encounter with
George. Not only does he refuse to make a date then and there, but asks
George to call him again and, moreover, not this week. He in fact is violating the maxim of quantity by not giving enough information to George. Even
before Michael could finish, George interposes:

*George: Next week sometime.*
*Michael: Next week. Call me early in the week and we will set something up.*
*George: Okay, great.*

(Office Transcripts)

Michael is still controlling the situation and indicates when George should
call and George could barely contain his enthusiasm. It was indeed okay and
great for him that, though his self was somewhat undermined, all was not lost
since Michael had agreed to have coffee with him, "sometime next week."
   No doubt the cooperative principle was at work here too: Michael and
George cooperate by giving presence to their selves in their respective discourse. Michael by being stingy addressively presences a subordinated self
for George and a dominant self for himself while George by being voluble
does the opposite. These selves were carried over from earlier conceptions
and indicated the relevant statuses of each in larger structures of relations.

## The Maxim of Quality

In the course of ordinary conversations, as one speaks and gives presence to
his or her self, the other typically has to take these words and the self that is
presented as substantially true—at least for the time being. In this case, the
auditor can operate under the belief that the speaker is following Grice's
maxim of quality, which is expanded into two submaxims:

(a) Do not say what you believe to be false.
(b) Do not say that for which you lack adequate evidence.

(Grice 1989: 27)

Insofar as every statement that one makes to the other embodies a claim about the self of the speaker and the listener, a lie—defined here as a statement that the articulator knows to be untrue, insupportable with evidence—makes it difficult, if not impossible, to conduct an interaction. Such a lie in fact creates a disjunction between the "I" of the speaker and the "me" that he or she is creating: The other will grant him or her a self that he or she knows to be false to the extent that the other does not know that he or she is being told a lie. The initiator can operate in the interaction and the relationship on the basis of the self he or she has created by providing ill-founded criteria to the other. However, there is always the danger that the other will find out, sooner or later, the false basis of his or her relationship to the individual and alter the character of the relationship in one way or another.

If, however, the speaker offers a lie to the other to his face, and the other knows it to be a lie, he or she has one of two courses left open to him or her: (a) He or she can challenge it then and there, i.e., refuse to answer the proffered self, refuse to confer on the speaker the me that he or she has sought and face the consequences. The liar can then change his or her claims and substitute a different one that the other may accept, although by then this too will be under suspicion. Nevertheless, the self of the speaker will remain damaged and the interaction and relationship between the liar and his or her other will also remain problematic or else the liar can stick to his or her account and further transactions between him or her and his or her interlocutor will be terminated. (b) The recipient of the lie can pretend to believe the speaker, thus saving the speaker's face and perhaps one's own as well, and proceed with the interaction and use this experience to influence his or her relationship with the liar in the future. This liar will now have a referential self that will influence his or her relationship with the one to whom he lied as well as the others to whom the latter would communicate his or her findings.

## The Maxim of Relation

For this maxim, Grice provides only one recommendation: "Be relevant" (1989: 27). Grice expands on this as follows: "I expect a partner's contribution to be appropriate to the immediate needs at each stage of the transaction" (1989: 28). One obvious conclusion of being less than relevant is that the self being presented or addressed is not being fully realized in the interaction. One addresses the other in vain, and the addressor either gives up the interaction or changes the topic in order to draw the self back into the conversation. In more extreme cases, irrelevance in conversational exchanges is taken as a symptom of "mental illness" or neurologic disturbances. In such cases the self becomes absent or irrelevant to the ongoing proceedings. Indeed, one way to absent one's self from the ongoing proceedings is to deliberately violate the maxim of relation and ask in the midst of a monologue from the other, "What were you saying? I was not paying attention." Another way is to say something that was totally unconnected to the preceding statements and change the topic. Grice's example makes this point:

"At a genteel tea party, A says *Mrs. X is an old bag.* There is a moment of appalled silence and then B *says The weather has been quite delightful this summer hasn't it?* (1989: 35)

With this maneuver B has disassociated himself from A's remark, indeed from A's self and its addressive imputations, refused to be answerable to it, and moved his self into a new position and in a different direction.

In either case—that is when one provides unwittingly an irrelevant remark, one that is unconnected *narratively* to the earlier one, as well as when one deliberately disconnects the relationship to the earlier remark—the relation to the self is evident. In the first case, the self could be said to have been absent insofar as it was not connected to the earlier remark and in the second case one particular self was rejected and a new one substituted. The controlling of relevance, it appears, is managed by self and other in various ways: One brings the other by one or more remarks back to relevance, deliberately ignores the other's remark to make a point, or else one disattends the other's remarks and proceeds to the important business at hand. The latter can be seen in the following excerpts. The participants are selecting a date for their next meeting:

*Susan:*     *I am not back from vacation until July 10th.*
*Mary:*     *I am leaving on the 17th.*
*Susan:*     *I am gonna read those two books on vacation.*
*Anne:*     *Isn't that funny. The 10th and the 17th. I have two things none of which would interfere, one is the dentist . . . and that is during the daytime. (laughing)*
*Mary:*     *How about the 12th?*
*Judy:*     *Is Wednesday the 12th?*

(Book Club Transcripts)

Anne's statement here violated the maxim of relation: The two things she has to do between the 10th and the 17th of July in the daytime are of no consequence to the meeting of the book club. Her statement is routinely ignored by the next two speakers, who in fact set the date for the next meeting between the 10th and the 17th when Anne had the two things to do. Lacking relevance, and therefore lacking addressivity, she is not answered, essentially canceling her self, for the time being at least.

## The Maxim of Manner

By the category of manner, writes Grice,

> I understand as relating, not . . . to what is said, but *how* what is said is said, I
> include the super- maxim—"Be perspicuous"—and various sub-maxims follow
> such as:
>
> 1. Avoid obscurity of expression.
> 2. Avoid ambiguity.
> 3. Be brief (avoid unnecessary prolixity).
> 4. Be orderly.
>
> (Grice 1989: 27)

The implication of these maxims for the presencing of self are manifold.
Obscurity of expression when it is directed at the other in a conversation will
make it difficult, if not impossible, for the recipient to define the self of the initiator and address it in return. In fact, the addressive self of each participant will
be diminished if not actually absent, making interactions and relationships difficult to sustain. And certainly the nuanced and graded self that emerges in the
course of ongoing conversational interactions will fail to emerge. The extreme
case here would be someone whose language is foreign to the recipient of the
communicational moves so that he or she understands little or nothing. In such
encounters, it is safe to say, only fragmented selves emerge interactionally and
addressively and even referential and reflexive selves may be affected
adversely. Consider the case here of the Japanese exchange student Yoshi Hattori in Louisiana who dressed in a Halloween costume and in the company of
an American friend went looking for a party on Halloween. Here is a summary
of the description of the events of the night by Yoshi Hattori's friend at the trial:

> We knocked on the side door and hid in the bush. A woman opened the door. We
> jumped out of the bushes and scared her. She screamed and shut the door. After
> that, I told Yoshi that maybe we were at the wrong house. So, we turned and
> started to walk back toward the car and then we saw a light come on and heard
> the door open again. I told Yoshi that maybe this is the right house. We turned
> around to face the side door and a man came out. The man yelled "freeze," but
> Yoshi continued dancing and jumping toward the man in a fast pace. I suddenly
> noticed that the man held a gun in both hands with it pointed toward Yoshi. At that
> point I got real scared because I knew Yoshi didn't understand English that well.
> Yoshi got within a few feet of the man, and he shot Yoshi. Yoshi fell backwards.
> The man lowered the pistol, stepped back into the house and shut the door.
>
> (Vanderhoof 1997)

The occupant of the house sees an unusually, perhaps alarmingly, cos-
tumed young man who could not explain his presence. He could only speak
a phrase about the party. The occupant shoots the young man, killing him.

He is later acquitted on charges of manslaughter. The addressive presence of the young man was ambiguous to the occupant: Visually he looked strange and threatening, his manner was exuberant, and he was present in a territory to which he was not entitled. These anomalies could have been obviated by a verbal explanation that he, being not fully tutored in English, could not provide nor could he understand the imperative "freeze." It is clearly in one's best interest to claim the right self, reflexively and addressively, by using the appropriate locutions to avoid ambiguity.

Interactions in which one elects to remain silent can also be taken as extreme examples of obscurity: The self of the person is unavailable for interaction. Examples of such elective silences, the consequent absence of self-presence, and the erroneous or undesirable imputation of self, are those who are accused of crimes and choose not to reveal crucial information. Julius Rosenberg, it was believed, would have had his death sentence commuted to life imprisonment if he had elected to reveal the members of his coterie of spies (Pilat 1952). If he had done so, he might have saved his life and that of his wife Ethel, but he would also have changed the presence of his self: He would have acknowledged that he was in fact an agent of the USSR and a member of a coterie of spies. He remained silent and obscure and years later people were debating the nature of his self.

Grice's interest in ambiguity and its implications for conversational interaction are confined to those that are deliberate and intentional. We must consider, however, both forms of ambiguity, the intended and the unintended. To take up the first, in such presentations of ambiguity, a self is achieving its presence as one familiar with the nuances of language as well as one possessing complex attitudes. Grice's own example indicates this: the general who captured the province of Sind in India for the British sent a message to the Foreign Office in London with just one word in Latin "*Peccavi,*" which can be translated as "I have sinned." He had reason, no doubt, to believe that those in the Foreign Office knew enough Latin to understand his code. The pun involving two languages, however, also reveals something about the general's attitude: The taking of the Sind was not a totally noble enterprise and that, though he and the British may now have Sind, they have also sinned. Further, it also reveals a general given to wordplay and hence to play, a self that is both or alternately (ambiguously?) religious and playful.

In producing deliberate ambiguity in one's communications he or she can also intend to deceive the other and claim a self that is not warranted. A man having spent his last five years in jail may well answer the query about his whereabouts with "I was out of local circulation." This can signify that he was (a) traveling overseas, (b) living in another part of the city or country, (c) in a mental institution, or (d) in prison. The recipient of this statement may choose not to probe further and demonstrate his tact or choose to probe further and demonstrate his inquisitiveness. There are, however, special relationships in which the latter course of action is mandatory—for example, in interviewing someone for a job in which the history of the self of the applicant is relevant.

Unintended ambiguity results from either careless use of locutions or, in the use of certain phrases that are inherently ambiguous, being interpreted in one way rather than another. A burglar is holding a gun to a policeman and the policeman says, "Give that thing to me" and the burglar's accomplice, standing a few feet away from the burglar himself, says, "Let him have it, Chris." Chris, the burglar with the gun, shoots the policeman and he is wounded. A few minutes later Chris shoots and kills another policeman. In the trial of the two men—Chris Craig and Derek Bentley—Bentley's lawyer argued that the phrase "Let him have it, Chris," was a response to the policeman's request, "Give that thing to me," and was a conciliatory move. That Bentley was also standing apart from Chris, was already in the custody of another policeman, and did not make any move to be either aggressive or to escape indicated circumstantially that Bentley could have signified to Chris to surrender the gun. The prosecution, however, argued—and police witnesses claimed as well—that Bentley had in fact "incited" Chris to shoot the policeman. The jury, with strong incitement from the Lord Chief Justice of England, who presided over the trial, convicted both for murder. Chris Craig, who had in fact pulled the trigger and killed the policeman and who was also the leader of the other, was sentenced to life in prison, because he was sixteen years old, while the slightly older Bentley was sentenced to death and eventually hanged.[5]

In this instance, an ambiguity that was not intended and was a result of a clash of the colloquial significance of an expression and the literal one resulted in the conviction of Bentley. Colloquially, "Let him have it" can signify, "Let him have the works" and be taken to be a demand that Chris Craig kill the policeman. In this case, however, Bentley's usage was a *continuation* of the policeman's demand, "Give that thing to me": the "have" in Bentley's expression *reciprocating* the policeman's "Give" and the "it" in Bentley's expression referring to the "that" of the policeman. The plausible interpretation here was that Bentley, having already surrendered to the police, was asking Chris Craig to surrender the gun as well as himself. In the circumstances in which he found himself—gunfire around him, police officers in control of him and of the proceedings—Bentley also had to be brief, all too brief as it turned out. The expression he used came to be taken as an expression of an aggressive, rebellious, and murderous self, a self of a proletarian character with no respect for property and its ownership, as the Lord Chief Justice defined him for the jury.

The relevance of Grice's observation becomes more apparent when we examine what he describes, in a later paper, as "further reflections about the proliferation of the senses." As an antidote to the unhappy consequences of such proliferation, Grice notes,

I would like to propose for acceptance a principle which I might call Modified Occam's Razor: Senses are not to be multiplied beyond necessity. Of course the application of this principle would depend on what was to be counted as necessity. (1989: 47)

If only Bentley had used a noun, instead of a pronoun . . . yet, I do not want to claim that Bentley was hanged for using a pronoun . . . or do I?

In the less momentous encounters—in everyday conversations, courtship, discourses, quarrels and so on—clarity and the production of the "senses" of words and sentences that are subject to Occamite principles may present and display selves with which it would be easier to cooperate. Nevertheless, there is no doubt that such precision is difficult to achieve in everyday encounters. In such encounters, unlike the case with Bentley, there is the chance for the other interlocutors to ask for clarification, specification, and so on if and when necessary and if the imputation of a particular identity to the self is made addressively, it can be denied in the response and a new attribution elicited.

This can occur in ongoing discursive interactions as they proceed with various bumps and grinds. Each input into the conversation uses various words that the other can take to signify a subtly different meaning than was evident on the surface, either reject it or expand on it on his or her own, and redefine the ensuing communication as well as the selves involved in them. These ambiguities provide opportunities for individuals to *shade* their selves in varying colorations and contours as the conversational interactions proceed. These plays of differences do not so much obviate the presence of self as give it the means for the implying of a complex and variable self.

In the following discussion in the book club there are seven participants, but only a few of them speak—Judy, Mary, and Anne.

| | |
|---|---|
| *Anne:* | *Mary, is this going to be our last meeting for . . .* |
| *Mary:* | *I am not. . . .* |
| *Anne:* | *For the season?* |
| *Mary:* | *This is a democracy; this isn't my agency, for Christsake.* |
| *Judy:* | *This is the first time we have talked about there being a leader.* |
| *Anne:* | *Well, we assumed.* |
| *Mary:* | *You assumed too much.* |
| *Judy:* | *Who is the co-ordinator then?* |
| *Anne:* | *The cat wants its dinner.* |
| *Judy:* | *We have had meetings in the summer, or later.* |
| *Mary:* | *Yeah.* |
| *Judy:* | *I remember wearing sandals.* |
| *Anne:* | *It will be kind of fun. In the other book clubs I have belonged to, there is a leader, the leader you know first reads the book then might do some research about the author and if we are reading a period piece you know, you might do a little research about what's going on in at that time and it is kind of fun.* |

| | |
|---|---|
| *Judy:* | *I have been in a book club like that. I like that.* |
| *Anne:* | *Which is kind of fun, so it gives you a kind of reference.* |

(Book Club Transcripts)

Anne's question, "Is this going to be our last meeting?" is addressed to Mary and this imputes to Mary a leadership role. The mere putting of the question addressed to Mary is enough to allow this imputation to be made. Mary counters with "This is a democracy; this isn't my agency for Christsake" and rejects the imputation. Not only has Mary interpreted the question as one that regarded her not merely as a leader but as a dictator or autocrat. This is the absent word that is signified by the alacrity with which Mary jumps to the word "democracy"—a word with rich implication in American society. In the usage adopted here, it does not refer to an organized political system but to an egalitarian and consultative pattern of relationships in everyday life. Mary is keen, in fact, to indicate that her self is not either a dictatorial or autocratic one, but a democratic one, a standing of her self achieved by using one word and then qualifying it by saying "This is not my agency," with additional emphasis provided by the blasphemy "Christsake."

Judy retracts the imputation of autocracy, if indeed there ever was one in Anne's question, by using the word leader in her locution: "This the first time we have talked about there being a leader." Anne rushes in with "Well, we assumed." Mary is once again quick to shield herself, this time, of being even a "leader": "You assumed too much," she says and continues to shade her presence. Judy continues to save the situation by using a more, shall I say, democratic title now: "Who is the co-ordinator then?"

A cat has wandered in and is demanding attention. Anne changes the topic by referring to the cat. The remark about the cat is of course irrelevant to the topic at hand, but the visible presence of the cat and the fact that it was making a noise makes the remark acceptable and will not indicate either a deranged or absent self for Anne. Far from that being the case it turns out to be an adroit move by Anne to divert attention from the uncomfortable moment that is developing. In fact, it indicates a coloration of Anne's self as one that is attentive to her surroundings and concerned with maintaining decorum. Judy gets back to the main topic: "We have had meetings in the summer." And she remembers wearing sandals. Anne enters the scene now with a long statement that addresses the remark with which this entire episode began—her question to Mary that made her a leader: "In the other book clubs I have belonged to, there is a leader. . . ." This statement speaks to the earlier remark, justifies it, and seeks to persuade Mary, or someone else, to become a leader, because it was "fun." Anne had redeemed herself as one who does not deliver ill-advised questions, but as one who knew what she was doing; she has reshaded herself into this by giving significant detail about the leader's role and responsibility in the other book club. Further, this move softens the situation by introducing "fun" as the reason to have a leader rather than a desire for an autocracy. This is consistent with her earlier interjection about the cat as a means of diffusing conversational tensions.

It is clear that the presence of variations in the interpretation of the texts that are available in the course of interactions allows for the emergence of shading in the construction of self, shades and shifting differentiations that result from the existence of multiple significance of words. An individual can use this property of discourse to introduce ambiguity deliberately and achieve an incoherence to one's self, or to both accept an imputation and alter it to one's advantage by deliberate shadings. This can be seen clearly in the following exchange. It is a point in a telephone conversation that Joseph and Sam were having.

| | |
|---|---|
| *Joseph:* | *The reason I called, I'm gonna be in the city office tomorrow so you won't reach me.* |
| *Sam:* | *I thought you go on Thursdays now.* |
| *Joseph:* | *I'm gonna alternate. I'll take the day Thursday, you know Thursday is a bad day for me because I have school Thursday night. Normally it would be okay 'cause I can leave. I'm downtown already, but, I tried the last time and I got there like an hour and half, two hours early and there was nothing to do. I was just wasting time.* |
| *Sam:* | *Oh, okay.* |

(Office Transcripts)

Sam is subtly asking Joseph for an explanation of Joseph's movements, and the change in the normal routine of his duties. Joseph colors his explanation with a lot of details about his condition: his "school" in the evening, the waste of his time. To his explanation, Sam says, "Oh, okay."

Joseph goes on and introduces another shade by an apparent case of stuttering—a self that is uncertain, apologetic:

| | |
|---|---|
| *Joseph:* | *Well, I don't I'll I'll probably do it tomorrow. I am I'll, I'll. . . .* |
| *Sam:* | *I figured you go on Thursdays.* |
| *Joseph:* | *Yeah.* |
| *Sam:* | *Your leg still bothering you?* |
| *Joseph:* | *Yeah. It cleared up for awhile and then it flared up again because I keep walking on it when I had gout. I just forced myself. I pulled a tendon in my foot so it is very irritating.* |
| *Sam:* | *Can you drive?* |
| *Joseph:* | *I can drive, because it is my left foot.* |
| *Sam:* | *I know.* |
| *Joseph:* | *Because I have to use the elevator, I can't go where there are stairs.* |
| *Sam:* | *Yeah.* |

(Office Transcripts)

It can be seen in this exchange that each participant was seeking to create a presence with his discursive acts, but a presence that was subtly varied as the exchange proceeded: It begins with Sam as a demanding and uncompromising boss and then abruptly shifts to a Sam who is solicitous about Joseph's health. This, too, is shaded presence: on the one hand it shows concern and on the other it is a question about Joseph's capacity to continue the work he has been assigned to do. Sam is able to present himself as aloof and interested, solicitous and calculating, domineering and compassionate within the confines of a brief interaction. Joseph, in turn, gives answers that are detailed descriptions of his physical condition, saying that in fact he is handicapped, but qualifying it by saying that as long as there are elevators, he can still do the work. The subtly shaded implications are accepted by Joseph—who is after all in a subordinate position—and it is reshaded by him in equally subtle ways.

Shading a self is an ongoing activity that results from the multiple significance that words have and acquire in given situations and interactions. This shading can occur spontaneously in ongoing conversations, or they can be used with forethought so that a vivid self is not made available to the other. Such shadings are used to imply a self for the other as for the individual himself or herself.

The submaxim "be brief" brings in the idea of parsimony again and indeed overlaps with the maxim of quantity. Grice expands it with "avoid unnecessary prolixity." In other words, there is a socially and situationally determined *measure* of necessary prolixity in discourses. Consider the following exchange, the concluding moments of the discussion in a book club. They are discussing the date of the next meeting:

| | |
|---|---|
| *Mary:* | *How about the 12th?* |
| *Judy:* | *Is Wednesday the 12th okay?* |
| *Mary:* | *Yes.* |
| *Susan:* | *Oh, I think.* |
| *Mary:* | *OK, where?* |
| *Judy:* | *1350, 174th Street.* |
| *Susan:* | *174th?* |
| *Judy:* | *174th.* |
| *Susan:* | *Could you repeat the address?* |
| *Judy:* | *1350 174th Street.* |

(Book Club Transcripts)

Clearly there was no unnecessary prolixity in this discussion: parsimonious, to the point, and the social and situational purposes of the discussion were fully realized. Consider an alternative:

| | |
|---|---|
| *Susan:* | *I am not back from vacation until July 10th. John and I and the kids are going to Crete. We were there last year too and we want to see Knossos again. The kind . . .* |
| *Judy:* | *Okay, It is the 12th then.* |

It would have been appropriate for Judy to have cut Susan off at this stage and brought the discussion back to the main topic even though Susan's discourse was an attempt to give some color to her self by giving details about her vacation plans. Insofar as the topic was the date of the next meeting, Susan's detailed description of her vacation was unnecessarily prolix. If indeed the topic on the table was Susan's vacation plans, her discourse was necessarily correct and parsimonious: It gave details of where she and her family were going and answered the implicit question of why they were going to the same place they visited the previous year. That is, the prolixity or brevity of the discourse depends on the self that is suitable to be presented at defined occasions.

The last of the submaxims, be orderly, however, depends on the degree of orderliness that one can expect in a conversational discourse. Needless to say, a certain degree of orderliness is necessary so that the other can answer the discourse intelligently and fruitfully. However, conversational analysts have discovered many structures to discourses that on the surface may seem disorderly but do nevertheless fulfill a variety of pragmatic purposes. These structures of everyday discourses, discovered and painstakingly documented by the conversation analysis—topic generation, turn-taking, interruptions, overlaps, side-sequences, embeddedness, preliminaries to conversations and preliminaries to preliminaries, corrections by others and corrections by self, repairs of conversational inputs by self or by other, listing, and closings—add complexity to interactions and achieve rich communicative goals. They in fact systematically *qualify* the self of the addresser and addressee and *shade* their respective presences in the interaction. Yet, one can take this complexity of structures in one's discourse to extremes and prevent the other from answering him or her. Indeed, if one is thoroughly disorderly, it would be taken as a symptom of mental illness. Consider this:

> Losh, I don't know what it is, you see—she says I don' know, I'm sure. There is Cinderella. There is a much better play than that. "I don't know" I said. He is an awful idiot. Oh dear God, I'm so stupid. That is putting two and two together—saying I really don't know—saying Cathie, and so I observe—and flowers.

> (Henderson and Gillespie, 1944; in Abse, 1971:55)

The allusions, the side-references, and the pronominal references are all in such disarray that no commensurate answers could be provided for this discourse. Compare this to a discourse from a member of the book club:

> *I went to that Monticello, which has been really fixed up, beautifully restored a few years ago and I've read a lot of these things that he had written and there is no question that he was a racist. On the other hand that was one of the most interesting places I have even been. He was so incredibly brilliant. I mean the breadth of his mind and the things he did. He was a philosopher, and you know*

*this, a scientist who did all these real innovations in terms of farming techniques.*
*He is an art collector. He's it is just amazing, in Monticello. A wonderful house.*

(Book Club Transcripts)

A long disquisition on Thomas Jefferson and his famous home, and it is without a doubt a rather disorderly one. After the initial announcement of her visit to Monticello, Susan says, "which has been fixed up; beautifully restored." This is on the surface a disorderly redundancy but on close inspection it will be seen that the second phrase introduces additional qualifications to the first: "fixed up" is a colloquialism more properly used to work on a small scale, on an unimportant place, whereas "restored" alludes to major and significant enterprises. The word often occurs in conjunction with art and sculpture, and archeology; a damaged work of art is restored, broken sculpture is restored, the palace at Knossos was restored by Arthur Evans. With the adverbial qualification of restored by "beautiful," the Jeffersonian home has been elevated in stature to that of a work of art or an archeological find. The redundancy here succeeds superbly in conveying significant information and, above all, the attitude of the speaker. Immediately, however, she adds another qualification to her attitude: "No question that he was a racist." She may well admire Jefferson and his home, but she must acknowledge, by using another disorderly intrusion, that she knows that he was a racist and that she does not condone that: "No question," about that. Again this intrusion indicates another of her attitudes. But she is off again indicating her admiration for Jefferson by cataloguing, not in the simple form of listing them, but by a series of sentences with a number of qualifying terms, the extent of Jefferson's achievements: brilliant, breadth of mind, philosopher, scientist, innovator. The disorderliness of this discourse functions to indicate both the contradictoriness of the man about whom the address is being made and the complexity of the attitudes that the speaker had toward him—indeed the complexity of her self.

In formal exchanges, such as the examination and cross examination of witnesses in courts of law, these embedded structures will not be allowed. Any disorderliness, going into side-sequences and giving embedded answers, would be, typically, truncated and the witness brought back to the main thread. A minimal self is all that is required in these interactions: I was there, this is what I saw, not what his friend thought about what he saw and not what his friend's wife, who is a doctor, thought about it. No doubt, however, that orderliness of one's utterances—that is, productions that are not embedded with allusions, side-sequences, and conditionals and contractions, not to speak of contradictions and syntactical, semantic, prosodic, and metaphorical infelicitous—need to be avoided. To violate this maxim systematically is not only to achieve obscurity of communication, but it also makes one become socially ineffective and to absent one's self from the felicity of being in a world of others.

To conclude, to debate whether the self exists and if so what is its "form" or "shape" and ask whether it has a content and, if so, what is the nature of the substance that is its content, are questions that betray an entrapment in substantivist metaphors. Phenomena can exist in the world without having to possess a finite shape or a finished form, without being a container in which various items are stored or concealed. Some phenomena, or perhaps all phenomena, exist as moments in ongoing processes of definition and redefinition, their contours and boundaries changing and rearranging themselves, but always subject to logic of differentiation. The self is such a phenomena: An individual gives it presence by various acts, discursive and otherwise, and others respond to it. In the course of such transactions a self, of varying shades and contours to be sure, is constituted and sustained, with various degrees of efficiency and success. Such a presence for the self is achieved by the discourses that the individual has with himself or herself as with the others. Insofar as any given individual is always in communion with himself or herself, as with the others, presumptive or real, a self is always present.

Such a self exists as the *relational* positing of a subject vis-à-vis an other in a verbal and visual drama of human relations. It is a relational position because it is achieved only in the presence of others, real or imagined, and, with their cooperation and support, may have to be surrendered, sooner or later, and be replaced by another. As such, the self is not a mere center of the discourse and does not claim any a priori privilege. Such claims would lead to solipsism. Rather, an individual speaks and expects to be heard and answered as he or she hears, and listens to, and answers the speeches of the others. As one speaks he or she expects to be not only heard but answered as well, that is, supported or rejected, accepted or contradicted, with varying shades in between these binary opposites.

## NOTES

1. In recent years the individual as an amnesiac has become the favored version in some theoretical perspectives. In ethnomethodology the individual is viewed, as a matter of *policy* always in his or her situated capacity and accomplishing a reality in the situation itself all by himself or herself—though even these pronouns may be unsuitable in this context. John Heritage (1984: 242), in his discussion of conversations as "context-shaped" and "context-renewing," conspicuously disprefers, if I may say so, a discussion of context-remembering, not to speak of situation-remembering. Boden and Zimmerman express this situational specificity of ethnomethodology very succinctly as follows: "Structure . . . is accomplished in and through the moment-to-moment turn-taking procedures of everyday talk in both mundane and momentous settings of human intercourse" (1991:17) and advance the view that one can consider social structure only in this manner. It is no doubt true that structures are "accomplished" in this manner. However, the people who do all these "accomplishments" are

irrefutably minded creatures who know their places in the relevant structures before they begin all their momentous and mundane accomplishments and remember them and use them. Not only do they use their recollections, they use them in cognizance of the consequences of the particular uses to which they are putting them. If there is no remembering there can be no generalization and continuity of action with the past.

In a discussion of Giles Delueze's and Felix Guattari's theories of the subject, William Bogard too argues for a view of the human as "body" that attends to the immediate context of its "desires" in the world and thereby becomes a "subject." He puts it this way: "And the whole problem of the subject—its genesis and historical development—is a problem of how desire is actualized (segmented, ordered) on the surface of bodies, that is, as the sense of bodies" (1998: 56). If desire is actualized in this way in the genesis of a subject, it still will presumably remember it and allow it to influence the next actualization. From Bogard's rendition one gathers, however, that in facing a new situation, this "body" will not remember that he or she was a subject in an earlier one and will have to start all over again and become a new subject insofar as it is only a "body." This view of the subject as being born, again and again, to suit the "desires" of every situation leads Bogard to an egregious misrepresentation of the work of G. H. Mead and Herbert Blumer. Bogard opines, "Deleuzian (and Guattarian) 'subjects' are not the selves of interactionist and constructionist theories, which magically conjure themselves into existence in the process of speaking or communicating" (Bogard 1998: 65). There is neither magic nor conjuring involved in the presencing of selves in interactions; rather, each individual remembers his or her past "desires" and remembers the meanings they elicited and gives presence to them as his or her self, verbally and gesturally. The claim here is that any given infant (as a body?) enters an already constituted society and is transformed into a self, that is, endowed with a rich memory as it undergoes various experiences, a memory that is both emotional and cognitive.

To deny the presence of a remembered self is to commit one's theories to a position that can only be described as solipsistic fascism: every man and woman his or her own dictator constructing a world without attending to his or her own memory and the memory that is shared with others in the shape of institutions and history. The approaches to the "subject" that Bogard recommends and to "structures" that Boden and Zimmerman recommend so enthusiastically are truly awesome in their virtuosity—like the tricks performed by Houdini. They initially put various constraints on themselves with what may be termed epistemological locks and chains and fight their way out, impressing themselves and a few others. In dealing with the nature of the subject this procedure consists of inventing certain a priori *conditionals* and then showing how one particular theory does not meet these conditions and then proposing another theory. These procedures are no doubt excellent as tricks, and amusing too, but quite unnecessary and unproductive in the work of sociology.

2. These features of conversations—openings, topics, turn-taking, interruptions, overlaps, closings—are derived from the work of Harvey Sacks, Emmanuel Schegloff, and Gail Jefferson. They have been described variously as the "technology" of conversations and as "devices." I am using these devices here to investigate the pragmatic consequences of their occurrence in interactional talk. The work of Sachs, Schegloff, and Jefferson is described and discussed in Heritage (1984), Boden (1994), and Boden and Zimmerman (1991).

3. In fact in many societies the ritual phrases used in closing a conversation express goodwill or suggest that there will be further interactions. In English "goodbye" has been used from at least 1709 to leave someone and "cheerio" has been used in England from 1910 to say farewell, I gather from the dictionary. "Farewell" itself indicates the required sentiments for leave-taking. "Good day" and "good morrow" again express the wishes of the leave-taker for the other. If one leaves the other with these sentiments, he or she can hope for and expect a resumption of interaction in the future. In the Indian subcontinent and Sri Lanka one leaves an interaction by saying "I will go and come back"—often contracted, interestingly enough to "I will come now." In Tamil for instance it is "nan varan" and in Sinhalese it is, "mama gihan eneva." In Marathi, it is again "I will come back": "mi yeto." In these rituals and their vocabulary, then, the solidarity of the interactants and their hope of continuing the same are expressed and affirmed. This is nicely paralleled in the American "see you later" and "see you soon." In French "adieu" again expresses goodwill and fare wellness with the help of God, while "au revoir" indicates further interactions. One can, of course, leave the other by using hostile forms. He or she can say, "drop dead" or "fuck off" or "damn you" or the Shakespearean "away, slight man," and obviate further solidary connections.

4. In this chapter, I am using three kinds of conversations: one made up by me to make a point, recorded conversations made at an office of law enforcement, and the discussions at a book club. The latter two are reproduced in italicized form, while the made-up examples are in standard type. The excerpt from Ribeiro is reproduced in the same form as the original.

5. This is a famous incident that occurred in England in 1953 and has been made into a film, *Let Him Have It* (Vermillion Productions, Peter Medak, Director). It has also generated a number of books, songs and a social movement dedicated to clearing Bentley's name even after these many years. In late 1998 he was exonerated by a judicial commission. An authoritative account of the case can be found in Yallop (1990).

# Chapter 6

# The Plays of the Self

So I wish you first a
Sense of theater; only
Those who love illusion
And know it, will go far:
Otherwise we spend our
Lives in confusion
Of what we say and do with
Who we really are.

W. H. Auden

A dictionary provides a column describing the various significations of the word "play." Among these, I would like to choose a few to indicate the meaning in which I want to use the word in association with self. To begin with, to play is "to perform or act (a role or part) in a dramatic performance." The dictionary gives the following significations:

To pretend to be; mimic the activities of: *The boys played cowboy*. To compete against in a game or sport. To take advantage of (another's attitudes or feelings) for one's own interests: *He played on her sympathies*. Activity engaged in for enjoyment or recreation. A move or action in a game. The condition of a ball, puck, or similar object in active or legitimate use or motion. Used in phrases *in play* or *out of play*. Action, motion, or use: *the play of the imagination*. (*American Heritage Dictionary of the English Language*, 1973: 1005)

One can take these varied meanings of play and claim that a self is in play while it is being performed. Not only, however, can the self be *in play*, but it can also be *put* into play either in the sense of a ball or puck being put into play or as in the sense of the play of the imagination. In such plays, the self can be said to be in action and use insofar as it is an objectified feature of the minding processes of the individual. Such a conception indicates that not only is a self performed but it is *put* into play by moves of differing deliber-

221

ativeness and purposiveness by the minding organism. That is, in putting a self into play in the performance of a role and keeping it in play, an individual is seeking to achieve certain fulfillments and consummations just as he or she may be seeking to control others in his or her own interest.

Putting the self into play is not, then, the same as performing a role. In interactions one surely performs, but he or she also puts a selected aspect of his or her self into play. Such plays of the self can occur in one's encounters with the material objects in his or her world or the human ones. In an extensive discussion of what he calls the "contact experience" of objects, distant or near, Mead argues that the "perceptual function" of the self is able to take the role of the material object itself and imagine and anticipate the nature and quality of the object:

> When the individual assumes the attitude of pushing a heavy object, its character as ponderous is more than stimulation to exercise effort. It is a sense of the pressure or *inertia* which the body will exert upon the individual. It is true that memory images of past expenditures of effort upon it or like objects may arise, but these images will be of the efforts expended aroused by the stimulation of what we call the resistance of the object. They do not of themselves carry with them the location of the resistance in the object, nor is this location of the resistance given in the definition of the boundaries of the objects through sight and touch. What has taken place is the "*feeling one's self into*" the object. (1938: 310, my emphasis)

One feels one's self into the object, or one puts one's self into it, *assuming* the quality of the resistance it will offer initially and then actually *experiencing* it when contact occurs.

> One, then, identifies the mere stimulation to exercise more effort with the expenditure of force on the part of the object because this playing of the role of the heavy object has excited one's response in advance of the actual contact with the object. (Mead 1938: 311)

How do these observations apply to the mundane tasks of everyday life? One can in fact extend Mead's argument here to suggest that in all encounters in the world, whether with distant heavy objects or immediate light ones, and whether they are ponderous, inanimate objects or animate humans of varying degrees of ponderousness, an individual confronts them in similar ways and puts the feelings of his or her self into it. Indeed, he or she puts his or her self into play in such encounters. Consider a human who encounters an automobile or, even more mundanely, a toaster. Let us construct a scene: A man comes down to breakfast and his daughter says, "Daddy the toaster is broken." He says "That's okay, I will take my tools and repair it." He proceeds to do so. In undertaking these acts the man has put into play many of the moves that Mead had described for the heavy object that his man encountered. With these moves, the man has objectified his self as one who can repair a broken toaster and put his self into play: In his imagination he has assumed the resistance the task will offer and is able to say to himself that he could handle it. This play can have one of two outcomes; he can successfully repair the toaster and enhance the standing of his self in his eyes and the eyes of his daughter, or else he can fail and feel the commensurate effects on his self. In his encounter with the toaster he not only put the "feeling of his self," in Mead's words, into the object, but also put his self into play by seeking to repair it. Indeed, contact with all and any material object in the world gives a human a chance to put his or her self into play.

In interactions with humans, too, one not only performs a role but also puts a self into play. Consider again a simple example: A man is introduced to a woman he finds attractive at a gathering and he has to decide what to do next: Does he do the cool, aloof, and formal bit? Does he do the warm and friendly bit? Does he do the aggressively flirtatious and erotic bit? Does he do the indifferent and contemptuous bit? Each of these is a performance, but with each of these moves he is putting a self into play. Each such move will meet its own destiny in the responses from the other with commensurate reverberations to the self of the man in question. He may be cool and aloof and formal, but the woman may decide to be aggressively flirtatious, thereby making him develop either a new set of acts or continue in the original role. If he has originally acted warmly, she may in turn act aloof and contemptuous, and if he has sought to be flirtatious and erotic, she may rebuff him. In each of these acts the individuals are putting their respective selves into play and expecting return acts in a state of uncertainty. Putting the self into play is then a gamble, as Goffman has described in many of his essays on the rituals of interaction (1967), always a signifying moves characterized by uncertainty and dependent for its meaning on the return moves of the other. In other words, the resistance to the efforts one puts into these acts comes from the return acts of the others. Each partner in such encounters can be said to have put a self into play and waited for the outcome.

In putting a self into play, what Mead calls the "I" is acting and the responses that the acting elicits become incorporated as the "me" of the individual in question, bringing at least the possibility of novelty, creativity, and initiative to an action. (Mead 1934: 177–178). The "I" then, in Mead's view, allows for a creative and structurally untrammeled act to be executed by a conscious self. In these acts, a self, constituted in earlier acts, is put into play and the consequences of such playing experienced and used subsequently to define further aspects of the self. In such moves, the self is put into play, just as a ball may be put into play or a pair of dice, and the consequences of the act are *cognized* and *felt* and accepted as a meaning for the self. An act is then initiated and as it is initiated it carries the fate of the self with it; as the act matures, it can be expanded, qualified, truncated, jettisoned prematurely, or allowed to run its course. It can also be frustrated, thwarted in its course, qualified, and amended or allowed a consummation by the acts of the other or by the obdurate material world. This capacity of the plays of the self to elicit responsive plays from others and create obligations for the initial player to respond to them is an essential element of the interactive process. These plays occur in a trajectory as a continuum of commuting variables. At each moment in the continuum the play can either increase the emotional intensity of the self and its social value or diminish it.

It is in this capacity to put the self into play that one will find the intimate relationship between emotions and the self. Indeed one individual puts his or her self into play by introducing it into the self of another and inducing various emotional responses and reactions from it. In such proceedings the initiator may have control at the beginning, as well as choice and authority, but there is always the chance that the emotions generated may not be the ones that were wanted because the other has control over his or her responses. The fact that each individual puts his or her self into play by choosing one response rather than another means that the emotions and the character of the play that ensues cannot be predicted with any certainty. Emotions are not immanent and self-existing phenomena that can be reduced to given basic forms, nor are they "constructed" in the abstract or independently of situations. Rather, they are constituted *in* and *through* situated interactions and become manifest when selves are put into play in structures of experience—either imaginary or overt.

The agentic capacity of the individual, his or her ability to take action, accept or resist the power and influence of external structures, and thereby exist as a person in his or her own right, is manifest as plays of the self. Agency is an essential ingredient in the ontology of the human individual, a feature of his or her being as a sociolinguistic creature. If through labor a human being creates this world and also creates himself or herself, such "life activity," as Marx (1963: 127) called it, is really a manifestation of his or her agentic capacities. The obstacles to agentic expressiveness are social and cultural ones and socially and culturally constituted psychological ones. To be an agent is to be a self, conscious and cognizant of one's presence in a world and a community of others and having the capacity to act, to put a self into play, if not always the opportunity to do so. For a human individual, being is doing, and if he or she does not get the chance to "do" he or she may be forced to find some secondary substitutes—light a cigarette, get a drink and yet another drink, knit, crochet, play cards alone, watch somebody else act, and so on.

In putting the self into play, then, an individual involves it both cognitively and emotionally in a field of others by means of various acts. He or she puts his or her ideas, images, and conceptions of self into play and awaits validation or rejection. Similarly, in putting a self into play, an individual is also putting his or her emotions into play and awaits their development, and consummation or frustration. Conceptions of self, as of emotions, then, are not owned as such but used, put into play, in an ongoing series of acts, each act extending or truncating earlier ones.

The proceedings in which individuals put their selves into play and experience the consequences are ubiquitous ones in social life. An individual, in putting his or her self into play, typically draws another into it and the ordinary moments in life then are characterized by a series of plays—however unobtrusive they may be at times and however muted the emotions generated by them may be. In other words, there is a fundamentally agonistic quality to human acts, and it may be found in all social acts. In some it is the central *motif* of the encounter—for example, a quarrel or a debate or a transaction between a salesman and a customer, while in others it may only be a *leitmotif,* as in a sociable conversation. Further, one can also distinguish between *routine* acts, with only a minimal capacity to offer resistance and to excite emotional resonances, and *extraordinary* ones where there is greater resistance and the possibility of complex emotional resonances. The former may be put on one end of a continuum labeled *ennui* whereas the latter may be put at the other end and called *ecstasy,* with most human acts falling at points between the two.

A good example of ennui, an absence of the quality of the agonistic in one's experiences of life, is the worker in a modern assembly line. His or her work consists of repetitive performances on a moving platform and it is always the same series of acts. The worker, says Harvey Swados, who lived and worked among automobile workers in Detroit, hates his work because it "is mindless, endless, stupefying, sweaty, filthy, noisy, exhausting, insecure in its prospects and practically without hope of advancement" (1962: 111). The job is "mindless" and "stupefying" because it lacks the agonistic element, does not offer a sufficient degree of resistance, and one repeats the moves "endlessly," i.e., without dramatic development or a possibility of a denouement. Ennui sets in and the worker finds the job and the products he is making hateful and degrading.

True ecstasy, of course, occurs but rarely and most human experiences may be only a few short degrees away from ennui, though occasionally they may move toward the pole of ecstasy. In such moments of ecstasy, one puts a self into play and feels its presence in heightened moods and differing shades and colors. Here is a description by Fanny Trollope of a state of ecstasy that she witnessed in nineteenth-century Cincinnati:

> And now in every part of the church a movement was perceptible, slight at first, but by degrees becoming more decided. Young girls arose, and sat down, and rose again; and then the pews opened, and several came tottering out, their hands clasped, their heads hanging on their bosoms, and every limb trembling, and still the hymn went on; but as the poor creatures approached the rail, their sobs and groans became audible. . . . Young creatures, with features pale and distorted, fell on their knees on the pavement, and soon sunk forward on their

faces; the most violent cries and shrieks followed, while from time to time a voice was heard in convulsive accents, exclaiming "Oh Lord!" "Oh Lord Jesus!" "Help me, Jesus!" and the like. ([1832] 1997: 63–64)

Ecstasy is a state of feeling, an experiencing of intense emotionality in which mind and body participate jointly, often giving the mind extraordinary powers of perception and intuition, or, in the converse, blindness and dullness, and the body unusual strength and vigor. *Ecstasies are the processes of stepping out of the routine states of being, of leaving our current selves for a time and entering another such state or phase of the self.* The "stepping out" leads to the creation of the new phase, and once it is created it may take a life of its own and determine the subsequent moves of the individual.[1]

The reaching of different states of feeling is achieved by the acts of putting the self into play. Typically, once it is put into play and the emotionality achieved and experienced, there is an end to it and a return to a state of normality. The reaching of a peak experience of emotionality and its resolution is what writers from Aristotle to Kenneth Burke have called "catharsis," a "purging" or "releasing" or "relieving" of the emotions. For Aristotle, as for others since, catharsis meant the purging of emotions by vicarious participation in the enactments of a tale, a safe involvement that does not present any real physical danger to the participant. Jonathan Lear has argued, with textual support from Aristotle's writings, that catharsis is the experience of

tragic emotions in an appropriately inappropriate environment which, I think, helps to explain our experience of relief in the theater. We imaginatively live life to the full but we risk nothing. The relief is thus not that of releasing pent-up emotions per se; it is the relief of releasing these emotions in a safe environment. (Lear 1992: 334).

Such "theaters" to use Lear's expression, are not found only within the confines of a theater, but can be found wherever humans foregather. In these theaters of everyday life individuals put their selves into play and achieve catharsis even in environments that are safe only in varying degrees. The catharsis is achieved by a deliberate act of the self, by in fact putting the self into varying degrees of danger and experiencing the aftereffects.

Werner Stark (1987) has argued, however, that catharsis is a recurrent release or suspension from social constraints. Religious rituals and carnivals, which provided such release in traditional societies, he notes, have been replaced in modern societies by dances in discotheques, music concerts, and sporting events. If the cathartic events in traditional societies amounted to continuous orgies for a number of days, as in carnivals, the modern forms, Stark notes, are "splintered orgies"—periodic indulgences for a few hours in an evening in a dance hall, auditorium, or stadium. These are the new theaters for cathartic experiences.

The concept of putting the self into play does not actually occur in Erving Goffman's monumental work, but many aspects of it nevertheless imply it. One can examine his early monographs on the presentation of self in everyday life (1959) and his analysis of role-distance (1961), then move to the essay on where the action was to be found (1967) and see a natural progression in which putting the self into play from routine events to slightly unusual events to events bordering on the ecstatic are described. In the first work Goffman argues, "When an individual appears before others he knowingly and unwittingly projects a definition of the situation, of which a conception of himself is an important part" (1959: 242). This claim occurs at the end of a long study in which he gives examples of the many ways in which an individual *projects* a "conception of himself." Among the many such examples, I will first select his citation from a fictional account because it captures neatly the notion of putting the self into play in ordinary life.

Preedy is an Englishman vacationing in Spain and undertakes various moves to convey different impressions of his self.

> If by chance a ball was thrown his way, he looked surprised; then let a smile of amusement lighten his face . . . looked around dazed to see that there *were* people on the beach, tossed it back with a smile to *himself* and not a smile *at* the people, and then resumed carelessly his nonchalant survey of space.
>
> But it was time to institute a little parade, the parade of the ideal Preedy. By devious handling he gave any who wanted to look a chance to see the title of his book—a Spanish translation of Homer, a classic thus, but not daring, cosmopolitan too—and then gathered together his beachwrap and bag into a neat sand-resistant pile (methodological and sensible Preedy), rose to stretch himself (big cat Preedy), and tossed aside his sandals (carefree Preedy, after all). (Sansom 1956, in Goffman 1959: 4–5)

In each of the actions that Preedy took, he put his self into play and added a new dimension to it so that in the end he emerged as a very complex character: kindly, methodical, "big cat," carefree. Putting a self into play is then an active and deliberate and self-conscious move. In a later essay on roles and role playing Goffman describes individuals who strive to show a certain detachment from the roles in which they are currently engaged. For example, he describes a group of middle-class schoolgirls who go to a park while on a vacation and "do horse-back riding." By using a variety of moves, they are able to put the self of a "non-horsey set," "non-upper class," "inexperienced rider" into play to the audience. "The six I observed," Goffman writes,

> came in clothing patently not designed as a consolidation of the horsewoman role: pedal-pushers, cotton leotards, ball-type flats, frilly blouses. One girl, having been allotted the tallest horse, made mock of the scene by declining to get

on because of the height, demanding to be allowed to go home. When she did get on, she called her horse "Daddy-O," diverting her conversation from her friends to her horse. (1961: 111)

In Goffman's investigation of "where the action" was to be found (1967), he finds it in gambling and in various other activities in which individuals took chances, put their "character to the test," engaged in contests, and experienced their "consequentiality" and "fatefulness." These plays are designed to produce extraordinary meanings for the self, generate more intense emotions, and achieve novel and complex signs with which an individual can define his or her self. With these moves selves can be put into play and the risks of victory and loss—of face, property, life—experienced. If the uncertainty is confronted and the risks taken, there is of course the likelihood of winning new esteem for the self. It is this phenomenon that Georg Simmel, who originated inquiry into acts of this sort in the mundane life, calls "adventures." He writes,

> One of two experiences which are not particularly different in substance, as far as we can indicate it, may nevertheless be perceived as an "adventure" and the other not. The one receives the designation denied the other because of this difference in the relation to the whole of our life. (1971: 187)

That is, a sexual encounter will not be an adventure for a prostitute but for an adolescent having his first sexual experience it certainly would be one because he would be crossing a "threshold." Simmel writes,

> Viewed purely from a concrete and psychological standpoint, every single experience contains a modicum of the characteristics which, if they grow beyond a certain point, bring it to the threshold of adventure. Here the most essential and profound of these characteristics is the singling out of these experiences from the total context of life. (1959: 255)

In stepping over the threshold, in crossing a boundary, a self steps out of its routine presence into another moment, another presence for itself. These are "liminal" events, to use Victor Turner's reworking of a concept from Arnold von Gennep. "Liminality," Turner notes, "is marked by three phases: separation, margin (from *limen*—the Latin for threshold) . . . and reaggregation" (1974: 231–32). Turner finds such liminality in major transformations in the trajectory of a life. However, it is possible to find such liminality in lesser occasions as well. In the liminal moments in an ongoing trajectory of the individual's life, he or she is called upon to put his self into different arenas or differently defined interactions and experience heightened emotionality. Such "liminals" are experienced for awhile, and then the individual returns to the routines of everyday life.

Simmel compares the adventurer to artists and writers:

> For the essence of a work of art, is, after all, that it cuts out a piece of the end-lessly continuous sequences of perceived experience, detaching it from all con-nections with one side or the other, giving it a self-sufficient form as though defined and held together by an inner core. (1971: 189)

Like the artist the adventurer also has to take charge of the situation, even if he or she does not always initiate it himself or herself, and has to use it to put the self into play and anticipate the consequences. These adventurous moves—the acts of putting the self into play and experiencing the fruits thereof—achieve for the individual heightened emotionalities of varying duration and intensity. Once the moves are made, the individual is able to also experience spontaneity, since the next move has to be made without much aforethought and circumstantiality—that is, responding to the acts and moods that emerge from the situation.[2]

In these plays of the self not only are selves presented but they are con-stituted and reconstituted, the character of the self defined and redefined, and its emotionalities given an objective standing in the responses it is able to receive and feel. Further, the self is conferred an identity: champion, hero, winner, one who did not yield, fearless, courageous and so on, or loser, cheat, incompetent, one who yielded and so on. The individual's identity becomes qualified with new adjectives or restated in new noun-phrases and is used as the sign of the self for further relationship with others. From these observations one can see that the various acts of putting the self into play and the experiencing of the emotions that accompany them move seam-lessly from ones that are characterized by low problematicity and intensity of emotion and then cross the threshold to very high ones in a continuum. At each moment in this trajectory, there is always the possibility of one trivial act or series of acts developing into more serious ones with high emotional-ity and exploding into extreme intensities. These developments are depend-ent on the responses each act elicits from the other and are results of the ongoing interaction of the acts and the selves involved in them.

## PRACTICAL PLAYS

Individuals put their selves into play either in direct ways in which their minds, selves, and bodies get involved, often with real physical effects on the latter, or in their imaginations. In practical plays an individual actively under-takes moves that connect him or her to other individuals and physical objects as well as the environment, eliciting responses from them all and incorpo-rating them as a meaning for the self. These may be called *practical plays* and may be distinguished from imaginative plays or *fantasies*. In fantasies the individual puts his or her self into play only in his or her mind but nevertheless experiences emotional involvement. Practical plays can be further divided into encounters, contests, duels, combat, and hunts.

## Encounters

Encounters are occasions in which individuals engage in "focused interactions," as Goffman, who first used the term in this context, puts it (1961). In focused interactions individuals address each other as social objects and seek to influence each other. While Goffman focuses on human interactions, I would include interactions with material objects and animals in this category. In such encounters humans put their selves into play but there is neither an overt conflict nor do they typically generate extremes of emotionality. Encounters have two moments to them: one, routine encounters, and two, adventurous encounters. Often routine encounters of everyday life can be made to generate novelty and uncertainty and heightened emotionality and can be transformed into adventurous ones. One may escape from the ordinary into a liminal duration in such encounters, experience the self at play, and return to the routine.

One arena in which various encounters become transformed into adventurous plays of the self are those ubiquitous gatherings known as parties. Parties are of many kinds and some are organized to enhance and solidify the identities of the official life. There are also parties, the more frequent types, which are organized to be breaks from the routine organization of everyday life, and various licenses are given to the participants to engage in conduct that is different from those of everyday life. Parties are liminal moments in the life of an individual: Typically they separate the individual from earlier roles, rules, regulations—indeed a self—and draw a boundary between them and the new moments of the party. Once the party is over, he or she returns to the original state, albeit somewhat altered. Parties in everyday life are thus comparable to medieval carnivals. In carnivals a day or two are set apart from the normal functioning of everyday life. In Mikhail Bakhtin's words a carnival is

> A boundless world of humorous forms and manifestations that *opposed* the official and serious tone of *ecclesiastical* and *feudal* culture. In spite of their variety, folk festivities of the carnival type, the comic rites and cults, the clowns and fools, giants and dwarfs and jugglers, the vast and manifold literature of parody—all these forms have one style in common: they belong to one culture of folk carnival humor. (1984: 4, emphasis added)

Not only do they have one style in common, but the activities of a carnival are also defined by their opposition to the religious and political institutions of the day. In other words, carnivals are parties of the large-scale, more complex and loose at the same time, marking nevertheless a liminal moment. Social parties of course are not "boundless" as carnivals are and may not have all the features of a carnival; rather they are carnivals on a small-scale.

Parties as a social form can be described as a gathering of individuals, some of whom are known to each other whereas others may be newcomers who hope to find friends. The people come to parties on the basis of invitations, others may come as friends of the guests, and some may even force themselves into the gathering. Usually alcohol and various consumables will be served at the party, the alcohol serving to relax people and enable them to interact in less inhibited ways. It is within this frame that individuals come together and engage in various activities in which the self is put into play. In parties then, definitionally an individual has to put at least certain aspects of his or her identity away and typically present one that bespeaks unseriousness, ludicity, and, at times, foolishness. Further, one has to thrust oneself forward, initiate conversations, participate in them, say appropriate words, and engage in witty banter, in joke telling, anecdote telling, flirtations, seductions—all of which are achieved conversationally. All of these are activities in which and through which selves are put into play and various emotionalities expressed and experienced. Typically in such gatherings a certain mix of gender is arranged so that the smell of sexuality is present—to be sure of varying degrees, depending on the nature of the party and the age of the participants. Furthermore. many people in the party will seek to play roles and present selves that are different from the ones they did in earlier occasions and will again on later ones. Like a carnival, a party can find itself with fools, clowns, and jesters—with one or more of the guests either electing to or being induced to play one or more of these roles. In other words, they suspend their usual selves and put a new self into play—for the time being.

It does not mean, however, that this occurs in all parties. In some parties, one's power and status and prestige from elsewhere may be put into play all over again, and put to the test though in a different setting —including one's sexual power and attractiveness, social graces and interpersonal skills, and so forth. Simmel calls this kind of phenomena a "social game" and contrasts it with other kinds of "sociation," commenting:

All the forms of interaction or sociation among men—the wish to outdo, exchange, the formation of parties, the desire to wrest something from the other, the hazards of accidental meetings and separations, the change between enmity and co-operation, the overpowering by ruse and revenge, in the seriousness of reality, all of these are imbued with purposive contents. In the game, however, they lead their own lives; they are propelled exclusively by their own attraction. . . . To the person who really enjoys it, its attraction rather lies in the dynamics and hazards of the sociologically significant forms of activity themselves. (Simmel 1950:49–50)

Social games are ends in themselves, played only for the sake of sociability, of playing, of enjoying the interactions and interrelationships and agonistics as such. The social game that Simmel uses as an example is coquetry and is described as follows:

> This freedom from all gravity of immutable contents and permanent realities gives coquetry the character of suspension, distance, ideality, that has lead one to speak, with a certain right, of its "art" not only of its "artifices." (1950: 50–51)

In engaging in coquettish behavior an individual undertakes various acts whose task is to engage the attention of a male. Simmel notes, "The nature of feminine coquetry is to play up, alternately, allusive promises and allusive withdrawals—to attract the male, but always to step short of a decision, and to reject him but never to deprive him of all hope" (1950: 50–51).

In these moves an individual can be said to be putting her self into play, awaiting a completion in the acts of the other:

> Yet in order for coquetry to grow on the soil of sociability . . . it must meet with a specific behavior on the part of the male. As long as he rejects its attractions or, inversely, is its mere victim that without any will of its own is dragged along by its vacillations between a half "yes" and a half "no," coquetry has not yet assumed for him the form that is commensurate with sociability. (Simmel 1950: 51)

Nowadays coquetry may not be played with the artfulness with which it was done in earlier centuries; nevertheless, in parties one does put a particular self into play, does play "social games," and does wait for the consequences to develop. Here is a young woman describing an experience at a party. I have deliberately chosen, employing a Durkheimian strategy, the most ordinary of encounters with none of the elements of a grand passion or a serious romantic quest—to show how even here a self is put into play, a threshold crossed, and an adventurous moment created. The following is an account given by a student in one of my classes:

> Upon my arrival at the party I was greeted by my friend at the door. As I walked in I had an awkward feeling that I was the center of attraction. Not knowing where to look, I stuck myself to a wall and looked down. Later on when I began to relax I was able to glance around the room and take in some old faces as well as new ones. Suddenly my eyes focused upon this person whom I had seen a few times in the neighborhood. I felt as though I were in a movie and the crowd seemed to disappear as all my attention was focused on him. But soon I snapped back to reality, aware of the fact I was not alone. He did not see me looking at him, which gave me a sense of safety and control. He appeared not to know very many people, and the people he knew I did not know. My heart

began to slow down as I kept telling myself that I would probably never meet him. At the same time I was hoping that someone I knew, knew him. The party seemed to be dragging along while I still watched him from the corner of my eye. Then I saw him walk over to the closet and get his coat. All my hopes had faded. I knew now that I would never meet him and I was angry at myself for letting my fears win. I felt even more defeated and depressed as he walked out of the door. About half an hour had passed and I danced a few numbers with a friend of mine. I was just getting ready to leave when he walked through the door again. I felt such a relief that I had the urge to run up and hug him but I contained myself. He sat across the room from me and again I felt the excitement. I realized the things I liked about him, he was a casual dresser and from what I could see a comfortable person to be around. A few minutes later a friend of mine walked through the door and came over to me. I explained to her my predicament and to my surprise she knew him. Before I could say another word he was standing directly in front of me. She introduced us and all my fear faded away because I realized in talking to him he was not my knight in shining armor that I imagined. We talked like we had been old friends. He told me he was from California and he would be returning in a couple of days. We had lunch together the next day and that was the last I saw of him. All the things I had felt before I met him had vanished and other feelings of regret and sadness had taken over.

The assumptions I made were based on feelings not yet confirmed by the other. Like many people I was taken strictly by appearance. Later, through communication I was able to know more about the person and realize that it would be simply a friendship and nothing else. This being the first time I experienced this particular situation, I could understand the misleading signals that occur between two people. The assumption on my part was that I felt as though once in his presence he would automatically feel as I did. Hoping that something permanent was to come of this, I was deeply hurt to find out differently.

The experience I described is a common one. But it is important in life to take chances and many times expressing your true feelings can be the biggest chance of all.

In this description a young woman initially experiences, shall I say, a nothingness, where she is able to perform no acts of her own nor to be a party to someone else's acts. The situation soon changes and she is able to put her self into play and reap certain consequences, even though they were not the ones she had anticipated. Her feelings were heightened and her self given a presence as a result of her attraction to the young man, the encounter with him, her sense of disappointment when she thought that he had left the party, and the relief she felt when he appeared again. The encounter continued the following day and the upshot was her realization that nothing worthwhile would "come of this." She was "deeply hurt" at this discovery. Needless to say, there could have been more of the adventurous in it had he been more attracted to her, but this quasi adventure was good enough for the time being: It broke the routine for the young woman and put her self and her emotions into play.

**Contests**

When individuals encounter each other they relate to each other in terms of their respective selves. Gesture, appearance, and words present each self, identified according to relevant particulars, to the other and anticipate commensurate responses from the other. Such encounters are typically managed by the rules of decorum, honor, status and by the exercise of implicit or explicit moves of power. Often such encounters become overt confrontations between the selves of the participants and can emerge as contests for control and domination by one or the other. In such contests, individuals put their best selves forward, either with verbal skills or with physical prowess. At times, such displays of verbal skills will lead to physical attacks. A striking example of contests can be found in the various verbal games that black young men play with each other. There seem to be a great variety of these games—"signifying," "rapping," "to hip," "the put down," "playing the dozens," and "joning" (Hannerz 1969; Abrahams 1974: 240–241). Hannerz, in a field study of some of these games, describes joning as follows:

> The exchanges can occur between two boys who are alone and it is even possible for them to *jone* on some third absent person, usually one of their peers, but the typical situation involves a group of boys: while a series of exchanges may engage one pair of boys after another, most members of the crowd function as audience, inciters, judges—laughing, commenting upon "scoring" and urging the participants on. . . . (1969: 129)

These contests, whether it is of the playful sort described by Hannerz or not, are ubiquitous in social life. Consider the following episode described in Hans Toch's fine study of violent men. He recounts an incident between Jimmy and a police officer that eventually leads to a situation of confrontation and conflict. In this interaction Jimmy and the officer have both put their respective selves into play, with each seeking to best the other. The initial move is made by the police officer who refuses to admit Jimmy to a dance in the school. The school dance is no ordinary dance; rather, it is a special occasion for an adolescent in which he or she can display a self and its social and sexual presence, an arena for the gathering and garnishing of honor.

It is into this charged arena that Jimmy sought entry, and a policeman refuses to let Jimmy enter it. Jimmy in turn seeks to avenge himself, challenging the professional self and honor of the officer by singing a song that questions the manhood of the police. Jimmy describes these events on a later occasion as follows:

> *Interviewer:*     *So you wanted to show him that you didn't like him; so you put this can down. And is that when you started singing?*
> *Subject:*          *Yes.*

| | |
|---|---|
| *Interviewer:* | *Can you give us a little demonstration of how you were singing?* |
| *Subject:* | *Well, it wasn't nothing, you know, that I could . . . I remember all the words, you know . . .but I was.* |
| *Interviewer:* | *What were the lines about?* |
| *Subject:* | *No . . . I will tell it . . . you know, this song about his son, you know. A song . . . "fuck" and all that, you know. "Got jumped on . . . his daddy's a police, you know. His daddy's a punk." All that you know. But he couldn't hear . . . he could hear me singing but he couldn't hear the words.* |
| *Interviewer:* | *Could he hear it now and then, like "son," and "police" and "punk" and key words like that?* |
| *Subject:* | *He could probably hear something like "police" possibly. . . . I say it out loud "police are sissies."* |
| *Interviewer:* | *So he did have an indication that this song you were singing might have something to do with him, huh?* |
| *Subject:* | *Yeah. He might have, you know. It was . . . it was against the police department, you know. So, well, I guess since he's a part of the police department, he gotta, you know . . . so I told him, "It ain't nothing, anyhow."* |
| *Interviewer:* | *But so far, you think this is all pretty amusing?* |
| *Subject:* | *Yeah. I knew it was irritating him. That's why . . . that was my purpose of doing it.* |
| *Interviewer:* | *How did he show that he was irritated?* |
| *Subject:* | *Well, when he hit me, you know, it showed that he was irritated. I hadn't provoked him to hit me by . . . I mean, I didn't swing at him, and I didn't say nothing to him directly that would provoke him like that, but you know . . . What I was saying, I guess, that could have provoked him, when I kept on singing and "shining" him on, knowing that he was walking aside of me, and he kept on telling me to shut up and I wouldn't shut up, cause I was off the school grounds. He had no . . . I mean freedom of speech, you know.* |
| *Interviewer:* | *Let's get this game a little bit in detail. You start singing and he was showing that he doesn't like this singing?* |
| *Subject:* | *Yeah.* |
| *Interviewer:* | *And he's showing this by what? By telling you to stop?* |
| *Subject:* | *Yeah.* |
| *Interviewer:* | *In a tone of voice that kinda gave you the feeling that . . .* |
| *Subject:* | *He didn't like it.* |
| *Interviewer:* | *Did your volume increase or decrease?* |
| *Subject:* | *Increase as soon as I passed those gates.* |
| *Interviewer:* | *Your volume increased as soon as you'd passed through the gates, and he kept on telling you to stop? Then what? He didn't hit you right away . . . he told you not to walk?* |
| *Subject:* | *He told me to shut up.* |
| *Interviewer:* | *He told you to shut up . . . and certainly you weren't doing that.* |
| *Subject:* | *No, I wouldn't shut up.* |

| *Interviewer:* | *So then what was his next move?* |
|---|---|
| *Subject:* | *He said, "Come here," and I said, "Man, well, I'm going home." You know, like that. And he said, "What are . . .?" He said something funny, he said, "Well, this'll teach you to shut up." Or something like that. And that's when he hit me, you know. It just glanced off and you know, and tears started coming down my eyes.* |

(Toch 1969: 68–71)

Here, Jimmy is describing in detail his contest with the police officer. At every stage in this contest Jimmy takes the offensive and, using various provocative techniques, put his self into play: A courageous young man, with a certain degree of verbal felicity and poise who could, despite his youth and inexperience, handle a mature agent of officialdom, indeed, a policeman who represents authority and manhood in his own presence. Every discursive act that Jimmy addressed to the other was an assertion of his self, a move that puts his self in to plays that demanded a particular answer— one that he eventually obtained. The contest proceeds in various stages, each stage characterized by Jimmy's increasingly provocative playing of his self and getting satisfaction from the observation that the other was irritated and angry. Nevertheless he is surprised that this contest led, crescively, to a violent response from the other. Jimmy thrusts his self into play in very overt and direct ways, whereas the policeman was responding to them with parries and glances until the last violent thrust.

## Duels

Duels are also contests in a very general sense but duels are governed by systematic and formal rules. In their classical form they were contests that were defined by elaborate rules of etiquette and decorum in which the honor of an individual was put on the line. It was an activity undertaken by an elite and was designed, V. G. Kiernan argues, to defend the esteem of an individual as well as to protect the status of a class. He writes:

> Gentlemen must be ready to fight but with decorum and dignity, not like the noisy plebeians they often resembled. Everything in the ceremonial of the duel was of a kind to stamp it as the affair of an elite.(1989: 136)

The rules by which these duels were conducted were many and admitted many regional variations. Nevertheless, they were all derived from the medieval tradition of chivalry. One must defend one's "honor" (i.e., the self) at the risk of one's life, face death with equanimity and poise, display an indifference and emotional control, as well as observe the strict rules of procedure in the actual confrontation. These rules, drawn from many regions, were collected and codified by the Irish aristocracy in 1777 and came to be known as the "Twenty-six commandments" (Kiernan 1989: 145).

In such contests an individual employs swords and guns to wound or kill another in order to gain esteem for one's self. In duels there is a presumptive equality between the participants. Indeed, in the classical European duel, the parties must be of equal rank in every dimension before they will agree to engage in a duel (Kiernan, 1989). In my usage of the concept of duel, there is no claim that an equality of social rank is needed; rather there must at least be an equality in the capacity of the other to retaliate and participate in the "good fight." Hence a contest between an adult and a child cannot be called a duel, nor can one between an old and decrepit man and a strong young man. One may in fact look upon duels as interpersonal confrontations, subject to certain rules, between individuals in which one presents the other with various tokens—words, gestures, appearance, space— and challenges the other to provide commensurate responses. In such encounters, he or she puts a self forward, announces its presence in various ways, and anticipates it being treated with the proper rites.

In everyday life an individual faces many instances of such duels. For example, there are the formal debates that are staged according to well-defined rules. In courts of law, again, there are duels between opposing counsel as well as between the witnesses and counsel. In various social gatherings individuals often engage in informal debates that are also subject to various rules of decorum. Interactions between members of formal committees often take on the character of duels as well. In all these encounters selves are put into play and various consequences are recorded. The games that individuals play may be considered duels too. There is no doubt that in and through them, selves are put into play by adhering to certain definite rules.

It has been customary in both philosophy and the social sciences to use "games" as metaphors and exemplars to either illustrate or to elucidate a problem. G. H. Mead uses games as a metaphor for the type of regulated interaction that children experience and use to constitute their selves (1934). For others games represent the height of rational and calculated behavior (Gibbons, 1992). In Goffman's work on "where the action is," he also uses games as a model with which to understand "character contests" in everyday life (1967). In Wittgenstein's philosophical investigations, games play their part as a model for the uses of language: Language is used, he argues, according to certain more or less precisely defined rules within certain parameters that make them into "language-games" (1958). In each such usages of the notion of a "game" there is an assumption of what exactly a game is: while Mead and Wittgenstein address its rule-bound nature, the game-theorists and Goffman stress their confrontational character. To be sure, both of these features distinguish games: They are constituted by precise rules and they are contests.

While these features make them useful as metaphors for a variety of purposes, one can nevertheless investigate the uses of games as such—rule-bound and confrontational structures that they are—in everyday life. The use of language, that is, may be like a game of cricket but what of cricket itself? Insofar as games themselves are defined by precise rules that are expressed in carefully phrased commandments, one can of course say that while the use of language and the construction of meaning is like a game, games themselves are dependent on language. Cricket and tennis and football themselves become not only games of skill, but also language-games in themselves in which action is based on the interpretation of these commandments.

In these games, there are engagements between two individuals or two teams that are conducted on the basis of these rules. These rules are often enforced by the players themselves but more frequently there are officials whose task it is to enforce the rules. These engagements are essentially contests in which various stratagems and techniques are used by the players to put their respective selves into play and simultaneously demean, undermine, and outplay the self of the other. In such contests blood is typically not spilt nor overt physical violence perpetrated—except in boxing and wrestling—but selves are nevertheless put into play and tokens of self won or lost. The striking feature of the games of skill is that the participants can get involved in them physically, emotionally, and intellectually. Indeed, these games are truly wondrous structures for the symbol-using animal: *The body, mind, and self are simultaneously implicated in them.* Further, the plays that are made within the game are addressed to various others: fellow players, antagonists, fans, and one's primary groups. Not only, then, are the self, mind, and body unified into the acts of the game, but the social is also addressed through them.

In tennis how the ball is to be hit, the place where it is allowed to land, the system of scoring, and the manner in which the score is to be accumulated are the elements of the game. The manner of handling these elements becomes a *token for the self,* a handling that can be readily counted and used as a measure of the self: If one gets a certain number according to a certain pattern, he or she is endowed with an enhanced self, and conversely the one who does not obtain the magic number experiences a diminishment. In successfully executing these moves and countermoves the player puts his or her self into play against an opponent who is more or less evenly "matched." Every move he or she makes is one that carries the fate of his or her self with it and the outcome of each move becomes a measure of it. These moves are surely analogues of words and gestures used in everyday life with the advantage that they are more precise and clear in their significations, devoid of ambiguities and uncertainties, and readily and immediately accessible to both initiators and respondents. One can see this clearly in the following description of a move in tennis. Describing the opening serve in a tennis game Linda Bunker and Robert Rotella describe a process that should be familiar to anyone who has read G. H. Mead:

The serve is the stroke that you have complete control over. You and you alone *can* decide when, where and how you will put the ball into play . . . In this situation, you initially need a broad external focus before you serve so that you can bring together all the important information. Ask yourself which serve your opponent would rather return? Are more errors being produced on the backhand or forehand side? What will my opponent expect from me? If I shift to the backhand corner of the service box where is the return likely to come? (Bunker and Rotella 1982: 48–49)

While in Mead's work the aim is to explain how successful communications and interactions are constructed by taking the role and attitude of the other, it takes a more complex turn in the above quotation. No doubt, the player wants a successful game to occur and continue as he or she makes the moves, but he or she also wants to ensure that, while he or she takes the role of the other, the capacity of the other to take the role of the server is diminished: The receiver can anticipate the angle of placement, spin, and velocity of the serve only within certain boundaries because the server would take pains to disguise them. The serve is presented in such a way so that the other *cannot* successfully predict its angle, placement, velocity, and spin.

Once the ball is served and put into play, all the rational calculations made about the execution of the move and the responses that can possibly be made by the receiver recede into the background and an opportunity for quick judgment and spontaneous movement presents itself to the one who receives the ball: The ball may bounce in unexpected directions depending on the forcefulness and tightness of the racket that sent it, spin in an unpredictable way, and be influenced by the quality of the surface on which it was bouncing. All of these contingencies must be handled readily and with alacrity, a condition that gives the game the necessary element of unpredictability. Nevertheless, tennis gurus advise preparing oneself for the return to limit the unpredictability. Bunker and Rotella say,

As you wait for the oncoming serve, all the pressure is on you. You must watch the ball leave the server's racket. You must simultaneously be aware of subtle changes in racket position, react to the speed and spin of the serve, and then execute the stroke which will place the ball in the desired place on the opponent's court. (1982: 55)

That is, the server takes the role of the receiver and will serve in such a way that the receiver will find it difficult to return it. Conversely, the receiver takes steps to predict the nature and placement of the serve so that he or she can return it in such a way that the server will find it difficult to return it. Each is watching for the thrust of the other so that he or she cannot only parry it, but also thrust in return.

In tennis, and in many other games, the emotions that are generated during the course of the game need to be kept under a strict control and discipline if a successful outcome is desired. Indeed, one can say the moment one player gives in to an excess of emotions, his or her performance would be impaired. In other words, the acts that have to be executed would suffer in efficiency and effectiveness. The consequences of not being able to manage one's emotions are described by Bunker and Rotella as follows:

> On important shots, hands and feet turn cold; on important serves I rush my shot even though I am not set; if I lose the first few games, I tend to have great difficulty throughout the match; if I have to hit a backhand overhead, I cringe before I even hit it. (1982: 75)

To be able to overcome these problems, a player has to systematically practice a form of emotional discipline. Such a discipline of emotions does not, however, involve only the emotions that can detract from one's performance; rather, other emotions are garnered to enhance performance as well. Bunker and Rotella write,

> When you are happy and excited about your progress, your emotions can be a great source of motivation. But when you are having problems, your feelings can really work against your continued motivation. You must learn to *use* your emotions to help you when they are useful and *block them out* when they can hinder your continued improvement. (1982: 75, my emphasis)

In addition to the play of emotions during the game itself, there are the emotions generated by the winning or losing of a point, a set, or the whole game and match. In each such moment of a game, one or other emotion is generated and felt and given play—all of them achieved by putting the self into play. The tokens of self that were put into play during the game, or rather the plays of the self that were executed by means of these tokens, are counted as measures of the self and used by the individual himself or herself as by the others to measure the self. As measures of the self, they have currency within given primary groups and social circles—not to speak of their capacity to elicit the other more universal currency, money, when one becomes a professional player and meets with even a modicum of success. They in fact become markers of identity, labels of distinction: champion, winner, loser, two-time loser, "always a finalist, never a champion," "a good loser," or a "sore loser," and so on.[3]

These games in fact are duels, played according to a strict code, in which selves are put into play, emotions generated and felt, and various effects experienced for the continued presences of the selves involved.

## Combat

These are confrontations, not between two individuals as in duels, but between two groups that are presumptively equal. The "rumble" between two street gangs is an example of combat, as is a confrontation between supporters of different soccer teams in England. The key process in combat is the identification between given individuals with each other and often with something "external" to them. In old-fashioned warfare there were "platoons," or "squads," of soldiers who identified with each other, and perhaps with the larger units of the army and the "nation" or "country" on whose behalf they were putting their lives on the line. Shils showed in an analysis of "primary groups" in the American Army (1950) and (with Janowitz) in the Wehrmacht (1948) in the Second World War that such identifications were important in maintaining morale and commitment. In a study of the latter, they write,

> When the individual's immediate group, and its supporting formations met his basic organic needs, offered him affection and esteem from both officers and comrades, supplied him with a sense of power and adequately regulated his relations with authority, the element of self-concern in battle, which would lead to disruption of the effective functioning of his primary group, was minimized. (1948: 281)

It is this minimalization of "self-concern" that I call identification with the group. In the typical organization of street gangs there is also identification with each other, while each gang identifies itself in relation to a neighborhood, street corner, ethnicity, or religion. Such groupings typically contain males and constitute a bonding of like-minded individuals, peers who hang out together, share territory, emblems, and insignia of membership, and develop fierce loyalties.

In engaging in combat against other platoons—as they may be called—whether they are military units on the offensive or street corner gangs or ethnic or neighborhood assemblages, each member is able to put into play several aspects of his or her self. To begin with, for gang-based platoons, there is the identification of self based merely on belonging to a group who are related by being close in age and by living in the same neighborhood. Each member of the platoon is known to each other for sufficiently long periods of time and this, by itself, confers an identity on the self of the member. Second, those members who live in the same neighborhood are very likely to belong to the same socioeconomic class, which automatically grants them a shared identity as well as a structure of individuals, values, neighborhoods, opportunities, and institutions to which they are opposed. In addition, there is often an ethnic and religious identification of self as well. Finally, there is the gender identity: Maleness as an identity as defined in many societies demands certain types of conduct, predicated on a certain type of self. In a study of violence by spectators in soccer matches in England, Eric Dunning, Patrick Murphy, and John Williams call this "aggressive masculinity," and describe it as follows:

> One of the effects of [the circumstances under which lower-class children are raised] is the conferring of prestige on males with a proven ability to fight. Cor-

relatively there is a tendency for such males to enjoy fighting. For them and their peers who strive to emulate them, it is an important source of meaning, status, and pleasurable emotional arousal. (1986: 257)

Such meaning and status and arousal as they experience in engaging in combat with fans of the opposing side, however, are achieved not only by giving expression to their "aggressive masculinity" but by giving play to a self of many dimensions. In addition to the masculine and aggressive self, the individual who performs in such acts of violence does so as a member of a larger structure that he recognizes and acknowledges. Furthermore, these acts are performed in the presence of his significant others and in antagonism to a group that is collectively hated by his relevant associates.

This is also true for soccer "hooligans," as Dunning et al. call them (1986). While soccer hooligans are not gangs in the conventional sense of the term, they nevertheless share certain characteristics with them. Soccer fans are, to begin with, an amorphous assemblage of people who identify with one team or other. Immediately before and during games some of them break away and coalesce to form a platoon and engage another platoon that supports the opposing team. This enables each member of a platoon to share feelings of identification with each other. In participating in combat of this sort, English soccer fans are able to experience ecstasies of identification, not only with one's "mates" from one's neighborhood but also with hitherto anonymous fellow supporters of "their" team. To this may be added the element of social class—always a significant feature of English social life—and we have a potent brew that can induce ecstasies of identification. In one fell swoop a fan is able to put many aspects of his self into play by his violent maneuvers —class, race, gender, region, and neighborhood. Such acts of self-play take many forms in soccer matches in England. Here is Dunning's, Murphy's, and Williams's summary of such acts:

> Football hooligan confrontations take a number of different forms and they can take place in a variety of contexts besides the football ground itself. They can, for example, take the form of hand-to-hand fighting between just two rival supporters or between two small groups of them. Alternatively, they can involve up to several hundred fans on either side. In the most serious incidents, weapons— lightweight and easily concealed Stanley knives are favored at the moment—are sometimes used. Football hooligan confrontations can also take the form of aerial bombardments using as ammunition missiles that range from innocuous items such as peanuts, bits of orange peel, apple cores, and paper cups, to more dangerous, even potentially lethal ones, such as darts, metal discs, coins . . . broken seats, bricks, slabs of concrete, ball bearings, fireworks, smoke bombs and, as happened on one or two occasions, crude petrol bombs. (1986: 246–247)

Each such occasion on which any of these moves were made were ones in which certain identities were claimed and confirmed and relevant selves put into play. And each of the instruments used—from the fists in the hand-to-hand combat to the peanuts, from the apple cores to the petrol bombs—were semiotic instruments used as much to achieve certain effects in the other as in the self: They affirm the identity of the self and put it into play. Such moves often lead to ecstatic and agonistic moments of an extreme sort—point of culmination of the self at play, as can be seen in the following description by a fan:

> I go to a match for one reason only: the aggro. It is an obsession, I can't give it up. I get so much pleasure when I am having aggro that I nearly wet my pants . . . I go all over the country looking for it. (Harrison 1974: 604)

In combat then, a group of members, arrayed as a platoon, engage another group that is similarly arrayed and put their individual selves into play, along with the collective identity of the platoon itself and its external relevancies, and achieve certain emotional and personal fulfillment, sometimes leading to moments of ecstasy.

## Hunts

Hunts are plays of the self in which an individual or a group of individuals seek a victim and engage it in order to achieve esteem for his or her or their selves. In hunts, unlike duels, there is a definite want of balance between the parties: Hunters have more advantages, to begin with, than the hunted. The hunted are often animals or humans defined as animals; outsiders, aliens, enemies. In fox hunting, for example, the gentlemen-hunters mounted on horses, aided by plebeian and canine assistants, pursue a lone fox, "run it to ground," and destroy it. In other forms of the hunt, big-game hunting for example, the advantages are all on one side, too. In both kinds of hunts there is a boundary that is very important: It is the human world against the animal world, it is the masters of the world, the chosen ones of God, the ones to whom God gave dominion over the earth and for whose benefit, in Judeo-Christian mythology, the animals were created, pitted against these animals. The hunt is in fact a reenactment of the relationship between God and man on the one hand and the animals on the other that is depicted in the Judeo-Christian scriptures.

Such hunts, however, are not confined to the pursuit of animals: Humans of particular sorts can be defined or redefined as "animals," i.e., huntable creatures, and like the fox in English hunting, not full members of the moral community.

Consider an incident in Howard Beach, New York, in which three black men, after experiencing a breakdown of their car, walk to a nearby shopping center, call a repairman, and sit down at a pizzeria to eat. They accomplish all of this without incident or comment from an all-white community. In the meantime, however, a number of white young men are at a party and someone comes in and says that there are a "couple of niggers" at the mall—the very word defining the outsider, the alien, the huntable. The young men take umbrage at this, gather various weapons, get into cars and reach the black men. They find them and chase them in their automobiles as they run. One of the black men runs into a passing vehicle and is killed. For a large group of men to best a much smaller group in a fight is not typically considered heroic or honorable, and little esteem can be garnered from it—except when the victim is perceived as an outsider and an alien. In such cases the hunters are defenders of the boundaries between insiders and outsiders. That is to say, violating the rules of chivalry, sportsmanship, and decorum, outsiders—outsiders of color or religion and those insiders who become outsiders by violating some cherished rule of the group—can be readily assaulted or killed and the selves of the hunters embellished by the signs that these acts would generate.

In many ways, this violence by the many against an outsider, one or a few, is similar to head-hunting. Head-hunters are players who go outside the community and find the means of generating emotions and achieving esteem among the insiders by killing these others. In such contests the outsiders are not likely to honor the winner, and the signs that are thus generated have currency only among the insiders. Consider the facts of the case among the Ilongot of the Philippines, described by Michelle Rosaldo. Among the Ilongot, she argues, the self, its presence, and esteem in their world, is defined by *liget.* It can be translated as "anger, energy, passion," she notes, and has been used by Ilongot in the following locutions:

(a)   (When hunting) I am *impassioned* when game nears and my heart thumps.
(b)   It's the women who are, in a sense, the angry *energetic* ones in the household, because they are always getting up.
(c)   When we headhunt, we don't eat sugar cane, so that our *anger* will not be cooled.

(Rosaldo 1980: 247, my emphasis)

In social life among the Ilongots as among others, there are many opportunities to feel these angers, energies, and passions. Once they are felt and expressed, the act and the responses they elicit become features of the self. Sometimes these features are negatively valued: if a young man bests his grandfather or grandmother in a fight, there may be only dishonor and disesteem in it; if he bests a member of his own group of equal strength, there may be some esteem. If, however, he bests a common enemy or outsider, there is much to be gained. The Ilongot, for instance, distinguish between a proper head-hunting raid and the storming of alien households and the improper killing by stealth in a supposedly friendly household (Rosaldo 1980: 208). They elicit different degrees of honor and esteem.

Head-hunting, therefore, becomes a perfect arena in which *liget* can be felt and articulated and its effects experienced and incorporated into selves. In the head-hunting expeditions, the elders tutor, guide, and finally allow the youngsters to take a head and achieve honor, esteem, and status. Second, head-hunting becomes the sign that separates the elders (those who have heads) from the youngsters (those yet to win a head) and the Ilongot (those who take heads) from the outsiders. Rosaldo sums up the consequences of head-hunting as follows:

> Headtaking, as a moment of great emotional release and expansive and tran-scendent satisfaction, represents, for Ilongots, the point in the human life cycle when vitality is at its fullest, limited neither by childish constraints of "fear" and lack of "knowledge" nor by the deterioration of "energy," skill, and independence that accompanies marriage. . . . By taking heads young men revitalize the working rhythms of their homes and think as well of fame that will keep "shame" and "fear" from limiting their voyages abroad, of ornaments that communicate to all the new and forceful *liget* in their hearts . . . com-manding distance, calling hearts, cutting others while remaining safe from danger. Headhunters typify Ilongot ideals of potency, productive health, and beauty—and in their songs, ornaments, boasts, and dance, they show that, "angered" and renewed by a fresh victim's life, men can turn disturbing facts of daily worlds into the substance of a collective and transcendent joy. (Ros-aldo 1980: 148–149)

While these examples of the hunt involved groups of people attacking others, hunts can be undertaken by single individuals. Often the quest may be individual but the hunter may have a staff to help him or her: Big-game hunters, for example, have various others facilitating the process. At other times, the quest for self-fulfillment and emotional play may be a lonely one, but the rewards in agonistic ecstasies are real enough. Here is an example from a study of violent criminals by Lonnie Athens:

> I was just cruising around with some friends of mine drinking wine, smoking dope, and eating a few reds. We came to an intersection and slowed down to make a turn when this black dude in a Thunderbird coming the other way cuts us off in the middle of the intersection while he made a turn. Then he drove by us with a big grin on his face throwing the bone. The friend of mine who was driving just turned and started going the other way, but I suddenly said to myself "that dirty jive nigger flipping me off and grinning—now he thinks he's one bad nigger. Then I grabbed the wheel and said, "Turn around and catch that nigger driving that Thunderbird. "We started following him, but after he made a couple of turns, we lost him. . . . I said, "Well, he's got to be somewhere in this neigh-borhood so let's just keep driving around here until we spot that Thunderbird, because I'm out to book that nigger." I could still see his big grin when he shot us the bird, and it was driving me up a wall. There was just no way that I was going to quit looking for that motherfucker. I was outright determined to have his ass one way or another.
>
> Finally I spotted his car in a driveway in front of a house and told X who was driving to pull over and park in front of the house. Then I snapped my

shotgun together and loaded it. One of my friends said, "Hey, what the hell is your trip?" I said, "It's just my trip" and jumped out of the car. I didn't care about anything but having that nigger's ass. All I thought was, "I'm going to kill this punk." I walked up to the house and knocked on the front door. He answered the door, but as soon as he saw it was me, he slammed it shut in my face. I ran through the house after him and jammed him as he was climbing over the back fence. I leveled the barrel of my shotgun at his head and said, "Nigger, get off that fence." After he did, I said, "Head back into that house." I wanted to fuck him up in the house so nobody would see it, but when we got to the back door, he stopped and said, "Man I haven't done anything to you, please don't hurt me." His sniveling made me madder. I shoved the barrel into his back and said, "Man, go into that house." He still wouldn't go in, but just kept begging me not to shoot him. This pissed me off even more. I lost all my patience and said "Fuck it" and shot him right where he was standing. (Athens 1989: 29–30)

In this incident the self that the protagonist had put into play and the identities claimed are multifaceted. To begin with, there is the identity of the man who is outraged by an injustice: His car was illegitimately "cut off" in the middle of the intersection. This is accompanied by the identity of class: The other fellow is driving an expensive and ostentatious car. In American society an automobile is not just a form of vehicular transportation. It is rather the symbol of power and domination, of wealth and status, of masculinity and assertiveness. The bigger the car and the more expensive it is, the greater the value it will mobilize as a sign of the self. Furthermore, this other man is audaciously provocative: He makes the standard gestures of contempt and challenge, he grins and "throws the bone"—the uplifted middle finger. Finally, he is the classical outsider and scapegoat of American society: "The dirty jive nigger flipping me off and grinning—now he thinks he's one bad nigger." "Bad nigger," of course, is code for "uppity," arrogant, and overly self-confident black man, the exquisite anathema of all white racists.

Multiple identities of the self are put into play in this hunt: a man, a driver with rights on the streets, a man of honor who does not overlook slights or take challenges lightly, a man, moreover, who is no doubt aware of his membership in a dominant race, which is entitled to certain privileges but is nevertheless deprived of certain identity-defining consumer goods like expensive automobiles. The pleading from the black man creates further emotionalities: It annoys the protagonist even more and impels him into immediate action. This hunt, while not that of a group against another one, nevertheless has all the elements of what will be acknowledged in many social circles as a heroic presentation of self. It defines the protagonist as a man who stood his ground and was willing to fight for what he considered was right: No one has a right to humiliate the other overtly. Yet, the agents of the society in which he lived, unlike the ones of Ilongot, did not recognize the "heroism" in it and sent him to jail for aggravated assault, since his victim survived the gunshot.

The third example I would like to use here is the phenomenon known as "wilding." In this kind of activity a group of young men who habitually hang out together select a target and attack it, often committing rape and murder. There were a spate of such attacks during the last decade. The defining feature of "wilding" is the calculated selection of a weaker target, usually a woman, and the ritual violation of the person without any provocation from her or him. There is no violation of territorial rights in acts of wilding, no property is taken from the victims, and no immediate acts of the victims are taken as calling for revenge and retaliation. There is no issue of defending the honor or esteem of a member of the gang or of the gang itself. For instance, in Atlanta, Georgia, six men and a boy went on a "wilding spree . . . resulting in the gang rape of a woman and the slaying of a man who begged them not to attack his wife" (Scruggs 1991: C;1).

Similar attacks have been reported in Boston and Los Angeles and most famously in New York. In this incident a group of black teenagers saw a young white woman jogging, accosted her, held her captive, and some of them raped her while the others beat her and then they left her. No property was taken, she was not known to any of the assailants, and she had not invited their attention in any way. What elements of self and emotion were put into play by these young men in this attack? To begin with, there was the thrill of experiencing solidarity in the joint participation in a venture with members of one's primary group. The venture itself had the smell of both power and sex: One could overpower this woman and have sex with her. All the assailants were both young and black, making the slightly older white woman an alluring target: She was, from their point of view, aloof, rich, fit, and white—a socially distant and culturally forbidden fruit. While sexual activity occurred, it was quick, violent, unreciprocated. It was more a collective ritual of violation than a fulfillment of sexual desire. It was indeed a hunt, emotion-laden, intensely active, risky, but endowed with the qualities of pursuit and the possibilities of reinforcing one's feeling of fellowship simultaneously within age strata (the gang), ethnic strata (black), and social class. Indeed it would be a mistake to take this incident as merely a racial one; rather, many aspects of the respective selves of the participants were put into play in these acts, many selves were given presence and validated. There was male adolescent braggadocio and sexual quest in the assault and the affirmation and celebration of gang solidarity; there was ethnic and class resentment and assertiveness. Sexuality, class, race, gender, and group solidarity mingled to create an explosive mixture. Had they been able to get away with it they would have provided material for future boasts and bragging, leading to further opportunities to put their selves into play. As it happened, the attackers in the park were arrested and most of them sent to prison.[4]

## FANTASIES

In addition to these practical forms in which selves may be put into play, it is possible to put them into play in one's imagination. These may be termed fantasies. "Fantasies" are a more inclusive category in that engaging in "fantastic" plays of the self, one can also duel or hunt or engage in combat and even have adventurous encounters. The distinguishing feature of plays of the self in fantasy is that they are imaginary exercises in which the body of the individual is only minimally involved. They are acts in which the individual participates vicariously and, nevertheless, is able to achieve both dramatic realizations of their respective selves and ecstasies and catharses.

In such actions and involvements, selves are put into play by a process of identification. In an extensive study of what he called "the range of rhetoric" Kenneth Burke argued for supplementing the term "persuasion" in theories about rhetoric with the concept "identification" and sought to show that successful persuasion is achieved through the managements of the processes of identification. In a striking analysis of John Milton's *Samson Agonistes*, Burke showed how the poet in his composition of the long poem identified with Samson:

> A prisoner chained "eyeless in Gaza . . . blind among enemies" because he could not keep "the secret of his strength" . . .
> himself his "sepulchre" . . . himself his own "dungeon" . . .
> his sightlessness in captivity a "prison within a prison"
> enraged with himself for having,
> divulged
> The secret gift of God to a deceitful
> Woman.

For having given up his "fort of silence to a woman" he hugely laments his "corporal servitude" (1969b: 3–4). Since Milton himself had suffered certain vicissitudes in his own life at this time—though not as a result of betrayal by a woman—he then can be said to be identifying with Samson's plight, vicariously experiencing both his own blindness and social isolation. Such processes of identification occur here in an *act of composition* wherein various literary devices—rhyme, rhythm, imagery, various tropes, plotting, characterization, and so on—are used to create what Burke calls *consubstantiality* with the object being written about. He describes this as follows:

> A is not identical with his colleague, B. But insofar as their interests are joined, A is *identified* with B. Or he may *identify himself* with B even when their interests are not joined, if he assumes that they are, or is persuaded to believe so. Here are ambiguities of substance. In being identified with B, A is "substantially one" with a person other than himself. Yet at the same time he remains unique,

an individual locus of motives. Thus he is both joined and separate, at once a distinct substance and consubstantial with another. (Burke 1969b: 20–21)

Another way of describing the exercises that Burke has presented here is to say that Milton in his composition of the poem cast his self into a drama drawn from the defining text of his civilization and allowed his self to be *identified* with that of Samson and participate in all the trials and tribulations that Samson underwent—indeed, he appeared to experience a vicarious ecstasy by the composition itself, just as he may have felt similar emotions on later reading it. The process by which this identification is achieved is the placing of the self in one category or another and experiencing the perquisites that go with it. *Fantasy here involves the imaginative projection of the self into a story and participating in the characterizations and feelings and developments in it as they occur in the text.* The identifying subject finds a place and a role for himself or herself in the acts that are performed within the text and in the evolving plot they constitute and feels the emotions that are generated in and through them. In submitting his or her self to this process of identification, an individual experiences a transformation of the self. Milton, by identifying with Samson and his fate, including the fact that while destroying his enemies by bringing the temple down he killed himself too, was using this "murder-suicide" motive, as Burke argues, as "terms for transformation in general" (1969b: 11) insofar as death is the ultimate transformation. Identifying with another, while composing a text, or while reading it, one in fact achieves a transformation of self, however temporary.

In such a process of identification the rhetorical move is to persuade, not others, but the individual himself or herself that the action being construed or seen somehow involves its own self. Identification as conceived here is not a "psychological" event, not a subjective thoughtway, but an *act* that an individual undertakes and with which he or she enters into a *dialogue* with the text he or she is construing, or for that matter, an event he or she is watching, or an object that he or she is apprehending. Bakhtin wrote in one of his early essays that a "life is a responsive, risk-taking, open, act of becoming." And it is with these risk-taking acts that an individual deals with the world.

> For my participatory consciousness it [the world] is an architectonic whole, and is arrayed around me as around a singular center from which issue my acts: it locates itself with respect to me to the extent that I go out of myself . . . in my visualization-act, thought-act and deed-act. (Bakhtin in Roberts 1989: 121)

The "world" that we are interpreting, all the texts that we read, then have an architectonic—a subtle and systematic interrelation of its various elements, and it is this architectonic that elicits responses. The rhetoricity of a text, then, is intertwined with its architectonic with certain arrangements of a text eliciting given responses and readings while others elicit differing ones. This architectonic exists prior to the act of interpretation having been set up by other processes. There is no immaculate text or world, rather an arranged world, an addressed text. A text, in other words, is not a passive and inert entity. Rather, it is active in the sense that its form and structure can be taken as the *representamen* of the author's designs. The various elements of the text are signs produced by the author that a reader *considers* in confronting the interpretive tasks at hand.

This process of interpreting texts—responding to their rhetoricity or architectonic—and identifying with one or more of the characters in them and with the stories that they are made to enact may be termed *narrative semiosis*: the acts of *composing* a text out of other texts, as Milton did in his *Samson Agonistes*, or the acts of *reading* a text and responding to its rhetoric and architectonic. In such semiotic exercises an individual constructs an interpretant to a sign, to be sure, but both sign and interpretant are complex and dynamic functions and the processes of semiosis are ongoing constructions. This involves the construing of the elements of the narrative—the characters, their interrelations, and the developments they were undergoing, the ideas and emotions they were generating, the times and spaces and locations in which the actions were occurring, and the motives and themes they were enacting—as signs and responding to them in complex ways.

These moves may result in a masterpiece like Milton's, of course, but I want to extend this kind of exercise to include a variety of processes that are more mundane as well as decidedly less majestic than Milton's. That is, while some narrative semiosis or compositional activity may result in sublime fields of identification, all humans engage in some form of semiotic activity in which they put their selves into play and enjoy the fruits thereof in responding to either enacted or written texts. These activities can be creative acts in their own right, as Milton's was, or else they can be imaginary acts of putting one's self into play through texts, written or enacted, texts that are already in existence, or are being performed.

In reading a novel, for example, an individual achieves his or her satisfaction by identifying with one or more characters in it, disidentifying from others, participating vicariously in the development of the plot, and savoring its ultimate resolution. Similarly, when watching a play or a movie or a football match one puts one's self forward in his or her imagination, identifies with one or more of the characters, disidentifies with others, and participates in the ongoings of the event. In reading a text or watching an event one also participates in the generation of the various emotions, feels them, and savors them as well. In successfully achieving these results, an individual must engage in various steps that are tantamount to composition: He or she must recognize the logic of the plot that is unfolding and be able to respond to it, identify the characters, and recover and incorporate the acts the characters undertake into his or her own intelligible universe. In short, the reading of certain texts involves the construction by the respondent of an *answering narrative* to the one with which he or she is presented, and casting his or her self in it. Such a reading involves a certain empathy with one or more of the characters in the story, with their experiences and destinies, the justice or injustice of their acts and fates, the fitness of the denouement, and the general plausibility of the entire proceedings. Not only do we read a narrative but constitute our own version of it—shifting the emphasis in some places, bringing the characters to our own measures, rendering their motivations intelligible according to our own worldviews.

When one writes a novel, a narrative poem, a play, or a movie script, he or she is undertaking a composition, and in reading one, too, one composes complex structures of meaning in which the self is put into play by means of acts of identification. In composing *Samson Agonistes*, Milton identified with Samson; in reading it, one may identify with Samson too, or in special cases, identify with Samson and Milton. Other mortals, however, may be able to identify only with Hercule Poirot and Agatha Christie. Edmund Wilson ([1946] 1974) dismissed the whole genre of detective fiction by asking "Who Cares who Murdered Roger Ackroyd?" alluding to a popular novel by Agatha Christie. The answer, of course, is that many do, many more in fact than care about the murderer of old Hamlet or old Laius.

The meaning of a text, its cognitive and emotional *import*, to use Susanne Langer's word for the complex content of artistic forms (Langer 1953), is apprehended in the dialogic interaction between the cognitive and emotional *competencies* of the reader and the significations of the text. The reader is able to identify with all or some of the features of the text and enter into a dialogue with an active text because it possesses, in Burke's terms, a certain rhetoricity and what Bakhtin calls an architectonic. The architectonic will guide particular interpretations, indeed provide limits, accounting for similarities of interpretation among a variety of readers. In each such case, the text's architectonic may guide one particular interpretation or other but the influence of the identity of the reader cannot be discounted. Norman Holland puts this very well. The similarities of interpretation, he argues,

> come from similar hypotheses applied to the same text, hypotheses formed by gender, class, education, race, age or "interpretive community." The differences come from differing hypotheses out of individual beliefs, opinions, values, neuroses, in short one's identity. (1994: 1–2)

It is not necessary, however, to give priority either to the text or to the reader. Rather, one can conceive of a simultaneity and a situatedness of the connection between the architectonic of the text and the identity of the reader, a dialogue between them.

One must accept the independent facticity of the text and the valences of its constitutive details in eliciting certain given responses from the reader, just as one must allow the reader to participate actively in constructing the meanings of the text, a process that I have called narrative semiosis. In these compositional activities a reader brings the details of his or her biography, the stresses and tensions it has undergone, the emotional definitions and socialization to which it has been subjected, and the religious, philosophical, and ethical principles the individual has accepted and made a part of his or her identity, not to mention the theories of character, motivation, and plot that he or she may have learned or invented. Such an individual takes the material given to him or her and uses the material, composes a dialogic response in which and through which he or she puts his or her self into play by means of identification. Indeed, in developing a theory about the interaction between reader and text, one needs, as has been argued (Fish 1980; Holland 1992), an enriched definition of the reader: An active and complex individual, a member of not only an "interpretive community," but also of other more mundane communities, competent in linguistic and social skills, one with a history, one who knows his or her history and, above all, one with an active and imaginative cognitivity of his or her own self and its identifying loyalties.[5]

The rhetoricity and architectonic of a text may be found in the way in which a text has been organized. That is, events in real life follow a certain temporal order, but a writer can rearrange this order to achieve particular effects. Gerard Genette calls this *anachronies*. Further, in the narrating of a story, events that occur later can be anticipated in the text, a phenomenon that Genette calls *prolepses*. Stories have a duration within them: Joyce's Ulysses traveled only for a day, but Homer's did for several years. In telling a story, the narrator can either compress the duration or elongate it as it suits his or her narrative purposes. In narrating a story, a writer also has the freedom to allude to an event just once or call attention to it again and again to some purpose. Genette calls this *frequency*. Stories can be told with a certain closeness to the narrative by the narrator or from a certain distance and Genette, drawing on the usage in grammar, calls this the *mood* of the narrative: "One can tell *more* or tell *less* what one tells and one can tell it according to one point of view or another; and its capacity and modalities of its use are precisely what our category of *narrative mood* aims at" (1980: 161–162). The final element of narrative discourse that Genette identified he calls *voice*. This is a description of the narrator's relationship to the story being told and the moment of its telling and the development of these relationships as the story evolves. Genette describes three types of narrating voice: prior narrating or *predictive narrating,* where narrating precedes the story, *simultaneous narrating,* where the narrating occurs as the story unfolds, and *subsequent narrating,* where a story that has already happened is recounted. In the literatures of the world often all three are used in varying combinations (Genette 1980: 217).

Genette, having described the elements of narrative discourse with the above formulation, develops its implications further. The major consequence of narratives having these features is that they enable the authors, be they writers and composers of narratives that are claimed to be "factual," "fictional" or "mythical," to have a relative freedom to arrange and rearrange events and characters in order to develop particular themes and purposes: That is, to give them a particular architectonic so that they possess a certain rhetorical power and elicit one set of responses and reading rather than another. Yet, there is no gainsaying the claim that this will not guarantee success to the author: The reader still has the power to interpret these architectonics and either fulfill the expectations of the author completely or partially or subvert them or thwart them. Writing a "subsequent" narrative an author can treat two unrelated events that happened in separate temporal sequences as causally related ones and impute a purposiveness to the unfolding story of a destiny being fulfilled. The atypical birth of a child can, for example, be related to the subsequent heroic activities of the grown man as causally related sequences. In "prior" narratives, the same purpose can be achieved: By selectively arranging various observations and writing them into a thematic relationship, various social and political purposes can be fulfilled. Science fiction and utopian and distopian novels as well as religious tracts do this and present various selected versions of a future. "Simultaneous" narratives enable an author to give disciplined analysis and comparative examination of the ongoing events and explicate the themes as they unfold.

These and other architectonic features of narratives, intrinsic to the texts themselves, all or many of which can be found in all narrative forms, bring an organization and a discipline to the texts, certainly. *They also enable satisfactory identifications to occur by managing the unfolding of the narrative in such a way that they are able to engage the emotions and the intellect of the reader and elicit his or her emotional engrossment and cognitive commitment.* In other words, the features of narratives that Genette has identified are rhetorical instruments designed to elicit particular responses, within a certain range of such responses, that will lead to successful identification by the reader.

In reading these constructed texts, as a reader moves along the story, the first significant entry of the self into narrative is to *cast* himself or herself as a participant or an interested observer. Such an entry may initially be that of a mere voyeur or a discoverer. Once such an initial move is made, he or she may come to identify with some of the complex roles in the plot. He or she may become, more relevantly, a protagonist in the narrative, a vicarious actor. He or she can now be a hero or heroine, suffer the passion and the anguish of the character or characters chosen for identification, enjoy the triumphs, bemoan the defeats, suffer the injustices, and celebrate with the just, the proud, and the beautiful, not to speak of participating in their loves, lusts, and unfulfilled desires. Or else he or she, being a competent reader in other fields and having loyalties and commitments to other perspectives, may consider the rhetoric and the architectonic of the texts, its narrative discourse, and evaluate them in terms of these fields and perspectives and stand aloof from the text in question. That is, he can become a "critic," an "ethicist," and "moralist," or even perhaps an editor, and read it accordingly.

The ubiquity of such narrative semiosis on the part of the reader is attested by the fact that, while the responses of readers to a text may vary, the variations are about the interpretation of the *common elements* of the text. The variations in interpretations are usually about the different weight to be given to the various elements of the text, their collective import and significance, and their derivative relevancies. Nevertheless reading a novel—however complex its theme, structure, and plot, or however simple, involves the reader casting himself or herself into the narrative and participating with varying degrees of involvement in it. These moves would enable him or her to give play to his or her self vicariously and participate empathetically in the emotionality of the developing sequences. Yet, however much the self gives itself play by these acts of narrative semiosis, it is the elements of the text that draw these responses and induce the interpretations. There is in fact no gainsaying the claim that the relationship between a reader and a text is a dialogic one. To use Bakhtin's terms once again, the texts that a reader encounters are invested with addressivities that elicit particular answers—though not always the same answers, from different readers.[6]

## Reading the Self

I would like to examine Conrad's *Heart of Darkness* in the light of these observations in order to indicate how different selves are put into play in the reading of it. In this much-discussed novel, written in the last years of the nineteenth century, Conrad has a character go out to middle Africa in search of Kurtz, an adventurer, who had gone into the interior of the country and never returned. He has apparently abandoned his post and his mission and gone "mad" or "native." The narrative of these events is recounted to a group of sailors assembled on a ship that is stranded in the Thames estuary in London, waiting for the tide to turn in their favor. Marlow is the narrator of the story of the expedition to Africa but there is also another narrator who narrates Marlow's narrating of it. Marlow narrates his own story, narrates the story of Kurtz, draws the "moral," not to speak of the political, implications of the events, and has the assembled crew enthralled and involved in various ways with the story. They do not play their customary game of dominoes but choose to listen to Marlow's tale—as indeed the reader will too.

He or she will put aside his or her game of dominoes and play, with Marlow, his game. By having Marlow narrate a story in which he himself plays a part and having another narrator narrate Marlow's telling of it, Conrad has, from the beginning itself, trapped the reader into an engagement. The carefully arranged scene in the stranded ship, the waiting for the tide to turn, and the interrupted game of dominoes can apply to any potential reader: He or she is also waiting for something interesting to happen to him or her, he or she is also waiting, playing a game of dominoes to while away the time. It is easy, given these settings, for a reader to assume that he or she is also on the ship like the narrator and the sailors, smoking a cigar and listening to Marlow. Marlow begins to tell a story that has already happened—a subsequent narrative—but in the course of the telling, it becomes a simultaneous telling as Marlow describes his own experiences and then pulls back to comment on them as in a subsequent narrative, thereby giving the reader very complex identificational opportunities. He or she can identify with the listeners to Marlow, on board the ship that is stranded in the Thames, can switch to identify with Marlow, and return back to the ship in the Thames estuary again.

In a commentary on the novel Paul O'Prey discusses the play of the metaphors of "dark" and "light" in the opening lines of the novel. He notes,

> In the opening scene, the sky is a "benign immensity of unstained light" and the only darkness is over Gravesend and the city of London, "a mournful gloom, brooding, motionless"; and the familiar ground of London assumes a sinister and unreal nature as the sun falls "from glowing white changes to a dull red without rays and without heat, as if about to go out suddenly, stricken to death by the touch of that gloom brooding over a crowd of men," as Marlow suddenly announces into the carefully prepared silence, "And this also . . . has been one of the dark places of the earth." (O'Prey 1989: 7)

Marlow is about to tell the assembled associates about his trip to the heart of darkness in the Congo and he announces, with a daring touch of cultural relativism, that England, the fount of civilization and the very source of enlightenment to many Englishmen of those times, was also a "dark continent" or at least a dark island, when the Romans came there two thousand years or so earlier.

A little further into the text, Marlow finds himself in a city across the Channel, presumably Brussels, which Marlow says, "makes him think of a whited sepulchre." In this, a double metaphorization is involved: A modern city with its white-washed walls can be fruitfully compared with a sepulcher with white walls to it. There is also a biblical allusion here: A white sepulcher is also one that is outwardly clean, that is "white," but inwardly corrupt, that is, "dark." One reader may catch only the first metaphor while a second reader may catch both. The second reader, in catching and savoring both, is able to put an authoritative and knowledgeable self into play and agonistically enjoy the catch that the author has surreptitiously sent his way. This sensitivity to the play on words, on light and dark, black and white, the physical and literal light and dark, the metaphorical lightness and darkness, continues throughout the work. O'Prey observes,

> In the story Conrad further exploits the imagery of black and white, "light and dark," in a number of ways. Darkness is night, the unknown, the impenetrable, the primitive, the evil. Yet, when he reaches Africa the colors of skin invert the accepted associations of the contrast. "White" is above all ivory, the beautiful luxury of civilized man which is the root of all evil in the darkness, and which obsesses the *white* men until they, like Kurtz, come to resemble it. (O'Prey 1989: 9)

The reading of these allusions and verbal refractions, the reflections and interpretations they elicit from the reader, and the *alertness* to them, constitute a compositional activity, in itself, involving a play of the reader's self by the choices it may make. The self of the reader manifests itself in the authoritative sensitivity to the multiple meanings of the material that is presented to him or her. Such a deconstructive reading of the text is undertaken—can be undertaken—only by a self that is conscious of its powers and capacities to interpret it this way rather than another way, one that in fact is putting a self into play in achieving these interpretations. For these alert and informed interpretations are not, after all, solipsistic exercises: They are communicated by the self to itself, in a shared and public vocabulary, as an I to a me, and their qualities appreciated and enjoyed and then, sooner or later, communicated to others. The interpretive responses to these plays on words and the reconstruction of the implicit allusions in them is very much like the response to riddles in everyday life: A puzzle, a verbal and intellectual problem is constructed by an author that is unraveled by an auditor. A self is given presence to itself and to whoever else may be around.

O'Prey's reading of the novel can be contrasted with that of Johanna Smith. She reads *Heart of Darkness* as a textualization of two interrelated ideologies—the ideology of imperialism and the ideology of patriarchy. Her essay is an extremely detailed and intricate analysis of the work, and I will give here a short quotation that exemplifies her reading:

> By examining the women in Marlow's narrative, we can identify the patriarchal-imperialist blend that requires the kinds of women he creates . . . Such rethinking about the *Heart of Darkness* reveals the collusion of imperialism and patriarchy: Marlow's narrative aims to "colonize" and "pacify" both savage darkness and women. (1989: 180)

Imperialist enterprises convert the people they conquer into a subjection and a dehumanization, she argues, just as on the domestic front males conquer and colonize women and dehumanize them. For Smith there is a parallel between the imperialistic construction of the "savage" and the patriarchal construction of the "woman," and in Conrad's novel they are splendidly integrated. This reading puts Smith's self, as an ardent anti-imperialist and feminist, into play. It is her feminist, liberationist, and progressive self, besides a critical one, that she is putting into play and giving expression in her own text. The roles that are depicted in the novel, the plot, theme, and characterization, are inescapably masculine in nature. The activities depicted in the novel define the male role in certain cultures: daring, courage, adventuresomeness, enterprise, initiative, work in the outside world, confronting the wilderness (as opposed to the feminine domain of the home). Furthermore, Marlow, after having confronted the wilderness and the wilding of the European Kurtz and its "horror," comes back to the domestic front and reports untruthfully to Kurtz's "intended" that the last words on Kurtz's lips were her name. Marlow's lie restores the validity of the domestic life: From the farthest reaches of "civilization" and amidst all the "horror," Kurtz's memory is that of the "girl he left behind" and all that it represents. Women—other than those with the self and consciousness of a Johanna Smith—can no doubt read the novel and understand women's role in that particular culture: allow your men to go out on the hunt, wait patiently for their return, and pay a price for it in loneliness, and at times abandonment.

There is no doubt, however, that both males and females may be able to put their selves into play in Conrad's work, but they will find different places for their selves in the worlds it creates, making literature also a powerful instrument of socialization into customarily accepted roles. The text reinforces the connection of the male as an adventurer and go-getter and the woman as the stay-at-home, entertaining patiently, and no doubt chastely, romantic fantasies. The intricacies of the identifying processes, and the roles with which one can identify are such, however, that they are girded only by the limits of one's imagination. It is possible for women also to identify with Marlow, or the entire imperialist mission, or with the "white man's burden," and achieve ecstasies and catharsis.

Other selves can also be put into play in reading this novel. Another reader, Chinua Achebe, has called attention to the rampant racism in the work. The Africans in the novel, he contends, are dehumanized, denied the power of speech, and made out to be "frenzied," practicing "barbaric rites," and "waiting silently for a chance to eat one or other of the people they encounter." Achebe writes, further, that in the novel

Africa as a setting and backdrop . . . eliminates the African as a human factor. Africa is a metaphysical battlefield devoid of all recognizable humanity, into which the wondering European enters at his peril. Can nobody see the preposterous and perverse arrogance in thus reducing Africa to the role of prop for the breakup of one petty European mind? The real question is the dehumanization of Africa and Africans with this age-long attitude which has festered and continues to fester in the world. (1989: 12)

Achebe is reading the novel as a modern African intellectual who is informed with the intellectual and social and political history of European colonialism and racism. It is this self that he is putting into play in this reading.

One can ask, however, to whom was Conrad addressing the novel when he composed it? And who was this Joseph Conrad, intellectually speaking? Conrad was addressing his work to the English and the Europeans, and he was no doubt giving expression to a particular view of social and cultural psychology and history current in Europe in his time and considering its implications and contradictions. This theory held that human communities can be put on a scale in which complexity, and simplicity, heterogeneity and homogeneity of structure were the measures. Societies on the complex end of the scale were considered "civilized," while those on the simple end were considered "primitive." The foremost exponent of this view, Herbert Spencer, says, "The change from *homogeneity* to *heterogeneity* is multitudinously exemplified; up from the simple tribe, alike in all its parts, to the civilized nation full of structural and functional unlikenesses" (Spencer, 1898; reprinted in Parsons et al. 1961: 143). From this it followed that psychologically, too, the members of "primitive communities" were wanting in some or many ways. They were in fact inferior to those who lived in complex societies, which had themselves evolved from earlier primitive forms to their current status as civilized forms. "Evolution is an integration of matter," Spencer writes, "and concomitant dissipation of motion; during which the matter passes from an indefinite, incoherent homogeneity to a definite, coherent heterogeneity, and during which the retained motion undergoes a parallel transformation." Martindale quotes this from Spencer and comments, "This formula was believed to apply to the universe, to the evolution of the earth, and to the development of biological forms, the human mind, and human society" (1960: 66).

Conrad's view of the Africans and Europeans as depicted in this novel, as in some others, is truly a representation of the view that Europeans were higher on the evolutionary scale and Africans—the very people whom the Europeans were seeking to exploit and dominate—were lower, and moreover, needed to be controlled and managed by the higher life-forms. Spencer gave expression to these views in scores of books, and they were avidly consumed by the cognoscenti of England. Lewis Coser notes the widespread success of Spencer's works and observes,

> His evolutionary theory provided the solution for a dilemma that faced men of ideas at the time. His theory made it possible to reconcile the newly discovered variety of human behavior in different cultures with the principle of the psychic unity of mankind. (1971: 121)

We are all human beings, that is, but some are not as fully evolved as others. This theme of the return to the antiquity of the human species and its world represented by Africa is depicted metaphorically by the river that Marlow traverses: "Going up that river was like traveling back to the earliest beginnings of the world, when vegetation rioted on the earth and the big trees were kings" (Conrad, 1989: 66).[7]

Spencer's theories provided the ideological justification for the imperialism and the patronizing racism that engulfed Africa after Europeans came into contact with it. The question of interest for us here is the response of the reader imbued with Spencerian theories to Conrad's work. He or she would be able to put this Euro-self into play, his or her social-Darwinian self, imperialist self, and white supremacist self, too, and achieve emotional and cognitive ecstasies by immersing himself or herself in the narrative and identifying, not only with Marlow, but the entire thematics that Marlow narrates, illustrates, and analyzes in eloquent prose. The response here is not merely that of an informed reader, but one who is able to use the information to illuminate larger themes and serve grander purposes. Such readers were rampant in Conrad's time, and they are not sparse even now. And Conrad's exquisite craftsmanship provides ample opportunities in the details that the novel contains—its architectonic— for them to allow their respective selves to wallow in them.

What were these contemporary reader s able to get out of the readings? In Conrad's text, there are "savages" performing various "barbaric rites," given to cannibalism and quite incapable of interacting with Europeans. As Achebe pointed out they are denied the "power of speech," rendered voiceless, and they become available to the reader only through the observation of the Europeans. The Europeans in the novel are aggressive and in control—features highlighted by the fact that one of them lost control and went "native" with horrific consequences. A white supremacist, as an ordinary European, would find all this very gratifying and would be able to identify his self with one or the other of the European characters or identify with the larger themes, give play to it in his or her imagination.

Nevertheless, it is possible also to read Conrad's novel as an ambiguous and ironic text that, on one level, represents the European interest and attitude to Africa and the Africans and, on another level, raises questions about them. The Europeans whom he presents in the novel—with the exception of Marlow—are not quite exemplary characters and they are depicted as being uncomfortable, out of place, and out of sorts. Murfin cites Edward Garnett as having written an early review of Conrad's novel claiming that it was about the "immorality of whites in Africa" (Murfin 1989:98). Conrad himself said that his novel was about "criminality, of inefficiency and pure selfishness when tackling the civilizing work in Africa" (Murfin 1989: 98). That it was a civilizing mission was never in doubt in Conrad's mind. For him, the white man's burden can, at times, be borne by unworthy representatives. The destiny of Kurtz himself is no model for other European adventurers to emulate. Indeed, it could very well be a warning to the ivory-colored people to stay away from Africa and the Africans and from the seductions of the ivory trade and dreams of colonization unless they had the purest of motives and the most sterling of characters. The lie that Marlow tells Kurtz's "intended," that her name was on his lips as he lay dying, may be said to depict the deceit and hypocrisy on which patriarchal and imperialist adventurism were based and a female reader—or for that matter a male one too—would have seen it for what it was. The lie speaks to the fiction on the basis of which male adventurers left home and wife to seek fortunes: It was for the sake of the wife and children. Once again there is an ambiguous and nuanced representation of both patriarchy and imperialism: Imperialist patriarchs are liars and deceivers. Indeed both the imperialist and patriarchal postures may be said to be exposed as hollow and devious in Conrad's work, ones that lead to betrayals and self-destructions.

Insofar as the same text evoked, or can evoke, such a variety of responses, the question that arises is this: Did the text *determine* these interpretations, extract them as an imperious existent? Or, did the reader respond to it in his or her own free-enterprising individualistic ways? "Neither" seems to be the correct answer. In fact, Umberto Eco calls a commitment to one or other of these positions "epistemological fanaticism" (1990: 24). There are limits to the interpretational freedom of the reader just as there are such limits to the significance that an author can put into his or her text (Perinbanayagam 1982: 12–17; Eco 1990). Conrad's text provided the basic structures, the architectonics, to which the readers addressed their own selves and produced a responsive interpretation, which were varied because the selves that addressed them were varied. In Peircian terms, the text was a *complex* sign-system that had power of its own to which the readers produced their interpretants, each selecting certain aspects of the original sign-system to address. The variety of responses that the sign-system, which the *Heart of Darkness* is, has been able to elicit demonstrates that, while the text sets definite parameters, in reading it and responding to it the self of the reader is put into play. When an individual puts his or her self into play in fantasies, it is not as a subjectivist activity; rather it is a dialogical activity in which a reader uses the structures available in the text to experience the ecstasies of his or her self.

## Watching the Self

One of the most ubiquitous of human activities is to watch others play, in two senses of the word: play games of skill and strength and play parts in enacted dramas. The watching of dramas on stages or screens and the watching of games in arenas or on screens, too, can elicit both cognitive engrossment in the ongoing proceedings and emotional involvement. Such spectatoring is also an inescapably dialogic process in which the rhetoricity and architectonic of the drama or the game—their respective structurings and characterizations, temporal and spatial ordering, and other elements of a narrativization—elicit particular cognitive and emotional responses. The performances on the stage or the arena are thus able to allow the spectators to identify with the proceedings presented to them, identify with the characters, plot, and theme of the performed text, and experience various degrees of ecstasy by engaging in narrative semiosis.

Such a semiosis and interpretive responses in which the self gets full play occur frequently in the watching of sporting contests. Today millions of people, often on a worldwide scale, watch certain games—soccer, for example, and at times cricket. In the United States, football has become a sport that millions watch on a weekly basis during the season. Some of this watching is done in stadiums and arenas, but most people nowadays watch the games on television. Such watching is indeed an active and involved pastime and demands that the audience read the game as it progresses. In watching games, in getting actively involved in them, a spectator puts his or her self into play and experiences both emotional engrossment and intellectual engagement. Such a semiotic activity, to be at least minimally successful, demands a number of a priori conditions. A spectator must know the game, understand it, and indeed engage in certain activities that may be termed "preparatory work" to participate in the ongoing game. The first task that he or she must accomplish is to master the rules of the game. *Indeed it could be said that baseball, cricket, football, soccer, tennis, and so on are not merely games that are played with bats or rackets and balls but are structures of activity through which rules are put into play.* Those who play the games, as well as those who watch them with the necessary understanding and appreciation, are participating truly in an affirmation and celebration of the rules. The rules become alive and manifest in the moving flesh and bones and brains of the players. And for the spectator the rules define the meaning of the moves on the arena. On a very general level these rules establish a system of acceptable and unacceptable moves, each of them defined very precisely. They also define the moves by which one side in the game can gain or lose advantage over the other, advantages that are once again very precisely measured. Further, these rules also define the way time and space are to be handled in the course of the playing of the game. Games are played within given spatial limits and, in certain games, the game must be played within given time frames. Second, a spectator must know the teams that are playing in the game, their respective lore and history, the particular character and competencies of the players and the place of this particular game in a series of other such games.

One can take American football and examine how certain rules about roles, moves, space, and time are put into play through the deployment of various human agents and how they are able to elicit engrossment and emotional

involvement. The game is arranged as a pattern of roles that define given relationships with each other. The hierarchy in these roles is limited with the quarterback occupying a certain superiority in power and control. Nevertheless,
everyone is presumptively equal to one another and every role is crucial to the
game. A division of labor is achieved in its most pure form in football—a division that leads to what Durkheim called organic solidarity, thereby solving the
problem of social order within the team. Thomas Hobbes notes,

> Nature hath made men so equall, in the faculties of body, and mind; as that
> though there bee found one man sometimes manifestly stronger in body, or of
> quicker mind then another; yet when all is reckoned together the difference
> between man, and man, is not so considerable, as that one man can thereupon
> claim himselfe any benefit, to which another may not pretend, as well as he.
> (Hobbes in *Leviathan* 1651; reprinted in Parsons 1965: 99)

To ensure that these claims are enforced, humans enter into a "contract" with
each other and create a state to accomplish it. In the real world a man or
woman may pretend to such benefits as another, but typically he or she cannot get away with it because he or she is circumscribed by the facts of caste,
class, ethnicity, gender, and other variables of stratification. They limit, a priori, the benefits that a person can claim. In football, however, these limitations are eliminated. On the field everyone can claim the benefits. The contract holds and everyone is subject to its provisions—though the referee
functions as the state to ensure that serious departures from the contractual
obligations are corrected. It is in football, as in other games, that one finds
such a contractual order in the most perfect form: Everybody is, a priori, equal
and has an important contribution to make to the total effects of the organized activities. In the event, some of the members may be found to be making a bigger contribution than others, but there is nevertheless a presumption
of equality among the role-players. There are no classes, castes, and estates
within the team, only roles that contribute to the well-being of all.

A system of rules that are clear and unambiguous defines and executes the
relationship between the various roles. These are statements made in the
form of imperatives by either a body of individuals or transmitted over the
years by members of larger and more nebulous organizations. Officials specifically appointed for the purpose, as well as members of an organization in
interactional situations, enforce them. They exist as forms of *shared* knowledge—even the usually unarticulated behavioral rules can be put in the form
of a statement—and have a systematic quality to them. The existence of this
knowledge bespeaks, in fact, the existence of a social organization.

In the case of football the rules were made by a body of individuals and
are enforced by officials. The rules are imperatives of what is permitted and
what is forbidden in the field of play. If a player accomplishes one of the
negative imperatives, his team will be penalized, and if he accomplishes one

of the positive imperatives, the team will be credited. Interpretation and enforcement are swift, immediate, and typically unchallenged and unappealed. There are no grounds for complaining of the "law's delays and the contumely of office." Offenses against the collective conscience—the rules of the game—are punished by small penalties against the whole team and sometimes by big penalties of the offender being expelled from the game. The errant player, the persistent offender against the collective conscience, is exiled and made to suffer the consequences.

The game begins with one team kicking the oval-shaped ball to the other side. One member of the opposing team retrieves the ball and runs with it toward the other end of the field. Usually he is interrupted soon after, and after this the quarterback and his offensive team take to the field, take the ball, and seek to advance it to the opposing end. The quarterback passes the ball or hands it to one member of his team, the latter tries to catch and run with it, until he is interrupted by members of the opposing side. If he is not interrupted he runs to the other end of the field and scores a "touchdown." Often the quarterback is prevented from passing the ball at all by being "sacked" by members of the opposing team. Besides the interruptions by the opposing side, the game can come to a halt if the officials espy a foul and call it. However, if the quarterback successfully passes the ball and the receiver takes the ball and is interrupted before he moves ten yards, the side gets three more chances to move the ball the requisite ten yards. If the side succeeds in moving the ball the requisite ten yards, it gets another such chance until the goal line of the opposite side is reached. This final moment is called a "touchdown," whereas the earlier ones were called "downs" with numerical qualifications "first down," "second down," and so on. *The game in fact consists of episodes that are begun and certain narrative developments achieved and then terminated, only to begin another episode with an interval between the episodes. Each episode and their fruits develop further into whole plots with a denouement at the end.* The activities that occur in each episode, even the most minute event within it, are defined and made existentially possible and given value and importance by the operation of the rules of the game.

The rules that define the roles and relationships of each player are operational within very precisely articulated space-time coordinates. The game is played within a bounded arena of a given length and breadth. This arena is marked with various spatial coordinates: there is the outer boundary within which the game is played, and within this area space is marked in terms of yards. In addition, there is an area marked as the "end zone" in which all the moves made earlier come to a consummation and a rest.

Time is fundamental to the game—time broken formally into quarters and halves, the time of the entire game, the time between a move by the quarterback and the moves by the receiver or the interrupters, the time between the quarterback receiving the ball and passing it, the last two minutes of each half of the game, and periods called "time-outs," which are not counted as part of the overall time of the game. It is not only rules that are put into play in a game, but so is time. The vast open-ended nature of time's unfolding is contracted into measured units with precise endings, a halftime, the full time preceded by the last two minutes, defined and announced to all, and other subunits within them. The game in fact is organized to provide the spectators with both contracted and delimited timings in which their selves may be put into play, retrieved for the time being, and reactivated again. In such plays of the self, time itself is experienced sensuously and viscerally as fleeting moments that are soon arrested only to begin again.

Consider a single episode in the game: The quarterback gathers his players in a "huddle" in which the next move in the game is presented to the team, with each player assigned a particular task. They move to the line of play and the ball is passed, shall I say, to a receiver. He catches it and runs with it for a few yards, dodging and ducking the defenders from the other side, until eventually he is tackled and his run ended. The game comes to a standstill at this moment, albeit temporarily, and the entire proceedings begin all over again. A spectator identifying with the defending team can feel fear that the move will be completed and, if it is in fact completed, can have this fear reinforced and experience the disappointment of the defending team as his own, just as one identifying with the advancing team can feel elated if the move is successively completed. The episodic structure of football is such that each spectator can experience these emotions successively or alternatively, giving ample opportunities to put the self and the attendant emotions into play.

The systematic use of certain elements of narratives—order, duration, mood, and voice—serves to ensure engrossment and emotional play and the commitment of a self to the proceedings on the field. Unlike more conventional narratives, football follows a simple linear order: no anachronies or prolepsis. Its progress is however nonlinear: It is interrupted often and the narrative line reset after every such interruption, particularly after an interruption in which a score or an interception or fumble has occurred. The game's most fundamental narrative feature is the frequency with which each move is repeated. In fact, it could be said that the central motif of the game is the repetitive structure of the moves, with each repetition, however, having a different *value* in the overall narrative scheme: Something is added to it or subtracted from it. Mood, too, is important in eliciting an audience's response to the game. In narrative theory mood is defined as the point of view from which a story is told. One must manage, that is, the degree of *distance* from the details of the narrative that is being unfolded as well as appreciate the *perspective* from which the narrative is being presented (Genette 1980: 161–162). In football games, the mood is simple: The story the game tells is from the point of view of the quarterback, *his* defenders, *his* receivers, and their attackers. His are the main scoring moves and he gives shape to the narrative line of the game. In following and appreciating his moves a spectator truly gets very close to the narrative that is unfolding on the field and views it from his perspective. Occasionally the perspective shifts to a goal-kicker or punter, but the focal point of the game is the quarterback. If it is the quarterback of the team one is supporting, then one follows his moves with anticipations of advancing on the space of the field within the allotted time and effecting a score and with a fearful anticipation that he may be thwarted. If on the other hand the ball is being maneuvered by the quarterback of the oppos-ing side, then one watches in fearful anticipation that he may score and in hopeful anticipation that he may be interrupted. The voice in which the game is narrated is an immediate presentist one: It is happening in front of one's own eyes and the action that is seen is seen to be related to the actors on the field and read or heard as such. There is no intervening process and no other narra-tive voice. The time of the narrating is identical to the narrative time. It creates no unusual complexity and follows a linear, albeit interrupted, pattern. In short, the unfolding is no doubt a narrative unfolding, but characterized by a classi-cally simple line.[8]

While the focal perspective of the spectator is on the quarterback, he or she can nevertheless shift his or her point of view by following the move-ment of the ball. Each such moment of the plays in time and space is fraught with a dizzying alteration of the point from which the moves on the field can be viewed. To begin with, there is the moment of the throw: The spectator sees the move from the standpoint of the quarterback. This is changed soon after this to the point of view of the receiver and from that of the receiver to that of the players who are trying to tackle him or chase him if he has eluded the tackle. Each such perception places the spectator in a unique point, and, depending on the identification that he or she makes with either the attack-ing team or the defending one, unifies the perception and emotion. If the spectator identifies with the attacking team, his or her perception and emo-tion would begin with the quarterback's moves and then shift to watch the ball's parabola as it moves into the hands of the receiver and feel elation when it is caught and moved further toward the goal line. This final denoue-ment will be experienced as a feeling of emotional consummation develop-ing out of earlier moments of elation when the quarterback and the receivers executed their moves successfully.

The coordination of time and space enables a spectator to see the moves of the players and the ball in their "*simultaneity, to juxtapose and counterpose* them dramatically . . . to get one's bearings in the world," and "to conceive all its contents as simultaneous and to guess at their interrelationships in the cross-section of a single moment," as Bakhtin says, discussing the relationship between time and narrative in Dostoevski's poetics (1984: 28). In these games, time is transcended and space traversed, making the game into what Bakhtin calls a "chronotope." He writes, "We will give the name *chronotope* to the tem-poral and spatial relationships that are artistically expressed in literature . . . in the literary artistic chronotope, spatial and temporal indicators are fused into one carefully thought-out concrete whole" (1981: 84). James Joyce's *Ulysses,* for example, embodies the chronotope of a single day and the streets and public areas of a single city, while Conrad's *Heart of Darkness* embodies several years and several locations in different cities, villages, rivers, and continents. The time of the novels and the space in which they are situated speak to each other and the characters find their presence and achieve their dramatic realization in these times and within these spaces. There is a union between time and place and the moves of the characters serve to define them. In football, too, there is an organic fusion of time and space in which various characters, i.e., players, perform their roles in accordance with the specific time-space coordinates that are watched by the spectators and experienced as such. *On each occasion in which an episode is watched by a spectator, its full import understood and appreciated, his or her self is put into play in and through these space-time coordinates.* The constantly shifting point of view and the placement of the perception in the particular locale by the spectator's self allows it to achieve a potent mixture of emotion and identity.

These proceedings can be best understood by using St. Augustine's discussion of temporality, which has recently been refurbished by Paul Ricoeur to develop a theory about the narrativity of time and the temporality of narratives. Ricoeur writes, "Time becomes human to the extent that it is articulated through a narrative mode, and narrative attains its full meaning when it becomes a condition of human temporal existence" (1984: 52). Claiming that "there is no pure phenomenology of time in St. Augustine" (1984: 83) Ricoeur quotes from Augustine's confessions: "The mind 'performs three functions, those of expectation [expectat], attention [adtendit; this verb recalls the intention praesens], and memory [meminit]'" (Ricoeur 1984: 19). From the spectator's point of view in football there are the following temporal and narrative stages:

(a) The preparations by the quarterback and the team—Augustine's "expectation."
(b) The quarterback's pass and reception and run by the receiver—Augustine's "attention."
(c) The interpretation of the moves of the receiver and ending of this sequence, allowing the spectators to recall and reconsider the earlier moves—Augustine's "memory."

In each of these latter two moments there was the possibility of the moves being either fulfilled or thwarted. If the moves were fulfilled, the spectator would have been able to experience emotions of consummation and fulfillment; if the moves were thwarted by the other side, there would have been the feeling of sorrow and disappointment to be experienced. Both these feelings are only for the "time being" because a new move is about to begin that will open the opportunity for the further experiencing of expectation, attention, and memory. The expectation phase in the experiencing of football has another enriching element to it: The possibility of *peripeteia*. Ricoeur has observed that one element of a narrative unfolding is the possibility of *peripeteia*—the occurrence of "reversals" in the plot. "To follow a story," Ricoeur writes, "is to move forward in the midst of contingencies and peripeteia, under the guidance of an expectation that finds its fulfillment in the 'conclusion' of the story" (1984: 66). In football with the "interception" and the "fumble" that is recovered by the other side, one has the perfect example of such peripeteia. Here is a spectator, all filled with the memory of the previous move and its outcome, attending to the current moves of the quarterback, expecting him to consummate a pass to his receiver, and suddenly an antagonist catches the ball and runs in the opposite direction and scores a touchdown. The story is interrupted, the conclusion postponed, the destiny reversed, but if there is still time, there will be opportunities to remember, attend, and anticipate and, above all, there may still be further opportunities for another reversal or re-reversal. The result is that, in Augustine's words, "the future, which it expects, passes through the present to which it attends, into the past, which it remembers" (Ricoeur 1984: 19). The remembered past and the anticipated future occur in the nowness of the attentive moment. It is the human mind, capable of functioning with "signs, rules and norms" that is then able to narrativize experience this way. *Remembering, attending, and anticipating are in fact the temporal modes of the self's presence.* The self, however, needs external narrative structures in which to give it this presence. In football, watching it and interpretively responding to it, the spectator is able to narrativize the self's presence by using the structures provided by the game itself.[9]

The simplicity of the narrative line in football enables spectators of varying personal styles and complexities to identify their selves with the proceedings on the field. Yet football has other characteristics that make it a suitable field of identity in certain societies. The watcher is typically a male and in American society, football, the playing of it, the understanding of it, the watching of it, the talking of it, and the appreciation of it, is a sign and measure of one's masculinity. It is the occasion for being with other males, it is a topic of conversation with them, and it is an instrument for constructing personal loyalties and commitments. These become features of the self of the watcher, and the watching becomes an occasion for putting this self into play. Above all, football represents one of the prime responsibilities of maleness: putting one's life and limb at risk for one's own benefit as well as for the common good. No doubt the audience—predominantly male—identifies with the strong, classically proportioned players and their activities almost totally. Clifford Geertz, in his study of the Balinese cockfight, notes that among the Balinese males there was a direct identification between the cock, the bird, and the cock, the penis (1973). They play with their birds as fondly as they may play with their cocks and as Geertz puts it, the fact that cocks are "masculine symbols par excellence is about as indubitable, and to the Balinese about as evident as the fact that water runs downhill" (1973: 418). I have no evidence at this stage to claim that football spectators have this complete an identification between the ball and their penises. Nevertheless the sensuous fondness with which young boys and young men handle the ball while playing "catch" in backyards, frontyards, and streets makes one wonder whether this elongated object, soft and yet hard, is a symbolic equivalent of the cock, an "ambulant genital with a life of its own" in Geertz's potent description of the cock in Balinese society (1973: 417).[10]

The maleness itself that football represents is a mixture of a variety of traits—not all of them connected to roughness and insensitivity. In a remarkable study of the culture of football, Michael Oriard cites different aspects of manliness that different observers found in football from the very early days of its emergence:

(a) To bear pain without flinching, and to laugh at the wounds and the scars of a hotly-contested game, is very good discipline, and tends to develop manliness of character. (1892, *Frank Leslies's Illustrated Weekly*, quoted in Oriard 1993: 189)

(b) The manly qualities which are necessary to the building up of a successful player call forth the best class of college men, and the wholesome attributes which the game itself promotes are shown in the splendid examples of mental and physical manhood found to be among football men. This is true only if the game is played in the proper spirit. (From *Outing* 1901, quoted in Oriard 1993: 189–190)

Here we have two versions of "manliness," as Oriard calls it and he adds many others as he proceeds in his discussion: "manly" qualities of temperance, patience, self-denial, and self-control (1993: 193). Articles in periodicals and newspapers in the early days of football, Oriard argues, reinforced these notions. "Implicit in many of them lay the idea that football offered a rite of passage into manhood. As a cultural text, it dramatized all the uncertainty and competing possibilities in the male's metamorphosis from youth to adulthood" (1993: 198). This metamorphosis involves months of practice and training.

The "manly" self that a typical watcher brings to the game may not have all the aspects of manhood described here—and that self is not one that is committed to brutality or mindless violence. There is a science in it and a craft in it and the violence is really mindful violence, and a training to endure hardship and defeat, pain and suffering. And in an afternoon of watching, a self that bears some or many of these aspects of manhood can put them into play and experience varying degrees of ecstasies. Nevertheless, there is no gainsaying the claim that these very "manly" qualities are the ones necessary to be a successful warrior—soldier, sailor, or marine, a thug, bully, or marauder—and conduct wars of territorial aggrandizement, national or personal pride and prestige, and genocide or individualized acts of violence against the weak and the powerless. The "space" of football and the members of the opposing team can be readily transformed into territory to be won or lost and enemies to be killed or captured, honor and prestige to be gained or lost, with the "tackles" and "sacks" becoming the weapons.

This is not all there is to the self that watches the game. He or she is also a "fan"—that is a fanatic follower of a team, one who identifies with its fame and fortune or lack thereof. Such "fanning" of a particular team is a characteristic feature of identifying processes in modern society. There are many American males who in the course of a their lifetimes change jobs, houses, cities of residence, and wives but stay rooted in the loyalties to the teams of their childhood. This process of identification is both emotional and cognitive and material: enjoying its victories and feeling it in one's bones; sorrowing over its failures in "one's heart"; gathering information and "stats" about individual players, the team's history, and its legends and lore; collecting objects that represent the team—caps, shirts, cards, buttons, and so on.

Yet, ultimately such identifications are played out in the moments of play. It is the arena in which the identities are manifested and the self that bears these identities are put into play. Often a fan is unable to go to the arena and is forced to watch it on the screen. He or she is aided in this project by the dramatic and narrative skill of the commentators who "call" the game on television. To call a game is in fact to narrate the game as it occurs, emphasizing the meaning of every move and providing analysis, whenever necessary, of the character of the individual players and officials, their social background, piquant stories from their respective pasts, and so on. The commentators in fact play a Marlow to the viewers at home. Furthermore, the technology is able to enrich the memory phase of the watching by providing "instant replays" of the moves on the field and the attention phase by shifting the focus of the camera very precisely to the movement of the ball. All these factors can make the home viewer, even without the smell of the crowd and the noise of the cheering, feel a sense of intense participation. Here is a rather poetic and perhaps extravagant description of the cognitive, emotional, and behavioral manifestation of this process of identification achieved through watching a game on television:

> Each weekend I traveled fifty odd miles from Glacial Falls to Watertown, where I spent Friday night and all day Saturday in some sustained whiskey drinking, tapering off Sundays with a few bottles of beer at *The Parrot*, eyes fixed on the television screen, cheering for my team. *Cheering* is a paltry description. The Giants were my delight, my folly, my anodyne, my intellectual stimulation. With Huff I "stunted" up and down the room among the bar stools, preparing to "shoot the gap"; with Shofner I faked two defenders "out of their cleats," took high swimming passes over my right shoulder and trotted, dipsy-doodle-like,

into the end zone; with Robustelli I swept into the back fields and with cruel disdain flung the flat-footed, helpless quarterbacks to the turf. (Exley 1968: 2)

Watching a game in a stadium or on a screen, then, enables a spectator to
put his or herself into play, as his or her emotions, and experience both exs-
tasies and catharses. The episodic structure of football also enables the spectator to experience catharsis in ways that are unique to it. *Catharsis must not
be viewed as a simple hydraulic process in which certain emotions are
"released" or "purged" but as processes in which various emotions are given
play.* Emotions are not unitary and readily classifiable elements in the internal
and interactional life of an individual but are rather intricate and multivalent
feelings that are often mixed-up and interact with each other. In watching a
drama or a game the spectators may be said to be putting their emotions into
play, activating them and experiencing them rather than merely releasing
them—the varied emotions of joy and sorrow, awe and dread, fear and security, love and hatred and pity and so on.

In tragedies and other literary forms the emotions are stirred, given play,
and then lead to what Kenneth Burke calls a "final resolution" (1959). In
football there are a number of small resolutions that lead to a final one. In
each move in the game the quarterback raises the emotionality, and then
either dashes the hopes of the watchers or fulfills them. In either eventuality
there is a resolution and settling of the emotions, a small expressivity, a
release, a purging if you will, but also the alternating feelings of joy and sorrow, elation and frustration, pity and fear. And, very carefully, the structure
of American football creates the opportunity, in its episodic structure, for the
watchers to identify or dis-identify with a "victim" in it. "Catharsis," writes
Burke, again expanding on Aristotle,

> involves fundamentally purgation by imitation of victimage. If imaginative
> devices are found whereby members of rival factions can weep together, and if
> weeping is a surrogate of orgiastic release, then a play that produced in the
> audience a unitary tragic response regardless of personal discord otherwise
> would be in effect a transformed variant of an original collective orgy (such as
> Dionysian rites from which the Greek tragedy developed). (Burke 1966c: 186)

In the watching of football, spectators can be said to be "weeping together" if
their team was losing and "laughing together" if their team was winning. The
structure of the game enables this to occur in what may be termed "uncertain
succession." One group of supporters may watch the ball that was passed by
their quarterback, interrupted by either an interception, or a block short of the
necessary yardage, leading to a weeping and identification of self as victim.
Simultaneously, supporters of the other team may feel joy and fulfillment and
become victimizers. This situation can be reversed by the next move and the
victims become victimizers and victimizers become victims. The availability of

these alternating structures of experience within a short compass enables watchers to give play to a variety of emotions and give it a thorough airing. The episodic structure of football is such that each spectator can experience various complex emotions—including "fear" and "pity" that figured so prominently in Aristotle's work (Nehamas: 1992), successively and alternatively, giving ample opportunities to put the self and the attendant emotions into play.

## NOTES

1. Peter Berger has a different take on the meaning and significance of ecstasy in everyday life. He opines, "As soon as a given role is played without inner commitment, deliberately and deceptively, the actor is in an ecstatic state with regard to his 'world taken for granted'" (1963: 136). I am using ecstasy here not only as an act of stepping out of oneself but of actively stepping into another self with attendant emotionalities. There is no deception involved, no performance in "bad faith," as Berger argues, but a transcendence, with varying degrees of intensity from one self into another or from one emotionality of the self into another such emotionality.

2. Stanford Lyman and Marvin Scott (1975: 147–158) have expanded on Simmel's concept and given various contemporary examples. See also Charles Axelrod (1977) for an excellent statement that places Simmel's essay on adventures in the body of his sociological concerns.

3. Games of the kind in which individuals engage others in agonistic contests—whether they are verbal ones "like playing the dozens" (Abrahams 1974), where wit, verbal dexterity, narrative inventiveness, and emotional control are put into play, or physical contests where bodily and psychological skills are put into play—are instruments with which children are socialized into the management of emotions. "Poise," "self-control," "graciousness" in defeat and in victory, and a general capacity to bring one's emotions into a *disciplined relationship* to the situation in which one finds oneself, are learned in these games. See also Elias and Dunning (1986) for a study of the role of sport and leisure in "the civilizing process."

4. The "hunt" practiced by the English aristocracy moved through the local territory. This pursuit of the fox was, besides being a sport, about claiming and enforcing the right to move over the local territory by the aristocracy. The chase measured these rights and announced them to the local populace. Elias sees the emergence of fox hunting as part of the "civilizing process," insofar as the hunter does not actually do the killing himself but allows the hounds to do it (1986: 149–174). This claim may well be true—but only as far as it goes and it does not go far enough to consider the class structure of the hunt. Letting someone else do the "dirty work"—whether peasants and serfs, foot soldiers or hounds is—after all, the standard form of the relationship between the elite and the proletariat. In the hunt in Howard Beach, the claim that was being enforced was the right to exclusive dominion of a territory by a racial category. See Charles Hynes and Bob Drury (1990) for a detailed description of the events in Howard Beach.

5. However, Norman N. Holland goes further. He writes, "Readers make meaning, indeed construct the whole experience by exploring a passive text with schemas" (Holland 1994: 64).

The problem with this view is that there is no such thing as a passive text and the relationship between a text and a reader is a truly interactive one where each speaks to the other and establishes a series of dialogical moments. The text itself, as a sign-system has powers of its own, "sign-power," as Ransdell puts it. He writes,

> Sign powers are in the signs themselves, and any changes in these powers, or the accruing of such powers to objects not previously having them, are due primarily to the signs themselves and *their* actions not to people's actions (though the action of people is usually contingently instrumental in this respect). (1980: 151)

Holland's theory of "reader response" to texts, and the views of the doconstructionists, despite the many differences between them, share an attitude that may be described as "fear of the other"—or even fear of the author. In seeking to escape the extremism of "text-active" approaches to the problems of interpretation in literature, Holland seems to have slipped into an untenable solipsism by claiming that the reader is a sovereign I, even in his rendition of him or her as a "Critical I" (1992).

6. For an analysis of fantasy and its place in everyday life and its connection to political economy see Farberman (1980).

7. John Savesson (1972) has discussed the Spencerian influence in Conrad's early works, *Almayer's Folly, An Outcast of the Islands,* and *Lord Jim.* He finds strong evidence of Spencer's evolutionary psychology, described in the latter's *Principles of Psychology,* in Conrad's characterizations. Strangely, he does not find any affinity between the contrasts that Conrad draws between Africans and Europeans and the evolutionary sociology of Spencer in *Heart of Darkness.* For another reading of Conrad's work from an antiracist and anti-imperialist standpoint—i.e., by an anti-racist self—see Edward Said (1993).

8. See Holquist (1990) for a very perceptive discussion of time, narrative, and point of view and their relationship to the theory of relativity, as they occur in Bakhtin's work.

9. Michael Oriard discusses the narrativity of football too in a multifaceted study. His approach to its narrativity is different from mine but is compatible with it, nevertheless. Oriard also calls attention to the importance of written accounts of given games appearing in newspapers and magazines as providing a sort of secondary narrativity to the game. John Caughey has discussed the emergence of "imaginary social relationships" between fans of sports figures. He describes spectators having relationships with sports figures that range from admiration to fantasy (1987: 19–33).

10. Geertz also argues that the cockfight draws on almost every level of Balinese experience: "animal savagery, male narcissism, opponent gambling, status rivalry, mass excitement, blood sacrifice. . . ." (1973: 451) What cockfights do for the Balinese, Geertz argues, is to catch up "these themes—death, masculinity, rage, pride, loss, beneficence, chance—and, ordering them into an encompassing structure, presenting them in such a way as to throw into relief a particular view of their essential nature" (1973: 443). All of this may well be true of American football, too. No one actually dies on the field nor is the sacrificial element overt, but the calculated violence that occurs on the field and the severe injuries that occur often no doubt bring the themes of death and sacrifice into the game. The plays and the players enshrine the theme of the male role as that of being specialists in violence who confront death

for the sake of securing territory for the tribe. In addition, football presents vividly the theme of sexuality. The men display their muscularity, strength, aggressiveness, and dexterity while the cheerleaders—representatives of the feminine—cavort seductively on the sidelines when the team scores or is in need of encouragement, displaying their limbs and underwear. The activities of the "robust" males on the field and those of the "delicate" females on the sidelines together constitute a dance of symbiotic eroticism.

# Epilogue

In seeking to understand and explain human existence, it is not "being" or "self" as such that one must begin with but the social act. As each individual, whether he or she is a philosopher or a scientist, an artist or an artisan, observes himself or herself and the others around him or her, he or she will see only the moves and countermoves each makes. It is the acts that these individuals prosecute, however simple or complex, that become the criteria with which each of them will construct an image and a theory of each of them—including himself or herself. In addition, an observer of his or her own acts would discover that these moves are nearly always thought-full and delayed actions, moves that would consider the significance of the act to himself or herself, the context and situation in which the act is occurring, and the probable consequences of the act. The observer in prosecuting these acts in these ways has in fact become a self. The self is then discovered in the act. Once it has been thus discovered it is given presence in further activities. Act and self are inseparable, coterminous, intertwined, and they live and develop and will finally die together. One is not prior to the other either in an existential or logical sense though the act is prior to the self in its emergence. Once the self has emerged, act and self exist in a dural and practical simultaneity.

Such a consciousness of self and the significance of its acts is an essential feature of the human condition as a linguistic creature, an element of its condition as a species. To be a linguistically competent creature is to be able to use words and sentences to observe, refer and classify—*exquisitely and systematically*—one's own presence in the world and that of others. Such uses of language enable an individual to allow the meanings of the various acts it prosecutes, as well as the meanings of the acts it encounters from others, to be sedimented and organized into a concept. This concept of a self will be featured in the consciousness and memory of the individual and used to influence the performance of further acts—performances that would immediately and directly affect the self.

Selves, and the identities they bear, are defined and given presence in the discursive activities that occur between individuals and in communities.

These discursive activities are able to achieve twin ends: one, they are able to name the entity, classify it, attend to it, and feel for it—in short, to objectify and identify it; two, they enable others to objectify the self of the individual with whom they are dealing. Such discursive activities convert the identification of self, the naming and classification, i.e., the *identification*, into a logical, rhetorical, and poetic process.

In the absence of the logical resources of the language, *intelligible* interactions between individuals will become impossible. To become a self is also to understand one's separation from others as well as to recognize one's continuity over time. The dictionary says that "self is derived from Latin *ipse* and signifies a concordance with the subject or pronoun to indicate emphatically that the reference is to the person or thing mentioned and not to some other" (*The Oxford English Dictionary* 1989:905). The grammatical use of the word, then, is to indicate identity in a logical sense, the claim that one—in this case a fleshly body with the capacity for thought and action—is to be differentiated for all essential purposes from another such entity. Each such self, and the entity in which the self is embodied, has, for all *practical purposes,* a separate and independent trajectory through time, and such a trajectory constitutes a life. Such a self is placed in categories and classifications that are, to begin with, external to the individual and eventually become meaningful to the self.

The notion of the identity of the self, identity as a logic of separation, is fundamental to any conception of a self that can emerge. Such an imperative of identification demands a system and process of *naming* so that such identifications can be used in discursive processes by an individual. A human individual is a self in relation to others and acts as a self in such a relation where it is able to treat itself as an I and me, as the situation warrants, and treat the other as a you, and in turn is treated as a you by the other. Once its identity becomes meaningful to the self, he or she would be able to use it to identify the self in various moves. As an individual undertakes these acts, he or she identifies himself or herself, just as others do, and in this simultaneity, the self finds its presence. A self always has an identity, though it may selectively vary as the time and place changes, and such identities affect the acts that are undertaken.

Insofar as an individual, in his or her interactions with others, has to successfully *appeal* to the other to enable him or her *to be*, just as he or she must *respond* to the appeals of the other and allow the other to be, interactions, and the selves that are enmeshed in them, become involved with rhetorical activities. Further, insofar as rhetorical activities involve all the resources of language, they also make selves and interactions poetic enterprises. Wherever there are selves and interactions there also will be rhetoric and poetry.

Such selves are not static conceptions but are given play and continue to exist as eddies in the ongoing current, poised tremulously on the edge of an abyss or a plateau, either to fall or to advance. This gives the self a narrative character—one that the individual recognizes and plays and performs accordingly. In fact the individual finds himself or herself in twin narratives: one in which he or she is the protagonist and another in which he or she is able to identify with a protagonist in various religious or secular narratives and experience varied emotionalities. In the former, he or she puts his or her self into play in practical ways and in the latter it is done in the imagination.

In sum then, a self is not a thing that can be measured, nor is it a sponge that can become saturated, nor is it an entity that can be abandoned and reclaimed or made to vanish by changing historical, social, cultural, or calendrical circumstances. Rather, it is a logically and poetically and rhetorically constituted concept that a linguistically minded individual puts into play whenever it acts, in its consciousness as in the external world. A theory of mind, self, and society, in fact, must begin with a philosophy of the act.

# References

Abrahams, Roger. 1974. Black Talking on the Streets. In *Explorations in the Ethnography of Speaking,* ed. R. Bauman and J. Scherzer. Cambridge: Cambridge University Press. 240–262.

Abse, Wilfred D. 1971. *Speech and Reason.* Charlottesville, Va.: University of Virginia Press.

Achebe, Chinua. 1989. *Hopes and Impediments.* New York: Doubleday.

Amelunxen, Clemens. 1991. *Of Fools at Court.* Berlin: Walter de Gruyter.

*American Heritage Dictionary of the English Language.* 1973. New York: Random House.

Anderson, Dave. 1997. Tiger Woods Needs to Apologize for Distasteful Jokes. *New York Times,* April 24. Section 8:2.

Anderson, James. 1975. Introduction to *Summa Contra Gentiles,* by Thomas Aquinas. London: University of Notre Dame Press.

Apel, Karl-Otto. 1981. *Charles S. Peirce: From Pragmatism to Pragmaticism.* Amherst: University of Massachusetts Press.

Aquinas, St. Thomas. [1258–60] 1975. *Summa Contra Gentiles.* London: University of Notre Dame Press.

Athens, Lonnie. 1989. *The Creation of Dangerous Violent Criminals.* London: Routledge.

Austin, J. L. 1975. *How to Do Things with Words.* Cambridge, Mass.: Harvard University Press.

Axelrod, Charles. 1977. Towards an Appreciation of Simmel's Fragmentary Style. *Sociological Quarterly* (Spring) 18, no. 2: 185–196.

Baker, Russell. 1997. Food, Race and Tragedy. *New York Times,* May 3. Section 1: 23.

Bakhtin, Mikhail. 1981. *The Dialogic Imagination.* Austin: University of Texas Press.

———. 1984. *Rabelais and His World.* Bloomington: Indiana University Press.

———. 1986. *Speech Genres and Other Essays.* Austin: University of Texas Press.

———. 1990. *Art and Answerability.* Austin: University of Texas Press.

Baldwin, F. E. 1926. *Sumptuary Legislation and Personal Regulation in England.* Baltimore: Johns Hopkins University Press.

Barash, David. 1977. *Sociobiology and Behavior.* New York: Elsevier.

———. 1978. Evolution as a Paradigm for Behavior. In *Sociobiology and Human Nature,* eds. M. S. Gregory, A. Silvers, and D. Sutch. San Francisco: Jossey Bass. 13–32.

———. 1979. *The Whispering Within.* New York: Harper and Row.

Barbu, Zevedei. 1960. The Emergence of Personality in the Greek World. *Problems of Historical Psychology*. New York: Grove Press. 69–144.

Barker, John. 1974. *Race*. New York: Oxford University Press.

Barthes, Roland. 1980. Proust and Names. In *New Critical Essays*. Berkeley: University of California Press. 55–68.

Beard-Williams, Diana. 1996. White America Can Now Exhale (O. J. Simpson and the Civil Trial Guilty Verdict). <http://www.afronet.com>

Berger, Peter. 1963. *Invitation to Sociology*. New York: Doubleday.

Bergmann, Jorg. 1993. *Discreet Indiscretions: The Social Organization of Gossip*. New York: Aldine De Gruyter.

Bharati, Agehananda. 1985. The Self in Hindu Thought and Action. In *Culture and Self: Asian and Western Perspectives*, eds. A. Marsella, G. DeVos, and F. Hus. New York: Tavistock Publications. 185–230.

Bickerton, Derek. 1990. *Language and Species*. Chicago: University of Chicago Press.

Boas, Franz. 1911. *Handbook of American Indian Language*. Part I. Bulletin 40. Washington D.C.: Bureau of American Ethnology.

Boden, Deirdre. 1994. *The Business of Talk*. Cambridge: The Polity Press.

Boden, Deirdre, and Don Zimmerman. 1991. Structure in Action: An Introduction. In *Talk and Social Structure*, eds. D. Boden and D. Zimmerman. Berkeley: University of California Press. 3–21.

Bogard, William. 1998. Sense and Segmentarity: Some Markers of a Deleuzian-Guattarian Sociology. *Sociological Theory* 16, no. 1: 52–74.

Boler, John. 1964. Habits of Thought. In *Studies in the Philosophy of C. S. Peirce* (2nd series), eds. E. Moore and R. Robin. Amherst: University of Massachusetts Press. 382–400.

Bourdieu, Pierre. 1972. *Outline of a Theory of Practice*. New York: Cambridge University Press.

———. 1980. *The Logic of Practice*. Stanford: Stanford University Press.

Bowman, William. 1931. *Charlie Chaplin: His Life and Art*. New York: The John Day Co.

Brinnin, John Malcolm. 1955. *Dylan Thomas in America*. Boston: Little, Brown and Company.

Brothers, Leslie, 1997. *Friday's Footprints*. New York: Oxford University Press.

Brown, Penelope, and S. Levinson. 1987. *Politeness: Some Universals in Language Use*. Cambridge: Cambridge University Press.

Brown, Richard Harvey. 1977. *A Poetic for Sociology*. Cambridge: Cambridge University Press.

———. 1987. *Society as Text*. Chicago: University of Chicago Press.

Brown, Roger, and A. Gilman. 1972. The Pronouns of Power and Solidarity. In *Language and Social Context*, ed. P. P. Giglioti. New York: Penguin Books. 252–282.

Buber, Martin. 1965. *Between Man and Man*. New York: The Macmillan Co.

Bunker, Linda, and Robert Rotella. 1982. *Mind, Set and Match*. Englewood Cliffs, N.J.: Prentice Hall.

Burke, Kenneth. [1935] 1965. *Permanence and Change*. Indianapolis: Bobbs-Merrill.

———. 1959. On Catharsis, or Resolution, with a Postscript. *The Kenyon Review* 21 (Summer): 331–375.

———. 1961. *The Rhetoric of Religion*. Boston: Beacon Press.

————. 1966a. What are Signs of What? In *Language as Symbolic Action.* Berkeley: University of California Press. 359–379.

————. 1966b. Terministic Screens. In *Language as Symbolic Action.* Berkeley: University of California Press. 44–62.

————. 1966c. I, Eye, Aye—Concerning Emerson's Early Essay on 'Nature,' and the Machinery of Transcendence. In *Language as Symbolic Action.* Berkeley: University of California Press. 186–200.

————. 1969a. *The Grammar of Motives.* Berkeley: University of California Press.

————. 1969b. *The Rhetoric of Motives.* Berkeley: University of California Press.

Callinicos, Alex. 1990. *Against Post-Modernism.* New York: St. Martin's Press.

Caughey, John. 1987. Mind Games: Imaginary Social Relationships in American Sport. In *Meaningful Play and Playful Meaning,* ed. G. A. Fine. Champaign, Ill.: Human Kinetics Inc. 19–34.

Childe, Gordon. [1926] 1970. *The Aryans: A Study of Indo-European Origins.* New York: A. A. Knopf.

Clark, Candace. 1990. Emotions and Micropolitics in Everyday Life: Some Patterns and Paradoxes of "Place." In *Research Agendas in the Sociology of Emotions,* ed. T. Kemper. New York: State University of New York Press. 305–333.

Clark, Katerina, and M. Holquist. 1984. *Mikhail Bakhtin.* Cambridge, Mass.: Harvard University Press.

Coady, C. A. J. 1992. *Testimony: A Philosophical Study.* Oxford: The Clarendon Press.

Colapietro, Vincent. 1989. *Peirce's Approach to the Self.* Albany: State University of New York.

————. 1990. The Vanishing Subject of Contemporary Discourse: A Pragmatic Response. *Journal of Philosophy* 87, no. 11: 644–655.

Collins, Randall. 1988. The Micro Contribution to Macro Sociology. *Sociological Theory* 6, no. 2: 242–253.

Collins, Steven. 1982. *Selfless Persons: Imagery and Thought in Theravada Buddhism.* Cambridge: Cambridge University Press.

————. Nirvana, Time and Narrative. *History of Religions.* 215–244.

Conrad, Joseph. 1989. *Heart of Darkness.* New York: Penguin Books.

Coser, Lewis. 1971. *Masters of Sociological Thought.* New York: Harcourt, Brace.

Cuddihy, John Murray. 1978. *No Offense: Civil Religion and Protestant Taste.* New York: Seabury Press.

Culler, Jonathan. 1981. *The Pursuit of Signs.* Ithaca: Cornell University Press.

————. 1989. Paul de Man's War and Aesthetic Ideology. *Critical Inquiry* 15: 777–783.

Czikszentmihalyi, M., and E. Rochberg-Halton. 1981. *The Meaning of Things: Domestic Symbols and the Self.* New York: Cambridge University Press.

Daly, Mary. 1973. *Beyond God the Father.* Boston: Beacon Press.

Daniels, Jessie. 1997. *White Lies: Race, Class, Gender and Sexuality in White Supremacist Discourse.* New York: Routledge.

Das, Robin, and Doyle McCarthy. 1986. The Cognitive and Emotional Significance of Play in Child Development. *Sociological Studies of Child Development.* Vol. 1: 35–53.

David, Kenneth. 1973. Till Marriage Do Us Part. *Man* 4: 522–35.

Deacon, Terrence William. 1977. *The Symbolic Species: The Co-Evolution of Language and the Brain.* New York: W. W. Norton and Co.

Derrida, Jacques. 1972. Structure, Sign, and Play in the Discourse of the Human Sciences. In *The Structuralist Controversy*, eds. R. Macksey and E. Donato. Baltimore: Johns Hopkins University Press. 265–272.

———. 1981. *Positions*. Chicago: University of Chicago Press.

Dore, John. 1989. Monologue as a Reenvoicement of Dialogue. In *Narratives from the Crib*, ed. K. Nelson. Cambridge, Mass.: Harvard University Press. 231–262.

DuBois, W. E. B. [1903] 1982. *The Souls of Black Folk*. New York: Penguin Books.

Dumont, Louis 1983. A Modified View of Our Origins: The Christian Beginnings of Modern Individualism. *Contributions to Indian Sociology* 17, no. 1: 1–27.

Dunning, Eric, P. Murphy, and J. Williams. 1986. Spectator Violence at Football Matches: Towards a Sociological Explanation. In *The Quest for Excitement: Sport and Leisure in the Civilizing Process*, eds. N. Elias and E. Dunning. Oxford: Basil Blackwell. 245–266.

Durham, William. 1991. *Co-evolution: Genes, Culture and Human Diversity*. Stanford: Stanford University Press.

Eco, Umberto. 1990. *The Limits of Interpretation*. Bloomington: Indiana University Press.

Eco, Umberto, V. V. Ivanov, and M. Rector. 1984. *Carnival*. New York: Mouton Publishers.

Elias, Norbert. 1983. *The Court Society*. New York: Pantheon Books.

———. 1986. An Essay on Sport and Violence. In *The Quest for Excitement: Sport and Leisure in the Civilizing Process*, eds. N. Elias and E. Dunning. Oxford: Basil Blackwell. 150–174.

Elias, Norbert, and E. Dunning. *The Quest for Excitement: Sport and Leisure in the Civilizing Process*. Oxford: Blackwell.

Ellis, John M. 1989. *Against Deconstruction*. Princeton: Princeton University Press.

Ellison, Ralph. 1952. *Invisible Man*. New York: Doubleday.

Erikson, Erik. [1950] 1992. Psychological Issues: Identity and the Life Cycle. In *Social Psychology*, eds. M. Kearl and C. Gordon. Boston: Allyn and Bacon. 237–238.

Ervin-Tripp, Susan. 1969. Sociolinguistics. In *Advances in Experimental Psychology*, Vol .4, ed. L. Berkowitz. New York: Academic Press. 91–159.

Exley, Frederick. 1968. *A Fan's Notes*. New York: Random House.

Farberman, Harvey. 1980. Fantasy in Everyday Life: Some Notes on the Intersection of Political Economy and Social Psychology. *Symbolic Interaction* 3, no.1: 9–27.

Fish, Stanley. 1980. *Is There a Text in This Class?: The Authority of Interpretive Communities*. Cambridge, Mass.: Harvard University Press.

Fitts, Dudley, and R. Fitzgerald. 1977. Trans. *Sophocles: The Oedipus Cycle*. New York: Harcourt Brace.

Fodor, Jerry. 1998. The Trouble with Psychological Darwinism. *The London Review of Books* 20, no.12: 11–13.

Fok, Vladimir. 1971. Quantum Physics and Problems of Philosophy. *Social Sciences* (USSR Academy of Sciences) 4, no. 6: 69–81.

Foote, Nelson. [1951] 1970. Identification as the Basis of a Theory of Motivation. In *Social Psychology through Symbolic Interaction*, eds. G. P. Stone and H. Faberman. Waltham, Mass: Ginn-Blaisdell. 480–488.

Fortes, Meyer. 1969. *Kinship and the Social Order*. Chicago: Aldine Publishing Company.

Foucault, Michel. 1979. *Discipline and Punish*. New York: Random House.

———. 1986a. On the Genealogy of Ethics. In *A Foucault Reader*, ed. P. Rabinow. London: Harmondsworth. 340–372.

———. 1986b. *The Care of the Self.* New York: Pantheon Books.

———. 1988. *The History of Sexuality*. Vol. 1–2. New York: Vintage Books.

Francis, William. 1906. A Gazetteer of the South Arcot District. In *Omens and Superstitions of Southern India,* ed. Edgar Thurston. New York: McBude, Nast and Co. 121–136.

Franks, David. 1985. The Self in Evolutionary Perspective. *The Foundations of Interpretive Sociology,* eds. H. Farberman and R. S. Perinbanayagam. Greenwich: JAI Press. 29–64.

Freud, Sigmund. 1949. *An Outline of Psychoanalysis.* New York: W. W. Norton and Co.

———. 1960. *The Ego and the Id.* New York: W. W. Norton and Co.

———. 1965. *New Introductory Lectures in Psychoanalysis.* New York: W. W. Norton and Co.

Friedman, Jerome. 1987. *Blasphemy, Immorality and Anarchy: The Ranters and the English Revolution.* Athens: Ohio University Press.

Geertz, Clifford. 1973. Deep Play: Notes on the Balinese Cockfight. In *The Interpretation of Cultures.* New York: Basic Books Inc. 412–453.

———. 1976. From the Native's Point of View: On the Nature of Anthropological Understanding. In *Approaches to Symbolic Anthropology,* eds. K. Bass and H. Selby. Albuquerque: University of New Mexico Press. 221–237.

Gerhardt, Julia. 1989. Monologue as a Speech Genre. In *Narratives from the Crib,* ed. K. Nelson. Cambridge, Mass.: Harvard University Press. 171–230.

Genette, Gerard. 1980. *Narrative Discourse.* Ithaca: Cornell University Press.

Gentry, George. 1952. Habit and the Logical Interpretant. In *Studies in the Philosophy of C. S. Peirce,* eds. P. Weiner and F. Young. Cambridge, Mass.: Harvard University Press. 75–92.

Gibbons, Robert. 1992. *A Primer in Game Theory.* Princeton, N.J.: Princeton University Press.

Gibbs, Raymond. 1994. *The Poetics of Mind.* New York: Cambridge University Press.

Giddens, Anthony. 1984. *The Constitution of Society.* Berkeley: University of California Press.

———. 1991. *Modernity and Identity.* Stanford: Stanford University Press.

Goffman, Erving. 1959. *The Presentation of Self in Everyday Life.* Garden City, N.Y.: Doubleday.

———. 1961. *Encounters.* Indianapolis: Bobbs-Merrill.

———. 1963. *Stigma.* Englewood Cliffs, N.J.: Prentice Hall.

———. 1967. *Interaction Ritual.* Garden City, N.Y.: Doubleday.

———. 1974. *Frame Analysis.* New York: Harper and Row.

———. 1983a. Felicity's Condition. *American Journal of Sociology* 8, no. 1: 1–53.

———. 1983b. The Interaction Order. *American Sociological Review,* 48: 1–17.

Grice, Paul. 1989. *Studies in the Way of Words.* Cambridge, Mass.: Harvard University Press.

Grunbaum, Adolf. 1984. *The Foundations of Psychoanalysis: A Philosophical Critique.* Berkeley: University of California Press.

Hamilton, Sue. 1996. *Identity and Experience.* London: Luzac Oriental.

Hannerz, Ulf. 1969. *Soulside*. New York: Columbia University Press.

Harre, Rom, and Grant Gillett. 1994. *The Discursive Mind*. Thousand Oaks, Calif.: Sage Publications.

Harrison, Paul. 1974. Soccer's Tribal Wars. *New Society* 29: 602.

Heisenberg, Werner. 1958. *Physics and Philosophy*. New York: Harper and Row.

Helgerson, Richard. 1992. *Forms of Nationhood*. Chicago: University of Chicago Press.

Henderson, D. K., and R. D. Gillespie. 1944. *A Text-book of Psychiatry for Students and Practitioners*. London: Oxford University Press.

Henry, Jules. 1973. *Pathways to Madness*. New York: Random House.

Herder, Johann. [1803] 1969. *On Social and Political Culture*. London: Cambridge University Press.

Heritage, John. 1984. *Garfinkel and Ethnomethodology*. Cambridge: Polity Press.

Hobbes, Thomas. [1651] 1961. Of the Natural Conditions of Mankind. In *Theories of Society*, eds. Talcott Parsons, E. Shils, K. Naegle, J. Pitts. New York: The Free Press. 99–101.

Hobsbawm, Eric, and T. Ranger, eds. 1983. *The Invention of Tradition*. New York: Cambridge University Press.

Holland, Norman. 1992. *The Critical I*. New York: Columbia University Press.

———. 1994. Reader-Response Already is Cognitive Criticism. *Stanford Humanities Review* 4, no. 1: 65–66.

Holquist, Michael. 1990. *Bakhtin and His World*. New York: Routledge.

Hynes, Charles, and Bob, Drury. 1990. *Incident at Howard Beach: The Case for Murder*. New York: Putnam.

Jeremias, Joachim. 1971. *New Testament Theology: The Proclamation of Jesus*. New York: Scribner and Sons.

Johnson, Barbara. 1980. Nothing Fails Like Success. *SCE Reports* 8 (Fall): 7–16.

Johnston, E. H. [1936] 1984. *Asvaghosa's Buddhacarita or the Acts of the Buddha*. Varnasi, India: Motilaldas Banarasidas.

Jones, Ernest. 1963. *The Life and Work of Sigmund Freud*. New York: Doubleday.

Kalupahana, David. 1987. *Principles of Buddhist Psychology*. Albany, N.Y.: State University of New York Press.

Kaplan, Abraham. 1964. *The Conduct of Inquiry*. San Francisco: Anne Chandler Publishing Company.

Kaysen, Susanna. 1993. *Girl, Interrupted*. New York: Random House.

Kiernan, V. G. 1989. *The Duel in European History*. New York: Oxford University Press.

Kohn, Hans. 1959. *Nationalism: Its Meaning and History*. Princeton: von Nostrand.

Laing, R. D., and A. Esterson. 1964. *Sanity, Madness, and the Family*. New York: Penguin Books.

Langer, Susanne. 1953. *Feeling and Form*. New York: Scribner's Sons.

———. 1967. *Mind: An Essay on Human Feeling*. Vol I. Baltimore: Johns Hopkins University Press.

———. [1942] 1970. *Philosophy in a New Key*. Cambridge, MA: Harvard University Press.

Lawler, Edward, Cecilia Ridgeway, and Barry Markovsky. 1993. Structural Social Psychology and the Micro-macro Problem. *Sociological Theory* 11, no. 3: 268–290.

Lear, Jonathan. 1992. Katharsis in Aristotle's Poetics. In *Essays on Aristotle's Poetics*, ed. Amelie Rorty. Princeton, N.J.: Princeton University Press. 315–340.

Lee, Dorothy. 1959. *Freedom and Culture*. Englewood Cliffs, N.J.: Prentice Hall.

Lemert, Edwin. 1970. Paranoia and the Dynamics of Exclusion. In *Social Psychology Through Symbolic Interaction*, eds. G. P. Stone and H. Farberman. Waltham, Mass.: Ginn-Blaisdell. 652–667.

Levi-Strauss, Claude. 1966. *The Savage Mind*. Chicago: University of Chicago Press.

Lienhardt, Godfrey. 1961. *Divinity and Experience: The Religion of the Dinka*. Oxford: The Clarendon Press.

Lowe, E. J. 1989. *Kinds of Being: A Study of Individuation, Identity and the Logic of Sortal Terms*. Oxford: Basil Blackwell.

Luke, Carmen. 1994. Childhood and Parenting in Popular Culture. *Australian and New Zealand Journal of Sociology* 30, no. 3: 289–302.

Lyman, Stanford, and M. Scott. 1975. *The Drama of Social Reality*. New York: Oxford University Press.

MacIntyre, Alasdair. 1958. *The Unconscious: A Conceptual Analysis*. London: Routledge.

MacPherson, C.B. 1962. *The Political Theory of Possessive Individualism*. Oxford: The Clarendon Press.

Maines, David. 1993. Narrative's Moment and Sociological Phenomena. *Sociological Quarterly* 34 (Spring), no. 1: 17–38.

Malcolm, Norman. 1966. Knowledge of Other Minds. In *Wittgenstein: The Philosophical Investigations—A Collection of Critical Essays*, ed. George Pitcher. New York: Doubleday and Co. 371–383.

———. and M. Moliseed. 1986. The Obsessive Discover's Complex and the "Discovery" of Growth in Sociological Theory. *American Journal of Sociology* 92 (July): 158–164.

Mallory, J. P. 1989. *In Search of the Indo-Europeans*. London: Thames and Hudson.

Martindale, Don. 1960. *The Nature and Types of Sociological Theory*. Boston: Houghton-Mifflin.

Marx, Karl. [1844] 1963. *Early Writings*. Ed. Thomas Bottomone. New York: McGraw Hill.

———. [1865] 1965. *Capital*. Vol. I. Moscow: Progress Publisher.

———. [1869] 1963. *The 18th Brumaire of Louis Napoleon*. New York: W. W. Norton.

Mbabuike, Michael. 1996. The Cosmology of Igbo Anthroponyms: Life Continuum and the Liturgy of Culture. *Dialectical Anthropology* 21, no. 1: 47–65.

McCarthy, Doyle. 1984. Towards a Sociology of the Physical World: George Herbert Mead on Physical Objects. *Studies in Symbolic Interaction* 5: 105–121.

———. 1996. *Knowledge as Culture*. New York: Routledge.

McCorkel, Jill. 1998. Going to the Crackhouse: Critical Space as a Form of Resistence in Total Institutions and Everyday Life. *Symbolic Interaction* 3: 227–252.

Mead, G. H. 1904. Image or Sensation. *Journal of Philosophy* 1: 2.

———. 1932. *The Philosophy of the Present*. Chicago: University of Chicago Press.

———. 1934. *Mind, Self and Society*. Chicago: University of Chicago Press.

———. 1938. *The Philosophy of the Act*. Chicago: University of Chicago Press.

———. 1964. *Selected Writings*. Ed. Andrew Reck. New York: Bobbs-Merrill Company.

Merton, Robert. 1968. *Social Theory and Social Structure*. New York: Free Press.

Michaels, Walter Benn. 1977. The Interpreter's Self: Peirce on the Cartesian "Subject." *Georgia Review* 31: 383–402.

Miller, James. 1993. *The Passion of Michel Foucault.* New York: Simon and Schuster.

Mills, Peter J. 1982. Misinterpreting Mead. *Sociology* 16, no. 2: 116–131.

Milnes, Mattison. 1988. Conceptualization of the Person: Hierarchical Society and Individual Autonomy in India. *American Anthropologist* 90: 568–579.

Mizuno, Kogen. 1982. *Buddhist Sutras: Origin, Development, Transmission.* Tokyo: Kosei Publishing House.

Morgan, Jane, C. O'Neil, and R. Harre. 1979. *Nicknames: Their Origins and Social Consequences.* Boston: Routledge.

Morris, Charles. 1888. *The Aryan Race: Its Origins and Achievements.* Chicago: S. C. Griggs.

Muhlhausler, Peter, and Rom Harre. 1990. *Pronouns and People: The Linguistic Construction of Personal Identity.* Oxford: Basil Blackwell.

Muller, Max. 1898. *Auld Lang Synge.* New York: Scribner and Co.

———. 1905. *The Biography of Words and the Home of the Aryas.* New York: Longmans, Green and Co.

Murfin, Ross. 1989. *Joseph Conrad: Heart of Darkness. A Case Study in Contemporary Criticism.* New York: St. Martin's Press.

Mus, Paul. 1964. The Thousand-Armed Canon: A Mystery or a Problem. *Journal of Indian Buddhist Studies* 6, no. 1: 1–33.

Navasky, Victor. 1980. *Naming Names.* New York: Penguin Books.

Nehamas, Alexander. 1992. Pity and Fear in the Rhetoric and the Poetics. In *Aristotle's Rhetoric: Philosophical Essays,* eds. D. J. Furley and A. Nehamas. Princeton, N.J.: Princeton University Press. 257–282.

Nelson, Benjamin. 1981. On the Structures of Consciousness and the Omnipresence of the Grotesque. In *On the Road to Modernity: Selected Writings,* ed. T. Huff. Totowa, N.J.: Rowman and Littlefield. 202–212.

Nelson, Katherine. 1989. Monologues in the Crib. In *Crib Narratives.* Cambridge, Mass.: Harvard University Press. 1–26.

Newport, Frank. 1996. American Public Opinion Continues to Think O. J. Simpson Guilty <http://www.gallop.com>

Oakes, Guy. 1995. Straight Thinking About Queer Theory. *International Journal of Politics, Culture and Society* 8, no. 3: 379–388.

Olivelle, Patrick. 1992. *Samnyasa Upanishads: Hindu Scriptures on Asceticism and Renunciation.* New York: Oxford University Press.

O'Prey, Paul. 1989. Introduction to *Heart of Darkness,* by Joseph Conrad. New York: Penguin Books.

Oriard, Michael. 1993. *Reading Football: How the Popular Press Created an American Spectacle.* Chapel Hill: University of North Carolina Press.

Ortega y Gasset. 1956. The Self and the Other. In *The Dehumanization of Art.* New York: Doubleday. 161–187.

*Oxford English Dictionary.* Vol. 14. 1989. Oxford: The Clarendon Press.

Parsons, Talcott, E. Shils, K. Naegle, and J. Pitts, eds. 1965. *Theories of Society.* New York: Free Press.

Pears, David. 1988. *The False Prison: A Study of the Development of Wittgenstein's Philosophy.* Vol. 1 and Vol. 2. Oxford: Clarendon Press.

Peirce, Charles A. [1868] 1958. Some Consequences of Four Incapacities. In *Charles S. Peirce: Selected Writings*, ed. P. Weiner. New York: Dover Publications. 73–90.

———. 1955. Logic as a Semiotic. In *Philosophical Writings*, ed. J. Buchler. New York: Dover Publications. 98–119.

———. 1960. *Collected Papers*. Vol. 5. Cambridge, Mass.: Harvard University Press.

Perinbanayagam, R. S. 1982. *The Karmic Theater*. Amherst: University of Massachusetts Press.

———. 1985. *Signifying Acts*. Carbondale, Ill.: Southern Illinois University Press.

———. 1986. The Meaning of Uncertainty and the Uncertainty of Meaning. *Symbolic Interaction* 9, no.1: 105–128.

———. 1991. *Discursive Acts*. New York: Aldine De Gruyter.

Perry, John. 1975. *Personal Identity*. Berkeley: University of California Press.

Peterson, Indira Viswanathan. 1989. *Poems to Siva*. Princeton, N.J.: Princeton University Press.

Phillips, Denis. 1976. *Holistic Thought in Social Sciences*. Stanford: Stanford University Press.

Pilat, Oliver. 1952. *Atomic Spies*. New York: Plenum.

Pinker, Steven. 1994. *How The Mind Works*. New York: W. W. Norton and Co.

Plummer, Ken. 1995. *Telling Sexual Stories*. London: Routledge.

Poliakov, Leon. 1974. *The Aryan Myth*. New York: Basic Books.

Polkinghorne, Donald. 1991. Narrative and Self-Concept. *Journal of Narrative and Life History* 1, nos. 2–3: 135–153.

———. 1995. Narrative Knowing in the Human Sciences. *Journal of Communication* 45, no. 2: 177–184.

Raja, Kunjunni. 1963. *Indian Theories of Meaning*. Madras: Oxford University Press.

Rambelli, Fabio. 1995. Buddhism and Semiotics. *The Semiotic Review of Books* 6 no.1: 11–12.

Ransdell, Joseph. 1980. Semiotics and Linguistics. In *The Signifying Animal*, eds. I. Rauch and G. F. Carr. Bloomington: Indiana University Press.

Ribeiro, Branca Telles. 1994. *Coherence in Psychotic Discourse*. New York: Oxford University Press.

Ricoeur, Paul. 1981. *The Rule of Metaphor*. Toronto: University of Toronto Press.

———. 1984. *Time and Narrative*. Chicago: University of Chicago Press.

———. 1992. *Oneself as Another*. Chicago: University of Chicago Press.

Roberts, Mathew. 1989. Poetics, Hermeneutics, Dialogics: Bakhtin and Paul de Man. In *Rethinking Bakhtin*, eds. G. Morson and C. Emerson. Evanston, Ill.: Northwestern University Press. 115–134.

Roberts, Selena. 1997. Calipari Apologizes Publicly for the Slur. *New York Times*. March 24. Section B: 8.

Rohde, David. 1997. Endgame: *The Betrayal and Fall of Srebenica*. New York: Farrar, Strauss and Giroux.

Rorty, Amelie. 1976. *The Identities of Persons*. Berkeley: University of California Press.

———. 1992. *Aristotle's Poetics*. Princeton, N.J.: Princeton University Press.

Rosaldo, Michelle. 1980. *Knowledge and Passion*. Cambridge: Cambridge University Press.

Rose, Stephen. 1992. *The Making of Memory*. New York: Doubleday.

Rosenthal, Sandra. 1969. Mead, Peirce and the Logic of Concepts. *Transactions of the Charles Peirce Society* 5 (Spring): 173–187.

———. 1977. Activity and the Structure of Perceptual Experience: Mead and Peirce Revisited. *Southern Journal of Philosophy* 15 (Summer): 207–214.

———. 1986. *Speculative Pragmatism*. Amherst: University of Massachusetts Press.

——— 1988. The Third Alternative: Speculative Pragmatism. *Journal of Speculative Philosophy* 2: 312–317.

———. 1993. Giving Ourselves a Little Time for Mead and Derrida—and Why Bother. *Journal of Speculative Philosophy* 7, no. 4: 249–265.

———. 1996. Sign, Time and the Viability of Trace: Derrida and Peirce. *International Philosophical Quarterly* 35, no. 1: 19-28

Russell, Robert. 1991. Narrative in Views of Humanity, Science and Action: Lessons for Cognitive Psychotherapy. *Journal of Cognitive Psychotherapy* 5, no. 4: 241–246.

Said, Edward. 1993. *Culture and Imperialism*. New York: Alfred Knopf.

Samaraweera, Vijay. 1997. An "Act of Truth" in a Sinhala Court of Law: On Truth, Lies and Judicial Proof among Sinhala Buddhists. *Cardozo Journal of International and Comparative Law* 5, no. 1: 133–163.

Sampson, Edward. 1989. Deconstructing the Self. In *Texts of Identity*, eds. J. Shotter and K. Gergen. Newbury Park: Sage Publications. 1–19.

Sansom, William. 1956. *A Contest of Ladies*. New York: Reynal Publishers.

Sarbin, Theodore. 1986. *Narrative Psychology: The Storied Nature of Human Conduct*. New York: Praeger.

Savesson, John. 1972. *Joseph Conrad: The Making of a Moralist*. Amsterdam: Rodopi Press.

Scherbatsky, F. T. 1962. *Buddhist Logic*, Vols. 1 and 2. New York: Dover Publications.

Schuman, Hans Wolfgang. 1973. *Buddhism: An Outline of Its Teachings and Schools*. London: The Theosophical Publishing House.

Schutz, Alfred. 1964. *Collected Papers: Studies in Social Theory*. Vol 2. The Hague: Martinus Nijhoff.

Scribner, Robert. 1988. Ritual and Reformation. In *The German People and the Reformation*, ed. R. Po-Chia Hsia. Ithaca: Cornell University Press. 122–144.

Scruggs, Kathy. 1991. Gang Rape Slaying Mark Night of Wilding. *Atlanta Constitution*. May 19. Section C:1.

Seidman, Steven. 1994. Queer Theory, Sociology: A Dialogue. *Sociological Theory* 12, no. 2: 166–177.

Shapin, Steven. 1994. *A Social History of Truth*. Chicago: University of Chicago Press.

Shils, Edward. 1950. Primary Groups in the American Army. In *Continuities in Social Research: Studies in the Scope and Methods of the American Soldier*, eds. R. K. Merton and P. F. Lazarsfeld. Glencoe, Ill.: The Free Press. 16–39.

Shils, Edward, and M. Janowitz. 1948. Cohesion and Disintegration in the Wehrmacht in World War II. *Public Opinion Quarterly* 12: 280–315.

Shotter, John, and K. Gergen. 1989. Texts of Identity. Newbury Park, Calif.: Sage Publications.

Silva, J. A., and G. Lochak. 1969. *Quanta*. New York: McGraw Hill.

Simmel, Georg. 1950. *The Sociology of George Simmel*. Ed. K. Wolff. New York: The Free Press.

———. 1959. *Essays in Sociology, Philosophy and Aesthetics*. Ed. K. Wolff. New York: Harper and Row.

————. 1971. The Adventurer. In *On Individuality and Social Forms*, ed. D. Levine. Chicago: University of Chicago Press.

Singer, Milton. 1984. Personal and Social Identity in Dialogue. *Man's Glassy Essence*. Bloomington: University of Indiana Press. 74–103.

Smith, Johanna M. 1989. "Too Beautiful Altogether": Patriarchal Ideology in Heart of Darkness In *The Heart of Darkness: A Case Study in Contemporary Criticism*, ed. R. Murfin. New York: St. Martin's Press. 179–194.

Smith, Linda Anderson. 1996. Unique Names and Naming Practices among African-American Families. *Families in Society* 77, no. 5: 290–297.

Snow, David, and Leon Anderson. 1987. Identity Work among the Homeless: The Verbal Construction and Avowal of Personal Identities. *American Journal of Sociology* 92, no. 6: 1336–1371.

Spacks, Patricia Meyer. 1986. *Gossip*. Chicago: University of Chicago Press.

Spencer, Herbert. [1862] 1958. *First Principles of a New System of Philosophy*. New York: Dewitt.

————. [1898] 1961. The Nature of Society. In *Theories of Society*, eds. Talcott Parsons, et al. New York: The Free Press. 139–146.

Stark, Werner. 1987. *The Social Bond*. New York: Fordham University Press.

Stein, Gertrude. [1936] 1976. *The Geographical History of America or the Relation of Human Nature to the Human Mind*. New York: Vintage Books.

Stephens, Lynn G. 1981. Cognition and Emotion in Peirce's Theory of Mental Activity. *Transactions of the Charles S. Peirce Society* 17 (Spring): 131–140.

Stone, Gregory P. [1962] 1970. Appearance and the Self. In *Social Psychology through Symbolic Interaction*, eds. G. P. Stone and H. Farberman. Waltham, Mass.: Ginn-Blaisdell. 394–414.

Stout, David. 1997. Three Blacks Win $1 Million in Bauer Store Incident. *New York Times*, Oct. 10. Section A:16

Strauss, Anselm. 1959. *Mirrors and Masks*. New York: The Free Press.

Sullivan, Harry Stack. 1953. *Interpersonal Theory of Psychiatry*. New York: W. W. Norton and Co.

————. 1956. *Clinical Studies in Psychiatry*. New York: W. W. Norton and Co.

Suttles, Gerald. 1968. *The Social Order of the Slum: Ethnicity and Territory in the Inner City*. Chicago: University of Chicago Press.

Swados, Harvey. 1962. The Myth of the Happy Worker. In *Man Alone*, eds. E. and M. Josephson. New York: Dell Books.

Szasz, Thomas. 1961. *The Myth of Mental Illness*. New York: Harper and Row.

————. 1970. *Ideology and Insanity*. New York: Doubleday.

Tambiah, Stanley. J. 1976. *World Conqueror and World Renouncer*. Cambridge: Cambridge University Press.

Thomas, Edward J. 1956. *The Life of the Buddha in Legend and History*. London: Routledge and Kegan Paul.

Toch, Hans. 1969. *Violent Men*. Chicago: Aldine Publishing Co.

Todorov, Tvetzan. 1982. *Symbolism and Interpretation*. Ithaca: Cornell University Press.

Trevor-Roper, Hugh. 1983. The Invention of Tradition: The Highland Tradition of Scotland. In *The Invention of Tradition*, eds. E. Hobsbawm and T. Ranger. London: Cambridge University Press.

Trollope, Fanny. [1832] 1997. *Domestic Manners of the Americans*. New York: Penguin Books.

Tuan, Yi-Fi. 1982. *Segmented Worlds and Self.* Minneapolis: University of Minnesota Press.

Turner, Victor. 1974. *Dramas, Fields and Metaphors.* Ithaca: Cornell University Press.

van Buitenen, J. A. B. 1981. *The Bhagavatgita in the Mahabharata.* Chicago: University of Chicago Press.

Vanderhoof, David. 1997. The Germanville Halloween Shooting. <http//:www.uncp.edu>

Varella, Charles. 1995. Ethogenic Theory and Psychoanalysis: The Unconscious as a Social Construction and a Failed Explanatory Concept. *Journal for the Study of Social Behavior* 25, no. 4: 363–386.

Volosinov, V. N. [1930] 1973. *Marxism and the Philosophy of Language.* London: Seminar Press.

von Eckart, B. 1982. The Scientific Status of Psychoanalysis. In *Introducing Psychoanalytic Theory,* ed. S. L. Gilman. New York: Bruner and Mazel. 129-179.

Wacquant, Loic. 1992. Introduction. *An Invitation to Reflexive Sociology,* eds. Pierre Bourdieu and L. Wacquant. Chicago: University of Chicago Press. 1–15.

Wang, Zhigang, and M. Miklin. 1996. The Transformation of Naming Practices in Chinese Families. *Journal of International Sociology* 11, no. 2: 187–212.

Warren, Henry Clark. [1896] 1987. *Buddhism.* Cambridge, Mass.: Harvard University Press.

Weber, Max. 1958. *Essays in Sociology.* New York: Oxford University Press.

Weigert, Andrew, J. Smith Tietge, and Dennis Tietge. 1986. *Society and Identity.* New York: Cambridge University Press.

Weiss, Paul. 1967. 1+1=2 (One Plus One Does Not Equal Two). In *The Neurosciences: A Study Program,* eds. G. C. Quartron, T. Melnechuk, and F. O.Schmitt: New York: Rockefeller University Press.

Welsford, Enid. [1935] 1966. *The Fool: His Social and Literary History.* Gloucester, Mass.: Petu Smith Publishers.

Wheeler, John. 1984. Bits, Quanta, Meaning. Unpublished paper. Center for Theoretical Physics, University of Texas, Austin.

Whittaker, Elvi. 1992. The Birth of the Anthropological Self and Its Career. *Ethos* 20, no. 2: 191–219.

White, Harrison. 1992. *Identity and Control.* Princeton, N.J.: Princeton University Press.

Wiley, Norbert. 1994. *The Semiotic Self.* Chicago: University of Chicago Press.

Willeford, William. 1969. *The Fool and His Scepter.* Evanston, Ill.: Northwestern University Press.

Wilson, Edmund. [1946] 1974. Who Cares Who Murdered Roger Ackroyd? In *The Art of the Mystery Story,* ed. Howard Haycraft. New York: Biblo and Tannen. 18–32.

Wittgenstein, Ludwig. 1958. *Philosophical Investigations.* New York: Macmillan and Co.

Yallop, David. 1990. *To Encourage Others.* London: Corgi Publishers.

Yogananda, Paramahansa. 1977. *The Autobiography of a Yogi.* Los Angeles: Self-Realization Fellowship.

# Index

# About the Author

Robert Sidharthan Perinbanayagam received his early education at the University of Ceylon (now Sri Lanka) and later obtained his M.A. and Ph.D. in sociology and anthropology at the University of Minnesota. He is on the faculty at Hunter College and the Graduate Center of the City University of New York. He is the author of *The Karmic Theater: Self, Society and Astrology in Jaffna, Sri Lanka, Signifying Acts*, and *Discursive Acts*. His articles have been published in various scholarly journals in sociology, anthropology, and psychiatry. In 1998 he was awarded the G. H. Mead Award by the Society for the Study of Symbolic Interaction.

.